INTRODUCING SOCIOLOGY
A Symbolic Interactionist Perspective

JOHN P. HEWITT, *University of Massachusetts at Amherst*

MYRNA LIVINGSTON HEWITT

PRENTICE-HALL, INC., ENGLEWOOD CLIFFS, NEW JERSEY 07632

Library of Congress Cataloging in Publication Data

Hewitt, John P., [date]
Introducing sociology.

Bibliography: p. 369
Includes index.
1. Sociology. 2. Symbolic interactionism.
I. Hewitt, Myrna Livingston. II. Title.
HM51.H52 1986 301 85-6323
ISBN 0-13-477373-X

Editorial production and interior design: Serena Hoffman
Cover design: Joe Cureio
Cover art: Georges Seurat, *Sunday Afternoon on the Island of La Grande Jatte,* The Art Institute of Chicago
Manufacturing buyer: John Hall

PRINTED IN THE UNITED STATES OF AMERICA

10 9 8 7 6 5 4 3 2 1

ISBN 0-13-477373-X 01

PRENTICE-HALL INTERNATIONAL (UK) LIMITED, *London*
PRENTICE-HALL OF AUSTRALIA PTY. LIMITED, *Sydney*
PRENTICE-HALL CANADA INC., *Toronto*
PRENTICE-HALL HISPANOAMERICANA, S.A., *Mexico*
PRENTICE-HALL OF INDIA PRIVATE LIMITED, *New Delhi*
PRENTICE-HALL OF JAPAN, INC., *Tokyo*
PRENTICE-HALL OF SOUTHEAST ASIA PTE. LTD., *Singapore*
EDITORA PRENTICE-HALL DO BRASIL, LTDA., *Rio de Janeiro*
WHITEHALL BOOKS LIMITED, *Wellington, New Zealand*

Contents

11 Race and Ethnicity 255

12 The World of The Family 280

13 The World of Religion 308

14 The World of Politics 329

15 Symbolic Interactionism and Sociology 355

References 369

Index 375

Preface

This book is an introduction to sociology written from the symbolic interactionist perspective. Like other introductory textbooks, it strives to inform students about the nature of the discipline of sociology, as well as to convey its authors' sense of excitement about the field. Our goal is to show how sociologists look at the social world and then to describe some of what they have learned about it.

Unlike many other books, however, ours is not eclectic, but is written from a distinctive perspective—that of symbolic interactionism. Our aim is to use the insights of this theoretical tradition as the basis for an organized introduction to sociology. Symbolic interactionism provides an informing and guiding perspective—not a doctrinaire source of truth, but a vantage point from which a complex and fascinating social terrain may be viewed.

In writing this book we have been guided by several principles. First, because no book can say everything there is to say about sociology, we have necessarily been selective in our choice of concepts and substantive topics. Our use of symbolic interactionism as an orienting perspective has naturally had some effect on this selectivity. We give more attention to social process than to social structure, for example, and emphasize topics that interactionists will find congenial. But we have also avoided writing a book that mentions only those topics that symbolic interactionists have studied explicitly. Thus, in addition to chapters on the nature of human conduct, self and socialization, sex roles, social coordination, deviance, race and ethnic relations, and collective behavior—all of which draw heavily on the interactionist tradition—we have included chapters on social inequality, the family, politics, and religion—areas where symbolic interactionists have invested less effort.

Second, we have sought to introduce sociology, not write a general treatise on American society. Our book draws many of its examples from American and, more generally, Western society. In several chapters we do attempt to describe existing social arrangements, but ours is not primarily an effort to depict the nature of contemporary society. Instead, we have kept our focus on the understanding and application of sociological concepts.

Third, wherever possible we have tried to use historical materials as illustrations and provide historical accounts of the origins and development of current social arrangements. We have not devoted a separate chapter to social change. We have, instead, taken the view that a grasp of history is essential to an understanding of sociology. In our race relations chapter, for example, we devote space to a historical account of immigration to the United States. Our interpretations of social class and of the family are similarly informed by a historical perspective. We view this effort not only as necessary in itself, but also as consistent with the symbolic interactionist perspective. Human conduct does not exist in a temporal vacuum, but is embedded in the temporal flow of situations and social worlds. We live in a world we did not make, and our actions make a world with which our descendants must struggle.

Fourth, we have attempted to treat our readers as people capable of understanding and handling serious ideas. This book presents few facts to be memorized, but it offers, we hope, many serious ideas on which the student sociologist can chew. We have tried to write at a level that is clear, but not condescending, and to follow ideas through to their logical consequences, rather than assume that students will be content to memorize a set of definitions.

We have been guided in this effort not only by each other, but also by our children, Beth and Gary, who are college students themselves. Both have offered their unsolicited comments from time to time as they read over our shoulders. Both have participated in countless family conversations about the substantive topics with which sociologists deal. Both have generously, if unwittingly, contributed a share of the examples. In addition, Beth has read and commented on the manuscript from the perspective of a student reader, and the book has clearly benefitted from her work.

We have also worked profitably and enjoyably with the staff of Prentice-Hall—with Susan Taylor, who first contracted us to write it, and with Bill Webber, who took over and gave the book his strong support. Thanks are due also to Serena Hoffman, who saw the book through production. We also want to express our appreciation to the following reviewers, who saw early drafts of the manuscript and offered helpful criticisms: Mark Hutter, Glassboro State College, and Richard Sweeney, Modesto Junior College.

John P. Hewitt
Myrna Livingston Hewitt

Introducing Sociology

1

About Sociology

What is sociology? The question has no simple answer, for sociology is a discipline with many facets, and sociologists do many different things. Sociology can be defined as the scientific study of society, but not all sociologists feel their discipline is scientific in the same sense as physics or biology. Sociologists can be found studying the causes of crime or the condition of the nuclear family in contemporary America; but they can also be observed investigating the world economic system and its impact upon developing nations in the nineteenth century. Some do their research armed with large computers and massive amounts of data gleaned from social surveys or censuses, while others carry more modest gear: a notebook and tape recorder, or perhaps just a library card.

But for all the seeming diversity—even chaos—of sociology, there is a distinctively sociological way of looking at things that transcends particular methods of research, topics of inquiry, or even definitions of the discipline itself. In this book, we will attempt to convey the essence of the sociological perspective. While we want to acquaint you with a body of knowledge about human social behavior, our more fundamental aim is to make sociology available to you as an illuminating and useful way of looking at the human world.

SOCIETY

Perhaps the best way to understand a discipline is by examining the concepts it defines as central to its work. Among several concepts important to sociologists, *society* is paramount. It is a term that springs easily to the sociologist's lips, and more than any other concept it conveys the essence of what sociologists think is important about people and their conduct.

Society is a relatively common word. People use it like most words, generally taking its meaning for granted. When people talk about the "society pages" of the newspaper or about "American society," they have a more or less clear understanding of the word and how its meaning differs from one context to another. Seldom do people have any need for an explicit definition, and they sometimes have difficulty formulating one even when they understand what the word means.

Like the average person, the sociologist often uses the word *society* without giving it much thought. Thus, the sociologist understands the common-sense meaning of the word when it is used to refer to members of the upper class. Sociologists also recognize and sometimes use the word to refer to a nation-state—a political unit existing within definite boundaries. Thus, sociologists might speak of "Canadian society" or "American society."

But the sociological concept of society does not have the same meaning as these commonplace uses of the term. Like most scientific concepts that have counterparts in everyday speech (such as *energy* or *life*), *society* has a more precise meaning that differs significantly from conventional usage. For the sociologist, society is a complex and important phenomenon, not just a term for a segment of a population or for a politically unified state. In the sociological eye, what makes France a society is not simply its political system or the facts of its history and geography, but something more.

What is that something? In the most fundamental sense, *society refers to the fact that humans live together in groups and interact socially*. Wherever we see people, we see them in various kinds of social relationships. We see them as cooperative or in conflict, as lovers or enemies, as members of the same or different family groups, as superiors or subordinates, and in a great variety of other relationships. But always we see them associated with and oriented to other human beings.

From the moment of birth we are surrounded by people. This seems an obvious fact, but it is still a significant one. Unlike many animals, humans do not abandon or lose interest in their young soon after birth. Human young remain with adults (whether their biological parents or other kinfolk) longer than any other animal. Moreover, they remain helpless and dependent for a long time, requiring twelve or more years to begin sexual maturation and attain adult size. The length of time children remain under the care and control of adults varies widely. Adulthood comes with sexual maturation in many simpler societies, but may be postponed into the twenties in the modern world. Regardless, dependency lasts longer for humans than for any other animal.

Humans are not the only social animals, to be sure. Several species of insects live in very complex social relationships, and many of the higher primates live and travel in bands with identifiable patterns of social organization. Birds flock and fish school, so the simple fact of association is not all there is to society. Human society is distinctive because of the ways humans associate and interact with one another. Human conduct rests upon an immense amount of learning. We are creatures not of instinct, but of socially acquired ways of thinking, feeling,

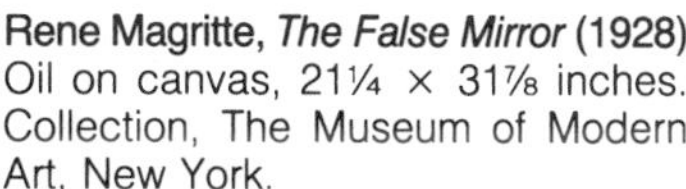

Rene Magritte, *The False Mirror* (1928) Oil on canvas, 21¼ × 31⅞ inches. Collection, The Museum of Modern Art, New York.

There are as many sociological "eyes" as there are perspectives on society. Each slightly distorts our vision of social reality, while enabling us to see other aspects more clearly. All try to overcome the inherent limitations of "common sense," which can often be a "false mirror."

and acting. Our biology does not dictate the form of our society. Instead, it is from society that we acquire the knowledge, skills, and attitudes with which we approach the world. And, as we shall see later in this chapter, human society rests upon the unique human ability to make and use symbols—a capacity that has not appeared in any significant way elsewhere in the animal world.

A VARIETY OF PERSPECTIVES ON SOCIETY

Although sociologists generally view society as the central concept in their discipline, they often sharply disagree about the proper approach to the study of society. There is no single theory or perspective upon which all sociologists agree. Instead, there are several competing perspectives, each of which has a more or less distinctive view of the discipline and its subject matter. Four sociological perspectives—functionalism, conflict theory, exchange theory, and symbolic interactionism—have been particularly important in the development of sociology. These perspectives emphasize different aspects of social life and have developed contrasting pictures of the nature of society. Supporters of each perspective tend to think that their theory captures what is most important about human social behavior and that the others fall short in important respects. Our goal here is to present the four approaches as fairly as possible and to indicate why we have chosen symbolic interactionism as the guiding perspective of this book.

Functionalism

In the eyes of many sociologists, what is notable about society is that human conduct is organized in complex, systematic, and highly predictable ways. Each individual is born into a society with established groups, organizations, social relationships, and patterns of conduct. These patterned social arrangements shape and constrain individual conduct. Society, from this perspective, may be thought of as a structure composed of various parts that function together to organize the activities and meet the needs of individual members.

The parts that make up society can be conceived in a number of different ways. One common way is through the concept of *institution*. An institution consists of patterned ways of solving common problems and meeting needs, solutions that are so widely used by the members of a society that they are taken for granted as the natural order of things. Thus, the family is an institution that provides for the regulation of sexual activity, the reproduction of the species, and care and socialization of the young. Similarly, economic institutions govern the production and distribution of goods and services, while political institutions regulate relationships between individuals, families, and other units as well as between societies. To the members of a society, their institutions seem the right and proper ways of doing things—indeed, they appear to be natural and inevitable features of the world.

Institutions and other social patterns are, of course, made up of the everyday acts of real people who must forge collective solutions to the problems that confront them. The important thing, functionalists say, is that the acts of these living and breathing people repeatedly amount to the same behavior, the same solutions to similar problems, and thus they are patterned social arrangements. Because of the overwhelming regularity of human life, they say, the patterns created and sustained by people are more interesting and important than the minute details of how they are created.

Crucial to this approach to sociology is the idea that society constrains the individual. Society is composed of institutions that exist prior to the birth of any individual, and thus they exert profound influence on individual conduct. From a functional point of view, individuals are born into a society with an established set of patterns, and they are repeatedly confronted by its requirements, its limits, and its demands.

The newborn infant is immediately confronted with an existing world that determines the experiences he or she will have. Who its parents are, the religion they espouse, the language they speak, the resources at their command—all of these things are beyond the child's control. As the child grows, his or her conduct will be governed by expectations invented by others. The child's opportunities will be many or few depending upon parental resources, the nature and extent of inequality in the society in which it lives, and the actions of many other people, such as teachers, over whom the child has little or no influence. When the child grows up, he or she will marry in accord with custom, raise children as he or she was raised, and grow old and die in predictable circumstances.

Although social structure consists of patterns of human action and interaction, functionalists believe it is useful to think of society as if it were more solid and real. This was the perspective taken by the great French sociologist, Émile Durkheim, whose views still echo in the halls of sociology. Durkheim (1964) argued that society could be conceived as a reality *sui generis*—that is, a level of reality of its own kind to be explained on its own level of analysis, rather than by reducing it to psychological or biological principles. Treat social facts as things—*commes des choses*—he advised, by which he meant not that social patterns *are* things, but that they are *like* things. That is, social patterns are external to individuals and exert constraints upon them. Patterns of conduct do not exist in the minds of individuals or in the behavior of one person, but in the conduct of many people over time. Hence, such patterns (Durkheim called them *facts*) are truly social, existing outside of the individual and constraining what the individual can do. According to Durkheim, social facts can be studied without regard to individual motives or psychological characteristics.

The durability and force of social patterns or social facts is explained in part by emphasizing their interdependence. Over time, social institutions and arrangements come to "fit" one another, each making a contribution to the society as a whole and each tending to "mesh" with the others. So, for example, the nuclear family in a modern industrial society contributes to the society as a whole by providing a milieu for the reproduction, care, and socialization of the young. At the same time, however, the way the family carries out its tasks must be congruent with other institutions. Because industrial societies require highly specialized skills, the family entrusts its young to more formal agencies of socialization—the schools—after the early years of childhood. And because many social relationships in contemporary society are impersonal and highly competitive, the family becomes a place of refuge and emotional support against life's insults.

Conflict Theory

Some sociologists have looked at social structure differently, seeing it more in terms of the use of power than as a benignly functioning set of institutions. In the view of conflict theorists, people respond not only to social institutions in which they believe but also to the unequal distribution of power among individuals, organizations, and social groups. Some scholars, for example, see society as fundamentally divided between those who control the means of production and those who work for them. How people behave, what they believe, and the opportunities to which they have access are a function of their class position. (These ideas are stressed by followers of Karl Marx, whose work will be discussed later in this chapter.) Others see inequality and conflict among *many* groups in a society rather than just between owners and workers. But whether two groups or many groups are involved, the underlying perspective is the same: Social life is not simply a set of harmonious relationships between people who interact cooperatively and in the best interest of society as a whole. Social life also entails conflict and coercion, and if people sometimes act cooperatively and out of loyalty to institutions, at other times their behavior is best explained as a result of less benign premises.

A conflict approach to society may take several different forms. Some conflict theorists, for example, take the view that humans are naturally inclined to pursue self-interest, that they will use whatever resources are at their command in order to do so, and that this naturally leads to conflict (Collins, 1975). In this approach, conflict is an essential characteristic of human nature; whenever two people interact, each will seek to defend or advance his or her own interests. Social structure is thus a product of human nature expressing itself in the myriad interactions in which people engage. Patterned relationships between husbands and wives, rules that govern business contracts, and recreational sports—all are either the outcomes of social conflict or themselves the arenas in which conflict takes place.

Other theorists believe that conflict is not a part of human nature but stems from particular configurations of social structure, especially from the allocation of scarce resources. Karl Marx's view of human nature (see Marx and Engels, 1848), for example, is comparatively benign. In the ideal society, which for Marx was a society without social classes, people would live in harmony with one another, and the needs of all would be met through common effort. Marx held that conflict exists in capitalist society because social classes exist—that is, because some control the forces of production and exploit the labor of those who have nothing except their labor. Therefore, an end to social conflict—and a just society in which all share equitably in society's resources and goods—can be attained only through the creation of a classless society.

Whichever approach is emphasized, conflict theorists see existing social arrangements as outcomes of conflict. Their views thus contrast sharply with those of functionalists. The latter would analyze the public schools in the United States as the primary agency of socialization that has evolved to meet the needs of an industrial society for trained personnel; schools convey a growing and increasingly complex body of cultural knowledge that cannot be conveyed by the family alone. Conflict theorists would agree that schools are an important agency of socialization, but they would point out also that schools are an agency of social control. What is taught in schools, they say, is designed to support and further the ideology of the ruling class. Thus, the "virtues" that schools teach, such as hard work, loyalty, and promptness, are virtues that tend to serve the interests of those who employ labor and who want their workers to be productive, loyal, and punctual (see Bowles and Gintis, 1976).

Conflict theorists are thus skeptical of a major assumption made by functionalists, who tend to see the members of society as cheerfully in agreement with one another and supportive of their institutions. Conflict theorists assert that there is less agreement than functionalists believe, and that society is in fact filled with conflict. And if people believe in their institutions, it is often because they have been duped into believing. From a conflict perspective, institutions are apt to consist of ideas and beliefs fostered by those who have power in order to exert control over those who do not.

Exchange Theory

A third general approach looks for the essence of society in the exchanges that occur between people in everyday life. Social interaction always involves the transfer of valued things from one person to another. A parent provides physical care and emotional nurturance to a child, who, in return, gives the parent respect, love, and obedience. Likewise, neighbors borrow and lend tools, watch one another's pets, and express mutual admiration of gardens or of children's accomplishments. These are examples of *social exchange*, in which goods, services, love, esteem, and other valued things are transferred from one person to another.

A prominent exchange theorist, George Homans (1974), bases his version of this approach on the principles of psychological behavior developed by B. F. Skinner and others. In the view of behaviorists, people, like all animals, learn to do what they are rewarded for doing. If the child has been rewarded by parents for being docile and obedient, then the child will likely continue this pattern of behavior in order to sustain their affection. If a neighbor who borrows a cup of sugar later returns it along with thanks and a sample of the cake he baked, this makes it more likely that the other neighbor will continue to lend things in the future. Moreover, exchange theorists hold that individuals choose among alternative actions on the basis of the rewards they will bring. The more rewarding an action (such as becoming rich by devoting every waking moment to work) and the greater the probability of actually getting the reward, the more likely that action will be chosen in preference to some other (such as devoting more time to family).

Over time, as individuals exchange various benefits with one another, they develop mutual expectations that their relationship will continue. Neighbors and friends believe they have the right to expect favors from one another. Parents and children come to look upon one another as dependable sources of valued rewards. These expectations are the source of people's ideas about what is natural and proper. In other words, once an exchange relationship develops between people, they expect that it will continue, and they become upset if someone fails to do what is expected. A friend who fails to agree to a reasonable request or a parent who seems indifferent to a gift eagerly offered by a child is, in fact, refusing to behave in the expected way. Their behavior is upsetting not only because it does not give the others what they expect, but also because it violates what they have defined as the natural order of things.

For Homans, the basic processes of exchange are the foundation of society. Institutions exist because people engage in patterned, systematic exchanges that come to be defined as right and natural. People are thought to be fundamentally self-interested, but the prevailing image of their conduct emphasizes the exchange of benefits rather than conflict. Power and conflict can be found in society, according to this approach, but they have to be understood in relation to exchange. The unequal allocation of social resources means that some individuals have things that others desire. Thus, exchanges are not necessarily equal. One person may have much of value to others but need little from them, in which case that person has considerable power to participate in exchanges on his or her own terms. And there is always the potential for exchange to be replaced by sheer coercion. However, even the interaction that occurs between thief and victim is a form of exchange; the robber who says "Your money or your life" is offering the victim a "choice" of which thing is more valued. Of course, it is the power of a gun that enables the thief to control these valued things, namely, money and life.

Symbolic Interactionism

Finally, symbolic interactionism views society as people interacting with one another. Sometimes interaction is predictable and routine, recreating familiar patterns of behavior. Much everyday interaction in families, on the job, at school, in banks and stores, and similar places falls into this category. At other times, people interact in unfamiliar settings, responding to changing circum-

Georges Seurat, *Sunday Afternoon on the Island of La Grande Jatte* (1884–86)
Oil on canvas. 81 × 120 3/8 inches. Helen Birch Bartlett Memorial Collection, © The Art Institute of Chicago. All Rights Reserved. Courtesy of The Art Institute of Chicago.

Different sociological perspectives lead to different views of this quiet park scene. Functionalists might emphasize the functions of leisure in urban society; conflict theorists, the fact that only middle-class people seem to be represented; exchange theorists, the mutual obligations binding these citizens together; and symbolic interactionists, the way social activities are coordinated in public places.

stances—as, for example, when people face natural disasters or band together to change society. Whatever the context, the symbolic interactionist image of society emphasizes social interaction.

Human beings interact with one another primarily by using symbols. *Symbols* are indirect ways of representing physical objects, other people, experiences, and even abstract ideas and thoughts. The role of symbols in human interaction was charted by the American philosopher and social psychologist George Herbert Mead (1934; 1938), whose ideas we will examine in more detail later. For now, symbols can be thought of as words, since the major systems used by human beings are embedded in language. Words—house, John, liberty—stand for objects. They are ways of depicting, representing, and talking about the world, both human and material, abstract and concrete.

Human society rests upon *symbolic interaction,* a term coined by one of Mead's students, the sociologist Herbert Blumer (1969), to characterize interaction that depends upon the use of symbols. Elsewhere in the animal kingdom, interaction is a matter of the direct and immediate response of one animal to another. One animal acts in a certain way, and the other immediately responds with an act of its own. A dog begins to move toward a cat, for example, and the cat responds by arching its back. Whether this interchange of behavior is learned or instinctive is, for the moment, less important than the fact that it is direct, immediate, and instantaneous.

Among humans, it is different. When we smile or frown, there is no automatic response produced in another. A smile might be a genuine invitation to friendship; it might represent a sexual proposition; or it might be the frozen smile of an airline flight attendant. A frown might be used to register disapproval of another or disapproval of oneself. For humans, there is not necessarily an automatic response engendered by even such simple acts as facial expressions. Instead we must symbolically designate these acts in order to respond to them. We must decide whether we are the recipients of a routine smile or a special invitation, label the other's act according to what we think is intended, and then form our own response. We must, in fact, determine the *meaning* of another's act before we can form our own.

Human conduct is formed as people confront objects, events, or other people, interpret them in symbolic terms, and then decide upon a course of action. In this process, *meaning* is everything. People must interpret the meaning of others' acts in order to respond appropriately to them. At the same time, it is the very capacity to *interpret* that makes the human world so much more fluid and flexible than the worlds inhabited by other animals. Because we respond to the world by interpreting the meanings of things rather than reacting immediately and directly, we can act more imaginatively and creatively. Our symbols give us the capacity to anticipate the future (although not necessarily accurately), to imagine alternative courses of action, and to escape some of the chains that bind other animals to immediate response to their environments. We are able to think, to contemplate the future, to imagine how others will respond to our actions, and to decide between one course of action and another.

These basic ideas about symbols and social interaction will be developed in greater detail in later chapters. For the moment it is important to understand that, for symbolic interactionists, what we are and what we do as human beings depend upon our capacity to act in and upon the world by symbolic means.

WHICH PERSPECTIVE?

Each of these perspectives throws a different light on society. Each has strengths and weaknesses, illuminating some aspects of social life while leaving others in relative darkness. Thus, functionalism calls attention to the connections among social institutions and emphasizes the ways in which society constrains individual actions. Conflict theory stresses that social institutions are not as benign as they may appear, that society seethes with self-interest, power, and conflict. And exchange theory provides an image of human conduct as driven by an effort to secure and hold on to various kinds of rewards. Symbolic interactionism introduces the concept of meaning, emphasizing that human conduct, above all else, is meaningful—that where people cannot find or create meaning as they interact with one another, they are paralyzed.

But each of these perspectives also has limitations. In focusing on society as a network of constraining institutions, functionalists can easily lose sight of the fact that these institutions continue to exist only because people act. By treating social facts as things, the sociologist may forget that society is an abstraction, not a material thing or an acting organism. By focusing on power and conflict, on the other hand, the conflict theorist is tempted to interpret everything in these terms, forgetting that people often engage in cooperative activity. Conflict is an important part of social life, but it is not everything. For their part, exchange theorists have little to say about why people find this or that activity rewarding. They say that we do what we are rewarded for doing, but do not tell us why we are rewarded or why we define one thing as a reward and another as a punishment. And symbolic interactionists, who stress that people act on the basis of their interpretations of reality, often credit individuals with more freedom than they actually have, ignoring the many ways in which behavior is shaped and limited by social forces.

In spite of the fact that each perspective has limitations, most sociologists, including the authors, adopt one of them, regarding it as the most useful way of looking at society. Each scholar must examine the available theories and choose one that makes the most sense to him or her. While such choices are made by a careful weighing of evidence for each, they are also—and perhaps more often—made on the basis of a "gut" feeling. One theory will seem "right" and others, although they contain much that is of value, do not seem adequate as guiding perspectives. Our choice is symbolic interactionism.

Why choose symbolic interactionism as an orienting perspective? First, its image of human nature, which we develop in depth in later chapters, seems to us to be the most accurate and comprehensive of all available perspectives. Each of the perspectives we have discussed has valuable insights into this question, especially conflict theory and exchange theory, which stress the importance of self-interest. But self-interest by itself provides too narrow a view of human nature, we believe, and does not address our distinctively human abilities.

Second, because it emphasizes symbols and meanings as the bases of human conduct, symbolic interactionism provides an especially good account of the actual formation of behavior as people interact. As we shall see, symbolic interactionists stress the importance of social interaction. Our analysis of interaction is more detailed than that of the other perspectives, and it is able to encompass a great variety of forms of interaction. Thus, symbolic interactionists can explain cooperative exchanges between people, but they can also account for conflict, competition, rivalry, friendship—for the whole spectrum of human interaction.

Third, symbolic interactionism can take social structure into account without *reifying* it, that is, without treating it as if it had an existence independent of those whose conduct creates and recreates it. Symbolic interactionists recognize that constraint is an important aspect of social life. Our lives are linked to the lives and activities of others, often in ways we are unaware of. And what we do reflects the power of others over us, not just our own perceptions and desires. Symbolic interactionists recognize these facts, but emphasize that *people* act, not society; that institutions constrain in great part because people permit them to; and that coercion and power are not just abstractions, but have their effects on people as they go about their everyday lives, pursuing their own ends and responding to the acts of others.

In this book, symbolic interactionism will serve as a guiding and organizing perspective, one that provides the major themes for our analysis. But our choice of this perspective is not meant to diminish or demolish the other perspectives. Throughout this book, we will try to be alert to the questions raised by these other perspectives—and to their criticisms of our perspective. And we will often seek insights from them, recognizing that if symbolic interactionism is to flourish, it must learn to deal with some of the very issues that other theories have taken as central to their explanations of social life.

SOCIOLOGY AND OTHER SOCIAL SCIENCES

Sociology studies human society, but so do a number of other disciplines: economics, political science, history, anthropology, psychology, geography, and communications studies. How does sociology differ from these fields? Why are there so many academic disciplines dealing with the same subject matter? Will they someday converge into one field?

Answers to these questions lie partly in history. As creatures of meaning, humans have always been interested in explaining themselves. In different eras of history and for different groups, such explanations have taken different forms. A major goal of religion, for example, has always been to explain the origins and place of human beings in the world. The Judeo-Christian account of the creation of the earth in six days, the expulsion from the Garden of Eden, the Flood, and other biblical events provides such an explanation, as do the creation myths of other religions. Philosophers have also attempted to explain the human world systematically by accounting for the nature of human nature, prescribing ideal forms of government, and setting forth ethical principles. One has only to think of the Bible, the Koran, and writings of Confucius and numerous other philosophers—Plato, Aristotle, Descartes, Spinoza, Kant—to realize how preoccupied humankind has been with the study of itself.

Yet there are crucial differences between religion or philosophy and such social sciences as economics, sociology, or anthropology. The most obvious difference is that these latter disciplines aspire to be sciences. Unlike religion, they place their faith not in unseen forces or supreme beings but in the power of reason checked by factual observation. Science does not accept what it cannot directly or indirectly see, taste, hear, and touch. Moreover, science does not seek to prescribe what the world *ought* to be like. It is concerned with what *is*. Thus, sociology and the other social and behavioral sciences are not in the business of telling people how to behave, but rather of describing and explaining why they act as they do.

The social and behavioral sciences became possible only after the idea of science itself took root in Western thought. The classical civilizations were capable of highly sophisticated thought and of considerable technical mastery of the material world. The ancient Greeks produced excellent philosophers and mathematicians, and the Romans were great civil engineers. But for the ancients, practical and theoretical matters existed in separate realms. Ideas were proved true or false on the basis of argument and internal consistency, not by any effort to test them in the world of facts. Men of practical affairs did not concern themselves with abstract ideas.

It took centuries for the idea of science, which combines abstract theory and a meticulous interest in the empirical world, to emerge and crystallize in Europe. The Church stoutly resisted challenges to its theological account of nature and the place of humankind in creation. Just as important, science was slow in coming because the occupation of scientist did not exist. Even after some individuals began to conduct scientific experiments, most people found it strange to think that a grown person could devote time to poking around the secrets of nature. It seemed odd, if not downright dangerous, to play with chemicals and machines, seeking to learn what was not yet known. It was only common sense to think that what was, was, and that the important mysteries of life were satisfactorily dealt with by religious dogma.

Yet, slowly, science—as an idea and as an activity—did emerge. By the seventeenth century in England, scientific discoveries were beginning to occur rapidly. What has happened in the centuries since is well known. Science and technology became wedded, so that the physical mastery of the world became dependent upon theoretical understanding of the principles of physics, chemistry, and most recently, biology. Just as important, science has become the accepted way of thinking about the world. We take for granted the existence of an unseen world of atomic particles that swarm and spin within observable things. We accept the idea (with sporadic resistance from some religious quarters) that more complex forms of life on earth have evolved from simpler forms.

With science reasonably well established by the end of the eighteenth century, it was perhaps only a matter of time before the idea and practice of science began to be applied to humans and their behavior. After all, if there is order and pattern to nature, is it not likely that the same is true of people and their societies? The development of social science did not occur spontaneously, however, but was stimulated by a number of factors.

One of the seeds of social science was provided by exploration and colonization of other parts of the world by Europeans, especially during the eighteenth and nineteenth centuries. The development of anthropology was especially fostered by contact with the "primitive" peoples of Africa, Australia, and the Americas. To some extent, colonialism required that these cultures be understood so that they could be more effectively controlled by the European powers establishing their rule over large territories. In addition, the nonliterate and less technologically developed societies bolstered Western ideas about the evolution of society and culture. According to this view, Western societies stood at the apex of evolution, and the "primitives" could be seen as living fossils, examples of the stages through which all human societies had earlier passed.

Anthropology is the social science that has generally specialized in the study of simpler societies and cultures. In Britain, social anthropologists focused on the cultures and societies of British colonies, especially in Africa. In the United States, North American Indians were a special object of study. For all anthropologists, nonliterate groups around the world became the special province of their discipline. As industrialization and urbanization have spread around the globe, many indigenous groups have disappeared, either having been absorbed into national cultures or, in some cases, exterminated.

In recent years, anthropologists increasingly have turned their attention to modern urban culture, so that in many cases they study precisely the same phenomena studied by sociologists. However, anthropology has several distinguishing features. Anthropologists have shown more interest in human biology; physical anthropology is one of the discipline's major divisions. Some anthropologists (called archaeologists) specialize in the study of the material remains of previous cultures, while others take a special interest in language. And anthropologists are apt to regard culture, rather than society, as their key concept. (See Chapter 3 for a discussion of this topic.) Many anthropologists regard their discipline as the most encompassing of the social sciences, and there are strong humanistic as well as scientific emphases in the discipline.

The development of sociology itself was especially stimulated by the rapidly accelerating pace of industrialization and urbanization during the nineteenth century. For centuries before, European society had been relatively stable, with change occurring quite slowly. Land was the major basis of wealth, cities were relatively small and specialized, and relationships between people were governed by a complex and slow-to-change set of traditions founded on church, family, and community. Men and women lived lives rooted in the place where they were born. Their relations with others were governed by traditional arrangements of status and authority. They believed the world to be an unchanging place in which the circumstances of their lives reflected the natural order of things.

The growth of the industrial system of production, slow at first but then with increasing rapidity during the nineteenth century, drastically changed the character of human society. People who for generations had worked as peasant farmers in the fields of England found themselves drawn to the cities, where they lived in squalid conditions while providing the labor power to tend the machines of the new industrial order. And it was not only where people lived

Preston Dickinson, *Industry* (pre-1924) Oil. 30 × 24 ½ inches. Collection of Whitney Museum of American Art. Acq#31.173.

Sociology owes its existence partly to the rise of industry, which transformed the social as well as the geographical landscape during the late nineteenth century. The discipline of sociology arose partly out of efforts to understand and control the resulting social changes.

and worked that changed. In the old order, men and women made, or had made for them, only what they needed. Now goods were mass produced, not made to order, and decisions about what was to be produced were made by those who owned the factories and the machines. People were uprooted from their families and communities as they moved to industrial centers, where they lived among strangers. In this new urban world, old status orders were disrupted, and the old traditions that had guided people's behavior began to lose their influence.

In short, industrialization and urbanization were powerful shocks to traditional social arrangements, and the rise of the social sciences, especially sociology, can be traced to these changes. Three especially towering figures of sociology illustrate this point. Karl Marx (1818–1883), the author of *Das Kapital* and (with Frederick Engels) *The Communist Manifesto,* was also a giant figure in the history of social science. His ideas about the historical forces that had brought about the capitalist economic system and about social changes still to come are the basis for a general theory of human society and not just the foundation of communist political ideology.

Writing somewhat later than Marx, the German historian and sociologist Max Weber (1864–1920) also attempted to explain how the social and economic changes associated with capitalism had come about. Unlike Marx, who emphasized material and economic forces, Weber placed more emphasis upon the role of ideas in history. He felt that the Protestant Reformation had unleashed ideas and motivations that were responsible for capitalism, a thesis developed in his book *The Protestant Ethic and the Spirit of Capitalism* (1930). Weber also wrote about that ubiquitous form of organization, the bureaucracy, describing its features and failings in a way that remains current today. The French sociologist, Émile Durkheim (1858–1917), was also stimulated by the vast social changes of the nineteenth century. Durkheim provided a systematic description of the methods and procedures of sociology (1895), examined the different forms of the social division of labor (1893), provided an explanation of the origins and nature of religion (1912), and developed an explanation of suicide (1897) that is still cited.

These scholars helped set the tone for modern sociology and influenced the work of sociologists in the United States. Here, the discipline began to emerge and to find a home within universities during the late nineteenth and early twentieth centuries. At various times, the discipline has emphasized different things. During the early years of this century, sociologists were concerned not only with explaining but also ameliorating the social consequences of industrialization and urbanization. American sociologists also paid attention to two important features of their society: the problems of racial conflict and discrimination and the large-scale immigration of Europeans to North America. Later, especially during the 1940s and 1950s, sociologists became preoccupied with the scientific status of their discipline, seeking for it the characteristics—and the prestige—of the natural sciences. Since the 1960s, sociologists have increasingly turned their attention to practical matters, some adopting an activist and often explicitly radical stance toward society, others seeking a role for scientific sociology in the formulation of public policy.

Economics and political science were emerging as distinct disciplines along with sociology. As their names imply, they are more specialized disciplines, each focusing on a single institution—one on the economy, the other on politics and government. In contrast, sociology has always tended to be a more generalized discipline, attempting to create a general theory of society and taking the position that institutions have to be viewed in relation to one another. Sociologists think that the economy and government influence and are influenced by families, communities, social inequality, and other social arrangements and institutions.

In recent years there has been considerable blurring of lines among the disciplines of sociology, economics, and political science. Sociologists can be found writing about economic life or about government; at the same time, many economists and political scientists have become interested in topics, such as crime, that were previously left to sociologists. And political scientists have been particularly influenced by methods of social research developed within sociology. Each discipline tends to borrow the methods and theories of the others.

The disciplines of psychology and communication studies stand in a somewhat different relationship to sociology. Psychology has similar origins in the nineteenth-century movement to explain reality in scientific terms. But where the chief level of abstraction for sociology, economics, and political science is social, psychologists focus instead on the individual. Social scientists regard groups, organizations, and society itself as profound influences on individuals, whose attributes and motives are seen as largely the product of social experience. For psychologists, the inner workings of the psyche are of prime significance, with social influences acknowledged but not emphasized. Sociology and psychology each provide a home for a subdiscipline called social psychology, which focuses on the behavior of individuals as it is influenced by the presence of others. Social psychologists within sociology and psychology tend to be oriented primarily to the literature and theoretical concerns of the parent discipline.

Communication studies is a more recent arrival on the social-science scene and is not found in all universities and colleges. Departments of communication studies usually have developed out of speech departments, and contain an amalgam of several emphases: the study (and sometimes the practice) of the mass media; the examination of rhetoric and persuasion; and the study of language, conversation, and interpersonal interaction. The last emphasis in particular has been influenced by linguistics, sociolinguistics, and by the methods and theories of sociology, social psychology, and psychology.

Finally, there is the discipline of history. It used to be fairly easy to distinguish history from the social sciences. History did not pretend to be scientific, nor did it seek to formulate scientific generalizations. Standing firmly within the humanities, not the social sciences, it focused on the narrative depiction of historical events as they unfolded, often with an emphasis on the unique configuration of events and circumstances. The history that many of us learned in high school and college was a history of a succession of wars, rulers, and nations.

Much has changed, not only in the nature of history as a discipline but also in its relation to social science. Historians today are much more likely to write about the same things that interest sociologists: families, communities, and the experiences and perspectives of ordinary people. They are more apt to use quantitative methods, and the historical study of population composition and change has become a thriving enterprise. They are more likely to use at least some of the insights of the social and behavioral sciences; for example, drawing upon the work of Freud to interpret the character of historical persons. And, for their part, sociologists have found interesting much of what historians do. Sociologists have begun to apply their own methods and theories to historical materials, seeking to understand the social causes of such historical events as the French Revolution.

The picture that emerges is one of greater contact and cooperation among the several disciplines that study humankind, but not necessarily a rapid convergence into a single discipline. There remain significant differences among the various fields, and although these differences are as much the result of historical accident as of real differences in subject matter, they are still important. Thus, historians place more emphasis on the writing of history as literature and remain justifiably suspicious of the sociologists' penchant for quantifying everything. Psychologists are apt to seem historically and sociologically uninformed in the eyes of other social scientists; for their part, pyschologists accuse social scientists of giving too much emphasis to social influences on the individual. Economists, particularly those who specialize in the complex mathematical representation of economic systems, may look upon the efforts of other social scientists as crude and unscientific. Political science contains a strong humanistic tradition as well as a policy orientation, in addition to its more recently developed social-scientific flavor.

These continuing differences may sometimes impede contact and mutual assistance among the several disciplines, but they may also have some value. The study of humankind is a vast and complex field, one which no single science or perspective can hope to master in the foreseeable future. Thus, diversity and even disagreement ought to be encouraged, and the existence of several disciplines may be one way of providing for such diversity.

CONCLUSION

In this chapter we have described sociology in a general way, showing how its major concept—society—can be approached from different perspectives. We have also made a case for symbolic interactionism, the perspective we will adopt in this book. And we have said something about the origins of sociology and its relationships to other social-science disciplines and to psychology and history.

In Chapter 2, we turn from the abstract to the concrete, from characterizations of sociology to examples of sociologists at work. We will examine several different kinds of sociological research, talk about the rules they follow, and examine the methods they use to study society and the behavior of its members.

SUGGESTED READINGS

Berger, Peter L. *Invitation to Sociology* (Garden City, N.Y.: Anchor Books, 1963).

Blumer, Herbert. *Symbolic Interactionism: Perspective and Method* (Englewood Cliffs, N.J.: Prentice-Hall, 1969).

Collins, Randall and Michael Makowsky. *The Discovery of Society*, 2nd ed. (New York: Random House, 1978).

Inkeles, Alex. *What is Sociology?* (Englewood Cliffs, N.J.: Prentice-Hall, 1964).

Madge, John. *The Origins of Scientific Sociology* (New York: Free Press, 1962).

Mills, C. Wright. *The Sociological Imagination* (New York: Oxford University Press, 1959).

2

How Sociologists Work

Sociology is the scientific study of society. This definition, which is fine as an abstraction, actually says very little about the day-to-day work of people who call themselves sociologists. How do sociologists study society? What is it about their work that makes it scientific, distinguishing it from the work of journalists or novelists? What kinds of tools do sociologists use? And what, specifically, do they study? In this chapter we will try to answer these questions by describing some of the research methods of sociology and by discussing examples of sociological research. Before we do, however, there are a few things that should be said about the nature of science.

SOCIOLOGY AS SCIENCE

Much has been written in an effort to describe science and the scientific method of pursuing knowledge. Although the philosophy of the scientific method is a complex topic, we think that the attitudes and behavior that characterize the scientist's quest for knowledge can be readily described.

Science is *empirical.* Its concern is with observable facts, not with moral or ideological preference. The job of the biologist, physicist, or sociologist is not to tell people how to behave, nor to specify what the natural or social world should be like. The task of the scientist is to make factual observations of what is: the conditions under which plants grow slowly or quickly; the behavior of atomic particles bombarded by other particles; the rituals people follow when they exchange greetings; or the effect of punishment on the subsequent behavior of convicted felons.

The scientist is obligated to follow certain rules in carrying out such observations. Whether the topic is the behavior of molecules or children, the scientific observer is supposed to report honestly what has been observed. All scientists have preferences, among them the wish to observe facts that will confirm their theories. Nevertheless, complete honesty is a prime virtue in science. One of the ways honest observations are achieved is through complete and open reporting. Scientists do not just report conclusions. They are supposed to report the methods they used to gather data, describe any instruments or mechanical devices employed, and detail any conditions that may have affected the outcome of their work.

By following such rules of observation and reporting, scientists seek to make their work capable of being replicated by others. If one sociologist observes that released prisoners who get financial assistance are less likely to end up back in prison than those who do not get such help, another sociologist should be able to use the same methods in order to test this conclusion. If the results of a study cannot be replicated, doubt is cast on the validity of the previous study, the care with which it was carried out, or perhaps even the veracity of the scientific investigator.

Science is also *theoretical.* The work of the scientist is not aimless, guided only by the whim of the individual observer. Instead, science is a generalizing activity in which there is a constant quest to organize observations into increasingly powerful explanatory theories. The scientist is usually not interested in the particular thing under observation, but in that thing as a sample or representative of a category of things. Thus, the biologist has no interest in the behavior of a particular animal in the laboratory on a particular day. Rather, the biologist's interest is in the behavior of that *kind* of animal under known conditions. Similarly, the sociologist studying prisons is not concerned with whether a particular Joe Smith ends up back in jail, but in the general conditions under which ex-prisoners either revert to criminal activity or succeed in the "straight" world. Scientists try to generalize from their observations.

Scientists also are led to make their observations on the basis of existing theories. A sociologist might theorize that it is the lack of money and job opportunities that forces released prisoners to turn once again to criminal activities, an "occupation" in which they already have skills and contacts. In order to test this theory, the social scientist might enlist the aid of authorities in order to design an experiment. (For a study that attempted just this, see Rossi, et al., 1980.) Some individuals would be offered financial and job-finding aid on their release, while others would not. Their subsequent activities could then be compared. Although a study such as this has a very practical aim, it is still guided by a theory, that is, by an attempt to generalize about the conditions under which people will behave in certain ways. Not all theories have such a practical bent; in many cases, the social scientist is simply interested in testing a generalization about society and has no practical goal in mind.

Much more could be written about the nature of science. But it is best characterized by this combination of interest in and respect for the empirical world and by the quest to develop theories that will organize and explain what is observed. In the final analysis, science is what scientists do. Whatever rules may be formulated to describe or guide scientific work, science consists of a community of people who follow these rules and do things they call science. Thus, to see what sociology is like as a science, we have to look at sociologists and examine their work.

TOOLS OF SOCIOLOGICAL RESEARCH

We can begin by saying that the job of the sociologist is to observe and theorize about society. But just how does the sociologist do this? What instruments or techniques are available, and what does the sociological eye perceive when using them? What is the nature of sociological observation? The sociologist has a diverse kit of tools with which to do the work of observation. Here we will describe and illustrate some of the more important ones.

George Tooker, *The Subway* (1950)
Egg tempera on composition board. 18 × 36 inches. Collection of Whitney Museum of American Art. Juliana Force Purchase. Acq#50.23.

Participant observation is possible wherever there is a vantage point from which to observe ongoing social life, including such public places as subway stations. But not everything that is meaningful to participants can be observed directly. Routine and public acts can be grasped readily, but it is impossible to know with certainty the feelings of the woman in this painting.

Participant Observation

One of the most important techniques of sociological research is *participant observation.* This method is especially favored by symbolic interactionists because they feel that research should begin where the action is—among those people in whose behavior the sociologist is interested and in the real situations where it occurs. This is not surprising if we remember that the symbolic interactionist perspective focuses on meaningful social interaction as the basis of society.

The method of participant observation entails just what its name suggests. The sociologist enters some location or situation—a factory, club, family, or neighborhood—and conducts observations while also participating in it. When engaging in participant observation, sociologists use many of the same skills they have learned and used as members of the society. The difference is that their goal as participant observers is not to be a part of the social world under study but to describe it, theorize about it, and understand it.

Everyday interaction occurs in settings such as families, jobs, schools, churches, and the like that are to some extent unfamiliar to the sociologist, who often must learn what others take for granted. This may mean learning a new vocabulary, new skills, and new rules of etiquette. In doing this, the participant observer often gains new insights into an activity.

An interesting example of how the sociologist can use participant observation, along with some other methods, to explore some facet of society is Harvey Farberman's study of the used-car business (Farberman, 1975). This study also shows how theory and observation affect one another in the course of research, and how luck and accident play a part in scientific work.

Farberman began his study with an interest in the bargaining tactics used by consumers, particularly low-income consumers, in dealing with higher-status sales and service personnel. He theorized (on the basis of previous research) that customers tried to gain an edge in their dealings with salespeople and service managers by treating them in a more personal way and attempting to be regarded as friends and not just as customers. Guided by this theory, he began participant observation at a used-car dealership, a place where interaction between customers and salespersons can easily be observed. Farberman had worked for the dealership as a student, so it was relatively easy to get the owners' permission to do his research.

What does a participant observer do? For almost two years (averaging one day a week), this researcher hung around the used-car lot, listening, watching, and taking notes on what was happening. At first primarily an observer, Farberman was gradually drawn into some kinds of participation—answering the telephone, delivering cars, helping around the lot. He carried a notebook to record observations and made his entries in full view of others, thus making clear his status as an observer. He also talked informally with people and socialized with members of the organization. After six months of observation, Farberman began to conduct tape-recorded interviews with these members. He did this in order to validate the insights and observations he had reached as an observer.

During his research, Farberman noticed something that was not directly relevant to the theory with which he had started, but which was nevertheless interesting. After a deal for a car had been struck, he noticed that customers would often give the dealer some cash as well as a check to cover the agreed price of the car. He began to focus on this transaction in an effort to discover what was going on. What was happening, he found, was a practice known as a "short sale." When a salesperson began to write up a sale, a state sales tax—a hefty 8 percent—would be added to the cost of the car. The customer would grumble about this, and the salesperson would suggest a way to reduce the tax; namely, if the customer would pay part of the cost of the car in cash and the rest by check, the salesperson would make out a bill of sale only for the amount covered by the check. The sales tax would be computed on the basis of the smaller amount instead of the total cost of the car. On a car selling for two thousand dollars, if fifteen hundred was paid by check and was the amount listed on the bill of sale, the customer could avoid sales tax on the remaining five hundred. The savings of forty dollars would be small, but still symbolically significant to the customer, who could feel the satisfaction of putting something over on the government.

This observation raised new questions in the researcher's mind. Although the customer gained a savings from the deal, what was the advantage to the dealer? Cash received in this manner would be unrecorded; that is, no sales contract or check would exist to show that the money had changed hands. Thus, the dealer could avoid taxes on this money, since its existence could not be detected by the authorities. But was this the sole motive for short selling?

Farberman pursued the topic by conducting more observations, asking more questions, and learning more about the automobile business as a whole. He found, for example, that used-car dealerships like the one he was studying relied on new-car dealers as their source of cars. New-car dealers take cars in trade on new-car sales, but they keep only a few trade-ins to sell themselves. The others are sold to used-car dealers. The new-car dealers are desperate to sell excess used cars as quickly as they can to recover their value, since the used car is accepted as part payment for a new car. To sell trade-ins, new-car dealers generally employ someone who specializes in this task. This individual is in a powerful position; he has something, namely used cars, that new-car dealers are anxious to get rid of and used-car dealers must have in order to stay in business. Frequently the price of doing business with him is a kickback; that is, he will sell cars to a dealer looking for them, but only if something is thrown in for him. This is where the used-car dealer can use the supply of cash generated in short selling, since kickbacks are generally not paid by check!

This finding led Farberman to another connection; the new-car dealer is chronically short of money. Large sums have to be borrowed from banks in order to finance the inventory of new cars, and interest on these loans is expensive. Automobile manufacturers are committed to a policy of volume sales at low per car profit margins; their goal is to sell cars in massive volume in order to realize economies of large-scale production. Manufacturers force their dealers to take a large number of cars as a condition for retaining their franchises. Faced with the need to finance a large inventory and with the profit per new car sold relatively small, the new-car dealer turns to other means to keep the cash flowing in. Getting rid of used cars taken in trade is one way of keeping the money flowing, of generating the revenues needed to stay in business. Another technique is to engage in a variety of rip-offs in the service department: overcharging customers, performing service that is not needed, charging for parts not used, and the like.

In pursuing this chain of connections, which we have sketched only briefly, Farberman supplemented his participant observations with interviews—asking various key participants how the system worked—and by consulting other research, congressional hearings, and similar documents. In doing so he followed an important rule of social science research: *triangulating* his observations (Denzin, 1978). That is, he did not rely on observation alone, but checked it by asking questions that were raised in his mind by his observations and compared his results with data available from other sources. He did not rely on a single method, but on several.

This study illustrates another important point, namely that research that begins with one theory sometimes goes in quite unexpected directions. As a result of his work, the author linked his observations to a theory known as the *criminogenic market hypothesis*, which states that illegal activity (in this instance short selling, kickbacks, service rip-offs) can often be traced to the legal activities of groups and organizations with the power to force others to violate the law. In this case, the volume sales and pricing policies of the major auto manufacturers place their dealers in a position where they feel they have to engage in or condone illegal activity to stay in business.

The advantage of participant observation is that it brings the investigator close to a particular social world. What occurs there is not a matter of speculation, but of direct observation. Moreover, by participating to some degree in the activities under study, the researcher can gain a closer and more valid appreciation of their meaning. To grasp the perspective of used-car dealers toward customers, for example, one has to associate with them as they interact with customers. Farberman found that the used-car dealer holds retail customers in great contempt because they are interested in the appearance of a car rather than in its mechanical condition, but also because the dealer is so dependent upon them. To grasp fully the relationship between dealer and customer, one cannot rely simply on questions, nor simply on the distant observation of their interaction. To know a social world and its meanings, one must participate to some degree in its activities.

Participant observation is not without its pitfalls. The researcher can be deceived by those whose activities are under study. Important areas of an organization or an activity may be closed to scrutiny. The observer may get uncomfortably close to illegal or even dangerous activities. And the participant observer may start to adopt the perspectives of those whose social world is being studied. For these and other reasons, triangulation—checking observations by several methods—is crucial. No method by itself can do the whole job of observation.

One final note about Farberman's study. Although the researcher began by studying the activities of a local dealer and observing the face-to-face business transactions there, it did not take long for the wider ramifications to become apparent. The single transaction between buyer and seller is a small part of a more extensive chain of connections among various levels of the automobile industry. What happens in a transaction is affected by decisions made by people with considerable power. The average customer doesn't know how the automobile industry works, nor does the president of General Motors have any interest in the individual sale. Nonetheless, these individuals are linked together by successive levels of the industry. Symbolic interactionists believe that it is crucial to study the meanings that are involved in everyday interaction, but they also feel it is essential to show how the microscopic world of everyday life is connected to larger and more complex social arrangements.

Asking Questions

Sociologists who observe what goes on in social life only see a part of what actually transpires. They can see people's physical movements, hear their conversations, and watch how they behave in one another's presence, but the full meaning of their actions cannot be grasped merely from observation. This is because, in addition to a person's overt behavior, there is also an inner, mental life that is not directly open to others' scrutiny. People make plans; they imaginatively rehearse what they will say or do next; they decide whether they think others approve or disapprove of what they are doing; they have private interpretations of their successes and failures; they have hopes for themselves or their children; they have a fund of experience and a set of opinions about all kinds of things. Although these inner matters are not directly observable, they are still an important aspect of what the sociologist studies. To understand and explain society, the sociologist must know something of people's thoughts, ideas, opinions, and plans. Asking questions is a key method for investigating this aspect of social life.

There are so many ways to ask people questions that it is impossible to cover all of them here. We will discuss and illustrate three kinds of question-asking activities that are commonly used by sociologists. First, we will look at a study in which *intensive interviewing* of a selected group of people was the chief research method. Second, we will discuss what is probably the method most commonly used by sociologists, the *survey interview*, in which a large number of people are asked a standard set of questions. And third, we will examine the use of a *mailed questionnaire* that is sent to respondents, filled out by them, and then returned to the researcher.

Intensive Interviewing Symbolic interactionists hold that in order to understand the way people participate in social life, it is necessary to understand things from their point of view. Often it is difficult to gain this understanding, for the sociologist may wish to study groups with whom he or she has had no previous contact and whose world is not understood. Even when a theory underlies the investigation, it may provide only sketchy guidance about what should be observed. Under these conditions, the sociologist often turns to intensive interviewing: sitting down with a number of individuals and asking detailed questions that focus on matters about which the sociologist wants to become informed.

This kind of interviewing calls upon all of the skills of social interaction and conversation at the researcher's disposal. People must be persuaded to answer the sociologist's questions and assured that what they say will be held in confidence. The sociologist must win their trust and confidence and do whatever can be done to elicit honest answers from them. And the researcher must be careful to let respondents answer questions in their own words and with their own ideas. It is *their* social world and *their* opinions in which the sociologist is

Fernand Léger, *Three Musicians* (1944)
Oil on canvas, 68½ × 57¼ inches. Collection, The Museum of Modern Art, New York. Mrs. Simon Guggenheim Fund.

Beneath the appearances and activities of these musicians (and of members of all occupations) lie unseen but important layers of meaning. Their aspirations, dreams, and disappointments can be detected only by the investigator whose questions probe beneath the surface.

interested, and great care must be taken lest the researcher put words in their mouths or misinterpret what they say. (To avoid this problem, interviews are often tape recorded.) The researcher must be able to think on the spot, for there is no way to anticipate every possible question that should be asked during the course of an interview.

Robert Faulkner's study (1974) of the career patterns of professional hockey players and orchestra musicians illustrates one of the many ways in which interviews may be used in the study of social life. Faulkner employed several different methods in his study; he conducted observations in work settings, took field notes, and consulted personnel records. However, the portion of the work to be discussed here is drawn mainly from his interviews with sixty symphony orchestra musicians and thirty-eight minor-league hockey players.

Why interview hockey players and musicians in the same study? These two occupations seem to have very little in common. Faulkner was led to these fields by his general interest in studying occupations, and especially by a desire to learn more about a problem that is common to many, but not all, occupations. Hockey and music are highly competitive; an individual entering one of these fields does so with high hopes for success. Each new player wants to succeed, to make it into the "big leagues" of sport or music. The orchestra players interviewed were members of good middle-level orchestras, and all either had or formerly had aspirations to advance in their careers—to become a principal player in their orchestra (for example, first violin) or, better still, to gain a seat on one of the prestigious "big five" orchestras, such as the New York Philharmonic. Similarly, the hockey players were on minor-league teams in the American Hockey League, just below the big-time National Hockey League, and their goal was to get a permanent spot for themselves on an NHL team.

In both professional hockey and symphony orchestras, the minor leagues are training grounds, providing a place where some players are prepared for future stardom. Future success in the majors motivates their efforts to perform well in their present positions. But in these two occupations more people aspire to reach the top of their profession than will actually get there. The majority of musicians will remain in lesser orchestras, and most hockey players will end their careers in the minor leagues. This fact of life presents problems for individuals and for the organizations in which they work. The individual who does not make it to the top must somehow learn to live with this fact. The organization still needs these people and must somehow encourage them to continue to work effectively, even though they are no longer motivated by the prospect of moving to a better team or orchestra.

Several questions were thus on the researcher's mind: How do people in these occupations know when the time has come to abandon hope for greater success? How do these men and women redefine themselves and their aspirations in order to adjust? And how does the organization fare as people scrutinize their careers and their accomplishments and change their outlook on the future?

These are questions that can be answered only by learning how people perceive themselves, their careers, and their chances for success. Faulkner theorized that *time* would be an important aspect of these perceptions. Members of each of these occupations would, he felt, share a set of ideas about how fast their advancement should occur and how old they should be at various career stages. For hockey players, advancement would be age-graded, if only because their sport places a premium on youthful athletic ability. And musicians, like members of other professions, would share the belief that chances for advancement diminish with the passing of time. To test the validity of his theorizing, Faulkner had to ask people about their perceptions.

He found that players indeed had definite ideas about the timing of success. You could stay in the minors only for a certain length of time before it became clear that you would not move up. Consequently, the first five or six years in hockey and the first ten to twelve years in an orchestra are seen as the time the person has to "make it." During these years, an individual feels he or she is establishing a foothold in the profession and trying to make a name. Success seems to be a realistic goal, and advancement seems possible.

When hockey players or musicians linger too long in the minors, they begin to define themselves differently. They start to view their present positions more favorably and the climb up the ladder of success as costing more than it may be worth. They strive for recognition rather than stardom, and they devote more of their time and energy to family and other things outside the job. These changes in outlook provide a way for the individual to retain self-esteem—to define the position attained as relative success rather than as failure to reach the top.

Such changing perceptions not only affect the individual player; they also are important for the organization. A middle-level orchestra may not be the big leagues, but it still wants its players to play well. If there were continuing bitterness and disappointment on the part of those who would rather be elsewhere, the orchestra as a whole would suffer. And owners and fans want a winning hockey team, whether it is major or minor league. A group of players who would rather be somewhere else can hardly make a winning team. Thus, personal adjustments of the kind Faulkner discovered contribute to organizational survival as well as to personal well-being.

Intensive interviewing is especially useful in studies where the researcher needs to learn the perceptions and opinions of individuals. Knowing little about their situation at the outset, but guided by some hunches and theorizing, the sociologist can focus questions on the areas about which knowledge is sought. Because the researcher wants to understand the ideas and perceptions of people, every effort is made to have them tell the story in their words. Even when questions are formulated in advance, the answers are recorded in the respondents' own words, not in categories or codes predetermined by the researcher. And the interview affords an opportunity to ask new questions, to explore in depth those topics that seem to be especially interesting to respondents, and to take the cues they provide for inquiring about what is important to them.

Survey Interviews The intensive interview is useful, but it is also an expensive and time-consuming research technique. Even fifty interviews of two hours each, and they are often longer, consume enormous amounts of time. For this reason, much sociological research uses less expensive methods that are capable of gathering information from larger numbers of people. Among the most common of these methods is the survey interview.

The survey interview has several characteristics. First, researchers using this technique ask a standardized set of questions. Each respondent is approached by an interviewer who, after introducing the study and its purposes, asks for the individual's cooperation in answering questions. The interviewer then reads a set of questions that have been prepared in advance and printed on an *interview schedule.* Often the researchers have established ahead of time the categories in which they desire respondents to answer. Questions about attitudes and opinions, for example, often call for answers such as "strongly agree," "agree," or "strongly disagree." These fixed alternative categories do not allow the respondent the opportunity to formulate an answer in his or her own words. Some questions, such as questions about occupation, may be answered in the respondent's own words, but even these will later be coded by the researchers into a set of categories.

Second, the survey interview is usually administered to people who have been chosen on the basis of precise and often very complex sampling techniques. A *sample* is merely a subset of people selected by some procedure from a larger set, or *population*, of people. Thus, one might select a sample of American adults, women lawyers, or eleventh-grade and twelfth-grade students. One common approach to sampling, called *random sampling*, entails procedures that ensure that each member of the population in question has an equal chance of being included in the sample. Sometimes simple random sampling is impossible, and procedures are developed to come as close to it as possible. Whatever the method chosen, the purpose of sampling is to learn something about a specified population without studying every member. By careful sampling, researchers can save time and money and still draw accurate conclusions about the people under study.

The use of sampling is not limited to survey interviews, of course, since any study that seeks to learn things from and about people can use a sample. In many studies of the kind represented by Faulkner's research, however, interviews will be conducted with members of one or a very few organizations (such as hockey teams or orchestras). This is done because the time and expense required for the researcher to conduct face-to-face interviews with people scattered across the country would be prohibitive. Unlike studies such as Faulkner's, in which the researcher does the actual interviewing, surveys usually employ people who have specialized training in interviewing and who work for companies specializing in conducting such studies.

A third characteristic of survey interviews is that the analysis of data is usually *quantitative* in form. In a study using intensive interviewing, there is usually little effort to count the number of people who answer a question in a given way. This is partly because the small number of interviews does not usually permit the use of statistics. But the decision to use *qualitative* rather than quantitative analysis is also based on the fact that the researcher is concerned with the perceptions, opinions, and beliefs of the respondents. The goal is often to describe things from their point of view.

In surveys, however, attention is more often focused on establishing relationships among variables. A *variable* is something that can assume more than one state. Thus, sex is a variable that has two states: male or female. Attitudes are also quite often variables in sociological research, and they are usually measured so that they assume states ranging from "strongly disagree" to "strongly agree." Income is a variable measured by dollars received and can thus range from zero to very large sums of money.

Often survey researchers are interested in establishing the relationship between an *independent variable* and a *dependent variable*, where the former is in some sense viewed as the *cause* of the latter. For example, a researcher might be interested in studying the influence of sex on a political issue. Are men more or less likely than women to favor nuclear disarmament? Here, sex is the independent (causal) variable, and attitude is the dependent variable. Tackling a research question of this kind requires answers to questions about arms control from a sample of men and women, so that the proportion of men favoring disarmament can be compared with the proportion of women favoring disarmament.

Survey interviews thus differ significantly from intensive interviews. They are cheaper to administer and yield data from a larger number of people. At the same time, the information they provide has less depth than that yielded by the intensive interview. The survey researcher does not interrupt the interview schedule to go more deeply into issues that arise. In fact, the interviewer may have only a limited understanding of the purpose of the research project, which has been designed by a scholar who may be hundreds of miles away and whom the interviewer never sees. In many cases, respondents have to adapt their attitudes and beliefs to the categories of the researcher.

These features of the survey interview can be looked at as either advantages or disadvantages. On one hand, this method does yield standardized information from large numbers of people. If a sample has been carefully chosen, it is possible to generalize to the population from which the sample has been drawn. Thus, for example, a survey of a few hundred men and women could yield useful information about the attitudes of men and women throughout the society. And surveys can be designed to provide information that can serve the needs of many researchers.

On the other hand, the survey researcher is distant from the lives and circumstances of the people studied. It is hard to anticipate all the questions that one might want to ask, and it is possible to ask questions that have little meaning to respondents. Moreover, because response categories are usually determined in advance, there is a danger of imposing the ideas of the researcher on the ideas of the respondents. They may view things in ways that a researcher just cannot anticipate. There is always the possibility that a survey will yield superficial or misleading information. Respondents may tell an interviewer what they think about disarmament, for example, but this does not mean that the topic is important to them. Finally, the survey interview tends to emphasize attitudes, opinions, and beliefs, matters about which it is relatively easy to ask people. These are important matters, but hardly more important than actual behavior in real situations.

For these and other reasons, symbolic interactionists in particular tend to be skeptical about social surveys, and especially about basing too many conclusions upon them. Like any method, the survey interview has limitations that must be recognized. So long as scholars do not rely on this method to the exclusion of all others, however, there is much to be gained from the use of surveys.

In recent years, an important development in the survey interview has been associated with the widespread use of computers. Data from surveys, now economically stored on computer tape, can be mailed or transmitted around the country and thus made available to scholars other than those who designed the survey. In this way, analysis of the data can be carried out by many different scholars.

This latter procedure, called *secondary survey analysis*, has become very popular. Those without access to funds to conduct their own studies can nevertheless gain access to data that they can analyze. One of the major resources for this kind of analysis is the *General Social Survey* conducted annually by the National Opinion Research Center at the University of Chicago (see N.O.R.C., 1982). This survey asks a large number of questions of a national sample of adults. These questions cover a variety of matters: the occupation, income, racial, ethnic, and religious background of respondents and their parents, opinions about important political issues, and attitudes and behavior regarding such diverse matters as illness, gun ownership, and abortion.

This kind of survey is very useful. Many scholars can gain access to the data to research a variety of questions. Moreover, because many of the same questions are asked year after year, it is possible for sociologists to track changes in important areas of belief, opinion, and behavior. They can determine whether people are becoming more or less interested in certain political issues, for example, or whether political attitudes are becoming more conservative.

Questionnaires Another tool frequently employed by sociologists is the questionnaire, a technique that eliminates the interviewer. Rather than have questions read to them, respondents receive a printed set of questions that they answer in writing, either by checking predetermined categories or by writing short answers. These questionnaires can be mailed, distributed through some agency such as a school, or administered to people in groups.

Questionnaires have several advantages. First, they can be administered much more cheaply than survey interviews since they do not require the services of interviewers. Second, like survey interviews, they are a useful way of gathering information from a relatively large number of people. And, in the case of a mailed questionnaire, a researcher can reach people who are geographically scattered or otherwise difficult to reach.

The questionnaire must be constructed with great care. Often there is no researcher present to explain questions the respondents do not understand, so it is critical that questions be worded clearly and directly. The respondents must be given instructions on which questions to answer (for example, the respondents must be told clearly to skip a block of questions pertaining to children if they have no children), and the answer categories provided must match the kind of question that is asked.

Questionnaires work best when they are focused on a well-defined topic about which the researcher knows a great deal and has very specific hypotheses to test. Faulkner's study of musicians and hockey players could not have been conducted successfully by using a questionnaire, since the researcher wanted to plumb the depths of his respondents' views of themselves and their work. Farberman's study would have been impossible using this technique, since he would have had no idea what questions to ask. But where the sociologist has a very specific idea of what information is needed, questionnaires can be very useful.

One of the authors of this book used a mailed questionnaire to study Jewish identity and identification (Hewitt, 1980). She wanted to determine the extent to which contemporary Jewish men and women think of themselves as Jews, maintain distinctively Jewish beliefs and attitudes, and engage in various religious and ethnic practices.

The researcher also wanted to test a specific theory about ethnic and religious identity. Many sociologists and others have taken the view that each successive generation of Americans becomes more and more assimilated until ethnic identities ultimately disappear. Evidence of assimilation could be found in the abandonment of traditional patterns and beliefs by the children and grandchildren of immigrants. The researcher theorized that something else had taken place. She postulated an alternative explanation—a theory of *ethnogenesis*—that she felt would better explain the realities of contemporary American ethnic groups. According to this theory, ethnic groups sustain their group identities by creating *new* beliefs, attitudes, and actions that better fit the new circumstances under which they live. A study of contemporary Jews was undertaken to test these competing theories.

Although the researcher had access to a study conducted using a large national sample of Jews, a secondary analysis of these data was not sufficient to evaluate the two competing theories. Thus it was necessary to obtain additional data. In deciding where to obtain additional information, she decided to choose a sample that would permit a rigorous test of her theory; that is, she wanted to select a group of Jews among whom it might be expected that identity would be weakest. She selected as her sample those men and women born during a single decade, from 1940 to 1950, who received their religious instruction and were confirmed in a midwestern Reform congregation. Reform is the least traditional of the three major Jewish denominations. Thus it might be expected that these persons, in their thirties and forties when the study was conducted, would have weaker ethnic identities. Indeed, it might well be expected, if the assimilationist view was accepted, that many of them would no longer consider themselves to be Jews. The study would then see if they continued to identify themselves as Jews, and if they did, whether they were continuing traditional patterns or developing new cultural patterns.

The questionnaire was specifically designed to assess the current attitudes, beliefs, religious practices, and self-definitions of this sample. Care was taken to make the questions easy to answer by having people circle alternative responses or by writing only a few words. In the effort to limit the length of the questionnaire and to make it easy to answer, depth was sacrificed. Still, respondents were asked a variety of questions, including whether they still considered themselves Jews, whether they engaged in various practices such as keeping kosher or observing the Sabbath, whether they sent their children to religious school, and the like. There were questions about holiday observances and an opportunity to express attitudes about intermarriage, the Holocaust, and Israel.

This questionnaire was to be sent to 108 men and women who had scattered to many areas of the country since reaching adulthood during the 1960s. A search was conducted relying upon parents and relatives, many of whom still resided in the same city and could provide addresses for their own children and sometimes for others as well. Eventually 90 percent of the individuals in the sample were located. Questionnaires were mailed to them with stamped return envelopes, and ultimately more than 80 percent returned them.

The results of this study generally supported the ethnogenesis theory of ethnic identity. The vast majority of those who responded considered themselves to be Jews and identified with the Jewish people. The abandonment of traditional practices (such as keeping kosher) did not mean the cessation of Jewish identification. New practices and attitudes were of greater importance. For example, there was a special emphasis upon Hanukah, the Jewish holiday that occurs close to Christmas. Religiously a minor holiday, its celebration, during which candles are kindled for eight days and gifts are exchanged, is seen by many Jewish parents as a way of providing their children with a substitute for Christmas and at the same time reinforcing their identities as Jews.

Because of this study's sharp focus, a mailed questionnaire was an appropriate technique. Another factor that contributed to its success was that the respondents seemed highly motivated to reply. They had an interest in the topic and wanted to express their views. The fact that the researcher was raised in the same congregation also helped; many of the respondents knew her and probably felt some sense of obligation to assist her in writing her doctoral dissertation. Mailed questionnaires are generally most successful under conditions such as these. Where the focus of a study is less clear and the sample is drawn from the general population, there is less motivation for people to answer the questions and return the form to the researcher.

Other Data-collection Techniques

Participant observation, interviewing, and questionnaires are the major techniques of data collection for sociologists, but they are not the only ones. In addition to these methods, sociologists make use of many other sources of information. Organizational records (such as personnel files, internal memoranda, or sales reports), letters, diaries, autobiographies, congressional and other legislative hearing records, newspapers, novels, films, television programs, and other kinds of written and/or recorded material provide grist for the sociologist's mill. Any product of human activity that can be found and examined is a potential source of information about the people who produced it.

In addition, sociologists make use of data gathered by others for particular purposes. The United States government, like that of most other nations, conducts a periodic national census. Since it was first conducted in 1790, the census has become more complex and comprehensive each decade. Information about occupation, income, age, sex, national origins, marital status, and many other facts about people are routinely gathered by the census takers. These data and the reports based upon them are a major source of data for sociologists.

In addition, the federal and state governments are avid compilers of statistics dealing with almost every facet of human experience. Births, deaths, accidents, diseases, unemployment, marriages, and other events during a person's life come to the attention of authorities and are recorded. Much of this information is available to the public and is useful to the sociologist in doing certain kinds of research. The sociologist interested in the topic of suicide, for

Mary Cassatt, *The Letter* (1891)
Colored acquatint, drypoint and softground, 247 × 225 mm. The National Gallery of Art, Washington. Rosenwald Collection.

Sociologists use a variety of human documents in their research. Letters and diaries are of particular importance because they reveal much about the ideas and activities of ordinary people in their everyday lives.

example, will have to rely in part upon official death certificates, which may list suicide as a cause of death. By collecting other information about known suicides, it may be possible to assess which population groups—men or women, blacks or whites, and so on—have the highest rates, and thereby add to our understanding of how social conditions affect suicide.

The example of suicide illustrates an important point; records kept by others for *their* purposes have to be scrutinized carefully. Because suicide is so strongly disapproved by many people, there is often a reluctance to list suicide as a cause of death, and researchers may thus not detect many instances of suicide. Moreover, some forms of suicide may be difficult to detect. Many single-car accidents in which the driver dies may, in fact, be suicides, but in the absence of a suicide note, such a death will be classified as accidental. Thus, official statistics on causes of death may understate the actual incidence of suicide, possibly affecting the sociologist's conclusions.

The varieties of information of possible interest to the sociologist are almost limitless. But whatever the source of data or the technique for collecting it, the sociologist is faced with the task of using observations to form conclusions. How do sociologists use data to create generalizations and to test theories? How do they transform their observations into conclusions?

COMING TO CONCLUSIONS

There are essentially three strategies—the experiment, multivariate analysis, and analytic induction—available to the sociologist for designing research projects, conducting observations, and coming to conclusions (Denzin, 1978:26–28). In the *experiment* the sociologist designs a carefully controlled situation of observation in which various factors can be manipulated and their results observed. In *multivariate analysis* the researcher tries to attain the equivalent of experimental control by the use of statistical techniques. And finally, in *analytic induction* the sociologist has neither experimental nor statistical control, but must painstakingly build generalizations by examining observations one by one.

Experiments

The scientific experiment is generally considered to be an ideal model to follow in the process of formulating and testing scientific generalizations. In its classic form, the experiment can be described quite simply. The researcher wants to determine the effects of an independent variable on a dependent variable; an observational setting is created in which the independent variable can be manipulated and its effects on the dependent variable directly observed. Generally this involves creating two groups or categories—an *experimental group*, which receives some treatment or in which the independent variable takes one state, and a *control group*, which does not get the treatment or in which the independent variable takes a different state. An effort is made to make certain that the two groups initially differ *only* with respect to the independent variable. If this condition is met, then any subsequent differences in the dependent variable can be attributed to the independent variable. Experiments typically require two periods of observation: first, before the independent variable is introduced; and second, after this variable has been introduced and has had time to take effect.

Returning to an earlier example, the investigator might be interested in determining whether the provision of financial assistance to recently released prisoners (independent variable) reduces the likelihood of their committing another crime and receiving another jail sentence (dependent variables). Working together, prison authorities, state legislators, and social scientists create a program in which some released felons (the *experimental* group) are provided with state unemployment compensation for a period of time after their release. At the same time assistance is not offered to another group of felons. These individuals—the *control group*—are similar to the experimental group in age, the nature of their offenses, and other characteristics. After their release, both groups are observed and records are kept of their success in finding jobs, any encounters with the law, and similar matters.

If those who have received assistance turn out to commit fewer crimes in the future, then it can be concluded that providing monetary assistance is a useful technique for reducing crime. This conclusion depends, however, upon the fact that the independent variable (the provision of aid) is the *only* difference between the experimental and control groups. If there are other differences between the two groups—if men in the experimental group are, say, older than the controls or if they have committed less serious crimes—then the observed effects on the dependent variable cannot be attributed solely to the independent variable. In a major study conducted along these lines by Peter Rossi and his associates (1980), the provision of aid did not have as much positive impact as the researchers had predicted.

Experiments are an ideal model for scientific research because they deal with several problems of logical inference. For one thing to be the cause of another, it must generally precede it in time; causes occur before their effects. Moreover, cause and effect must vary together; that is, there should be no instances in which an alleged cause does not produce a given effect, and whenever the effect is observed the cause should also be present. Finally, other possible causal factors should be eliminated; that is, it should be possible to demonstrate that no other possible causes are operating in an unseen way to bring about the effect under observation.

In their laboratories, natural scientists are able to exercise considerable experimental control over conditions and thus solve such problems. They can decide when to introduce a variable into the experiment. They can exclude other possible factors by rigorously controlling the conditions of the experiment—regulating the temperature, humidity, light intensity, or whatever physical conditions might be relevant. They can conduct experiments over and over again, seeking to determine the consistency with which effects are observed.

Social scientists face a more difficult set of tasks. It is a rare circumstance that permits the kind of social experiment described above. The idea of experimentation on human beings has limited acceptance within the world of medicine, but in our society we have not institutionalized the idea of conducting experiments to see if various social policies are effective. If someone has an idea to solve a social problem, we generally implement the idea politically rather than designing a careful experiment. And even when permission is secured to engage in social experimentation, the social scientist will face considerable opposition and political interference.

Outside the context of social experiments such as that described, of course, the social scientist is quite properly powerless to control the conditions under which people live and behave. The sole exception is the laboratory of the social psychologist, where considerable experimentation is done to investigate basic processes of social interaction and conduct formation. Social scientists have been debating for years the value of such experimental studies. Some argue that the laboratory is so artificial a situation that no conclusions about human behavior can be drawn. Others take the view that although considerable caution is required in the interpretation of findings, some basic processes of interaction can be studied by observing people interacting under controlled conditions.

One of the major problems of laboratory experiments is that people do not necessarily interpret the sociologist's actions in the expected way. Research has shown that research subjects often try to please the experimenter by doing what they think is desired. But what they interpret as the experimenter's wishes may not be his or her wishes at all. One way of dealing with this problem as well as with the general artificiality of experiments is to take the laboratory into the streets by contriving situations that seem "real" to participants, who may not even know they are part of an experiment. Several experimenters, for example, have staged heart attacks, seizures, and the like on buses and subways in order to study patterns of helping behavior.

Multivariate Analysis

Although the experimental method is an ideal, most of the topics sociologists investigate do not lend themselves to this method. Accordingly, social scientists have sought methods that approximate the controlled observation that characterizes the experiment. Multivariate analysis is a fancy name for the use of statistical techniques to approximate experimental controls.

Suppose the sociologist is interested in a particular dependent variable such as sexual permissiveness and wants to learn what factors cause people to be more or less permissive. This is the kind of research question that lends itself to the survey method. A sample can be drawn and questions asked in order to measure permissiveness. Questions that focus on the attitudes of some group toward premarital or extramarital intercourse, for example, might be a measure of the dependent variable. Obviously the sociologist can observe variations in permissiveness using the survey, but how can possible independent variables be identified and controlled? Identification of such variables is a theoretical matter; the sociologist examines various theories and selects one that seems to apply. Since the extent of education is a variable that affects many attitudes in American society, the researcher might theorize that those who have more years of education will be more permissive.

But how can the sociologist have any direct control over this independent variable? Actually, the researcher has no direct control. The researcher cannot decide to give one group of people more education than another in order to see if their attitudes change or increase or decrease the amount of education someone has attained. The approach taken by survey analysis is to *compare observations* made of various groups within a sample. Those with a college degree, for example, might be compared with those with less than a college education. If the latter have less permissive attitudes than the former, then there is evidence that suggests the independent variable affects the dependent variable in the manner predicted.

There is a problem with this approach, however. Men and women who differ from one another in educational attainment also may differ in other respects. They are likely to have different incomes, for example, since getting a college degree generally increases one's lifetime earnings. The members of various religious, ethnic, or occupational groups are also apt to differ from one another in educational attainment. Thus, an effect attributed to the independent variable may really be the result of other factors that are strongly associated with the independent variable.

This is where multivariate analysis enters the picture. The researcher uses a variety of statistical devices to *control* various extraneous factors that might be affecting the relationship between education and attitudes. For example, if income is suspected as a possible factor, the sociologist might divide the sample into several income categories. The relationship between education and permissiveness could then be investigated within each of these income groups. If higher level of education is associated with greater permissiveness at all income levels, the researcher has some added confidence that the independent variable is, by itself, having an effect on the dependent variable. There are also techniques available that let researchers decide which of two variables is having a stronger effect on a dependent variable.

The web of social life is complex. It is therefore rare to find simple cause-effect relationships between independent and dependent variables. In most cases, dependent variables such as sexual permissiveness are affected by many independent variables operating together. This is an additional reason why experimentation is difficult and researchers place so much reliance on the survey. There are so many variables possibly affecting conduct that it seems almost impossible to bring them into the laboratory and under experimental control.

Analytic Induction

The technique for drawing inferences and coming to conclusions that has been especially favored by symbolic interactionists is analytic induction. Like the two other approaches, it is a method for testing generalizations, but it is one especially suited to the analysis of data collected by participant observation.

Analytic induction is a case-by-case procedure for creating and testing generalizations about data. The investigator first examines one of the cases or instances observed during the study and tries to formulate a generalization about it. In Farberman's study, for example, a case might consist of an observed transaction between a salesperson and a used-car buyer. Observing a short sale, the researcher might generalize that this is a regular occurrence in such transactions and that the parties are motivated by a desire to beat the system. This generalization would then be tested by examining as many cases as possible, modifying the generalization if cases are observed in which the generalization fails to hold. One of the revisions in Farberman's generalization involved the discovery that beating the state out of some sales tax was not the only motive, and that dealers regarded the short sale as an important source of cash with which to pay kickbacks.

Analytic induction searches for generalizations that hold true *all* the time, not for statistical patterns. Thus, the procedure tries to be especially alert to negative cases; it tries as hard as possible to find cases that will contradict the generalization that is being formulated. Analytic induction is also a procedure that is employed while data are being gathered. The participant observer does not wait until all the observations are made to begin the process of making inferences. Instead, as cases are observed, generalizations are formulated and tested against observations. Further observations will be made based on this testing process; the researcher may decide to ask new questions, observe different people interacting, or otherwise adjust the data-gathering process in the search for generalizations and negative cases.

This procedure thus lends itself very well to participant observation, in which the researcher is in the field and able to constantly adjust observations to meet the needs of new theories. In this respect, analytic induction and participant observation are somewhat closer to the experiment than is multivariate survey analysis. Like the participant observer using analytic induction, the experimenter in the laboratory does not simply conduct one-shot experiments that are later subject to intensive analysis. Instead, a series of small experiments are often conducted, each one shaped to some extent on the basis of findings from the previous one. Similarly, for the participant observer, each observation is shaped by ideas derived from the previous observation.

This procedure thus contrasts markedly with the social survey, a method that generates a "snapshot" rather than a "motion picture" generated by participant observation. The survey is conducted once and is the researcher's only contact with the social world until the next survey is conducted. After the snapshot is taken, the researcher examines it in minute detail. Participant observation is a motion picture guided by the method of analytic induction. Analysis and data collection take place at the same time, and the researcher is able to observe events as they occur.

CONCLUSION

In this chapter we have tried to convey something of the spirit and approach of the sociologist as well as to describe some techniques of data collection and methods of inference. There is more to research methodology than we can discuss here, but you may now have a better understanding of how sociologists go about "doing sociology."

Not all sociologists conceive of the discipline as a science, of course. Many take the view that society and human conduct just do not lend themselves to scientific study. They see themselves as more akin to historians, philosophers, and other students of the humanities than to scientists. Their goal is to interpret human society, to bring a sociological perspective to bear upon its problems, and to make sense of the social world for themselves and others. But they do not believe it is possible to develop scientific generalizations of the same scope and power as those of the natural sciences.

We have tried to avoid this kind of debate in this chapter. Our conception of science is fairly broad. For us, people are engaging in science when they attempt to join careful, logically rigorous thought with empirical observation. There are some obvious differences between what sociologists do and what physicists do. Perhaps most important is the fact that sociologists are people and members of society; sociologists study their own kind, whereas physicists study more impersonal nature. Yet too much should not be made of this difference, nor should we think that a discipline is scientific only if it strongly resembles physics. Each discipline has to contend with its own problems and must overcome specific obstacles to inquiry. It is the spirit of science that is important, not the particular form it takes in any given field.

Sociology is an exciting discipline. It deals with matters that are important to us. It provides a method for studying these matters and a basis for interpreting the social world around us. Our task now, as we begin to pursue the study of sociology in more detail, is to take a closer look at its basic concepts and its view of human beings. These topics will occupy us in the next two chapters.

SUGGESTED READINGS

BOGDAN, ROBERT and STEVEN J. TAYLOR. *An Introduction to Qualitative Research Methods* (New York: Wiley, 1975).

DENZIN, NORMAN K. *The Research Act* (New York: McGraw-Hill, 1978).

GLASER, BARNEY and ANSELM L. STRAUSS. *The Discovery of Grounded Theory* (Chicago: Aldine, 1967).

LOFLAND, JOHN. *Analyzing Social Settings* (Beverly Hills, Cal.: Wadsworth, 1971).

SCHATZMAN, LEONARD and ANSELM L. STRAUSS. *Field Research: Strategies for a Natural Sociology* (Englewood Cliffs, N.J.: Prentice-Hall, 1973).

3

Society and Culture

Society is the single most important sociological concept. In this chapter we explore the nature of society in more depth and introduce a number of related concepts in the sociologist's toolkit. Among the latter, one of the most important is *culture*. These twin concepts—society and culture—are the foundation for a more detailed discussion of the symbolic interactionist perspective in Chapter 4 and of various aspects of society, culture, and human behavior in the chapters that follow.

THE NATURE OF SOCIETY

Society may be defined initially as people interacting with one another. This definition emphasizes that the essence of human society is people who live and act in one another's real or imagined presence. Society is constantly created and recreated as its members engage in symbolic interaction. It is a product of their activities.

But this definition leaves something to be desired. Although people give life to society and sustain it by their actions, they also experience society as a force in their lives, as an external and constraining reality. The social world exists *prior* to the individual, and it shapes the way individuals interact. The child is born into a family that has established ways of doing things before the new member arrives on the scene. People attend schools that attempt to shape their behavior. Men and women get jobs in corporations that tell them what to do, and they acquire responsibilities to care for their children or aging parents.

Moreover, a simple definition of society as people interacting does not adequately describe the array of social forces people confront in their everyday lives. Individuals are not born into "society," but into one of its constituent parts, called a family. Social interaction is not constrained by "society," but by several particular elements of society. Statuses and roles, groups, and organizations, rather than society as a whole, are the forces people feel as they go about their lives.

Finally, society has some characteristics not possessed by its constituent elements. First, when sociologists use the term *society*, they have in mind social interaction that is coordinated over fairly large numbers of people and relatively long periods of time. Everybody does not know or interact directly with everybody, but the members of a society are either directly or indirectly linked in relationships that tend to be enduring. Thus, for example, the activities of a New Jersey chemical worker mesh with those of a worker in a California electronics factory. The two do not know each other, but they are linked by a complex chain of intermediate people and their activities. For example, the New Jersey worker has a sister whose boyfriend knows the California worker's father. Moreover, the California factory buys some of its chemicals from the New Jersey manufacturer.

Second, societies are self-reproducing entities; that is, societies get members primarily through human sexual reproduction. Corporations hire employees and universities recruit faculty and admit students, but a society is a unit whose members are born into it and who usually leave it only when they die. (Societies also gain members through immigration and lose them through emigration, but these are generally not as significant as sexual reproduction.) This self-reproducing attribute suggests that society is a long-term affair. Ordinarily, the term *society* is reserved for social units that survive over at least a couple of generations.

Third, societies are self-defined entities. A large number of individuals who coordinate their conduct over a period of time and who reproduce themselves are a society only if they think of themselves as a society. *A society exists in the minds of its members.* Its size, location, and criteria for considering people to be members are matters of social definition. Thus, each time people who call themselves "Americans" speak of the "United States" or of "American society," they are asserting their collective consciousness of their society.

A society need not be identical with either a political unit or a geographical territory. Several million Americans live outside the political and geographical boundaries of the United States, yet they consider themselves a part of American society. And in a complex political entity such as Canada, with two major cultural and linguistic groups, French and English, the definitions of "Canadian society" held by the members of both groups do not always encompass members of the other. Thus, some French Canadians may feel themselves a part of a French-speaking society and not part of an encompassing Canadian society.

As this example suggests, there may not be consensus within a political unit on just who is and who is not part of the society. Illegal immigrants from Mexico and other countries hold jobs and reside within the United States, but they are excluded from full membership in both the political unit and the society. Every society has some conception of who its members are, but this conception may be complex. Thus, legal immigrants in the United States cannot vote until they have become naturalized citizens, but they are entitled to many of the rights of membership in the society, such as education and welfare, from the moment they enter the country.

Viewing society as a self-defined entity helps us relate this concept to other forms and levels of organization. A family is not a society, even though its members reproduce and act in a coordinated fashion over a long period of time. Rather, it is a constituent part of a society, and its members think of it as such. Similarly, a corporation is not a society but a part of one, and it is so defined by its members. And the whole world is not a society (although its constituent societies and political states are highly interdependent), but a set of self-defined societies.

Society may thus be defined as a relatively large-scale, self-reproducing social unit that endures for two or more generations and that is defined by its members as a society. Keep this definition in mind as we begin to explore the nature of society in greater detail by examining the several different kinds of elements or components that make up a society.

ELEMENTS OF SOCIETY

Sociologists have developed a number of concepts, including status, role, group, and organization, that describe the components of a society. These concepts help describe how everyday social interaction is socially patterned and constrained. We will begin by describing status and role, and then discuss groups and organizations. Before examining these social units, a word of caution is in order. One of the difficulties involved in studying society is the tendency to *reify* it—to treat various abstractions, including society itself, as if they were real entities. It is crucial to remember that society and its units consist of people interacting with one another. Statuses, roles, groups, and organizations are not things, but are merely *words* sociologists use to capture some of the patterns observable in this interaction.

Status and Role

One way of looking at society is as a network of imaginary points, or *positions*. For example, "father" can be thought of as a position within a network of other positions that includes "mother," "son," "daughter," "grandfather," and others. "Male" is a position in a network of two positions, the other being "female." Similarly, "professor," "lawyer," "bricklayer," "waiter," and "truck driver" are positions in a network of occupational positions. The term generally used for such positions is *status*. When used in this way, the term *status* has no connotations of unequal rank or prestige, but refers simply to a position in society.

The sociologist's conception of society as a network of statuses partially resembles our everyday conception of society, but also differs from it in some ways. Members of a society have various "mental maps" of it, including one based on a view of society as a set of positions. Just as people have a map of American society in terms of its geographical extent (fifty states) or criteria for membership (being born or naturalized as a citizen), so they also think of it as a set of positions: parents and children, husbands and wives, butchers, bakers, and candlestick makers.

Sociologists are more likely than other people to emphasize the position and to downplay the individual who happens to occupy it. Interested in discovering patterns of human activity, sociologists focus on the ways a given status constrains the behavior of its occupants. In the Farberman study cited in Chapter 2, for example, the focus is not on the motives or attitudes of the individual used-car dealer or customer, but on the way their positions shape or constrain their interaction.

To speak of a status as something that *constrains* the behavior of individuals is, of course, to engage in a bit of reification. A status is not a thing, but an *abstraction* used by the sociologist to talk about society. To some degree this is an inescapable result of trying to condense a complex and slippery social reality into manageable concepts. It may be worth noting that ordinary people also (and unavoidably) reify statuses. For example, they are apt to say things like, "A person in my position has to be careful," or "I have to do many things in my position that I don't like." When people talk this way, they are acting on the basis of a map of the society in which they live. Their map, like the sociologist's, tries to organize and simplify the myriad details and complexities of social interaction by identifying the many positions people fill.

Because the concept of status is *relational*, it encourages a picture of society as a network of related statuses. One cannot imagine one of the statuses within the family—"father," for example—without linking it to the other statuses that exist within that group. This relational quality of the concept helps capture an important part of the essence of society. Each person is linked to others in a vast web of interrelated positions, a web that exists to some extent independently of any particular individual and his or her actions. This social web constrains people because it is their map of the social world. People are born into a social world conceived by others in terms of this map. It confronts them as a basic "fact of life."

There are two major kinds of statuses. *Ascribed statuses* are those positions the individual generally attains at birth, and which are difficult if not impossible to abandon. "Male" and "female" are ascribed statuses that are attained on the basis of the appearance of the genitals at birth. (Gender reassignment at a later time through surgical reconstruction has become possible, but it is an uncommon event.) Religion is also an ascribed status; one is assumed to have the religion of one's parents, although it is somewhat easier for this status to be changed later on. *Achieved statuses,* in contrast, are those attained on the basis of qualifications. In an industrial society, for example, occupational statuses are generally achieved, since they are based upon the acquisition of skills. The individual's occupation depends upon the learning of these skills and is not assigned on the basis of birth into a specific caste.

Closely related to status is the concept of *role,* which refers to the behavior, rights, duties, and obligations associated with a status. For example, associated with the status "father" there is a role—a set of prescriptions about the obligations fathers have to their wives and children, the things they must do, and the rights they have within their families. Thus, fathers are expected to help support their families, and they have the duty and right to discipline their children. Similarly, professors have the right to assign work and the duty to be fair in grading it.

Like the sociologist's concept of status, the concept of role mirrors to some extent the way people think of themselves and their behavior. Individuals can picture society, or their part of it, as a set of statuses. The world consists of fathers, mothers, workers, policemen, etc. Similarly, people have ideas about the characteristic conduct of people who attain or occupy these statuses. People think of fathers as having rights, duties, and typical ways of behaving.

Again, care has to be exercised in using the term *role*. The term fundamentally refers to the characteristic ways in which the members of society *expect* those in certain positions to behave. (The account of *culture* later in this chapter will discuss these expectations in more detail.) A role is thus not a material thing, but an abstraction, whether used by the sociologist or anyone else. And like statuses, roles are constraining. People organize their own activities and their expectations of others' behavior by using these abstractions. (Chapters 4 and 5 will describe just how they do this.)

People occupy multiple statuses. They are mothers or fathers, but also employees, husbands and wives, citizens, members of associations and clubs, friends, and many other things. Thus, people are exposed to a great many expectations. Each status has its associated role, and although the individual's roles form some kind of more or less coherent bundle, there may sometimes be conflict or strain among them. For example, a woman in a hunting and gathering society may find that her primary roles are those of mother, gatherer, preparer of food, and builder of the house. In this case, the roles tend to "fit" rather well; no role conflicts with another. The tasks of raising or gathering food do not conflict with the tasks of child care.

This is often not the case in modern society, where a woman may simultaneously be a lawyer, wife, mother, and political leader. Frequently, the requirements of one of these roles are not compatible with those of another. In the complex world of modern society, some roles have requirements that interfere with our capacity to meet the expectations of other roles. Some roles have contradictory requirements built into them. And other roles make demands that people are not prepared to meet because they lack the necessary resources.

Role Conflict and Role Strain *Role strain* exists when people cannot meet the requirements of their roles. Two kinds of role strain can be identified. First, individuals may not have the resources necessary to meet role requirements. An unemployed father will find it difficult, perhaps impossible, to meet his obligations to serve as family breadwinner. A teacher may be expected to give individualized attention to students, but have too little time for the number of students demanding it. In both examples, a role requirement continues to exist even though there may be conditions beyond the control of the individual that prevent it from being met.

Second, some role strain reflects incompatible requirements built into a role. A factory foreman, for example, is expected to serve as a representative of management, enforcing its regulations and seeing that workers meet its requirements. At the same time, the foreman is expected to remain on good terms with the workers, from whose ranks he or she has come, and secure their co-

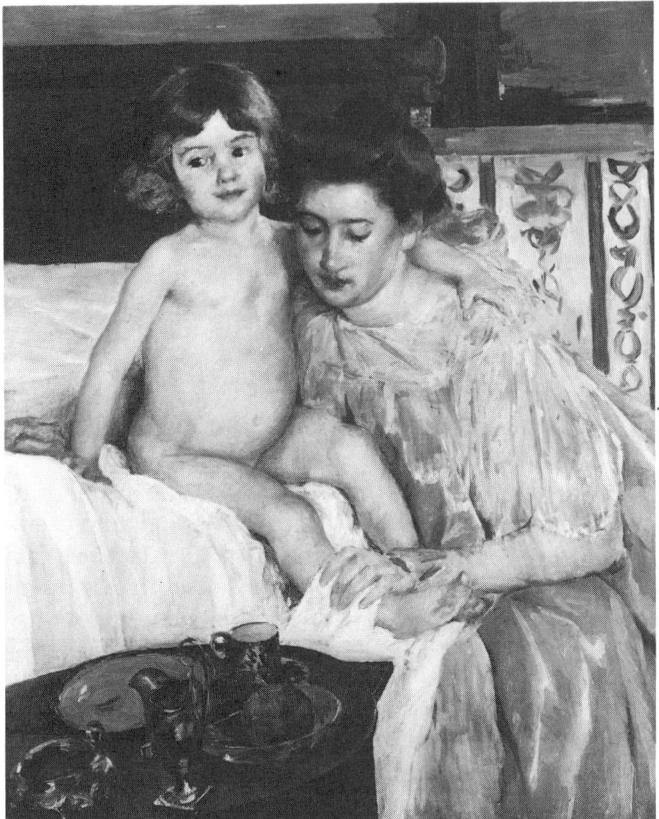

Mary Cassatt, *Mother and Child* (1909) The Metropolitan Museum of Art, New York.

The role of the nineteenth-century middle-class woman was defined primarily in terms of domestic responsibilities. Her contemporary counterpart is more apt to be expected to have a job outside the home as well as to care for her husband and children, and thus she often experiences role conflict.

operation. Considerable strain results from conflicting obligations to management and fellow workers; actions that meet one set of requirements may violate another.

Role conflict exists when the demands of one role conflict with those of another. Perhaps the most frequent arena for role conflict in contemporary society is in occupational and familial roles. The physician's role, for example, is a demanding one that requires a great investment of time and energy. At the same time, the physician is also likely to be a spouse and parent, roles which are also very demanding. Under these circumstances, fully meeting the requirements of one role interferes with the capacity to meet the demands of the other.

This kind of role conflict is apt to be particularly sharp in contemporary society. Women who pursue careers outside the home (whether due to preference or economic necessity) often find that the demands upon their time and energy as mothers and spouses have not diminished. Having added a new role, they find conflict between it and existing roles. Men can also be affected by this form of role conflict. Those men who wish to participate in more egalitarian patterns of family life, sharing child care and other household responsibilities with their wives, may find expectations on the job have not changed. They may be liberated, but their employers still expect a total commitment of time.

Role strain and role conflict exist because of the way roles are *defined*. Individuals may find it difficult to live up to the requirements of a particular role or to reconcile the demands of one role with those of another. They may feel frustrated in their efforts to do what they feel they are supposed to do, and they may find their commitments to some roles weakening. Regardless of their inner feelings, however, their roles continue to exist as external facts that shape their behavior. The physician may be unhappy that his profession makes him vulnerable to constant interruption of his family life. The working mother may be angry that her husband and children continue to expect her to cater to their every whim. Still, their roles continue to exist and to constrain them.

How can roles constrain people when those roles are only realized when people enact them through their behavior? How can role expectations be sustained, even though they are contradictory or inconsistent with the requirements of other roles? Three ideas help to solve this puzzle.

First, the network of statuses and roles seems natural and inevitable to the members of society, who find it difficult to think of things being organized differently. The terms Americans use to describe kinship positions (father, mother, sister, brother, uncle, cousin) and the expectations attached to each position seem to them to be descriptions of biological reality. That is "just the way things are." Thus, for example, American uncles may take an interest in their nephews, but they ordinarily have no special or binding obligations toward them. In other kinship systems, a child's uncle—his mother's brother, for example—may have both particular obligations to and special authority over the child. People growing up within each system assume that it is natural, and so it exerts a hold over their minds.

Second, the rights, duties, and obligations associated with each role are reinforced by the belief that it is right to live up to them and wrong not to do so. For example, the traditional American male believes he *should* be the major breadwinner for his family. Human beings develop ideas about what their behavior should and should not be in various circumstances. (These ideas, called *norms*, will be discussed later in this chapter.) Even when people wish to escape the demands of a role, they may feel bound by their conceptions of what they *should* do.

Third, roles are constraining because others are apt to take them seriously, even when the individual does not. The overburdened and frustrated working mother is confronted by a husband and children who act as if she should be able both to work and to meet traditional obligations. The husband and father with too little time to spend with his family is confronted with a demanding employer who accepts nothing less than full dedication to the job. Roles constrain not just because we and others believe them natural and right, but also because they are enforced. Others require us to shape ourselves to fit roles, even when we do not wish to do so.

Status and role are basic elements of any society. Whenever people interact, they are guided by their mutual sense of position (status) and by their ideas of appropriate and required behavior (role). Status and role do not rigidly dictate what people do, for social life is too complex for its script to be written out neatly in advance. But common-sense perceptions of status and role do shape and constrain behavior.

People take status and role into account as they interact with others. Their actual behavior, however, is usually contained within some kind of social unit that comprises a number of interacting people. The first and most basic of these units is the *group*.

Groups

A group may be defined as a set of people who interact more or less regularly with one another and who are conscious of themselves as a group. By this definition, a family composed of husband, wife, and children is a group. Similarly, people who meet regularly as a sociology class or who are players on the New York Yankees baseball team constitute groups. In contrast, several individuals standing at a street corner waiting for a traffic signal to change do not form a group. They do not interact regularly, nor do they think of themselves as constituting a group. Similarly, the whole population of the United States is not a group, since the members think of themselves as a society, not a group, and since each individual interacts regularly only with a fraction of the others.

The members of established groups share an image of the statuses and roles found within the group. Thus, for example, contemporary Americans think of the family as consisting of such statuses as mother, wife, son, and sister, each with an associated role. The "typical American family," as members of this society conceive of it, contains two parents and one or more children. Many real families, of course, do not have a full complement of members; a spouse might be missing because of death or divorce, or a couple might be childless. Nonetheless, the American image of the family remains that of the complete nuclear unit, and families that do not conform to this type are often seen as somehow falling short.

Social groups cannot be described, however, simply by listing the statuses and roles they are typically thought to contain. Shared definitions of such groups provide people with models for their conduct, but each concrete group to some extent shapes this model into its own unique set of patterns. People act on the basis of ideas about statuses and roles, but as real people interact over time, they modify and elaborate these patterns. Thus, Americans think of the small family as normal, but many families depart from this ideal definition. Even those families that fit the definition may vary considerably from one another. Some may be tightly knit groups that do everything together as families, while others are looser groups whose members interact less frequently and intensively. And the members of any family adapt the standard definitions of family roles to their own needs and interests. Roles provide guidelines for group members, not rigid prescriptions for each and every act.

A group is nevertheless constrained by what is *felt* to be normal and typical. Both the members of the group and outsiders tend to view it using a conventional set of ideas. A husband and wife may develop a unique relationship, but others will judge them by conventional criteria. Even their own children, who are privy to the unique features of relationships within their family, will compare notes with other children and will learn how their parents differ from those of their peers. Thus, a couple who love one another deeply but who argue frequently may be judged unfavorably by others, even by their own children.

Most groups are more complex than is apparent by merely listing their statuses and roles. A college class, for example, appears to be a simple group. Two statuses are represented—professor and student—and their roles seem straightforward enough. But, in fact, even in a semester's time the class will become more complex. Some students in the class will take the lead in asking questions or participating in discussions, while others will be more reticent. The professor will identify some students as truly interested, while seeing others as less involved in the class. Students will have similar perceptions of themselves and each other. As a result, new statuses and roles develop. For example, "interested student" or "class brain" become statuses, and the individuals who occupy these statuses play particular roles. Even though these positions are created within the class rather than existing beforehand, they become significant elements of the group. Professor and fellow students alike may turn to someone who occupies such a special position—the professor for support for his statements and the students for assistance. For all of them, the group includes not just the standard positions and roles of student and professor, but the created ones of "class brain" or "class dimwit."

Groups are major units of society. Like statuses and roles, they constrain and shape the conduct of their individual members. And they are external to the person; that is, they exist regardless of the individual's existence, and they stand "over and against" the individual as forces to be reckoned with. They seem real to us and thus have power over us, even though in the final analysis they only exist because people act. The family of Robert Smith exists only because several people interact with one another repeatedly and define themselves as a family. Yet, to each of them, this family is a fixed, given part of the world. Its existence is external to each of them as individuals, and they must each take account of it in their behavior.

Organizations

Between the group and the larger society there is another kind of unit, which sociologists call an organization. Organizations are larger and more complex than groups, and they do not have the self-sufficiency of a society. There are many different kinds of organizations. They include industrial corporations such as General Motors, as well as charitable associations such as the American Cancer Society. The Methodist Church is an organization, as are the American Medical Association and the Benevolent and Protective Order of Elks. Organizations encompass a multitude of types, purposes, and degrees of complexity, and they are central to the way social life is organized in modern society.

Organizations are distinguished from groups by their size and complexity. Thus, an organization such as the Boston Red Sox may well contain various groups. The players, who are in daily contact with one another and who think of themselves as a team, are a group. But the baseball club is more than a group of players, for it has managers, coaches, trainers, physicians, front-office personnel, groundskeepers, owners, and various other members. The totality of these participants, who occupy statuses, play roles, and are linked together by their contributions to the baseball club, constitutes the Red Sox organization. Interaction tends to occur frequently within each of the various groups who make up the organization, but less frequently between members of different groups. Thus, for example, ticket sellers may see the players only somewhat more frequently than the public does, and even the manager may be excluded from some areas of player interaction.

Organizations are also distinguished by the complexity of their *division of labor*. All social groups, no matter how small or temporary, achieve some kind of division of labor. In the family, for example, different responsibilities are allocated to fathers, mothers, and children. A newly formed group will quickly achieve some sort of division of labor, even if it merely entails simple distinctions between leaders and followers or speakers and listeners. But organizations are built upon more complicated allocations of role responsibilities to specific statuses. In the baseball club, it is not the job of the trainer to decide the starting lineup, nor will the pitcher sell tickets at the gate. Instead, each member has a sphere of responsibility, assigned tasks, and specific areas of authority. In general, the larger the organization, the finer the division of labor. A modern industrial corporation contains thousands of finely graded and often very narrowly and explicitly designed job definitions.

Another feature of an organization is that those who occupy specific statuses are, at least in theory, recruited on the basis of competence and are therefore replaceable. When General Motors hires an electrical engineer, it is presumably because of that person's competence to perform assigned duties. Accordingly, a worker who does not perform well can be let go or transferred to another job. This contrasts markedly with the situation that prevails in families or friendship groups. Parents and children obviously do not choose one another on the basis of competence, and they are stuck with one another for better or worse.

Another difference between groups and organizations is revealed by the different impact of the loss of members on each. When a family is disrupted by death or divorce, it changes very substantially. A parent might remarry, but the family group that results is different from the one that preceded it. Relationships have to be redefined, new relationships developed, and former patterns of family life changed to adjust to a new member. Much the same is true of friendship groups, which may be substantially changed when a member leaves or a new member is added. In contrast, General Motors remains much the same when workers leave or new workers are added. Departed members are replaced by others with equivalent competence. New members adapt themselves to its requirements without much affecting the formal structure of the organization.

To put it another way, organizations tend to adopt an *instrumental attitude* toward their members. So far as General Motors is concerned, the crucial question about a tool and die maker is whether the worker's skills contribute to the production of automobiles. Members of organizations are valued for their contribution to organizational goals. In contrast, within families or friendship groups, people and their interpersonal relationships are more likely to be valued for themselves, rather than simply as means to attain goals. To be sure, people in groups exchange various benefits—spouses exchange affection, for example—and come to depend upon the relationship as a source of these valued things. But relationships themselves come to be valued things, worth maintaining for their own sake.

Organizations also develop patterns of authority that are more complex than those found within groups. Organizations are generally arranged in a *hierarchy*, with some people accorded the right to command others. Returning to the baseball example, it is the owners of the team who determine how much money is to be spent hiring new players and who choose a manager. The manager, in turn, organizes training, selects the pitcher, determines the batting order, and controls game strategy. The manager's authority is based upon specific competence and a set of formal rules that define him as having the right to make certain decisions. Similarly, officers of corporations are assigned specific spheres of responsibility within which they can make decisions that govern the actions of their subordinates.

The authority exemplified by the baseball general manager or the corporate executive was termed *rational authority* by Max Weber (see Gerth and Mills, 1958). An individual who possesses this type of authority can influence the actions of others only within the context of a set of rules. The manager of a factory, for example, has the right to make certain kinds of decisions about how work will be done in the factory. But the manager's authority is not unlimited. It is more or less precisely spelled out, and the manager must obey rules in exercising this authority. Thus, a plant manager cannot decide to fire workers arbitrarily or elect to produce smaller quantities of a product than top management has commanded.

Although rational authority is the predominant type of authority found within modern organizations, other types can sometimes be identified. In organizations where a single individual remains in command for a prolonged period of time, members may feel that person's authority over them is legitimate because that individual is the *traditional* leader. For example, even after the Ford Motor Company issued stock and became a public corporation, it seemed "natural" for a time for Henry Ford, and later for other members of the Ford family, to play a major role in the corporation. Indeed, any time an individual retains a position of authority for a long time, elements of tradition are apt to creep in.

Organizations may also be influenced by charismatic leadership. *Charisma* refers to the capacity of some individuals to exert authority over others by sheer force of personality—magnetism, personal appeal, charm, or whatever it may be called. The emergence of a charismatic leader is often crucial to the formation, preservation, or growth of organizations. Martin Luther King, for example, was a charismatic leader whose personal strength and public magnetism were crucial to the impact of the Southern Christian Leadership Conference, the civil rights organization which King headed.

Groups may also have patterns of authority, but where they exist they are apt to be simpler and to rest upon different grounds from those characteristic of modern organizations. Parents have authority over children, for example, but this authority structure is relatively simple and it rests primarily upon tradition. That is, parents are traditionally accorded certain rights over children. Often groups have little in the way of authority structures. A group of friends, for example, have an egalitarian relationship, with no individual accorded the right to command the behavior of another. This does not mean that each member of a friendship group has equal influence over the others. Typically, some individuals will be more *influential*—others will look to them for advice or approval—and therefore play a leadership role. They have interpersonal influence, but not authority.

Finally, organizations exist for the pursuit of *specific aims*. Industrial corporations, baseball clubs, hospitals, universities, and professional associations each engage in a limited set of activities with specific goals in mind. It is true, of course, that there may not be full agreement about the purposes of an organization. Students and faculty are both members of the university, for example, but they may well see its objectives somewhat differently. Students will tend to define its purposes in line with their interests (acquiring knowledge and credentials) and faculty with theirs (doing research and attaining scholarly fame). And those who utilize the services of an organization may well see its purposes differently from its members. A corporation president may see the organization's basic goal as profitability, while the public may define it in terms of some basic service, such as energy or communications. In spite of such differing perspectives, however, there is generally some kind of consensual definition of the organization and its purposes that allows it to function.

Organizations are a ubiquitous feature of modern society; indeed, they are perhaps its most visible feature. People acquire such goods and services as food, health care, and education by turning to, and often by becoming members of, organizations. Jobs, for the most part, are contained within organizations such as corporations, governments, and schools. Organizations produce goods and services, they provide education, they structure religious activity, and they even shape people's leisure pursuits. To be a member of a complex modern society is to be deeply involved in organizational life.

CULTURE

Statuses and roles, together with the groups and organizations in which they are found, are the basic elements of society. But the capacity of human beings to interact as members of groups and organizations, filling positions and meeting the requirements of roles, depends upon their possession of *culture*. This concept, invented by anthropologists, helps to explain how people are able to interact with one another as members of society.

What is culture? Perhaps the most straightforward of the definitions devised by anthropologists is that of Kluckhohn and Kelley. Culture, they write, consists of all the

> . . . historically created designs for living, explicit and implicit, rational, irrational, and nonrational, which exist at any given time as potential guides for the behavior of man. (Kluckhohn and Kelley, 1945:91)

Whenever a human baby is born into a society, there already exist "designs for living" that enable him or her to solve problems and to know how to behave: what to do and when and how to do it. It is culture which provides each of us—both as individuals and as members of groups—with the patterns and guidelines that enable us to interact with other people.

The culture of a society is, for its members, a *guide to conduct*. It encompasses virtually all of life. It teaches people what and how to cook and sew. It tells them how to make love and war and when to experience joy or sorrow. It encompasses the rules for marriage and death, of parental responsibility and communal ties. It defines how friends and enemies are to be treated. It specifies which plants and animals are edible, which colors are perceived and named, and even what is sexually arousing.

Each culture provides standard designs for living, but there is wide diversity among the cultures of the world in the specific designs they provide. Each culture includes information on what and how to cook, for example, but definitions of what is and is not edible differ among cultures. Few Americans would enjoy eating dried, roasted cow's blood, as do the Nuer of Africa; an Orthodox Jew cannot imagine eating a ham dinner; and Hindus will not eat prime rib of beef. Whether you prefer your fish raw or fried, whether you drink milk, wine, or coffee, and whether you eat with a fork, chopsticks, or your fingers are matters defined in advance by culture.

Similarly, culture defines appropriate attire, and such definitions vary widely. During the last century, many European Christian missionaries, culturally trained to expect men to wear trousers and women to wear dresses, reacted strongly and adversely to the clothing preferences of non-Western cultures. They were scandalized by the "immorality" of women in other cultures who did not cover their breasts. In other cultures, different parts of the body require covering and provoke strong reactions when they are not. Among strict Moslems, women must veil their faces, and those who do not are considered wicked and immodest. Among the Cuna Indians of Panama, no proper woman would be seen without her nose ring.

Defining culture as "designs for living" tells us what culture does, but not what it is, and it leaves important questions unanswered. What kind of reality is culture? Where is it? How do we observe it? How do we tell the difference between behavior that is the product of cultural influences and that which is either unique to an individual or caused by biological forces? Does each society have one and only one culture? And, perhaps most important, how do people make use of culture and its "designs for living"?

The Nature of Culture

Culture consists of the accumulated knowledge, experience, rules, and values held by members of a society and its constituent groups and organizations. Its contents can be dissected in many ways, but in essence they fall into two categories. First, culture consists of practical ideas about the world which enable people to adapt to their environment and solve the problems they confront. It includes knowledge about how to grow crops, make artifacts, perform rituals, and explain why the world exists as it does. Second, culture consists of norms, rules, codes of conduct, and values that focus upon human conduct and guide the relationships that exist between people. It includes the proper ways of doing things in any society—the sexual codes and correct table manners, the ways that the young should treat the old, and who can talk to the gods. What is and is not acceptable is defined by culture.

Culture is an abstraction, not a tangible entity. It is not something that can be seen or touched. We see the reality of culture in the conduct of people, including what they say as well as what they do. For example, one idea found in many societies is the double standard of sexual conduct. This idea permits men to engage in sexual behavior with many partners while women are limited to their husbands. There is no way we can "see" a double standard except in the behavior of the members of society. When we see women condemned for behavior that is permissible (or even encouraged) for men, and when the sexual practices of men and women are clearly different, we can infer the existence of a double standard. The idea can be described because the behavior of members of a society reflects it.

Culture is, therefore, not observable itself, but is *inferred* from behavior, from what people do and say as they go about their affairs. It is not behavior, nor does it consist of the material objects created or used by the members of a society. It is simply the *ideas*—norms, values, beliefs, knowledge, and the like—

Paul Gauguin, ***The Yellow Christ*** **(1889)** Oil on canvas. 36¼ × 28⅞ inches. The Albright-Knox Art Gallery, Buffalo, New York. General Purchase Funds, 1946.

The crucifix, which has been a major subject of Western art, symbolizes not just an event, but a whole cultural complex of Christian religious ideas, beliefs, practices, and emotions. Among Christians it evokes culturally standard responses and serves as a tangible symbol of their culture.

that underlie behavior. Since culture consists of ideas, it is located in the minds of people. It does not float in some ethereal realm, but is firmly anchored in real human minds. Thus, if the double standard of sexual behavior for men and women is a part of a given culture, it is because culture exists as an idea in the minds of those who possess that culture.

Although culture exists in the mind of each individual member of a society, each mind is neither a carbon copy of the culture nor is it exactly like any other mind. Individuals are born into a society and gradually learn many of the details of its culture. As they do, they acquire ideas and skills that are very much like those acquired by others in the same society. Yet each person learns a version of the culture that is somewhat different from that learned by another. Personal characteristics, family ties, and place in the family are but a few of the factors underlying individual differences in the learning process. But regardless of the differences, there is enough similarity that sociologists can describe a society's culture. No one person may possess exactly that culture, yet it is the culture of the typical member of that society.

Even when there is individual variation in the learning of major parts of the culture, the dominant cultural ideas are still very important. Material success, for example, seems to be a major value of American culture. Yet not everyone adopts success as a value to the same degree. Some are content with less success than others, and those who are not very successful in material terms may tend to downplay the importance of this value. But the fact that success is an important value means that everyone must deal with the value in one form or another. If those who achieve success are led to feel they have been doing the right things, those who do not achieve it must explain why they have not. Thus, the successful businessperson will take pride in his or her energy and initiative; the person whose business fails may cite poor economic conditions or high taxes. Even individual departures from cultural norms and values take on meaning in relation to the norms and values.

Individual differences are not the only reason that different individuals learn somewhat different versions of a culture. In a society of any size or complexity, the culture is also apt to be complex. Consequently, every member of the society is not likely to learn all of the culture. For example, where the social division of labor is complex and the tasks of everyday life have been divided into many specialties and occupations, each person knows the specialized culture which relates to his or her job as well as the general culture that pertains to everyone in the society. Plumbers and sociologists alike are aware of the importance placed upon success in American culture. Plumbers, however, know how to sweat a joint, while sociologists are more apt to know how to perform a regression analysis.

Moreover, in all societies culture is *distributed* on the basis of sex and age. That means there are some things that a person knows because he is a male and other things he does not know because he is not a female. Similarly, the young not only know less of their culture than do the old, but often they cannot be taught some aspects of the culture until they reach certain ages. Among the Hopi Indians of Arizona, for example, the child is initiated into the Kachina cult between the ages of eight and ten. Only then do boys and girls learn that the Kachinas (costumed figures from the spirit world) that have regularly visited their villages have been impersonated by village men. American culture likewise has its myths—Santa Claus and the Tooth Fairy—that are presented to the young as facts and the truth about which is not revealed or discovered until they are older.

Elements of Culture

Culture comprises a number of separate elements, each of which is important in shaping the way the members of society interact with one another.

Knowledge Humans depend upon what they know to survive. Little guidance is provided by genetic programming, so they must rely upon what they have learned from their cultural traditions. Their physical dexterity, intelligence, and particularly the use of symbols have made humans so adaptable and flexible that their physical structure does not easily and automatically place them in an environmental niche. There is no obvious "human world" in the same way that there is a "fish world," where a combination of environmental conditions and the structure of organisms makes for little freedom in the organism-environment relationship. Fish are not only restricted to water, but the structure of specific species of fish determines what kinds of water they will inhabit and how they will feed. The human environment is far less restricted in this way, for culture is a major factor in determining the nature of that environment.

Culture is the repository of human knowledge, and can be organized generally into two categories: that which has to do with practical activities and that which is concerned with ideas and explanations. Much knowledge centers on the practicalities of everyday life and has to do with the activities in which humans engage to feed, clothe, and shelter themselves, as well as many other human activities that require practical knowledge. The second and more abstract type of knowledge consists of ideas about the nature and origins of the world, about time, space, and causality. Practical knowledge offers guidance in the details of everyday life; explanatory knowledge provides an integrating, encompassing framework within which human experiences can be organized.

Both kinds of knowledge can focus either upon the natural or the social world. That is, humans need practical guidance in their relationships with one another as well as in their adjustments to the environment. They interpret both social and natural events in terms of philosophical, religious, and other general ideas. They seek to explain such matters as the origins of social inequality, the nature of evil, or how life on earth began.

Much of what people know about the world takes the form of what Berger and Luckmann (1967) call "recipe knowledge"—how to fix a flat tire, how to read a map, how to bake bread, how to persuade a friend to do something, how to fool the teacher into thinking you've done your class assignment. This kind of knowledge is *instrumental*; it pertains to the way people go about attaining goals.

People who have learned "American culture" have acquired a great deal of this instrumental knowledge. When they were young, it is likely they learned how to use a telephone. They learned how to dial or to push the appropriate buttons. They either memorized the telephone numbers they would be calling or they learned where to find these numbers. To use this specific part of American culture, of course, it is also necessary to learn the more general skills associated with reading and number recognition.

Another piece of instrumental knowledge that many American teenagers learn is how to drive a car. This means they know enough about starting a motor, stepping on gas and brake pedals, using a clutch (if their family's automobile has one), and steering the vehicle through traffic that they can do what is called driving a car. In addition, driving a car assumes other kinds of knowledge—for example, that red lights mean stop, and green lights mean go. Shared knowledge of these social conventions makes it possible for one driver to anticipate another's behavior.

In contrast to this practical knowledge, people also have explanatory knowledge that focuses upon the "why" rather than the "how" of natural and social events. The scope of such knowledge is broad. It ranges from the elaborate systems of ideas about the world that we call science or religion to a host of much more mundane explanations of particular events.

Religion provides adherents with a more or less integrated set of propositions about the world, and especially about the place and destiny of humans in it. It gives meaning to the multitude of events that everyone faces in day-to-day life: earning a living, having a family, birth, death. Science plays a similar explanatory role in modern Western society, although its explanations of the natural and social world often conflict with those given by religion.

In addition to these systematic explanatory theories, culture contains many discrete theories that are used in everyday life. For example, in American culture when problems develop in a marriage or other interpersonal relationships, one explanation often put forth is that there is a "breakdown in communication." There is little scientific evidence that interpersonal troubles stem from communication failures, but the "explanation" is nevertheless a useful way of understanding a situation. Similarly, when a previously docile, oppressed population begins to rebel openly against its oppressors, as did black Americans in the fifties and early sixties, "outside agitators" are frequently held to be responsible for this development. Even though no evidence could be given to support this allegation, it "explained" the situation for many white Southerners (see Hewitt and Hall, 1973).

Everyday theories about people, their behavior, and even the natural world are as important a component of culture as the more systematic theories. Humans seem to require that their lives and the circumstances in which they live be meaningfully organized. Things are supposed to make sense, and consequently everyday theories about the problematic help fill the gaps left by more systematic explanations.

No person has a complete grasp of all the practical and explanatory knowledge that exists in a complex society. Most people know the specialized tasks that are related to their occupational and familial roles. And their knowledge is also limited by sex and age. Men have knowledge not possessed by women, and vice versa; children know less about the adult world and more about the child world than do their parents; parents have a fund of knowledge about child raising and development that is not shared by their children.

Even with these limitations, each person in society has considerable knowledge. How do people organize and keep track of this knowledge so that they can make use of it as the need arises?

Typification The concept of *typification* is a key to understanding how cultural knowledge is organized and stored by the individual (see Berger and Luckmann, 1967, and Hewitt, 1984). Much of the knowledge people acquire from their culture is knowledge of *types* of events, situations, and people. Think of certain words—professor, cocktail party, disaster, for example—and verbal and visual images spring to your mind. You will "see" in your mind's eye a certain kind of person as typical of a professor, particular forms of behavior as typical of a cocktail party, and certain happenings as typical of a disaster. Thus you might think of pretentiousness and stuffiness as typical attributes of a professor; utter panic and disorganization might be your image of a disaster such as an earthquake. These images are relatively standardized among the members of a society, and they tend to endure over long periods of time. Members have typifications of human beings as a whole, of particular occupations, of situations, and of behavior and feelings.

Most cultural knowledge is organized in the form of typifications rather than in the form of discrete bits of information and understanding. Because of this, humans are constantly on the lookout for clues and cues that will enable them to invoke the right typifications so that they can deal appropriately with a person or situation. Humans are not meticulous empiricists, carefully looking at all of the facts of the situations they encounter in order to decide what to do. Rather, they watch for cues, for bits of information about a person: mode of dress, style of speech, name, physical characteristics. On the basis of such cues, they infer the statuses, roles, and group and organizational memberships of others and decide how to interact with them. Much of what people "see" in their everyday lives is not seen at all but is assumed to exist because of the typifications they have learned.

People use typifications in many different ways. When they are looking for an attendant on an airplane, for example, they rely upon the typical appearance of a steward or stewardess. That is, they look for someone in a certain kind of uniform. Similarly, students rely upon a typification of professors to establish which person entering a classroom at the beginning of the semester is likely to be the professor. And typifications tell people when things are not going as they are supposed to. A crowd gathered in the middle of a busy intersection alerts people that something unusual is going on because it violates their expectation of what they will see there. That expectation is based upon typifications of busy intersections (dangerous places to walk) and of crowds (a crowd means something unusual is happening).

Typifications are necessary to the continuation of society. People could not organize all that they know nor could they respond appropriately to many situations if they had to piece together, bit by bit, an understanding of the events and people they encounter. Only by taking many things for granted are people able to act rapidly and efficiently. For example, people assume that a person pointing a gun at another person is dangerous unless the person with the gun is wearing a police uniform. In that case, they conclude that it is the person at whom the gun is pointed who is dangerous. People need not know the individuals involved, nor do they need to have had a gun pointed at them in the past to understand what is going on. Their knowledge of the culture permits them to make typifications regarding who has guns and who is dangerous.

What people know of the world and what they actually experience in it are thus powerfully shaped by cultural typifications. No two people learn exactly the same typifications. Still, each individual's stock of typifications closely approximates those learned by others in the society. Everyone has an image of a school, for example, yet the picture each person creates is not exactly like that of any other person—even those who attended the same school. Similarly, most Americans entering an unfamiliar bank would conclude that they were in a bank even if they had never been in that one before. How do they know it is a bank? They know because they have a typification of a bank that enables them to identify one when they see it.

Values Cultural knowledge of an explanatory and practical nature tells people what to expect in social life and how to accomplish what they wish to do, but it does not tell them what to do. Culture also provides people with guidance about desirable goals and states of affairs, and the term sociologists use for this guidance is *value.* A value is a standard or principle of judgment by which people decide upon desirable goals or outcomes. "Success," "justice," "loyalty," "efficiency"—these are values, for they represent very general criteria in terms of which people value their own and others' conduct, as well as the results of that conduct.

Like other aspects of culture, values are sometimes spoken about by their possessors, but often they must be inferred from behavior. For example, efficiency is a major value in American society, and it is often invoked as a justification for particular practices or decisions. Manufacturing industries change from one machine to another because their engineers tell them it will be more efficient; that is, the new machine will produce more products at less effort and cost. Values can be observed in operation not only when people use certain key words (such as efficiency), but also when, in using them, people seem to assume that questioning will cease and controversy will come to an end as soon as the value is invoked.

Values provide a framework of assumptions by which people conduct their lives and make important decisions. In much day-to-day activity, we do not see values. But just because values are hidden from view does not mean they are not present. They lurk in the background, existing as potential statements and utterances, as things taken for granted. For example, although efficiency is an important American value, people do not consciously make every decision on the basis of efficiency. Yet they do tend to do things in ways they would generally regard as the most efficient. To put it another way, many of the usual ways of going about everyday life fit existing values closely enough that it is not necessary for people consciously to choose behavior that "fits" the values.

This raises an important set of questions: If people generally take values for granted, when do they focus upon values? Does conduct sometimes depart from the values upon which it is presumably based? And if people sometimes abandon their values, how can they continue to exist as part of their culture?

Values tend to remain in the background until and unless something threatens them. As long as people's lives run smoothly, there is little need for them to question or even be aware of values. But if someone engages in or contemplates behavior that is contrary to a value, then the value itself comes into question.

In complex societies, values may often be in conflict with one another, and people are more likely to have to choose among conflicting values. For example, in addition to the value of efficiency that we discussed earlier, American culture includes a value that specifies that each person should be judged on his or her own merits. This value is often violated, for example, when workers are fired simply because they have grown older and are thought by management to be inefficient. When values conflict in this way, people become more conscious of them and have to struggle with what to do. They must reconcile themselves to violating one value while living up to the other, changing one of their values, or deciding that some values are more important than others.

In general, values help provide a sense of order in the social universe. They tell people what they should strive for, what the human condition should be like, and what they should define as pleasurable and good. Values may thus be thought of as providing a very general sense of direction to conduct.

This does not mean, however, that values provide a comprehensive, systematic, and neatly arranged set of directions. Culture contains many contradictory values. Moreover, the important values of a culture are not necessarily in harmony with human needs. Many observers feel that American culture has historically overemphasized success, so that few people can realize that value to the extent they feel they should. Thus, many individuals may find their self-esteem and energy reduced because a value is so emphasized that only a few can attain the goals all are supposed to reach (see Sennett and Cobb, 1972).

Norms In contrast to values, which provide guidance about the ends people ought to seek and the things they should consider important, norms offer much more detailed specifications of what people should do and how they should pursue values. Norms are *rules for conduct.* They define what people ought to do under specified conditions. Norms help establish the minute-to-minute and day-to-day definitions of what people expect others to do and what they think others expect of them.

Norms cover a variety of behavior and situations, from how to interact with friends, relatives, or subordinates at a party to general prescriptions about honesty or politeness. They define how one should eat food, with whom, when,

Dorothy Lee, *Thanksgiving* (1935)
Oil on canvas. 28⅛ × 40 inches. Mr. & Mrs. Frank G. Logan Purchase Prize, © The Art Institute of Chicago. All Rights Reserved. Courtesy of The Art Institute of Chicago.

The norm of reciprocity not only guides and limits conduct, but also creates social bonds. The women preparing Thanksgiving dinner in this painting probably feel bound to one another not only by ties of kinship, but also by a sense of mutual obligation developed through similar cooperative activity in the past.

and where one can engage in sex, and what one should wear to a formal dinner or a rock concert.

Like other aspects of culture, norms consist of ideas—ideas about what is proper or necessary behavior under various conditions. They differ from other ideas in two important respects. First, their main focus is the rightness or appropriateness of conduct itself, rather than the ends to which it is directed or the knowledge on which it relies. And second, norms entail rewards and punishments, called *sanctions*.

These ideas are well illustrated by what Alvin Gouldner (1960) has called "the norm of reciprocity." This norm refers to the idea that you are obligated to help people who have previously helped you and to avoid injuring people who have helped you. When you encounter a situation in which someone needs assistance, as when a friend needs a loan, the fact that the friend has previously helped you should weigh heavily in deciding whether to give aid. Other things being equal (and social norms generally carry an implicit qualification of this

sort), you should help someone who has previously
second part of the norm is likewise direct and simp
someone who has helped you.

Imagine, for example, that someone helped
tant exam by studying with you and lending you her
a general obligation toward her, a disposition to retu
reciprocity might come to play in one of two possible w
asks you for a favor, you will be disposed to grant it
to feel that it is wrong not to do so. And second, shoul
your action might injure the person, you will probably feel uneasy about taking such action. For example, you might feel reluctant to report the person if you hear she has cheated on an examination.

Behavior does not often fit norms very closely, and it often departs markedly from them. For example, the norm of reciprocity may be violated when a person finds ways to avoid helping someone to whom he feels obligated. But whenever conduct departs significantly from norms, the possibility of negative sanctions arises. These sanctions may be self-imposed or socially applied. *Guilt,* an inner feeling that arises when you violate a norm to which you have become deeply attached, is a self-imposed punishment for the violation of a rule. At other times, *sanctions* are applied by others, as when a mother scolds a child for failing to thank a relative properly for a birthday present, or when a person whose appeal we have not heeded reminds us disapprovingly of our obligation. There also tends to be both self-satisfaction and approval by others when one's behavior satisfies norms.

Norms can be classified in many ways, but three dimensions have seemed especially important to sociologists. First is the dimension of seriousness. If one imagines all of the social norms to which his or her conduct must conform, it becomes quickly clear that some are regarded with greater seriousness than others. Some norms, to which the sociologist William Graham Sumner gave the name *mores,* are taken very seriously, and when they are violated, sanctions are very strong. For example, rules about the taking of human life or the nature of sexual conduct generally fall into the category of mores. Those who transgress mores are usually severely punished. In contrast, *folkways* are norms which are of less consequence, and while there are sanctions, rarely are they serious.

A second dimension along which norms can be differentiated is the degree to which they are rationally and literally specified. Highly codified and systematized norms are called *laws.* They specify the rights and obligations people have under particular conditions. Those who violate laws are likewise subject to codified sanctions. Compulsory school attendance by children under the age of sixteen is a law whose observance is enforced through civil courts. If parents violate the laws by refusing to send their ten-year-old child to school without fulfilling certain alternative conditions, they will be subject to legal punishment.

In contrast, *customs* are norms that are much less formally stated. They are general practices that people feel to be right, but that are maintained by the force of opinion and common belief. If customs are violated, there may be ndemnation, but there are no legal sanctions. For example, American customs include eating turkey on Thanksgiving, having fireworks on the Fourth of July, and newly married couples establishing independent households. But if your Thanksgiving dinner is spaghetti and meatballs, if your town does not have fireworks, or if you and your spouse move into your parents' house, no punishment will befall you (other than perhaps a sense that things are not quite what they ought to be).

A third dimension of variability in norms lies in their origin. Norms that develop slowly over the generations are called *crescive*; that is, they have grown and become entrenched over a long period of time. Because of this, it seems like they have always been there. Laws which prohibit the taking of human life are examples of crescive norms. *Enacted* norms, in contrast, are those which have been created, usually by legislation or decree. Laws requiring people to file income tax returns or prohibiting the sale of certain drugs are examples of enacted norms. It probably does not come as a surprise that we have a greater sense of "rightness" about crescive norms, since they seem timeless and universal to us.

Like values, norms are ideas, and so they are not in themselves observable. They figure in what people say and do but can only be inferred from conduct. The norm of reciprocity, for example, is not something we can see. Its existence can be inferred by observing what people generally do and what they say about their conduct. As elements of culture, norms become part of individual minds, shaping the way these minds approach their environment and form conduct.

Although people frequently take them into account as they interact, in no sense do norms dictate conduct. Norms do not provide people with moment-to-moment guidance for their behavior. And people do not constantly focus their attention on norms, worrying about the right thing to do in a particular situation. Norms provide a general framework of expectations within which people generally steer their conduct. But norms do not tell people exactly what to do, nor are they always obeyed. And as we will see later, there often is conflict over whether a norm applies in a particular situation or whether it has been violated.

CONCLUSION

Society and culture constrain individuals and their actions and interactions. From the perspective of any single individual, society and culture are massive external realities that confront the person on every side. The child is born into an established family with its membership and customs largely settled matters. The individual has to master a complex body of cultural knowledge and often obey its many norms. Groups and organizations exist, and the person must adjust to their requirements. Culture and its typifications define the world for the members of society.

Yet society and culture exist only because individuals act. Statuses, roles, groups, organizations, knowledge, norms, and values depend for their continued existence upon the actions of men and women as they go about their lives. There would be no social norms if people did not take them into account as they act and talk about them when they are violated. There would be no groups or organizations without individuals who believe in their existence and interact with one another on the basis of shared ideas about their purposes, their division of labor, and the rights of their members. There would be no status and role without people who organize their perception of the social world into statuses and share ideas about how people occupying various positions should conduct themselves.

The concepts of society and culture are necessary to an understanding of human social behavior, for they are important constraining forces. But a full explanation of human conduct requires attention to the way people actually go about forming their behavior as they interact with one another. Chapter 4 will examine the nature of human conduct, the ways human beings act and interact. It will focus on the question of how people are able to act as human beings.

SUGGESTED READINGS

BENEDICT, RUTH. *Patterns of Culture* (Boston: Houghton Mifflin, 1934).

GEERTZ, CLIFFORD. *The Interpretation of Cultures* (New York: Basic Books, 1973).

HALL, EDWARD T. *The Hidden Dimension* (New York: Doubleday, 1966).

HALL, EDWARD T. *The Silent Language* (Greenwich, Conn.: Fawcett, 1959).

HALL, RICHARD M. *Organizations: Structure and Process* (Englewood Cliffs: Prentice-Hall, 1972).

HARRIS, MARVIN. *Cannibals and Kings: The Origins of Culture* (New York: Random House, 1977).

KANTER, ROSABETH MOSS and BARRY A. STEIN, eds. *Life in Organizations* (New York: Basic Books, 1979).

NIXON, HOWARD L. *The Small Group* (Englewood Cliffs: Prentice-Hall, 1979).

4

The Nature of Human Conduct

Society and culture shape human behavior but are also the result of that behavior. An explanation of this seeming paradox requires a closer inspection of the capabilities of human beings and the way they form their conduct. This chapter will discuss the evolution of human nature and present the basic ideas symbolic interactionists have developed to explain human action and interaction.

THE EVOLUTION OF HUMAN BEHAVIOR

The human species is a remarkable development in the evolution of life. Spreading virtually over the entire earth, its members have adapted to conditions as diverse as deserts, ice packs, tropical rain forests, and temperate lake shores. Humans have become the dominant species on earth, so successful that they have the power to destroy the very resources of air, water, and other living things upon which their own lives depend.

What is the basis for the extraordinary evolutionary success of the species? Scholars for generations have sought answers to this question. Some have held that the use of tools of ever increasing power and sophistication has set humans apart—that their ability to magnify the power of their own bodies permits them to harness more energy. But why have humans developed tools, ranging from simple tools for digging to complex electronic computers that can store and retrieve vast quantities of information? What underlies the ability to create and use tools?

Others have argued that the capacity for learned behavior sets humans apart from other animals. Because people can learn new ways of behaving, the human capacity to cope with the environment is greatly enhanced. Humans can adapt more swiftly than other creatures because their behavioral patterns are learned rather than genetically inherited. But again, although learning is clearly important, human beings are not unique in relying upon it. Other animals teach their young how to cope with their environments. The range of conduct that is learned may be far narrower for a lion than for a human, but learning still takes place.

Tools and learning are important, but they exist because of more basic capabilities that humans possess. For example, the use of tools rests partly upon the upright posture and opposable thumb of the species. Because humans can stand upright, their hands are freed for the use of tools. Their remarkable capacity for learned behavior depends upon the nature and organization of the human brain. And it is not simply the fact that humans learn that is significant. As we shall see, it is the way humans learn that is of greatest importance.

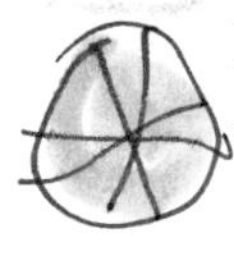

Organisms and Environments

The evolutionary success of any species depends upon the way its members relate to and act upon the environment. All living things exist in an environment, which can be defined as the set of surrounding conditions and events that affect organisms and influence their behavior. Whether we think of an infectious disease organism that has invaded the body or a human being living in a particular community, all life takes place in intimate and continuous contact with surroundings. Thus to understand what makes humans special, we must understand the relationship between ourselves and our environment.

Living things are *sensitive* to their surroundings. That is, each living organism has the capacity to respond to environmental events. For example, an amoeba is sensitive to the chemistry of the fluid in which it lives; if the fluid becomes chemically intolerable, the amoeba will move away. People are sensitive to the words and deeds of other people; if these are negative, people may move away from the irritation, strike back, or plead for better treatment. Not all organisms are sensitive to the same environment, for each lives in a world to which it is uniquely sensitive. People and fish live in different environments. If the pH level of water becomes very low (2 to 3), fish will die since they cannot live in acidic water. Similarly, people require air that contains about 20 percent oxygen. But at the same time, people cannot live under water, whatever its pH, and fish cannot live surrounded only by air, whatever its oxygen content.

Organisms respond to their environments in several different ways (see Becker, 1971, Chapters 2 and 3). The simplest connection exists when a single environmental event leads directly to a single response by the organism. A *direct response* of this kind, exemplified by a microorganism that automatically ingests a bit of food that it encounters, indicates a very immediate and restricted relationship between the organism and its environment. This type of interaction is referred to as direct because the organism responds directly to a stimulus.

A more complex form of response to the environment occurs when the organism is capable of *conditioning*. In this, the organism at first responds to an environmental stimulus; for example, a hungry dog salivates at the sight and smell of food. But suppose that an unrelated stimulus is presented to the dog along with its food. In the classic experiments of the Russian psychologist Ivan Pavlov, a bell was rung as food was presented to a dog. The bell had no intrinsic interest to the dog, but ultimately it became associated with food and, in time, the dog responded to the new stimulus in the same way as it had to the original. In Pavlov's experiment, the dog salivated when the bell was rung, even when no food was present.

Conditioned responses reflect the ability of the organism to respond to events that are not especially significant themselves, but which may be associated with biologically important events. These associated events are called *natural signs*, for they signify something of importance in the environment. This means that the organism has an enhanced capacity to cope with its surroundings, for it may be able to anticipate important events before they happen. The deer who hears the voices of approaching people and has learned to associate human sounds with danger is able to flee before hunters are actually present. Yet the organism still remains dependent upon its environment. The production of the signs themselves is not controlled by the animal itself. Pavlov, not the dog, rang the bell; people, not deer, make sounds that signify danger. Thus, although conditioning gives the organism more leeway and more power in its capacity to respond adequately to its environment, the environment is still very influential.

With the development of a third level of response to the environment, organisms begin to escape the whim of events beyond their control. This level is marked by the capacity for actively searching out and seeing connections between single events and conditions in the environment and then adapting. For example, a dog confronted by a fence will survey the scene and perceive an opening at the end that will allow it to pass through. In the same situation, a chicken would not be able to size up the total situation. It would pace back and forth along the fence, never perceiving the opening that would allow it to get to the other side. The dog is able to delay an overt act until it has surveyed the scene, but the chicken seems bound to make an immediate response to what lies directly before it.

A fourth level of response occurs when organisms respond to *symbols*, which are arbitrary signs of important objects and events. A symbol is like a natural sign in the sense that it is something associated with an object or event. It differs, however, because there is no inherent connection between the symbol and what it signifies. The connection exists only because those who use the symbol have agreed to use it in a certain way.

Although symbols take many different forms, the verbal symbol produced by human organs of speech is of greatest importance for an understanding of this level of response. A word, such as *boy*, is a symbol that stands for a particular object; it is associated with the object only because a particular community of users of that symbol agree that that is what it stands for. Symbols, embodied in language, do not merely stand between the organism and its environment. Symbols *are* the environment for organisms with the capacity to create and use them.

The key to understanding human behavior is understanding the nature and consequences of using symbols. So far as we know, humans are the only animals to create and use symbols to any significant degree. There have been a number of fascinating efforts to teach chimpanzees and gorillas to communicate with their masters. In a few cases, these animals have been painstakingly taught behavior that resembles rudimentary symbolic behavior. But it remains true that the use of symbols is a distinctive feature of human evolution that has appeared on its own nowhere else in the animal kingdom.

To see the significance of symbols, we must look at the way in which they function as the human environment, and to do that it is useful to speculate on the way in which they came into being during the evolution of the species.

Communication

We begin with the idea of *communication*. This word has a variety of meanings in everyday speech. It can refer to the instruments by which we convey information from one person to another, as when we speak of the mass media of communication such as newspapers, radio, or television. Communication can

Arthur Crisp, *Adam and Eve* (1918) Oil on plaster. 22 × 30 inches. Collection of Whitney Museum of American Art. Acq#31.156.

In the Judeo-Christian account of creation, human destiny was profoundly altered when Eve ate from the tree of knowledge of good and evil. The evolutionary account bases its explanation on the gradual emergence of cultural knowledge based on symbolic communication.

also refer to the transmitted information itself. And sometimes it is used to refer to the behavior of people as they attempt to pass information from one to another; people having a heart-to-heart talk about their problems often say they are "communicating" with one another.

Communication has a more fundamental meaning, however, which is present in each of these uses of the term. Invariably, communication implies *interaction.* And when we talk about interaction, we are really talking about the way in which the actions of one individual *influence* the actions of another. Two organisms interacting with each other are really influencing one another because they are a part of each other's environment. The deer that comes at dusk to a pond is part of the environment of the Eastern timber wolf; the wolf is sensitive to the deer's presence and its behavior is focused upon making the deer its prey. Similarly, the wolf and possible signs of its presence are part of the deer's environment, something to which it is sensitive as it tries to quench its thirst. Two birds engaged in a courtship ritual are also environmental to one another; each is sensitive to the other's presence and behavior, and the behavior of each influences that of the other.

Interaction involves the organism's sensitivity to that part of the environment composed of living things. Although we can speak of interaction whenever animals are sensitive to one another and influence one another's behavior, we generally use the term *social interaction* to refer only to the behavior of human beings. For example, interaction between the deer and the wolf is nonsocial. So too, the interaction that occurs between two courting prairie chickens is not social interaction in the human sense.

Communication exists when one organism is able to respond to the acts of another with acts of its own. More precisely, communication entails the capacity of one organism to respond to very small *fragments* of the acts of another and to treat these behavioral fragments as *signs* of impending behaviors that are more complex and of longer duration. Whether the signs are inherently (and perhaps instinctively) given, as they probably are in the case of the courtship rituals of birds, or whether the animal searches out cues in the behavior of the other and learns to be sensitive to them, communication entails mutual sensitivity to signs.

The idea that fragments of one animal's behavior can be treated by another as a sign is basic to George Herbert Mead's (1934) concept of action and interaction. Mead worked near the beginning of the twentieth century, when the ideas of the behaviorist John Watson were very much in vogue among psychologists. Behaviorists, then as now, explained behavior as a set of conditioned responses to stimuli, and much of Mead's work as a philosopher and social psychologist was an effort to correct what he felt were misconceptions of behavior introduced by Watson and his associates. One of these misconceptions was the idea that behavior is merely a series of simple momentary responses (eye blinks, movements toward and away from stimuli, reflexes). Mead thought that looking at an animal's behavior as a discrete series of responses made scientists lose sight of the continuity and basic organizing forces in nature. For Mead, the proper unit of analysis was something he called *the act*, which consists of a series of related responses that begin when an organism is somehow disturbed and end when the disturbance is removed. The organism gets hungry, it looks around and seeks food, it eats, and it is no longer hungry; this constitutes an act.

In a world where members of the same species exist in one another's presence, they naturally become environmental to one another. Dogs in a pack, for example, react not merely to the physical environment and to their possible prey, but also to one another. They compete for the same food or mates, bump into one another, and engage in various acts that we humans would call cooperative or competitive. In other words, *they interact*. Their interaction is made possible by their capacity to respond to signs, and these signs include the physical environment and other dogs' behavior. For example, when a dog bares its teeth and begins to growl, it is a sign to other dogs of impending attack. Whether by instinct or conditioning, another dog is able to react to this sign and begins its own act on the basis of this initial fragment. It may respond by growling in like manner and prepare to fight, or it may roll over and submit to the first dog. In either case, the dog has responded to the other's impending act. In Mead's language, a *conversation of gestures* has taken place. That is, each beginning part of one dog's act is a gesture to which the other dog responds; as it responds, the beginnings of its own act are a gesture to which the first dog responds.

This conversation of gestures is a form of communication. By responding to signs or gestures, organisms are able to adjust their conduct to one another and to form responses that are appropriate to the particular environment in which they are located. As we shall see, this kind of communication is the most rudimentary there is. Nothing we would think of as "information" is transmitted, nor is there any evidence that dogs and other organisms that interact solely at this level intend to communicate or have what we would call "consciousness" of what they are doing. Yet they do, as a matter of fact, coordinate their conduct in relation to one another.

Call Systems

Not surprisingly, some animals have evolved forms of communication and social interaction that are more complex and finely specialized. Among these, call systems are of major importance, for such means of communication precede human speech and the development of true symbols.

A *call* can be defined as a sound or other tangible sort of behavior that is produced by an animal in a specific situation as part of its response to that situation. Calls are the means by which information can be transferred among members of a species. They are limited in number, genetically fixed, and always interpreted in the same way by the members of a species.

Honey bees, for example, have a very complex system by which they are able to communicate to one another the distance and relative location of sources of nectar. One bee "tells" another where it can find nectar by means of genetically determined "dances" in which the speed of the bee's movements and their relative angle to the sun indicate location. Similarly, many animals have vocal calls that serve as signs of important environmental events. Calls may exist for food, danger, presence of others of the same species, territorial defense, and similar biologically important events.

Animals that use calls tend to have greater mastery over their environment than those who do not have this capacity to share information. For example, prairie dogs live in "towns" in which there are numerous holes and burrows. If one animal senses danger, it barks the call for "danger," and all the animals dart into the closest hole. The benefits of such a system are obvious. Each animal does not need to determine independently that there is danger present.

But while a call system is important for social cooperation among the members of a species, it is not a language and calls are not symbols. Call systems have several limitations that make them less powerful than symbolic language. For example, if we return to the prairie dog village in which the danger call has been made, we will see the animals scurrying for cover. Yet they do not know whether the danger is a rattlesnake, an eagle, or a person. Neither will they know exactly where the danger is. Their response to the call is not tempered by knowledge that the intruder is a friendly human tourist who simply wants to take their picture. Prairie dog calls do not distinguish the nature or specific location of an intrusion into their environment.

Humans, unlike prairie dogs, can use language symbols. These are more powerful than simple calls because they can be modified to address various situations. Consequently, humans are not restricted to the all-or-nothing responses of prairie dogs. For example, unlike the prairie dogs, humans can specify the kind of danger and indicate where it is located.

Origins of Language

How humans acquired the ability to use language symbols has been the object of much speculation. Two linguists, Charles Hockett and Robert Ascher (1964), have suggested one possible way that language could have evolved. In their reconstruction of human evolution (based upon established facts as well as conjecture), the prehominoids of the Miocene period, from which both apes and humans were later to evolve, encountered both changing climatic conditions and a shrinking forest area in Africa. Some were forced to abandon their homes in the trees, and as they did, they encountered many predators as well as a scarcity of food in their new habitat on the ground. Gradually, in response to such conditions, evolutionary selection favored upright posture and bipedal (two-footed) locomotion, both more advantageous in the new environmental conditions. And as these adaptations developed, the mouth and teeth of our ancestors no longer were occupied with the holding and carrying of food and could be used for other purposes. Hockett and Ascher's speculation about the consequences of unoccupied teeth and mouths is startling in its simplicity: our ancestors began to chatter.

Over time, chattering became an important basis for signaling. That is, a call system based upon vocalization came to be important in the survival of these social animals. The evolutionary advantage conferred by a call system was that it enabled better coordination in the search for food and for the defense of the band against predators. And patterns of behavior that confer an advantage tend to survive.

But what transformed the call system of our ancestors into what we know as language? What lifted the restrictions that are inherent in calls? Hockett and Ascher answer that our ancestors must have responded to their complex environment by *combining* simple calls. For example, let us assume there were distinct calls for "food" and "danger." How could our ancestors indicate a situation in which both were present? They did so by combining calls, so that a simple set of calls becomes expanded into a larger system. With more calls, they could designate and communicate about more varied and complex situations. When they did this, they introduced a revolutionary change into the world.

Over long periods of time, the bands who adopted an expanded system of calls had advantages. More and more composite calls could be created, and as they were, the use and interpretation of such calls would become more and more dependent upon *learning* rather than innate behavioral tendencies. Not only were the members of a species more able to respond to environmental events with calls, but they began to learn calls *before* they were needed in real situations. Members of the species were no longer restricted to the here and now, and they were able to use their calls in many situations.

Gradually the restricted call system of our ancestors became transformed into language. That is, the calls became numerous, highly differentiated from one another, and systematically interrelated, so that one call could be defined in terms of others. As this happened, calls became transformed into symbols.

They began to stand for events and objects in the environment, to be manipulated in advance of and away from the actual events and objects, and to be used to convey information from one individual to another.

The use of symbols confers a remarkable advantage upon the species that develops such a capacity. No longer is the organism tied to an environment to which it can respond only as important events occur. Instead, symbols enable the environment to be brought within the organism's mind, where it can be "manipulated" in ways not possible before. Without symbols, an organism must visualize events; with symbols, abstract thought is possible. Symbols codify various possible objects and events. Not only can they be used when the real events are not present, but they also promote abstract and categorical attitudes. To experience the world symbolically is to take a categorical attitude toward it. When an object or an event is given a name, one has taken the first step in creating a category of similar objects. And as we will see, the ability of people to see categories of things rather than concrete objects means they are able to respond to both their similarities and their differences.

The Emergence of Self

Symbols have one additional important consequence; they give rise to *consciousness*. To understand what consciousness is, we must recall that the emergence and use of symbols occurred in a social setting. The call system of many animals developed essentially as a way of coordinating activity among animals who lived in association with one another. And as calls gradually became transformed into language symbols, social coordination improved; our ancestors became more able to cope with circumstances and thus more adaptable.

But imagine what must have occurred among bands of our primate ancestors who were expanding their symbolic capacity. Calls, and later symbols, could be applied to events, to objects, to other animals, to circumstances, and, at some point, to individual members of the band itself. The first calls were very likely names for events and circumstances. Later, we can imagine, as calls evolved into symbols, objects were named, and still later, names were applied to individual members of the band itself. Such a development seems natural enough, for as members of the band began to refer to one another, their capacity to coordinate activities would be enhanced. Now it would be possible to locate events and objects in relation to specific individuals.

The next step seems simple, but it may be the single most dramatic event in the evolution of the human species. In a band that had names for individual members, each member would necessarily hear his or her own name along with those of others. And hearing one's own name implies the possibility of using it oneself, for if one can refer to others, one can refer to oneself as well. This possibility seems obvious, but its impact is revolutionary. An organism that names itself has accomplished something that no other animal has done: *It has made itself a part of its own environment.*

Once individual members of a band began to be designated, and once individual members had learned to apply and use their own names, the social organization of the band could become more complex and powerful. Now each member of the group could convey information about the environment (as they did in a simpler fashion with calls), and it also could convey information about itself. That is, it could relate information about internal as well as external events. And crucially, it could act not just in relation to a world outside itself, but in relation to itself. It had become a part of its own environment.

When we speak of consciousness as a distinctive capacity of the human species, we refer to the capacity of the individual to designate itself symbolically as a part of its world. Once an animal is conscious of itself, it can try out alternative solutions to problems by seeing itself as a part of its own situation. Of all animals, only humans have this ability.

Humans confront their environment, not immediately and directly, but through the medium of symbols. They act in their world not simply on the basis of overt trial and error, but also in their mind's eye, imaginatively trying out solutions to problems that confront them before the solutions are put into practice. They act self-consciously, aware not only of the world external to them, but of themselves as organisms in it. Not only the events of an external environment, but the events of the environment within are a part of the circumstances with which they must cope. And they act in a social world, one in which the self-consciousness of the individual is shaped by his or her relationships with others.

In the evolution of human life, then, two facts seem to stand out. First, symbols have made it possible for people to gain a considerable amount of control over their own conduct. By anticipating situations, inhibiting responses, and taking the self into account as a part of the context in which one acts, the human being gains a great advantage over other animals. This control is by no means perfect. People are obviously not always fully in command of what they do, nor is every solution to a problem the "correct" one. But compared with other animals, humans have an extraordinary degree of mastery over themselves. And second, control over their own conduct increases humans' mastery of their environment. Human beings are not free of environmental restrictions, of course, and the very fact that individuals can respond to their own actions and feelings is a complicating factor, producing more environment with which to deal. Even so, for good or ill, humans have a greater impact upon their environment than any other animal species.

SYMBOLIC INTERACTION

With these ideas in mind, we turn to a closer look at the way human contact is organized. The concepts we introduce here will be the foundation for more extensive discussions in later chapters.

Acts and Objects

In order to understand the nature of human conduct, we must first examine in more detail the nature of the act, a concept to which we referred earlier. Imagine a state of equilibrium or balance existing between an organism and its environment. Things are going smoothly, nothing is particularly bothering the organism, and it is meeting its needs successfully. Such a state of adjustment always exists in relation to some particular need or sensitivity. For example, in relation to the need for food, a person is in adjustment if he or she feels no particular hunger or thirst, as when food has recently been consumed and the person feels satiated. A person in this condition will, under most circumstances, not be especially moved by the sight or smell of food and will not think of food.

Sooner or later, however, the person grows hungry again. Hunger is a periodic deficit, and as the body digests food, the stomach empties and the internal state of the person changes. At this point, the smell or sight of food is apt to provoke quite a different response. As you sit studying or writing, for example, you may grow progressively hungrier until something—perhaps the smell of food cooking in another part of the house—makes you suddenly conscious of your hunger. When such an event takes place, when the internal condition of your body makes you alert to a particular kind of stimulation, such as the smell of food, an act has begun.

This beginning phase of the act is termed the *impulse* phase. At the instant when food is noticed, there is a generalized disposition or readiness to do something, although at that moment one has not formulated a particular plan of action. In the case of such periodic deficits as hunger, the generalized impulse very quickly gives way to a phase of *perception*, in which the individual focuses his or her attention upon the stimulus (smell of food) that has created the impulse, locates the source of the odor, and simultaneously labels himself or herself as hungry. Impulse and perception are often, as in this case, locked very closely together. To experience the impulse to act is to experience almost immediately the source of that impulse, namely, the need for food. Next comes *manipulation*, which refers to efforts to restore adjustment to the environment. In this case, one eats something to feel less hungry. When the person eats and eventually feels satisfied, we say that *consummation* has been reached; that is, the balance between the organism and the environment has been restored, and this particular act has come to an end.

Any act can be described in terms of these four phases: impulse, perception, manipulation, and consummation (Mead, 1934; 1938). Some acts occur very quickly, and we are scarcely aware of them. For example, an automobile driver automatically brakes to avoid a pedestrian in the flow of traffic. A person in front of the car is a source of disequilibrium between the driver and the environment and creates an impulse to act; the driver immediately perceives the person, applies the brakes (manipulation), and the adjustment is restored when the person is safely out of harm's way. In other cases, an act takes longer to move from impulse to consummation. For example, if awakened by a noise in the middle of the night, a person may first feel disposed to do something in response to the unusual sound, but may spend considerable time in a phase of perception before acting. As the sound penetrates sleep, the individual must first perceive its nature—a car horn or a fire engine's siren—and then determine whether it is near or far and whether it is relevant. Only when the sound is identified and labeled can one determine what action to take: going to the window to investigate, going outside to free one's own stuck car horn, calling the police, and so forth. The time interval between impulse and consummation may therefore be quite lengthy.

There is also a fundamental difference between reflexive action, such as braking for a pedestrian, and responding to a stimulus whose nature is at first unknown. In the former case, the act of braking for a pedestrian is automatic. We do not have to think about what we are doing, nor do we worry about what the person is doing in the middle of the street. We simply act habitually; if we did otherwise, there would be fewer pedestrians. But in many of our everyday acts, as exemplified by the way we deal with unknown noises, there are not habitual responses, and our acts are more carefully and self-consciously planned.

Unlike other animals, humans do not live in a world of stimuli to which they merely learn the appropriate responses. Rather, they live in a world of objects whose meanings must be grasped if they are to act in useful and productive ways. Consequently, people often are required to act toward objects whose meaning they must interpret before they can determine a proper response.

The term *object* has a special and very important set of implications. An object may be a tangible thing, such as a building or a rock, but it may also be something as intangible as an event, a thought, or an idea. A chair is an object, but so too are a cocktail party and the concept of liberty. When we use the term in this way we mean simply that *an object is anything that can be designated and toward which the individual can act.* A police siren, an article of furniture, the idea of democracy—these are all objects in this sense, since all can be designated or named by people, who can then act toward them in various ways.

Human beings are born into a culture, which can be thought of as a world of preexisting objects that powerfully shape their development and behavior. These objects exist in the concrete things and events people can see, hear, and touch. They also exist in the language they learn from other human beings. Humans are accustomed to thinking of their language as a means of communication, which, of course, it is. But in a more fundamental sense, *language is the human world.* It presents people with a vast array of names and ways of relating them, and so gives them a ready-made world of objects whose meanings they must learn and with which they must contend. Language, we might say, "carries" culture; it is the vehicle through which culture is learned, experienced, and passed on to others.

One of the tasks (and in some ways it seems an almost insurmountable

The Hunt of the Unicorn: III: *The Unicorn in Captivity* (late xv century)
The Metropolitan Museum of Art, The Cloisters Collection, Gift of John D. Rockefeller, Jr., 1937. (37.80.6)

Humans use symbols to name familiar objects in the world around them, but they also use symbols to create new objects. Unicorns and other imaginary beasts, as well as abstract ideas, are created by symbols. They exist because symbols shape, and do not merely reflect, the world in which we live.

one) that confront the infant and child is to learn the names of the objects that exist in his or her world. At first, this learning involves grasping the names of the concrete objects that are important to the child's well-being. "Mama," "Dada," "ball," "book," "dog," "cat," and the names of brothers and sisters are often the first words (names) a child learns. At first the words a child learns are associated with a specific object, but they are not distinguished from other similar objects. Thus, "mama" refers not only to the woman who is the mother but also to all females. Soon, however, a child learns that "mama" and "dada" refer to particular people with whom the child has a specific relationship. They do not refer to all adult males and females.

As the child learns the language of the community into which he or she was born, learning the names of things is quickly supplemented by learning the "things of names." That is, the child is confronted by many words for which there are no tangible referents, and whose meaning must slowly and painstakingly be sorted out. For example, words like "bad" or "pretty" do not label concrete things. They refer to more abstract ideas whose meanings must be inferred rather than grasped directly. Later in life, when we have more or less mastered our linguistic world, we take it for granted that the world *is* as our language has structured it. It seems "natural" to us, as if the world could only be the way it is. But in the beginning, it is a world we must discover.

From the perspective of the child, understanding this world and knowing how to behave are not merely a matter of learning what objects are called or of inferring the implications of more abstract objects. The child must not only learn the meaning of objects, but must grasp that the meaning of an object is likely to change from one context to another. In any situation, humans confront objects that are in some respects familiar to them, and yet they are also somewhat unknown.

Consider a chair. It is something in which to sit, but it may also be something to throw as a weapon, something with which to fend off a wild animal (as does the circus lion-tamer), something on which to toss clothing and books, or something on which to rest one's feet. A chair, then, may be considered to be not one object but several. The object it is at any particular time depends upon the way in which we are prepared to act toward it.

Human conduct depends upon our capacity to interpret and assign meaning to objects in particular situations. Language provides us with a world of objects, but in our moment-to-moment conduct we must interpret the specific meanings these objects have for us. Thus, the meaning of an object lies in its implications for our conduct; that is, in the responses we are prepared to make to it. Language gives us a world of possibilities, but it is our own efforts to interpret and assign meaning that produce a world of actualities.

In order to form their conduct, humans must not only interpret the meaning of objects, but they must also imagine alternative ways in which they can act toward these objects. For example, people are standing on a street corner and hear gunshots. They try to make sense out of the sounds. Are they really gunshots, or is it the sound of a car backfiring? Their responses depend on how they interpret the sound. If the noise is thought to be simply a car backfiring, they will probably continue whatever they were doing before. If people think the noise is gunshots, they will choose among various alternatives. They will look about to see who is doing the shooting and will probably move away from the street and toward the shelter of nearby buildings. In their minds, they are likely to run through various scenarios: Is a bank robbery taking place at the bank on the opposite corner? Is someone trying to kill another person? Is it a random shooting, or are people engaged in a domestic quarrel? Is there an assassination attempt against a prominent person? And what should they do—run for cover, try to help, look for the "action," or seek assistance from police?

An object is anything toward which a person can act. The capacity of people to interpret the meanings of objects and to imagine alternative ways of acting toward them would not exist if humans did not have the ability to make and use symbols. That is, it is only because they are provided with an extensive, preexisting world of cultural objects that people can "try out" various different ways of responding to a given situation. Humans, of course, must often engage in trial-and-error behavior when they encounter new situations. But much of this process of trial and error takes place in the imagination and does not need to be overt behavior. Humans approach problems by imaginatively trying out different solutions. This method enables them to make efficient use of past experience as well as of the culture that language makes available.

Social Acts and Social Objects

So far we have talked about objects, acts, and the process of interpretation as if only the individual mattered. But life is lived in association with others, and most of what people do in their everyday lives is strongly influenced by the interests and interpretations of others. Therefore, to the basic concepts of individual acts and objects, we must add the closely related concepts of social acts and social objects.

Social acts involve the coordinated conduct of two or more people whose individual acts are linked with one another for a period of time. A casual encounter with an acquaintance—"Hi! How are you?" "Fine, how are you doing?" "Oh, not bad."—is an example of a social act, for it involves the coordination of conduct between two individuals. So, too, making an out at a baseball game, having an argument, or performing in a symphony orchestra are examples of social acts, since all entail the coordinated acts of several individuals. These social acts are very different in other respects, to be sure. A casual encounter is very ritualized and people may be scarcely aware of what they are saying; an argument calls for the close attention of participants, each of whom must be very alert to what the other is saying; a musical performance relies on very precise timing and pitch. But whatever the case, conduct is coordinated and a social act occurs.

Social acts have social objects. People in the performance of social acts designate and act toward objects. They use the same process of symbolic interpretation that occurs in individual acts. But there are other factors at work in the social act. How are people able to coordinate their conduct and so create social acts and social objects? How do people know what social objects are being created as they interact with one another?

To understand how human social interaction works, we must return to an idea discussed earlier in this chapter—Mead's conversation of gestures. Recall that a crucial part of the conversation of gestures involved one animal's responding to the beginning fragments of another's act, treating them as signs of what is to follow. A dog, for example, might respond to another's growl as the sign of an impending attack. This kind of interaction occurs to some extent on the human level, but for the most part our conduct rests upon *symbolic interaction.* In symbolic interaction, as in the conversation of gestures, the beginning parts of an act are signs of the rest of the act, serving to indicate what will happen next. But in symbolic interaction, one person must *consciously* designate to himself or herself the meaning of the other's act. That is, instead of being able to respond automatically to a gesture, each individual must consciously think about the act and designate what the other is apparently doing.

Two (human) boxers, for example, engage in a conversation of gestures in a boxing match. Each movement by one is, to the other, a sign of subsequent movements; thus, a certain movement of the arm or torso would signal to the other that a particular punch is imminent, and a defensive response would begin. Much of the time this process is automatic and reflexive, and does not require thought. But in boxing, a movement by one fighter may not signify what it seems. The opponent's stance might indicate an impending left—but it might also be a feint, a deceptive tactic designed to make the other respond in one way so that a punch other than the one expected can be scored. If a boxer considers this possibility, he is better able to outwit his opponent. When such a conscious act of designating the meaning of the other's action occurs, symbolic interaction is taking place. The conduct of two boxers in this example is being coordinated not simply by reflex and habit, but also by the conscious designation of the intent of one another's acts.

A social act, then, is one in which two or more individuals coordinate their conduct by interpreting one another's intentions. In a social act, it is the social object that provides the "cement" that holds things together and makes it possible for people to interpret one another's intentions. People know, for example, that when they encounter one another on a city sidewalk, a polite exchange of greetings is called for. One could say that they know in advance that a particular social object is to be created. Knowing this, and assuming that the other knows it also, each can assume that the other intends the same object, an exchange of greetings. The action of the first person saying something like "Hi! How are you?" is the signal to the other that a polite exchange is about to take place. Both persons know the social object being created and can thus make the appropriate response. In general, when people interact, the actions of any one person have a threefold set of implications for the other. When people say "Hi!" it indicates that they plan to exchange greetings with the other person, that they expect the other person to do the same, and that they will engage in a conversation.

As Mead put it, meaning has a *triadic* nature. Each gesture by one individual simultaneously serves to indicate what that person is doing, what he or she expects the other to do, and the social object that both are engaged in creating. Meaning has this quality, whether the participants are engaged in a friendly chat, a game of chess, or an act of violence. The armed robber who tells you to lie on the floor while he empties the cash register is engaging in this triadic process every bit as much as a polite friend complimenting you on dinner. The implication of a gun and the phrase "Get down on the floor and don't move" is triple: I am going to rob you; you had best not try to stop me; and this is a stickup.

Definition of the Situation

People know what to expect of one another in various social situations—that is, they know which objects to create—because their culture has equipped them with a vast world of potential social objects. When people learn to speak the language of their community, they learn more than a way of communicating. They learn what the social world is, what possibilities it contains, and what forms of conduct are permissible or unthinkable. They also learn how to recognize from the words and deeds of others what they are going to do and what they expect. People are not born knowing that it is considered proper to talk politely with friends. But they gradually learn the social objects they are expected to create with others in various social situations, and in time they carry with them an immense stock of such socially important knowledge. (In Chapter 3 we examined the nature of that knowledge in some detail.)

Crucial to any social interaction is its participants' grasp of the situation as a whole and of their particular individual contributions and responsibilities. Before people can know what to do in a particular situation—what social acts will be performed and what social objects are to be found there—they must define the situation as a whole. The *definition of the situation* is an organized sense of what is going on at a particular place and time, of what can, should, and must not happen there. Most of the situations people encounter in everyday life are routine; people have encountered them or situations like them before and therefore generally know what to expect. Others are unexpected and even novel situations, such as the kind people encounter when they witness an automobile accident on a highway. These are more demanding, for participants must figure out how to act appropriately. But in either case, people must define a situation, identifying what is going on, who the participants are, and what is expected of them, before they can act in it.

Roles

Part of the definition of the situation generally includes an overall sense of the *structure* of the situation. For example, if you were to enter a large auditorium filled with people all paying attention to a person holding a baton, you would define the situation easily and spontaneously as a concert. The sense of the structure of that situation would include a set of terms you could apply to the various participants: musician, conductor, concertmaster, usher, audience, music critic, and the like. And you would see the situation not just as a physical place filled with bodies, instruments, chairs, and so on, but also as a social entity, as a well-organized assembly of individuals with coordinated responsibilities and rights.

The sociological terms for the labels people apply to participants in such a situation are, of course, *status* and *role*. For most or all of the routine situations they encounter, people have a sense of the activities to be engaged in and of the particular parts to be played by the participants. In a baseball game, for example, most Americans have an overall grasp of the structure of the game. They can visualize various positions—infielders, outfielders, pitcher, catcher, batter, and so forth—and they know each participant's contribution to the game as a whole. The duties, rights, and responsibilities that pertain to each position on the field make up a role, as was pointed out in Chapter 3. Thus, each player has a position to fill and a part—a role—to play in the game. Each is conscious of his or her own role, that is, each knows how the others expect him or her to behave in various situations—and each also has a grasp of the game of baseball as a whole, a sense of its structure and all its various statuses and roles.

Earlier we saw how the capacity to use symbols conferred an important evolutionary advantage upon humans. The ability of humans to coordinate their actions by use of symbols also increased our ancestors' social nature, and they became more dependent upon one another. In part, the increased dependence of human beings on one another rested upon a tendency to create a *division of labor*, a propensity to divide tasks among the members of a group and for some to engage in specialized activities. Male specialization in hunting and female specialization in agriculture are examples of a very basic division of labor. Such an arrangement does not require symbols, at least if it is genetically determined (for example, in the animal world, bees divide labor between the queen bee, workers, and drones). But the capacity to use symbols greatly increases both the possible complexity of specialization and the propensity to specialize. This is so for several reasons.

First, with symbols, tasks can be described in greater detail and coordinated over greater distances and longer spans of time. Symbols "refine" the world; that is, they make it possible to perceive and communicate more of the details of experience, they lead to finer distinctions, and they stretch out the memory of individuals and the group as a whole. Symbols make it possible for the members of a group to negotiate agreements about who will be responsible for doing what.

Second, and perhaps more important, symbols increase the propensity to specialize because they make it possible for each member of a group to experience the group as a whole in which he or she is included. As we said, symbols make self-consciousness possible. By providing each group member with a means of self-designation, symbols enable each member to imagine and talk about the complete group to which he or she belongs. Animals without symbols are literally unaware of themselves. They experience bodily sensations such as pain or hunger, to be sure; but they do not have any consciousness of themselves as separate and acting individuals in the company of their fellows. Humans do have such consciousness, and because they do, each member of a human group can imagine his or her contribution to the activities of the group as a whole.

Role-making and Role-taking

Another way of saying this is to point out that humans can not only experience the actions of others in a group setting and see their contributions to the group as a whole, but they can also make roles for themselves in the group. The creation and control of a role by an individual in a group setting is called *role-making*. This is an inherent and inescapable result of self-consciousness. As soon as our ancestors developed the capacity to use symbols and to create names for individuals, they acquired, as individuals, the capacity to imagine their own contributions to a group task and to communicate their intentions to their fellows. We can almost imagine a human in the distant past saying, "Look, you fetch the water while I get the fire going, and we'll soon have these roots cooked." This is role-making in its most basic form.

It is important to understand that, among human beings, a capacity for complex social coordination and consciousness of self go hand in hand, for one cannot really be imagined without the other. Without membership in groups, human beings could not be conscious of themselves; they could not have images of themselves. For humans, consciousness of self is essentially awareness of oneself as a member of a group. At the same time, the complexity of human social organization would not be possible without self-consciousness. Humans could not accomplish complex tasks requiring coordination of individual effort without the capacity for a member of a group to name others, to use his or her own name, and then to make roles and communicate intentions to others.

In an existing society, role-making takes different forms from that which occurred at the dawn of human history. Each person is born into a world in which roles are labeled, and learns, often painstakingly, over many years the rights, obligations, duties, and perquisites associated with each role. Indeed, social roles sometimes seem so clearly laid out that *role-playing* seems a better designation than role-making. The constraints that exist upon the roles of parents, children, teachers, physicians, clergy, janitors, bookkeepers, and many others seem so great that it often appears that people merely enact scripts that have already been written for them by tradition.

But even the most demanding and restrictive roles do not provide people with lines to read. Role-making is a process that depends heavily upon the fact that people perceive the social world in terms of roles and their requirements. But it is also a process that demands effort and creativity by people as they interact with one another. Therefore, to understand behavior we must look at the process of role-making, at the way in which people see themselves and others as they go about their everyday affairs.

The concept of *role-taking* is crucial to this process. This concept refers to the process whereby an individual adopts the perspective of another in order to be able to coordinate his or her own conduct. Whether we imagine a very routine and structured context, like that of a nuclear family in the United States, or a more novel and unpredictable occasion, such as a flood disaster, role-making goes hand in hand with role-taking.

Imagine parents and their children sitting at the breakfast table. It is a school day, and the children have finally dressed themselves and are eating hastily before the school bus arrives. Father notices that daughter's clothes look even grubbier than usual, but after a moment's reflection decides against saying anything, anticipating an argument. Mother, however, asks in an irritated tone of voice, "Why aren't you wearing the new shirt I just bought for you?" And the daughter, running out the door, replies that she wanted to, but decided that mother would say it was too good for wearing to school.

In this example, we have people engaged in taking one another's roles in order to make their own. In deciding whether to question his daughter's mode of dress, the father anticipates her likely response and decides the impending argument is not worth it. And in her earlier decision about what to wear, the daughter anticipated her mother's response and decided not to wear the new shirt. Father and daughter in this example have engaged in role-taking—seeing the other's likely response to his or her own possible act—in order to make their roles.

In this example role-making has taken place within the boundaries of fairly well-established social roles. Parents and their children are knowledgeable about the rights and duties attached to each. Parents know they can have control over their children's appearance, and children know they must answer parental questions. Yet these very basic parts of the structure of a family—its roles—do not provide a script that participants have to read. Instead, the roles provide a general framework within which people still must actively construct their conduct by taking the others' responses into account.

All social interaction among humans involves role-making and role-taking. In order for individuals to interpret the meaning of another's act, they must imaginatively place themselves in the other's role and examine the situation from the other's point of view. Based upon the interpretation of the other's intention, they are able to construct their own conduct in an appropriate way. Much of the time, people make and take roles within the context of established and familiar social groupings, like families and schools, where they have considerable knowledge of others' roles as well as of their own. They make use of what they know about the roles of teacher, for example, in making their own roles as students. In other circumstances where people encounter novel situations, they must act more imaginatively in order to create new roles for themselves and to interpret the roles of others. In either case, however, the creation of meaning in social interaction depends upon our ability to grasp a situation in terms of its role structure.

HUMAN CONDUCT AND THE SELF

It should be obvious by now that symbolic interactionists see human conduct in terms that differ markedly from the perspectives of some other social and behavioral scientists. Unlike many psychologists who are steeped in the behaviorist tradition, symbolic interactionists do not see conduct as simply determined by patterns of environmental stimuli and reinforcements. Instead, people are seen as acting consciously and willfully; they do not just respond to stimuli, but actively participate in making their environment. Ideas, goals, feelings, and other subjective states of the individual are, from the interactionist's perspective, not merely illusory experiences that bear only a superficial relationship to the forces that control conduct. Rather, they *are*, in large part, the forces that control conduct. And unlike some sociologists who see the behavior of individuals as essentially determined by the roles they are forced by society to play, interactionists see individuals as constructing their activity with some degree of freedom. The person is strongly influenced by the world of cultural objects and by the actions of other people. Still, the social control of individual conduct is not complete, for there is always a potential for innovation, for the creation of new objects and new meanings.

The Self

Perhaps the most crucial aspect of the interactionist approach to human conduct, and thus also to "human nature," is the attention and emphasis given to the self. More than any other concept, this one is identified with the interactionist perspective and helps to define its orientation.

The *self*—that is, an individual's ability to see himself or herself as an object—emerges in much the same fashion as other objects. Specifically, when we humans engage in role-taking and role-making and construct our own activities in coordination with others, we must be able to regard our own activities from the perspective of others. When we engage in role-taking, we see ourselves as we think others see us. It is, in fact, this capacity to see ourselves from the vantage point of another that makes it possible for us to form our own conduct.

But another aspect of this process can also be stressed. Seeing oneself imaginatively from the standpoint of another is a way of acting toward oneself as an object. To take the role of another toward oneself (for example, to see oneself as a patient imaginatively through the eyes of a physician or as a prospective date by a member of the opposite sex) is to consider oneself as a particular kind of object and to give that object meaning. In short, to take the role of another is to create a self.

The kind of object a person is—that is, the self that each of us is—depends upon the kind of social experiences we have. Over a lifetime, we are many different objects to many different people: a child, a student, a boy or girl, tall or short, able or incompetent, a member of various religious and social

Pablo Picasso, *Girl before a Mirror* (1932)
Oil on canvas, 64 × 51¼ inches. Collection, The Museum of Modern Art, New York. Gift of Mrs. Simon Guggenheim.

Humans are distinctive creatures because they can be objects to themselves. Society—its situations, roles, groups, and organizations—is the "mirror" that makes the self possible. We imaginatively take the perspectives of others and see ourselves as we think they see us.

class groupings, trained in a particular occupation, married or single, a parent or not. In these and many other ways, we are cast into roles that establish us as a particular kind of object, depending upon the role we are called upon to make at any given moment. What we are as persons is thoroughly and pervasively shaped by the social roles in which we engage, the social categories to which we belong, and our success or failure in constructing our acts and coordinating them with those of others.

To be sure, there are temperamental differences between individuals that should not be ignored. Humans differ from one another in strength, intelligence, quickness to respond to environmental stimuli, physiology, and so on. What people are is thus clearly influenced by inherited chracteristics over which neither they nor society have much control. Nonetheless, despite temperamental differences, individuals are very much a product of social experiences. They can know themselves only by adopting a perspective other than their own. People do not experience themselves directly or intuitively, but indirectly and from the standpoint of others.

This is so even when the person develops some degree of autonomy and independence. Children are very much tied to the judgments of others; they see themselves through the imagined eyes of their parents and peers. Later they become more attuned to generalized norms and moral standards and less concerned with the specific judgments of individuals in particular situations. Then they can apply expectations to themselves and do not need to imagine the responses of specific others. Even so, people remain fully social creatures, for the moral standards they adopt are those they have learned from others and continue to share with them.

Thus, not only the nature but also the very existence of the self depend upon social experience. At the same time, the existence of human society is dependent upon the existence of the self. The complex forms of social coordination that characterize human societies could not exist if people were not capable of acting toward themselves as objects. For without the capacity to imagine the possible results of their own conduct, human animals would not have the control that they do over their own acts. And, without the mental maps of the society and its component roles and groups that individuals carry, even simple forms of social coordination would be impossible.

CONCLUSION

The self is both dependent upon society and is the basis upon which society can exist. Society is the result of coordinated human activities. However, those activities could not continue if society did not imbue the individual with a consciousness of self, and this is possible only because humans have the capacity to respond to symbols. It is this set of relationships between the individual and the society that best characterize the symbolic interactionist view of the nature of human nature. Humans are socially dependent creatures, and yet the society that nourishes them and provides the capacity for them to be individuals depends for its existence and continuity upon their actions.

SUGGESTED READINGS

BECKER, ERNEST. *The Birth and Death of Meaning*, 2nd ed. (New York: Free Press, 1971).

FARB, PETER. *Word Play* (New York: Alfred Knopf, 1973).

HEWITT, JOHN P. *Self and Society: A Symbolic Interactionist Social Psychology*, 3rd ed. (Boston: Allyn and Bacon, 1984).

LINDESMITH, ALFRED, ANSELM L. STRAUSS, and NORMAN K. DENZIN. *Social Psychology*, 5th ed. (New York: Holt, Rinehart, Winston, 1977).

MEAD, GEORGE HERBERT. *Mind, Self, and Society* (Chicago: University of Chicago Press, 1934).

STONE, GREGORY P. and HARVEY A. FARBERMAN, eds. *Social Psychology Through Symbolic Interaction*, 2nd ed. (New York: Wiley, 1981).

5

Coordination in Social Life

Society is formed by the day-to-day symbolic interaction of human beings. This interaction is not random, but is patterned and coordinated. Out of the countless small situations and interactions of everyday life emerge coordinated lines of conduct that involve large numbers of people and span many years. This chapter will explore the variety of ways in which such everyday social interaction produces society.

BASIC FORMS OF COORDINATION

Society is an encompassing social unit containing regularized statuses and roles, groups and organizations. But it exists because people interact with one another in a great variety of very mundane situations—at the dinner table, on the job, at play, in the voting booth, in arguments and debates, and in many other places. There are several basic ways that people coordinate their activities in these situations and thus produce and reproduce society. First, people engage in routine role-making and role-taking, thus accomplishing coordination at the microscopic level of face-to-face interaction. Second, they transform the standardized roles of society into more personalized performances and relationships, creating interpersonal roles and relationships that make their own contributions to social order. Third, people coordinate their actions temporally; they share conceptions of time and expectations about sequences of activities. And fourth, people negotiate with one another in order to achieve their objectives and maintain orderly activities in their groups and organizations.

Role-making and Role-taking

We can begin to examine social coordination by looking at the simplest case, a single episode of interaction involving two people. A child "raids" the cookie jar and eats cookies that were to have been left for someone else. The "theft" is discovered by a parent, who confronts the child with the empty cookie jar, expresses anger or disappointment at the child's conduct, and administers punishment. The child is banished to his room, the parent attends to some other matter, and the episode ends.

This isolated and trivial episode illustrates the basic processes of role-making and role-taking that lie at the heart of every episode of social interaction. In order to define the child's act as something deserving of punishment, the mother must imaginatively occupy the perspective of the child. "You knew the last few cookies were being saved for your father," she might say, "and yet you deliberately ate them anyway!" In saying this, the child's mother has, in her imagination, examined the situation from the child's perspective and concluded that the child knew the cookies were not to be eaten. By the same token, the child's understanding of the mother's displeasure depends upon role-taking. He can grasp her attitude toward him only by looking at the situation from her vantage point, remembering how she planned to surprise his father with the cookies.

The mutual role-taking of mother and child in this situation is crucial to their success in making appropriate roles. The mother, for example, may realize that the child will seek to escape blame by claiming that he did not know the cookies were not to be eaten. Thus, she may take pains to emphasize that he did know: "I told you this morning not to eat any more cookies because I was saving them," she might say. For his part, the child may perceive that a possible way of escaping blame would be to claim that he did not eat the cookies. He may, however, decide not to do this because he knows that his mother knows no one else could have eaten them. To lie, he knows, would be to add a new infraction. Thus, he concludes, the safest course is to accept punishment quietly.

In their role-making, parent and child coordinate their conduct. Each anticipates the responses of the other to his or her own acts and adjusts those acts accordingly. Culture is an important element in this process.

Both parent and child in this situation invoke culture as a guide to their conduct. The parent, confronted with behavior that is displeasing or upsetting, will define the child's act in culturally typical terms. "Stealing" might be perceived as too harsh a term to apply to a child who has been caught with his hand in the cookie jar. But the child's mother might say that the child was "selfish" or "inconsiderate." These terms, which are culturally standard, provide the means by which both parent and child assign meaning to the child's act and to the situation as a whole.

Moreover, culture provides both parent and child with a more encompassing definition of the situation and with some standard behavioral paths within it. Each knows that a rule has been broken and that punishment is to be administered and accepted. Each has some notion of what a typical scene of "parent disciplining child" is supposed to look like, and to a considerable extent each attempts to act so as to create the appropriate scene.

This does not mean, however, that parent and child merely read the lines of a script already written. Culture does not provide them with detailed instructions for conduct. Instead, it provides images of the kinds of interaction that may occur. It tells people what objects—punishment, anger, remorse—may be found in a given situation. It instructs them about the emotions they might feel. But it is up to the participants themselves to create a scene that resembles the culturally typical scene, to act toward the appropriate objects, and to feel the right emotions.

Moreover, alternatives are usually available as people interact and create meaningful situations. Culture does not dictate the definition of a situation. Instead, people use culture to *create* meaning in situations. As a result, a given situation may be interpreted in more than one way by participants. In the preceding example, the parent could choose to be angry, disappointed, or tolerant.

Edward Hopper, *First Row Orchestra* (1951)
Oil on canvas. 31⅛ × 40⅛ inches. Hirshhorn Museum and Sculpture Garden, Smithsonian Institution.
People make and take roles as they interact, but the metaphor of the theater has its limits. In real life, the script is not fully written in advance, the actors direct their own performances, and the players of one moment are the audience of the next.

Whichever definition of the situation the parent chose would be culturally appropriate. People must find meaning in situations, but they also have considerable freedom in using the culture to create this meaning.

In an insightful analysis of how people define situations, Peter McHugh (1968) was able to show that people will go to great lengths to create and preserve meaning, even in situations that are, in fact, meaningless. McHugh presented individuals with a contrived experimental situation in which they were led to believe they were taking part in a study of a new approach to counseling. Each participant was asked to talk about a personal problem of importance to him or her, and then ask a counselor a series of questions to elicit advice about how to handle the problem. These questions would be given only "yes" or "no" answers, and after each answer by the counselor, the participant was to record on tape his or her interpretation of the meaning of the answer.

The catch in this procedure was that the answers were independent of the questions; they were given on a random basis. In many instances, therefore, participants would receive a very confusing and contradictory series of answers to their questions. The individual might be told "yes" in response to a question about whether someone in whom he has a romantic interest would make a suitable mate, only to be told "no" a short time later when he asks whether he should continue dating her. After a series of equally or even more contradictory replies, many participants expressed great frustration and anger. Nevertheless, they struggled mightily to find a pattern of meaning in the answers they received. And even though the answers were themselves meaningless, people frequently thought they could detect patterns of meaning. The person advised against continuing to date a desirable mate might conclude that the "counselor" was advising him to "test" his love for her.

By showing how people can construct meaning in an intrinsically meaningless situation, McHugh was able to provide some insights into the creation and maintenance of meaning in everyday life. We interact with others on the assumption that there is purpose to what they are doing, and it is usually hard for us to believe otherwise. We assume that social interaction will be orderly, and that even confusing developments will eventually make sense.

Role-making and role-taking in everyday life thus take into account both the culturally typical and the unique features of situations. As they interact, people strive to coordinate their conduct with one another. They also strive to align that conduct with culture, to do what makes sense in light of the actions of others, as well as to do what is culturally appropriate. People act as if the behavior of others is meaningful, and they use culture to establish its meaning. This is the very essence of socially coordinated conduct; it is the foundation of society.

Role-making and role-taking do not occur in a vacuum. In each situation participants have a sense of overall structure; they have a sense of who is responsible for which kinds of activity. This sense is implicit in each definition of a situation. The child being disciplined by a parent knows that it is a situation in which punishment is likely to be administered and that the participants in this situation will act from the perspectives of their roles as parents and children.

But roles do not shape behavior rigidly or automatically. People do not merely "play" or "enact" their roles; they act from the perspectives afforded by their own roles and those of others (Turner, 1962). They fashion performances that seem to fit the roles in which they are engaged and which, they believe, others will also agree fit those roles. Thus, the child being disciplined by a parent seeks to behave in a way it believes fits its role as a child, and the child hopes that the parents will find the performance acceptable.

Because we learn and share standard cultural definitions of roles, it is not surprising that our role performances tend more or less to meet cultural standards. The members of American society share (albeit with many subcultural variations) basic ideas about the roles of teenaged children in relation to their parents. Adolescents are expected to continue to be obedient to parental wishes, but it is also assumed they will sometimes be rebellious. Since parents and their adolescent children share these expectations, each uses the shared knowledge as a basis for role-making and role-taking. The teenager knows that parents expect that their wishes will be obeyed, and the parents are apt to tolerate a certain amount of willful disobedience because they believe this is how adolescents act.

Thus people do not give standard role performances merely because they try to meet expectations—to act in ways that live up to their conception of what a role calls for. Roles are not just models for our behavior, but are even more important as devices for *interpreting* behavior. Fathers do what they think fathers are expected to do, and thus model their conduct after a role. But people are apt to interpret the behavior of someone engaged in the role of a father as "fatherly" behavior unless there are compelling reasons not to. In other words, people are apt to define as appropriate role behavior almost anything that someone in that role does, unless that behavior departs so far from their expectations that they cannot make sense of it.

The limits of appropriate role behavior are frequently quite broad. In a controversial series of studies on obedience, social psychologist Stanley Milgram (1974) was able to persuade experimental subjects to administer what they thought were dangerous electrical shocks to other experimental subjects. Milgram constructed a situation in which subjects were led to believe they were participating in a study designed to measure the effects of punishment on learning. The shocks were not real, of course, and the individuals who purportedly were shocked were, in fact, confederates of the experimenter.

One possible explanation of Milgram's success in getting people to inflict pain and suffering on others is that they regarded Milgram as acting legitimately within the role of a scientist; that is, they interpreted his behavior as falling within the scope of his role. As the "shock" levels grew more intense and the reactions of the "victims" more vocal, the psychological discomfort of those administering the shocks increased, but many of them continued to cooperate with Milgram, even when they reached the point where "lethal" shocks were being given. Clearly a role—and the situation that contains it—exerts a powerful influence on the interpretation of other's conduct and the formation of one's own.

Many of the expectations people have of one another as they engage in their roles are normative. Parents feel their children *should* obey them, and their children may feel that they should not engage in behavior of which their parents disapprove. Yet role-making and role-taking encompass much more than a belief in norms. Much role-making involves *cognitive* activity in which normative expectations are not important. The adolescent, for example, knows that his parents disapprove of his drinking or using drugs. He may or may not share their disapproval of such activities, but he *knows* of it. Similarly, if you are shopping in a department store and someone approaches you to ask about a particular item of merchandise, you base your response on cognitive role-taking. You put yourself in this person's position and realize that he has mistaken you for a salesperson. It is then a simple matter for you to make your role by pointing out his error and directing him to someone who is a clerk.

Conventional and Interpersonal Roles

The roles we have used to illustrate various points in this discussion are examples of *conventional* roles. Mother, father, professor, student, child, salesperson, and similar roles are highly standardized. There is generally a high degree of agreement on the expectations associated with the role of a professor, for example. Those who have had some kind of contact with a college or university will have a fairly good notion of what professors do with their time and of what constitutes appropriate and inappropriate behavior. Although their knowledge of this role might have been formed through contact with only a few professors, the knowledge would be general enough so that it could be used as a basis for interaction with other professors.

Conventional roles guide much of our everyday interaction, particularly in a complex society. The salespersons, police officers, government officials, and business executives we encounter are frequently strangers to us. The coordination of activity in a large and complex society requires that people be able to interact with strangers, that they share enough knowledge of one another's roles to permit mutual role-taking. Thus, it does not matter if I am stopped for speeding in Wyoming or in Massachusetts, for the police officer and I share enough mutual understandings to be able to interact, even though we have not previously met one another.

People engaged in conventional roles are in some ways like interchangeable parts in a machine. To a store clerk, one customer is treated pretty much like any other. And to the customer, store clerks may often seem like faceless creatures who mouth a familiar set of lines—"May I help you?"—and run their cash registers in an impersonal manner. The interaction between the two seems highly standardized.

But to limit our discussion to such conventional roles would be a serious mistake, for much everyday interaction occurs between people who know each other fairly well. Store clerks and customers may be interchangeable, but husbands and wives, parents and children, and good friends are not. Husbands and wives do not face one another across the breakfast table as faceless roles, but as individuals who have interacted repeatedly over time. Accordingly, their interaction is shaped not just by the culturally standard roles of husband and wife, but also by the existence of an *interpersonal relationship.*

We might define an *interpersonal relationship* as a more or less durable bond between two individuals. Such a relationship may be formed on the basis of a conventional role pair, such as husband and wife, but it is sustained by the development of an *interpersonal role* (Shibutani, 1961). The latter is a role which is less culturally standardized than a conventional role, and which is defined by the unique characteristics of the individual who makes it.

"Friend" is a good example of an interpersonal role. People do have general expectations about the relationship that should exist between friends. They have culturally standard ideas about what friends owe to one another and the ways they should interact. But each friendship is also unique. It is shaped by the characteristics of the two friends and their history of interaction with one another. Thus, some of the mutual expectations of friends may be quite specific; one might be a regular tennis companion, while another is someone with whom you share very private feelings and experiences.

Interpersonal roles work very much like conventional roles in their coordination of interaction. When friends interact, it is the fact of friendship that establishes their mutual definition of the situation and sense of its role structure. They are aware of one another as friends and use this knowledge to anticipate one another's responses. Thus, friends may say things to one another that seem quite insulting but which they recognize as jokes. They can do this because they have a history of joking and kidding with one another. Their repeated interactions have established a mutual set of role expectations that permits them to make accurate interpretations of one another's acts.

Interpersonal roles are often associated with conventional roles. "Husband and wife" form a conventional role pair, and some of their mutual role-taking is conducted in relation to such roles. But if they have been married for some time, they are also an interpersonal role pair. Thus, the interpretations they make of one another's actions may depend upon their intimate and detailed knowledge of one another, more than upon their knowledge of the standard roles of husband and wife. Similarly, colleagues in a university or employees in a factory interact not only in terms of their conventional roles as professors or machine operators, but also as friends, enemies, rivals, and other interpersonal roles.

Interpersonal roles are as important to the coordination of behavior in society as are conventional roles. Although contemporary societies structure a great deal of interaction along the relatively impersonal lines of conventional roles, interpersonal roles remain important. They develop within families, peer and friendship groups of all ages, and on the job. They crop up wherever people interact repeatedly with one another.

Time

Everyday life consists of a multitude of situations in which people make and take roles—parents disciplining children, workers reporting for work, mechanics fixing machines, women giving birth, and countless others. But these scenes are not staged or distributed at random. They occur in more or less orderly sequences over time. An individual born into a conventional American middle-class family will pass through several life stages—infancy, childhood, and adolescence. He or she will be expected to progress through school year by year, and possibly to attend college. After graduation the individual will be expected to get a job, marry, have children, raise them, retire, and die. The countless scenes of a person's life are ordered by culture and its temporal expectations. Different cultures may order people's lives in different sequences, but all individuals are confronted with some set of cultural expectations relating to major life-cycle events or stages.

Time is a basic component of even the simplest social situation. A handshake is a sequence of individual acts that combine in a certain way to produce a social act. If one person delays too long in responding to the outstretched hand of another, the social act will fail to achieve its object. This may be viewed as evidence of social awkwardness or as an intentional slight, but whatever the interpretation, meaning has been constructed on the basis of *timing*. Similarly, if one grasps the hand of another for longer than usual, this may be interpreted as indicative of special warmth or affection. In handshakes and much of the rest of social life, timing is everything.

Moreover, situations are typically linked with one another across time. The members of a committee typically expect a series of meetings in which the business of the committee will be discussed. Each time the "Committee to Abolish Committees" meets, its agenda is shaped by past meetings and by its members' anticipation of the future. "Last week we decided that our Committee to Abolish Committees needed some subcommittees," they might say, "and so perhaps we should begin today with subcommittee reports." The past is prelude to the future, not only for us as individuals as we go about our affairs, but for the various social groupings to which we belong.

This leads to a basic insight. Individual and social acts are not discrete and separate from one another, but they are joined in linkages, often very complex linkages, over time. In a sense, any individual's life can be seen not as a simple series of acts, but rather as a set of "nested" acts—brief acts nestled within more extended ones. Some acts are completed in short order, while others take days or years to complete and may be interrupted many times by other acts.

Thus, for example, some acts are brief—one feels hungry, obtains some food, and eats it. But many acts are of longer duration. If a woman makes a date to have dinner with a man "next Wednesday," an act has begun that is not fully consummated until they actually have dinner together. In the interim, however, each will engage in many other acts. Most activities, for example, having out-of-town guests, are composed of smaller, temporally related acts; greeting the visitors to your home, entertaining them for dinner, showing them your neighborhood or city, and seeing them off to the airport are examples of social acts linked in sequence. And many of our individual and social projects are of even longer duration. Writing a book, seeking a promotion on the job, or passing a course in college involve us in sequences of acts that may last months or years. The common frame of reference for all such acts is *time*: a set of ideas about how individual and social acts are arranged in temporal sequence.

Time is an important factor in people's organization of their actions and conduct. "One's life" or "in the next year or two" or "ten years from now" are expressions that point to the importance of time for the person's organization of his or her acts. Few people think of themselves as having, much less writing, biographies. But they do frequently review past accomplishments and make plans for the future. In so doing—in thinking of what they would like to be doing in five or ten years—people order their futures.

Plans for the future help to lay out in advance a schedule of the situations to be encountered, those to be avoided, and what is to be accomplished in each. Thus, for example, a management trainee in a large corporation may contemplate his or her career, thinking ahead to what moves must be made, how to be alert to opportunity, how to impress those in command, and what to do if plans do not work out. Clearly not everyone plans in the same detail or for equal lengths of time. The military officer knows that promotions must come at a certain rate, and that to be passed over too often for promotion means certain retirement. The college professor knows that it is either moving "up" (given tenure and promoted) after the first six years in an institution, or "out." But the businessperson may have more flexible career plans, for there are a variety of avenues to success or failure. And some occupations provide a limited set of opportunities for career advancement. Most unskilled workers realize that their jobs offer few chances for promotion and that they will be doing the same work for many years.

Just as time organizes the acts of individuals, time is also essential in organizing relationships among individuals. Parents visualize the future with their children in mind, planning for their children's education, for example, or dreaming of (or dreading) the day when their children leave home. Teachers assume that their classrooms will be filled with students year after year, even though they do not know who these students will be. Indeed, each of us acts in the present and contemplates acting in the future on the assumption that others will be there and that they will act in predictable ways. Television executives, seeing that programs replete with sex and violence earn good ratings, plan more such shows for the future, assuming that people will continue to watch. Educators, seeing a shortage of engineers, decide to train more of them. A young couple buys a house with four bedrooms, anticipating as yet unborn children.

Quite obviously, people's best-laid plans do not always come to fruition—tastes in television change, educational institutions overproduce certain kinds of talent, and some couples remain childless. Yet, on the whole, such predictions are fulfilled more often than not. People do more or less what others predict they will do. A very considerable part of the social order rests upon such predictions and the temporal coordination of human activity they make possible.

Negotiation

There is one further way in which men and women coordinate their conduct and sustain their diverse groups and organizations. This form of coordination can be termed *negotiation*. Although it is implicit in each of the forms of coordination so far discussed, it merits independent attention.

Each of you has a common-sense familiarity with the concept of negotiation and can think of a variety of situations in which people negotiate with one another: talks between labor unions and management, diplomatic negotiations between countries, or conferences between lawyers representing parties in a lawsuit. In each of these instances of negotiation, people strive to come to an agreement of some kind. Union officials and management, for example, agree on what workers will be paid, how many hours they will work, under what conditions they can be hired or fired, and when the next negotiations will take place. Countries negotiate the terms of trade between them, what import taxes will be imposed, and whether each may locate trade representatives in the other's country. And lawyers agree to drop lawsuits if the other party will voluntarily pay damages for some alleged wrong.

These examples of negotiation differ in the matters at issue, but they have certain things in common (see Strauss, 1978). First, there is a specific time or place where other activities are suspended and the negotiations take place: labor and management closet themselves in a hotel or other suitable place; lawyers use their offices; and nations have diplomatic conferences where each detail of protocol is important to the success of the activity. Negotiation is itself a definition of a situation in which people interact in familiar ways in order to achieve certain objectives.

Second, negotiations lead to more or less explicit agreements between parties about their rights and duties in their relationships to one another. Not every detail need be worked out in advance, of course. Contract talks between labor and management often leave certain details for local decision or later negotiation. And a key feature of diplomatic negotiations is the use of diplomatic language, in which phrases are agreed upon that mean basically different things to each side, but which permit an agreement on other matters to be achieved. Often negotiators agree to ignore issues on which they are far apart so that they can achieve agreement on other matters.

Finally, negotiations usually result in agreements that hold for a certain period of time. Trade agreements and labor contracts do not run forever but for a specified number of years. Treaties often have provisions for review or renegotiation after a period of time. Agreements specify not only the obligations parties have to one another, but also when those obligations cease to be binding.

The very features that characterize formal negotiations are also found in many situations in everyday life, although people do not usually think of themselves as negotiating. In families, work places, associations, and countless other places and situations, people coordinate their conduct at least partly on the basis of agreements they have negotiated. These agreements have been explicitly arrived at, they spell out reciprocal rights and obligations, and they run for limited periods of time.

Within a family, for example, much of the division of effort between husbands and wives is achieved by negotiation. The conventional roles of men and women in any society provide definitions of women's work and men's work within the family. But these roles provide only the framework within which individual husbands and wives must establish their own arrangements. Similarly, although individuals learn that there are certain duties attached to their familial roles as husbands, wives, and parents, these are only made concrete in the actual course of living in a family. Who does the dishes and takes out the garbage, who gets up first in the morning, who is responsible for seeing that the children get to where they need to be, who cooks what kinds of meals, who initiates love-making, and who decides where the family will travel are matters settled not by the dictates of roles but often by negotiations between the parties concerned. "I'll get dinner tonight if you'll do the dishes." "How about if you take the kids to piano lessons, and I'll pick up your suit at the cleaners." These are examples of negotiations leading to very specific agreements which run for a particular period of time and which spell out mutual responsibilities.

In organizations, the processes of negotiation are more complex and more frequent, but the process is very much the same. The life of a bureaucracy —a university, for example, or a governmental agency—seems closely governed by rules and formal procedures, but there is a great deal left unspecified. First, there are always ambiguities in the rules, as well as cases where one rule conflicts with another. When such instances arise, some kind of settlement has to be reached. In universities, for example, such occasions for negotiation are numerous. Does a particular course meet a program requirement? Should a course taken at another university be given full credit? If Computer Programming counts as a substitute for a foreign language, what about Statistics for Social Scientists? Typically, when such questions arise people negotiate with each other and come to some particular agreement. "We'll count Statistics as a substitute for a foreign language," a faculty committee might say, "if you agree to take the course within the math department."

Just as there are ambiguities and inconsistencies in the rules, so there are also likely to be uncertainties about who is responsible for doing what, as well as conflicts among the members of an organization regarding what each would prefer to do or to avoid. Faculty members are apt to see themselves as the center of the university, for in their view it is their ongoing scholarly work that justifies the existence of the university and constitutes its central mission. Students are apt to place themselves at the center, defining the goal of the university as the transmission of knowledge and the task of professors as arousing interest in their subjects and conveying them accurately.

At any given time, a university consists of a set of negotiated agreements. Sometimes the agreements exist within a particular course, as when a professor agrees to spend more time on a particular topic, provided the students agree to come to extra class sessions. At other times, agreements are more formalized, as when students, faculty, and administration negotiate over whether the university will permit military recruiters to use campus facilities or continue to invest its endowment funds in firms doing business with particular countries. In either case, the organization we call the university exists over time because its members mutually agree to behave in certain ways. While much of this agreement rests upon the tacit acceptance of more or less clear cultural rules and expectations, some of it is explicitly created in various contexts of negotiation.

The amount of negotiation found in social life varies considerably from one organization or group to another. In their study of the school systems of two midwestern communities, Peter Hall and Dee Ann Spencer-Hall (1982) were able to identify a number of factors that affect how much negotiation actually takes place. They found, for example, that teachers perceived themselves to be powerless in relation to school administrators, and so made little effort to assert themselves by negotiating with their superiors about the school's goals or methods of attaining them. They simply accepted and carried out orders. Moreover, teachers were isolated in their classrooms, with only occasional and brief opportunities for contact with their colleagues, and students were usually bored. As a result, they simply wanted to "get through the day," and had little motivation to try to improve things. For these and other reasons, there was little incentive or opportunity to negotiate about anything. In general, the Halls concluded, there is apt to be more negotiation where activities require teamwork, organizations are larger and more complex, power is more equally distributed, leaders delegate authority, and an organization is undergoing change.

SOCIAL COORDINATION: POWER, EXCHANGE, AND CONFLICT

Up to this point, our discussion of social coordination has emphasized people's efforts to meet one another's expectations and to live up to cultural standards. Role-making and role-taking have been portrayed essentially as cooperative efforts in which people strive to coordinate their activities. But, of course, human conduct is not entirely benign or cooperative. People frequently—some would say usually—pursue their own interests regardless of the wishes of others, using coercion where they cannot secure cooperation. And social life often seems to be characterized not by harmonious and fruitful negotiations, but by serious conflict and disagreement. Thus, the discussion of social coordination must now turn to matters of self-interest, power, and conflict.

Linton Park, *Flax Scutching Bee* (1885)
Bed ticking, 31¼ × 50¼ inches. The National Gallery of Art, Washington. Gift of Edgar William and Bernice Chrysler Garbisch.

This painting shows people coordinating the productive work of individual families in a communal work party. A sense of reciprocal obligations doubtless underlies their cooperative efforts, but there may also be social conflict that is not reflected in the artist's somewhat idealized depiction.

Self-interest and Social Conflict

One way to approach these matters would be to propose that conflict is intrinsic to human nature. If conflict is to be found everywhere in human society, perhaps it is because humans are innately conflict prone and invariably turn to coercion when reason fails. Perhaps human beings are inherently driven by self-interest and strive to maximize individual advantage by whatever means possible.

"Human nature" is a notoriously poor explanation of behavior. Although conflict between people may appear to be an inescapable human fact—and it sometimes seems that there are no human relationships entirely devoid of conflict—such is not the case. Conflict is emphasized in some cultures and downplayed in others, and while some relationships seem to be founded on conflict, others avoid it whenever possible. For example, the relationship between opposing attorneys in a court of law is one of culturally prescribed conflict. Their conflicts within the courtroom are closely regulated by law and custom, and it is quite possible for lawyers who are enemies in the courtroom to be friends on the golf course. In their relationship, conflict is not an expression of natural tendencies, but is socially and culturally prescribed. The relationship between spouses in American society illustrates a context where conflict is culturally regulated. Husbands and wives expect to have some disagreements, but if they find their relationship contains considerable conflict, they are likely to feel that it is time to end the relationship and obtain a divorce.

Conflict, which is a variable phenomenon subject to social regulation, cannot be explained easily in terms of constants in human nature. Yet it is an important social process. To account for its existence and variety, we must look more closely at the way humans form their conduct and at the conditions under which they live.

Humans share with all animals the need to satisfy their basic needs and wishes—relief from hunger and thirst, protection from the elements and from predatory animals, sexual gratification, and the like. Other things being equal, people, like all animals, will eat in preference to starving, try to avoid freezing to death, and choose sexual activity over celibacy. We might say that the "natural" inclination of each individual living thing is to meet its needs as best it can and to overcome obstacles in its path as best it can.

Although needs are individual, they are met by humans through cooperative social activity. Indeed, society is the essence of human nature, for everything we do involves the real or imagined presence of others. If there is any single rationale for human sociability, it lies in the sharing of common tasks in order to meet the needs of individuals.

These two basic facts of human life—the individual nature of needs and the social nature of the response to them—create a considerable amount of strain. The actions individuals might take to satisfy their own needs or wishes are not necessarily actions that will contribute to the welfare of the community as a whole. This fact creates a recurrent dilemma in human life, and it is essentially the same dilemma for a hunter-gatherer as for a suburban gardener; should he or she carry back and share with others a choice piece of game or the plumpest strawberry, or devour it on the spot?

If humans are sometimes forced to choose between the pursuit of naked self-interest and the good of others, it is because they have the *capacity for choice*; that is, the gardener can anticipate the juicy taste of a strawberry on her own tongue, but she can also anticipate the enjoyment of someone else to whom she might offer it. Because humans can imagine alternative lines of conduct as well as the responses of others to their acts, they are confronted with the need to choose between what they want and what others may want or need. This is presumably not the case for most other animals, whose lines of conduct are less subject to their control and more at the whim of the environment and their own genetic constitution. Thus, the robin who returns to the nest to feed its young presumably does not choose to do so. Instead, its conduct is governed by innate responses.

For human beings, cooperation with others is not an automatic act governed by heredity. Nor is conflict an inevitable aspect of social life. Instead, cooperation and conflict involve choices. People can conceive of the idea of sharing as well as not sharing, of pursuing self-interest as well as serving the common good.

Looking at cooperation and self-interest in this way leads to a host of questions: What influences the degree to which human beings will cooperate with others in preference to looking out only for themselves? How do humans exert their will over others? If humans are capable of calculating individual advantage when they interact with others, how can there be any cooperative social behavior at all?

The balance between cooperation and conflict in a society is a result of many factors, one of which is culture itself. Within each society, characteristic solutions to human problems evolve and become embodied in culture. Thus, societies find differing ways of handling conflict. Some permit the unrestricted expression of physical violence, while others tend to attempt to transform physical aggression into verbal forms. In some societies, such as our own, cultural values encourage individuals to pursue their own interests where they can, to be constantly looking out for "number one." Other cultures encourage a very different attitude.

Among the Pueblo Indians of New Mexico and Arizona, for example, cooperation is an important value. Individuals are encouraged to think of the community before they think of themselves, and they are discouraged from seeking the limelight, even when they achieve some distinction (Benedict, 1934). Because of this, it is not unusual for famous Indian pottery makers to sign their own names to the work of others. They do this not in order to hoodwink potential buyers into paying more than an item is worth, but so they can share their good fortune with their neighbors.

Power and Inequality

Inequality is another major factor that influences the prevalence and form of conflict. Inequality is a feature of every known human society, although the degree of inequality varies widely. Within any society, people differ in their capacity to get what they want. Some people have more strength, more land, more money, more of whatever people in a given society value. Although some of this inequality results from individual differences in effort and talent, for the most part it is socially created. Occupations are unequally paid; people inherit land and other forms of wealth; and cultural beliefs define men and women as unequal in talent or social worth. Whatever the sources of inequality (a matter to be discussed more fully in Chapter 10), we cannot understand conflict and self-interest without considering them.

Power is closely related to inequality. *Power* can be defined as the capacity to follow a line of conduct without interference from others and to induce others to do what one wishes them to do. This definition follows that of Max Weber, who defined power as "the chance of a man or of a number of men to realize their own will in a communal action even against the resistance of others who are participating in the action" (Gerth and Mills, 1958:180). Individuals or groups have power to the extent that they can act without regard for the responses of others. Power is always a matter of degree, since people rarely have complete freedom of action or the capacity to enforce their will totally.

Power can be distinguished from *authority*, which is defined (again following the lead of Max Weber) as *legitimate* power. Sociologists speak of authority when individuals exercise power because they hold an office of some kind—such as mayor or church bishop—and when those over whom it is exercised accept it and view it as legitimate. As we pointed out in Chapter 3, authority may rest upon tradition, upon a rational set of laws or rules, or upon the personal appeal of the leader.

Power rests upon the unequal distribution of many different resources. In its most primitive form, power is derived from sheer physical strength or the capacity to inflict bodily harm. If one man is stronger than another or holds a gun while the other does not, the first has considerable power. He may take the other's money and jewels, force him or her to do slave labor, or otherwise secure desired ends without interference. Although the threat of physical force may seem to insure absolute power—ultimately those who are stronger, faster, or better armed have the power of life and death over others—power is in reality always limited. Coercion requires a considerable degree of direct supervision; one has to be in a position to carry out a threat in order for it to be effective.

Power rests on many other resources, and these are ordinarily of more import than naked force; these include money, land, and other forms of wealth, as well as knowledge. Those who control the means of production in a society, whether it is land in an agricultural society or factories in an industrial society, possess enormous power. Those who own land or manage factories have considerable control over decisions about what will be produced, how much will be produced, and who will get how much of it. And whatever the technology associated with a society, those who possess superior knowledge of that technology have an advantage. They can make better weapons, grow more food, or live in better houses, better protected from the elements. And in any society in which money is used, liquid wealth confers power, since one can use money to purchase goods or services, as well as use it to induce others to provide them.

No resource confers unlimited power, however, for the exercise of power invariably requires at least some degree of cooperation from those over whom it is exercised. If someone wields the power of life and death, one can, at least in theory, choose to disobey his or her threats—that is, one can choose death over life. If those who control the means of production set wages that are too low, workers can refuse to work and choose employment elsewhere or not work at all.

These situations are extreme, of course, but they do help clarify the nature of power and the way in which it is exercised. When people are confronted with a robber with a gun, the power that robber exercises depends upon the fact that people value their lives, and that the cost of disobeying the robber's order—loss of life—is too great for them to consider disobeying. Confronted with the command "Your money or your life," most people value their lives more than their money. We can think of the exercise of power in such a context as a form of exchange in which the robber "gives" a victim life in exchange for money.

Exchange and Power

As these examples suggest, we cannot understand how power works without considering how it influences and is influenced by social exchange. According to exchange theorists, whose views we discussed briefly in Chapter 1, any human relationship can be thought of as an exchange of benefits between participants. When the farmer trades corn for the artisan's finely made baskets, an exchange has taken place. Likewise, when an experienced worker gives advice to a novice in return for thanks and deferential treatment, each has given the other something of value. It is difficult to find an instance of human interaction in which nothing of value is exchanged. Not only material goods, but services, affection, respect, advice, deference, and other less tangible values are exchanged when people interact.

Exchange is inevitably a part of social interaction. Whenever people engage in joint actions, the acts of each person contribute not only to the overall coordination of their conduct, but also to the satisfaction of individual needs and desires. When someone solicits the help of another, asking to borrow a neighbor's power tools, for example, and the help is given, the social act of giving and receiving aid is accomplished. But in this social act, individuals are also rewarded. One person helps another and is either repaid immediately with thanks and respect or is tacitly assured that the favor will be repaid at some later time.

Human exchanges, like all human behavior, entail symbolic interaction and self-consciousness. People are aware of the benefits they bestow upon one another. Because exchange is a conscious activity, people can anticipate that a present activity will be rewarded in the future. By role-taking they can estimate the chances that they will be repaid for the benefits they bestow. If a man wants to borrow something from a neighbor, for example, he may, through role-taking, realize that there is nothing of his that the neighbor will want to borrow. He may still make the request, however, because he anticipates the neighbor will grant it out of a desire to maintain good relations. Exchange is thus based upon symbolic interaction, for when people engage in exchange, they are interpreting the meaning of one another's acts in terms of what they individually and jointly value.

Within any social relationship, benefits exchanged tend toward balance over a period of time. In economic relationships in modern societies, this balance is very precisely calculated. When a woman incurs a debt by buying a new car on credit, she owes the lender the amount of money she has borrowed plus accumulated interest. The bank will not be satisfied if she repays "most" of the loan, nor will she be happy to receive a car that is "more or less" what she bargained for. Nothing less than exactly what was agreed upon will satisfy the parties.

In other social relationships, calculations are far less precise. Friends do not reckon their obligations to one another with a banker's precision. Indeed, they could not do so, for American culture teaches that friendship, affection, respect, and similar values cannot be purchased or calculated in monetary terms. Nevertheless, friends do take account of what they have done for one another. If a friend is unwilling to give help when asked, or frequently asks for favors but is seldom willing to perform them, others are apt to think something is wrong—that they are putting more into the friendship than they are getting out of it.

Whether calculations are precise or vague, however, the principle of exchange is the same; people expect to receive values that are equivalent to the benefits they bestow on others. In many contexts of everyday life, this is precisely what occurs. Friends, spouses, employers and employees, colleagues, and business associates are part of relationships in which there is at least rough equivalence over time in the benefits that are exchanged.

Unequal power has a marked impact upon social exchange. In the example cited earlier, it is the possession of a weapon that gives the robber control over the victim's life. People do not ordinarily think of their physical existence as something under the control of others. But a robber with a gun has the capacity to kill, and so has the capacity to "give back" another's life. Similarly, the factory owner who controls the only factory in town participates in a very unequal exchange relationship with workers, particularly if they are not unionized. We think of the workers as exchanging their labor for money, which they can then use to exchange for the goods and services they need. But if there are no other employers, the worker does not have an effective choice about working for this employer and accepting the offered wages. The worker either accepts what the employer offers as compensation or does without work and pay.

Power is thus an element that affects how exchange occurs. Where people have roughly equal resources, they decide to enter exchange relationships or to refrain from entering them on the basis of their needs, the capacity of others to satisfy them, and the relative advantage of entering one relationship as opposed to another. Thus, you might decide to lend a neighbor a tool, even if he is not a friend, if he has something you will later need. But where some individuals have power over others, the exchange of benefits is not simply governed by their relative value to the participants. If one individual is the only source of a valued good or service, people will have no choice but to offer more to obtain it than they would otherwise be willing to do. Thus, you may give your employer forty hours each week if there is no other way to secure an income. But if you are part of a unionized work force on strike, your employer may give more than he or she would otherwise be willing to provide because there is no other source of workers.

It is thus the *scarcity* of valued things that underlies the exercise of power

and its impact upon exchange. Where valued benefits are plentiful and widely available, individuals can enter exchange relationships on more or less equal terms. But where some valued things are scarce—and particularly when they are scarce because some individuals have much and others have none—exchange is shaped by unequal power.

Unequal exchanges provide one of the contexts in which social conflict develops. We can define conflict as social interaction in which people pursue incompatible ends; that is, where, in order for one person or group to attain a desired goal, some other person or group must give up their goal in whole or in part. In conflict between workers and employers, for example, each side seeks to use whatever power it has to secure maximum benefits at minimum cost. The employer wants to minimize labor costs and maximize control, while the workers want to maximize pay and improve their working conditions. Ultimately, they will reach some kind of accord, each trading some of what it wants for other things it wants more. The process of negotiation to reach this accord is a highly structured form of conflict.

Conflict involves people pursuing incompatible ends. Yet it should not be thought that conflict as a form of social interaction differs dramatically from cooperation, in which people pursue the same or compatible ends. Both forms of interaction are symbolic. Both entail the basic processes of role-making and role-taking. In both kinds of interaction, people must be able to interpret one another's acts and anticipate lines of conduct in order to sustain their interaction. Thus, just as two people doing something as simple as shaking hands must define the situation, indicating to one another the joint action they are performing, so it is also with those engaged in conflict. Union negotiators at a bargaining table with their managerial counterparts must be able to anticipate how the opposing side will respond to their proposals. Each side must have a grasp of the resources of the opponent and an estimate of how these resources will be used. Will the workers be willing or able to stay out on strike indefinitely? Are the employers so strapped for cash that they cannot yield any more on wages, or so in need of business that they will yield anything? Conflict, no less than any form of social interaction, is symbolic interaction.

Although exchange is important, it is a mistake to see human beings simply as rationally calculating animals who seek to derive the maximum benefit at minimum cost from their relationships with others. Cultural values and norms profoundly shape the means and extent to which people seek to maximize their own rewards. In a capitalist society such as ours, there are powerful norms and social definitions that encourage and reinforce the pursuit of self-interest. The entrepreneur and the established corporation alike are acting in socially acceptable ways when they make decisions about wages, prices, and production with only their own advantage in mind. In the economic sphere, the calculation of costs and benefits is exact, and no enterprise can survive if it operates at a loss.

But in other spheres of life, even in a capitalist society, the concept of exchange seems out of place, and the notion that people act to maximize their gains and minimize their losses would sound strange to participants. Within the nuclear family, for example, it seems unlikely that parents calculate their actions toward their children with their own individual gain in mind. Parents do provide their children with many benefits—shelter, food, comfort, affection, and instruction in the culture. And children "repay" their parents with affection, services, and often just delightful companionship. Yet parents and children do not see themselves as motivated largely by selfishness, nor can their actions be explained solely on the basis of self-interest. Parents and children act as they do, and often at considerable cost to themselves, in part because they feel they must. They respond to cultural norms as much as to self-interest.

The pursuit of individual advantage in exchange relationships is thus not a universal principle explaining human behavior. Although benefits are exchanged in every relationship, exchange does not explain everything about relationships. The extent to which people seek their own advantage is not a function of human nature, but of the degree to which they are encouraged to do so by culture. It is culture, built up over lifetimes, that influences how much emphasis will be placed upon individuals' rights to pursue their own ends in relation to their obligations to others. And it is culture that specifies the social contexts in which people should be predominantly oriented to the needs of the group rather than to their individual interests.

Conflict and cooperation are social processes present in variable balance in human affairs. It is not very useful to see human behavior as inherently cooperative or as inherently filled with conflict. Human behavior is inherently symbolic, and humans may use their symbolic capacity to cooperate as well as to battle, to pursue joint as well as incompatible ends. Whatever the balance, however, power, exchange, and conflict are important social processes in any society, and they are basic to a grasp of the coordination of human activity.

Exchange and Coordination

The concept of exchange emphasizes the fact that individuals in a society, or in one of its constituent groups and organizations, are linked to one another over time by a network of mutual obligations. Not only do people expect that they will engage in joint activity; they incur debts to one another and come to depend upon one another for the satisfaction of important needs.

An exchange of benefits provides a cement that binds participants together and sustains their joint action. People in exchange relationships expect that mutual obligations will be honored and that there are actions they can take if they are not. If our neighbor refuses to help us with our garden, we can take back the tools we have loaned. If an employer refuses to meet an obligation to pay us, we can take him to court and have the contract enforced by the state. In either case, it is the expectation that people ought to and will "pay their debts" that binds people together in continuing relationships.

Exchange illustrates a basic idea about the coordination of social activity. Whether we speak of interaction between individuals or of relationships between groups of people, *expectations* play a powerful role in conduct. People develop expectations about what will happen at various points in their lives. Even in such relatively simple joint actions as shaking hands, they predict what others will do. They expect, and thus also predict, that their efforts on behalf of others will be repaid. These expectations are a blend of beliefs about what is right and what is likely. Thus, people feel it is right to repay the obligations they have incurred in exchange relationships with others. But they also make empirical predictions about the likelihood that others will behave appropriately. In either case, it is the expectation that permits people to coordinate their conduct with others, for role-taking rests ultimately on the capacity to anticipate how others will behave.

A sense of who owes what to whom—and predictions about whether obligations will be met—is therefore an important part of a more general sense of structure that people bring to social life. Just as individuals rely on a sense of role structure to organize their conduct and relationships with others, so they also rely upon a sense of how obligations are distributed. A circle of friends, for example, can be viewed as an exchange network; members do one another favors, provide mutual emotional support, invite one another to social gatherings, and in similar ways bestow the benefits of membership on one another. That sense of themselves as a group of friends sharing mutual obligations is as important an element in their coordination of activities as are their individual friendships.

Power and Coordination

Power is also a major factor in the coordination of activity. The linkage of joint actions over time and distance frequently depends upon their control by powerful individuals and groups.

One way of looking at how power affects social coordination is to examine how decisions made by different individuals and groups affect the society as a whole. For example, if an individual decides to buy a new automobile this year, that decision has a negligible impact on the automobile industry as a whole or the economy in general. Only if the decision is similar to that made by hundreds of thousands of others will it have a substantial effect—moving the economy toward prosperity or recession.

A corporate giant such as General Motors, on the other hand, can make decisions that profoundly affect the lives of many people. Whether automobile workers have jobs or not, what hours they work, and what they are paid are matters over which corporate executives have considerable power. If the company misjudges its markets and does not produce products that people will buy, it will lay off workers. Decisions corporate executives can make with a stroke of the pen have a profound impact on the everyday lives and perhaps the whole careers of the corporation's workers.

Corporate decisions also shape the everyday actions of people in far less visible ways. In Chapter 2, for example, we saw how the production and pricing policies of the major automobile manufacturers led to various illegal activities by car dealers and customers. In that case, decisions by a powerful organization have a coordinating effect by means of a chain of connections among various organizations and individuals.

The political realm illustrates another way in which the actions of a few individuals shape and coordinate the actions of many. Mayors, governors, presidents, and other public officials, by exercising authority, shape the way people live their lives. This is the most obvious sense in which the decisions of a few profoundly affect the lives of the many. If Congress passes tax legislation that makes it financially attractive to invest in thoroughbred horses, those with the resources will choose to do so. They may have no interest in racing, but are induced to make a decision to invest because they can secure a tax advantage through a loophole in the laws. The legislation itself may have been passed only because powerful interests were able to "buy" enough Congressional votes to secure laws favorable to them. But the effects are likely to be widespread. People with resources will invest in racehorses or other tax shelters instead of putting their money into more socially productive enterprises—new houses, new factories, or promising new products. Thus, some will go without jobs or houses while others take advantage of tax incentives.

These examples of power focus on the way in which decisions taken by the very powerful influence the actions of ordinary people. Power also enters into the coordination of activities in everyday life. Parents have power and authority over children, and teachers exert both over their students. How activities are coordinated in the home or the classroom depends upon who controls what resources. Parents and teachers get what they want not simply because they share values and norms with children, but also because they have power over them.

Power is also related to the basic processes of role-making and role-taking (Thomas, et al., 1972). To some degree, those with power over others have less need to be accurate role-takers, for they can often act without regard to the reactions of others. Parents can command what their children do, and while some role-taking is necessary, it may not have to be very precise. Children, on the other hand, must cultivate role-taking skills. To anticipate the actions of such powerful figures as parents and teachers, children must be very good role-takers.

It is important to stress the importance of power. If we do not, we are left with an unrealistic view of social life in which people seem to coordinate their activities because they always agree. The fact is, as we have suggested, people often have conflicting goals and sometimes use whatever resources they can to secure them. Social life is not invariably harmonious, as we all know, and an explanation of social coordination must take this into account.

Joseph Shannon, *Tasmania* (1971) Polymer. In the Collection of The Corcoran Gallery of Art, Gift of the American Academy of Arts and Letters, Childe Hassam Fund.

Common-sense images of social conflict often equate it with violence or angry confrontation and depict it as unlike cooperative social interaction. But conflict is frequently a highly structured and closely coordinated form of social interaction, with emotions held carefully in check.

Conflict and Coordination

Finally, social conflict itself must be counted as a major contributor to the coordination of social activity. This statement may seem odd, since on its face conflict would seem to embody the opposite of orderly social relations. Yet conflict is itself generally an orderly process, requiring coordinated activity on the part of participants. It thus figures in social coordination in several ways.

First, just as cooperation can be the basis for the expectations people have of one another, so can conflict. When people interact, they indicate to one another the nature of the social acts in which they expect to engage. Lovers signal each other that they wish to make love; robbers and their victims signal their mutual understanding that a holdup is in progress; and children engaged in a dispute indicate their readiness to fight. In each of these illustrations, people derive expectations of one another from their recognition of the social act in which they are engaged. It does not matter if the act entails cooperation or conflict, for role-making and role-taking go on in either case.

At both interpersonal and societal levels, social relationships involving conflict are as much a part of the social landscape as those involving cooperation. Thus we have enemies as well as friends, rivals as well as colleagues. The interpersonal relationships we have with friends are an important part of our social world, for they shape and guide our day-to-day conduct. But the same can be said of our relationships with enemies or rivals. The desire of two individuals to avoid one another where possible affects the way they behave—not attending the same parties, for example, or avoiding places where the other is likely to be found. They are coordinating their conduct every bit as much as if they were friends.

At a societal level, groups and organizations have orderly relationships of conflict just as they have cooperative ties. The American coal-mining industry, for example, has a history of labor-management conflict. Strikes in this industry have been frequent since the founding of the United Mine Workers union. The coal miners' and the mine owners' expectations of each other are governed by their previous behavior and by a sense of what they are trying to secure for themselves. Because of their long-standing dispute over compensation and job safety, each side expects to be in conflict with the other, and so the links between the two groups are founded on conflict. That is how they coordinate much of their activity.

Moreover, the conflict between union and management in the coal industry is a stable part of the environment in which other corporations operate. For example, electric utilities, which consume large amounts of coal, adjust their purchase of coal to the contract negotiations in the coal industry. If a new contract is to be negotiated and they anticipate a lengthy strike, the electric companies will increase their purchase of coal so that they will have large stockpiles. Thus, the way that one industry operates is affected by stable conflict relationships within another.

Georg Simmel (1908), a German sociologist and contemporary of Max Weber, argued that conflict was an important part of the social order. He found, for example, that conflict works to bind individuals to the social groups of which they are members. When the members of a group—a work group within a factory, for example—are engaged in conflict with another group, their loyalty and commitment to their group tends to increase. Workers who are being threatened by management with loss of their jobs unless productivity increases are likely to feel bonds with one another. They will define their situation as one in which they must identify with one another and their group in defiance of "the enemy." One direct result of this increased social solidarity is greater energy and motivation. People who feel strongly attached to a group are more likely to cooperate with one another to secure group objectives.

Social conflict also creates bonds between social groups. In wartime, for example, the existence of a common, external enemy helps to induce a spirit of cooperation among groups that might otherwise be in conflict among themselves. During World War II, a common dedication to the war effort diverted attention from social divisions in the United States—those between labor and management, for example. For a period of several years during the war, American society was integrated by its response to external threat. After the war, however, there was a marked resurgence of industrial conflict, with numerous and frequent strikes.

Conflict can be a binding force within a society even in the absence of external threat. There are ordinarily many cleavages within American society: those between young and old, black and white, Protestant and Catholic, working class and middle class, Northerners and Southerners. Because there are many issues, groups that are in conflict on one issue may well be allies on another. Thus, one conflict tends to be kept within reasonable bounds by the existence of shared interests on some other issue. In this way, social conflict provides part of the cement that binds the members of society together.

Social conflict is thus a key aspect of the coordination of social behavior within groups, organizations, and whole societies. Since resources are scarce and members of a society do not necessarily agree on what constitutes proper conduct, they may at various times find themselves in verbal or physical conflict, attempting to shape the future of the society or prevent others from doing so. Whatever the scope or means or forum of conflict, however, it is a major way in which individuals orient themselves to one another and to the groups of which they are members, and so it is a central part of social coordination.

THE SOCIAL CONSTRUCTION OF REALITY

Taken together, the ideas presented in this chapter go a long way toward explaining how the behavior of large numbers of people within a society is more or less coordinated and interlinked. One additional fact about social coordination must be addressed to complete this understanding.

People do not merely create a social order by coordinating their conduct with that of others; they also experience the society that their actions help constitute. To put this another way, people do not simply act within the framework of circumstances and situations that confront them. In addition, they "act toward" the very social world they have created. They talk about society or its groups, they complain about it, blame it for their problems, praise its virtues, and in similar ways objectify it; that is, they act toward it as an object in the sense in which we have previously used that term. Using a phrase introduced by Peter Berger and Thomas Luckmann (1967), we can examine this *social construction of reality* as an important process in its own right, one that contributes as much to social coordination as any of the processes we have so far discussed.

When sociologists speak of the social construction of reality, they refer to processes in and through which the nature of social reality is discovered, made known, and reaffirmed by the members of a society or one of its constituent units. Because human beings are dependent upon symbols, the "reality" in which they live depends to a great extent upon their perceptions of it. People act on the basis of their definitions of situations, on the basis of the way they perceive the world and their place in it, and not simply on the basis of how things actually are. If the members of a community believe that homosexuals are loathsome creatures or that God is inclined toward wrath and vengeance, for example, they will act on the basis of such beliefs, persecuting homosexuals or trying to avoid offending God and thus evade punishment. It follows that beliefs about social reality are an important determinant of social coordination, for what people do depends in part upon their beliefs about the world.

The simplest way in which social reality is constructed is through the *names* people attach to the society itself and its constituent groups and organizations. A crucial part of the concept of society is that its members are conscious of it as a society. The same might be said of any particular social unit; the self-consciousness of the members of a group or collectivity helps to determine the kind of social unit it is. Names organize consciousness. The labels people attach to a particular society or social unit—American society, General Motors, our family—summarize its reality in the eyes of its own members or those of outsiders.

Names are more than labels for groups or societies, however, for they are typically imbued with great symbolic significance. Names for social groups or whole societies or political subdivisions evoke responses that go beyond their mere cognitive identification of places or people. "California" stands for a way of life as well as a place—healthy, tanned bodies, experimental life styles, nude beaches. So, too, "my family" evokes an emotional response as well as a recognized group of individuals.

Names, labels, and their emotional baggage play an important part in sustaining the continuity of the social world. By naming and talking about various groups and entities, people help to sustain them merely by reminding themselves of their presence. A radar screen provides a useful analogy. As a radar beam sweeps across the countryside, the objects it strikes reflect energy back to the radar antenna, and this energy is converted to blips on the screen. The momentary phosphorescent glow of the blip begins to fade almost as soon as it appears, only to be reproduced again with the next sweep of the beam. So too, as people name and talk about the various groups that form their society, they continually refresh their memories. Names and talk periodically refresh their mental maps of the environment in which they live.

And it is not only the names of groups and organizations that are important as people talk to one another. Not just social reality, but all of reality—biological, geographical, psychological, religious, and conceptual reality—is embedded in the language spoken by the members of a society. Thus, every conversation is in some sense a contribution to the social construction of reality, for the very use of words to denote the objects that are important in a given culture reinforces prevailing ideas and helps to keep alternatives in the background.

Much everyday talk focuses on the problematic and thus helps to sustain beliefs about reality, even when people are attending to things that have gone wrong. According to George H. Mead (1938), it is the problematic situation—anything that actually or potentially impedes action—that arouses thinking. When things do not go as people expect and their pursuit of a goal is blocked, they consider alternative courses of action and attempt to determine what has gone wrong.

When people are engaged in joint actions with others, individual thought is coupled with discussion. That is, people engage in talk that is focused on ways of completing the social acts in which they are engaged. Suppose, for example, that a husband and wife have differing views on how much freedom their children should have. When a specific decision must be made—whether their child can go to the beach alone, for example—action cannot proceed until some agreement is reached. This agreement will be achieved through a conversation that focuses on this problematic situation. One parent may emphasize the busy highway that must be crossed to reach the beach, the lack of regular lifeguards, or the danger that the child may be molested by a stranger. The other might speak of the need to encourage a sense of autonomy and self-reliance, even if it means taking some modest risks.

In much of everyday life people have to overcome numerous obstacles as they pursue their objectives and adjust their conduct to the actions of others. As they do so, they are never far from general cultural ideas about what their conduct should be. The husband and wife in the foregoing example want to create a set of rules for their children, and they want them to be more or less in accord with their culture's ideas about children and their upbringing. As they talk about a particular situation, they invoke these cultural ideas, and by so doing they give them concrete form. An abstract idea such as "independence" becomes embodied in a specific set of activities. From the perspective of people who invoke such ideas, the goal is to decide upon a course of action. In a broader sense, however, the effect of their conversation is to make these cultural ideas real—to reaffirm their importance as the basic terms through which reality is perceived.

When people confront such problematic situations, they strive generally to *align* their conduct with cultural ideals (see Stokes and Hewitt, 1976). That is, they seek to act in ways that are consistent with culture or which others will define as consistent. Thus, while one parent invokes a cultural value of "self-reliance" in order to justify allowing a child to go out on his own, the other talks about the need for "supervision," thus also invoking a cultural value. Regardless of who prevails in the discussion, they have constructed an interpretation of their conduct that is consistent with cultural standards. They have aligned their conduct, not only in the sense that they have agreed on what they will do, but also in the sense that they have made it fit their culture.

Human beings seem to have a powerful need for reality, including social reality, to be orderly and familiar. As people seek to align their conduct with cultural ideas and expectations, their goal is not simply to do whatever conforms with cultural norms and values. Rather, and more broadly, they wish to *make sense* of their own conduct and the conduct of others in culturally familiar terms. They want the world to be an orderly and predictable place, one in which they can feel a secure sense that things are normal. Thus, for example, the parents in the previous example are not only trying to live up to cultural norms and values about child-rearing, for there are many such norms and values that often give contradictory guidance in specific situations. What these parents are attempting to do, as humans generally do, is to construct a more or less secure, orderly, familiar view of their world so that they can act with confidence in it.

As people align their actions with culture and create a sense of normality and orderliness, they make their cultural ideals concrete. Just as groups and organizations continue to exist only so long as people continue to identify with them and act as if they are important, so too with culture. Norms and values remain important as long as people believe that they are. And more generally, the reality that is designated by a given culture (and its language) remains alive as long as people orient themselves toward this reality and act "as if" it exists. If culture defines the gods as dangerous and fellow human beings as evil, they will talk about the world and act toward it as if this were reality—as they also will if the culture defines women as inferior to men and blacks as inferior to whites—and they will seek to defend their conceptions of reality from attack.

Human beings thus coordinate their conduct in part by sustaining their images of the material and social world in which they live. They do this by talking about their world and by reaffirming their conceptions of it, even when their own acts seem to violate these conceptions. They seek to align their own behavior with culture and, in a more general way, to make sense of all their experiences in terms provided by their culture.

CONCLUSION

In this chapter we have stressed the ways in which people coordinate their activities and thus create social life. Society exists because people coordinate their activities one with another and because they act toward the social order as if it exists. Various fundamental social processes are at work as people coordinate their conduct. These processes can be said to "produce" society, just as people produce society when they talk about it. In Chapter 6, our attention will turn to the way society produces new members through the process of socialization.

SUGGESTED READINGS

BERGER, PETER L. and THOMAS LUCKMANN. *The Social Construction of Reality* (New York: Doubleday/Anchor, 1967).

BLAU, PETER M. *Exchange and Power in Social Life* (New York: Wiley, 1964).

GOFFMAN, ERVING. *The Presentation of Self in Everyday Life* (Garden City, N.Y.: Anchor Books, 1959).

HEWITT, JOHN P. *Self and Society: A Symbolic Interactionist Social Psychology*, 3rd ed. (Boston: Allyn and Bacon, 1984), Chapter 5.

MCHUGH, PETER. *Defining the Situation* (Indianapolis: Bobbs-Merrill, 1968).

ROBBOY, HOWARD and CANDACE CLARK, eds. *Social Interaction: Readings in Sociology* (New York: St. Martin's, 1983).

STONE, GREGORY P. and HARVEY A. FARBERMAN, eds. *Social Psychology Through Symbolic Interaction*, 2nd ed. (New York: Wiley, 1981), Parts 1 and 2.

STRAUSS, ANSELM L. *Negotiations* (San Francisco: Jossey-Bass, 1978).

6

Becoming Human

WHAT IS SOCIALIZATION?
THE ACQUISITION OF SELF
- Language and the Self
- Stages of Socialization
- Elements of the Self

SELF AND THE CONTROL OF CONDUCT
- "I" and "Me"
- Society in the Individual
- The Self and Motivation

CONTEXTS OF SOCIALIZATION
- Socialization in the Family
- Socialization in the School
- Peer Socialization
- Adult Contexts of Socialization

The human being whose social behavior we have been examining is a complex and talented creature. In this chapter, we turn to the question of how humans become as they are. How do they acquire the capacity to interact with others, to engage in the basic processes of role-making and role-taking? What social forces shape the kinds of people they become—their values, ambitions, fears, skills, and failings? How is the human infant, the raw material of human society, transformed into a member of society? Under what conditions do individuals change, acquiring new attributes, skills, and orientations?

WHAT IS SOCIALIZATION?

Sociologists use the term *socialization* to describe the process by which human beings acquire, maintain, or transform the many attributes necessary for membership and participation in society. Socialization begins at birth and continues throughout life. It is a process in which humans acquire many things: the values, norms, and knowledge of their culture; a language; the skills needed to interact with others; the abilities to use society's tools and technology; and, crucially, the sense of self. It is also a process in which each person is an active, aware participant; people are not merely recipients of instruction.

The newborn human infant has no capacity to care for itself, and others must attend to its every need. However, if it is ultimately to care for itself and participate in human life, the infant must be socialized. That is, it must learn to feed and dress itself, speak the common language, perceive the world as others perceive it, learn what is valued and what is forbidden in its society, and acquire attitudes, knowledge, and beliefs considered proper for a member of that society.

Although socialization starts soon after birth, there is no clear point at which it comes to a halt. Each society identifies a certain age at which people begin to be treated as adults; for example, the age at which they can vote or marry without parental consent in our own society. But, sociologically speaking, there is no end to the socialization process. It occurs throughout life, both in childhood and in maturity. The forms and emphases of socialization shift from one stage of the life cycle to another, but the process itself is lifelong.

The young child receives instruction in the most basic features of the culture. By learning its language, it discovers the world of objects important to that culture. The child is instructed in the elementary rules of social intercourse—learning, for example, whom to address respectfully and who may be approached casually. In general, childhood socialization encompasses widely shared parts of a culture as well as knowledge and attitudes appropriate to the child's gender and age.

Adult socialization, in contrast, tends to be more specialized. Young marrieds, for example, are assumed to be adults who command the basic knowledge, beliefs, and values of their culture. Yet they too undergo socialization. They may seek information on contraception, be instructed in the rules of their religion regarding marriage, and learn how to live and relate to others as a unit rather than as single individuals. Thus, a married couple learn how to be married, and later they learn how to be parents, how to grow old, and even how to die. Similarly, workers enter the job market with some knowledge, but they continue to be socialized as they perform their work, learn new skills, change jobs, and adjust to failure.

Sociologists focus on many aspects of socialization: the agents of socialization, the results of socialization, and the processes of socialization. For example, one can attempt to determine who does what to whom—and where—in the course of socialization. In what social settings—such as the family, the school, or the peer group—does the socialization of children occur? Who has power over whom in these contexts? To what degree do agents of socialization such as parents, teachers, friends, and the mass media work together or in opposition to one another?

A sociologist also may examine the results of socialization. What values do people acquire as a result of childhood experience? What does the typical member of a society know and believe about the social and natural world? What basic aspirations are encouraged in a given society? Are people oriented primarily to hard work and to success, or do they value the good opinion of others over individual achievement?

Underlying any analysis of socialization is the fact that it is a process as well as a set of outcomes. From this vantage point, what is most interesting is how socialization actually occurs. What do parents do, for example, to teach their children appropriate behavior? Do they attempt to punish their young for misdeeds, or do they rely upon the rewarding of desired behavior? Do they dictate absolute behavioral rules, or do they attempt to explain the rules they have established?

As these examples suggest, the subjective perceptions of various agents of socialization are as important as who they are. To understand how children learn, or how anyone learns, one must know something about the goals and beliefs of their teachers. Every culture has a conception of what people are like, and its members rely on such ideas when they instruct others. Thus, children may be thought to learn different kinds of material best at different ages. Beliefs such as this will affect socialization procedures. In American society, children are often thought incapable of grasping the meaning of death until they are preadolescents. One consequence of such a belief is that young children are often sheltered from the facts of death, for example, by being kept away from funerals. As a consequence, they do not develop much of an understanding of this universal human experience.

Socialization must be analyzed from both the perspective of its agents and of those who are subject to it. Although the word *socialization* tends to conjure up a picture of active agents and passive recipients, such a portrayal is highly inaccurate. As former children, we all know (or once knew) that the child's response to adults is not simply to acquiesce passively to their demands. Sometimes adults make demands that seem unreasonable to children; they expect higher levels of obedience or self-control than the child can deliver. Frequently, the child has some difficulty figuring out just what rules parents are trying to enforce. While culture may inculcate various norms and encourage conformity with them through a standard system of rewards and punishments, there are no guarantees that parents will behave in a culturally standard way. Adults may enforce rules inconsistently. They can, and often do, attempt to enforce rules they themselves do not obey. Quite often, therefore, the child is in the position of attempting to figure out the logic of parental actions.

The perspective of the recipient of socialization is crucial for another reason. The most important development in socialization is the acquisition of selfhood. The initial development and the later elaboration and transformation of the self from birth through adolescence and beyond must be understood in order to understand socialization. Human behavior is self-conscious behavior. To grasp how people become human, it is necessary to understand how the self initially develops and how it plays a continuing role in the socialization process.

THE ACQUISITION OF SELF

The capacity of human beings to control their conduct rests upon the development of self. Because people can act toward themselves as objects, they can imagine alternative lines of conduct and choose among them. The essence of this process of self-control lies in an internal dialogue. If something happens to disturb an individual's adjustment to his or her surroundings—if, for example, a parent is upset by a child's display of bad manners—the event triggers the start of an act. The parent may begin to respond angrily to the child's behavior; then, as the act gets underway, the parent becomes aware of what he or she is about to do and begins to imagine the child's reactions. In doing so, the parent is engaging in role-taking—examining his or her own act from the child's perspective. The parent may elect to carry through with the angry response, or may decide to respond more patiently to the child. In either case, conduct has been controlled through a process of acting toward the self.

How does this capacity to act toward the self, and thus to control conduct, develop? At birth, there is no self and no capacity for the self-control of conduct. This does not mean that infants cannot respond to their surroundings, for they obviously do, as when nursing at their mother's breast, crying when they are uncomfortable, and responding to the sound and touch of other humans. But their responses do not initially involve self-conscious control of behavior. By age five or six, however, the child is a very different creature. Instead of being totally dependent upon others, it can take care of many of its everyday needs—dressing, feeding, and toileting, for example. And crucially, a child of this age has considerable control over its own behavior. It can make some choices about what it will do: whether, for example, to follow its own impulses or the wishes of others.

Organic growth and development are a part of the story of what happens to the child in the first years. The newborn infant can do very little, but within the first year it develops the capacity to hold its head up, to roll over from stomach to back, to sit up, to crawl, and to stand and take its first steps. It gradually learns to coordinate information gained through its senses and to distinguish between itself and the external world. Through toddlerhood and early childhood, additional developmental processes are at work and much learning occurs.

But growth and development are not the full story. Physical and mental development are necessary conditions for full participation in the human group, but they are not in themselves sufficient. Something else is happening in the early years of life that is directly related to the acquisition of self, and that is the development of speech.

Language and the Self

A child's first words are a momentous event, eagerly awaited and warmly rewarded by parents. Adults talk to children from the very start, and gradually children learn to make sounds, to imitate the sounds made by adults, and to associate these sounds with particular sensations. They learn the sounds associated with "Mama" and "Daddy," as well as the sounds associated with other important adults. Children learn that sounds are associated with all the things they encounter in their world, not only people, but animals, foods, toys, and everything else they encounter. And just as important, children learn that there are rewards to be had by using these sounds appropriately. The fuss that accompanies a child's first words conveys a powerful message—that words are important, that they command attention, and that using them is a key to securing one's goals.

Learning the names of things (and gradually learning how to combine words into sentences) literally opens up for children the world in which they and their parents live. The objects children learn about are those named and recognized within the culture of the group and society to which the child belongs. So children learn the names of tools, animals, places, buildings, activities, beliefs, ideas, and many other things. They learn the names of concrete objects, they learn the names of people, and they learn the names of more abstract objects—ideas such as God as well as colors, physical sensations, and emotions—that are not perceived directly but whose existence must be inferred from more concrete perceptions.

Moreover, in learning the names of objects, children also learn their meanings; that is, along with a label to be attached to an object, they learn that certain kinds of actions are possible in relation to that object. Thus, for example, children learn not just that "hot" is a label attached to a particular category of sensations, but also that this is a word that implies a possible range of actions. They learn that people drink "hot" coffee, that children should stay away from "hot" stoves, and that a car that has been stolen is a "hot" car.

A crucial part of the discovery that things have names involves the child and its relation to the family and other social groups of which the child is a part.

Three things are particularly important. First, children learn that people have names—that there is a regular and consistent association between the sounds "Mama," "Daddy," "Grandma," "Billy," and "Uncle Joe." Second, children learn that people have more than one name—that "Mama" is also called "Ruth" and that "Billy" is also called "your brother." And third, children learn that they themselves have names, that they are important objects whose names are regularly used.

When children learn that there is a name which is their own property, and that they can use this name just as others use the name, they have made a significant leap forward in the acquisition of self. When Susy or Billy can say "Susy" or "Billy" and identify this name with self, they have made a major advance. They can now visualize themselves as a part of the world in which they live. Their capacity for control over conduct is enhanced, for acquiring a name carries forward a general process of differentiating body and self from the external environment.

Yet the self that emerges when children first refer to themselves by name is relatively simple and undifferentiated. "Billy" is at first just a name that is associated with a body—his own body—and is nothing more complicated than that. In order for "Billy" to become a more complex and differentiated object, he must learn a more complex set of meanings associated with this object. How does Billy do this? How does he learn the meaning of this new and important object, himself?

The answer to this question lies in Billy's discovery that the others who surround him are themselves complex objects, and this discovery involves his learning the many names by which people are known. "Mama," he learns, is also called "Ruth" by "Daddy," who is called "Bob" by her and by others. "Mama and Daddy" are also sometimes "Mr. and Mrs. Jones." And everyone with whom Billy interacts is at various times known by other names—"I," "you," "me," "they," "he," and "she."

In discovering what must seem to be a bewildering array of names for people and for self, children are, in fact, being confronted with several things. First, they are confronted with the organized structure of the groups to which they belong. The first group they encounter is the family, with its array of personal names, relationship terms, and personal pronouns. Later they will be confronted with other groups, each with an organized structure of social relationships into which they must somehow fit. They will encounter schools, peer groups, clubs, and many others.

Second, children are confronted with a number of people who act toward them in different ways. If Billy belongs to a family in which his mother and father perform clearly gender-differentiated roles, he may find that his mother cooks his meals and dresses him, while his father plays football with him. Billy may also discover that the treatment he receives differs in some respects from that received by his sister Susy; that while both are subject to parental control, he has more freedom than she.

And third, children are confronted with a variety of perspectives from which they and their behavior may be viewed. Billy learns, for example, that pulling the cat's tail is met with squeals of delight from his younger sister, but that his mother takes a disapproving view of this behavior. In learning that different people respond in different ways to his conduct, Billy is really learning that he is a different object to these people. Just as they act toward him in different ways, so must he adjust his conduct to their expectations of him.

Gradually, children learn to fit themselves and their behavior to the family to which they belong. They learn that they have a place in this group that is defined by their relationships with others. They learn to make sense of the complex set of names by which people refer to one another. Billy learns that he is "Billy," "son," "brother," "child," and "grandson." He learns that he is "I" and "me," and he learns he is also "you" and "him."

In learning to fit behavior to the structure of activities within the family, the child becomes a more complex and differentiated object to self as well as to others. To adjust conduct to that of others, the child must learn their perspectives and begin to see things from their point of view. In doing so, the child also sees himself or herself from differing perspectives. Billy learns to see himself as his mother, sister, father, grandparents, and other significant individuals see him. He learns the attitudes they have toward him, the expectations they have for him. He learns what is expected of a child, of a male child, and of the particular male child who is "Billy." And he learns the general skill of role-taking, that capacity to view himself and his own conduct from the perspectives of the others with whom he interacts.

Stages of Socialization

These developments do not occur suddenly or immediately, but rather emerge over a period of time. Children gradually learn to make sense of the linguistic world in which they live. They gradually learn how kinship terms and personal names correspond, and how a set of personal pronouns are used to represent various positions in the family or in any context of social interaction. Mistakes are made, to be sure. Children will misuse personal pronouns before gaining a firm grasp of them. They will refer to all furry animals as "dogs," and they might even call all men "Daddy" in the beginning. The picture is one of gradual refinement in linguistic abilities.

Mead (1934) identified two major stages in the development of the self. In the first stage, called the *play stage*, the child has begun to acquire a vocabulary in terms of which people and objects can be represented. In this stage, the child perceives various roles in the activities of others; that is, the child perceives that mothers are engaged in a familiar cluster of behavior, as are police officers, mail carriers, or doctors. The child "plays at" these roles, enacting one, then another of the roles he or she has observed others playing.

This "playing at" roles has two aspects. First, the child is learning a repertoire of behavior, a set of words and deeds that can be used later in similar

Pablo Picasso, *Le Gourmet* (1901)
Oil on canvas, 36½ × 26⅞ inches. The National Gallery of Art, Washington. Chester Dale Collection.

Many kinds of learning occur in a single episode of socialization. This young gourmet is not only learning cooking techniques and what is culturally defined as good food, but she is also practicing a role and learning to see herself in this role.

or even different circumstances. Second, and perhaps of more significance, the child is learning to have a sense of itself as an object in the world. Indeed, since the child will play at several roles, it is learning to regard itself as one of several possible objects. Playing at roles, Mead wrote,

> . . . is the simplest form of being another to one's self. It involves a temporal situation. The child says something in one character and responds in another character, and then his responding in another character is a stimulus to himself in the first character, and so the conversation goes on. (Mead, 1934:151)

In acting toward the self in this way, playing two or more roles in rotation, the child is not merely imitating adult behavior. More important, it is learning to act toward the self as an object and is learning that the object has different meanings according to the way others act toward it.

In the play stage, the child has no real sense of the structure of the family or any other group as a whole, and so the grasp of each of the roles played is fragmentary and incomplete. In contrast, the second stage of development, the *game stage*, entails a more organized grasp of self as object.

The game of baseball, or any other organized game, illustrates what occurs in this stage of socialization. To play a role in a game—the role of catcher in baseball, for example—requires that you have a grasp of the game as a whole. You must have a composite, simultaneous idea of a baseball team, the various positions involved, the object of the game, and the relationship of the position you are playing to the activity as a whole. In other words, you have a grasp of yourself as an object in this organized activity by assuming the perspective not just of specific others, but also of the activity as a whole.

More generally, progression to this stage of socialization entails the development of the *generalized other*. In the play stage of socialization, the child responds to specific others and their demands. But in the game stage, the child responds to a more generalized set of expectations. That is, the child regards itself not only from the perspectives of specific others (such as mother or father), but also from the standpoint of the family as a whole (and later from the perspective of the society as a whole). This is exactly analogous to playing a role in an organized game in which the child must take the game as a whole into account in order to know what to do.

The *generalized other* represents the perspective of the whole group to which the individual belongs. We can think of the generalized other as a *perspective*—not as a specific other person or a specific role, but as a perspective of the society or group itself. The generalized other thus represents the most general and deeply held values of a society. Thus, a man who felt the urge to kill another might be repelled by this urge and prevent himself from taking such a disapproved action. This would be evidence of the generalized other in action. That is, the man acting in this way has taken the role of the generalized other and so has controlled his conduct.

In the beginning, during childhood socialization, the generalized other encompasses the general beliefs and values of the family. Later, as the child moves outside the world of the family and into peer groups, school, and later the adult world, the generalized other encompasses still more general beliefs and values. Indeed, in a complex society it is likely that more than one generalized other is formed. The existence of different religious, ethnic, and social class groups makes for cultural complexity, and thus also for the emergence of many different generalized perspectives from which individuals can view their own behavior.

Elements of the Self

During the game stage of socialization, the child becomes a more complex object as well as a more integrated one. The child learns that it plays a variety of roles in a variety of organized activities: within the family, in games, at school. In other words, the child learns that different behavior is expected in different situations, and that it is a different object to others depending upon the situation. Indeed, the child learns to adjust expectations of self to fit the expectations of different audiences.

But at the same time, the child learns that it is an individual. It may seem strange to think of people as having to learn this, but this makes sense in terms of interactionist theory. The child can view itself as an object only indirectly, from the vantage point of others and their roles. Since there are many others and many roles, the child becomes many objects to itself. Accordingly, the child must somehow learn that there is some thing or principle—a self—that unifies these diverse objects. Acquiring this sense of a unified, coherent self in which many facets are integrated depends upon social structure.

This understanding begins when we learn that we occupy certain statuses, that we have a stable place relative to others. At first this sense of place depends upon our membership in a family, but later it entails positions associated with occupation, religion, citizenship, and other statuses in the world outside the family. The sociological term for this sense of place is *identity*. This term refers to the individual's sense of who he or she is in relation to others. In each situation, an individual has an identity provided by the person's role in that situation. More generally, however, people develop more integrated and holistic identities that reflect a summing up and ordering of their particular identities.

Organized social life also provides people with a basis for forming *self-images*—pictures of their qualities, abilities, and attributes. From their participation in joint actions with others and from their responses to each other, people learn to think of themselves as strong or weak, intelligent or stupid, capable or inept. They learn what they do well and what they do poorly. These images of self derive from what other people communicate directly, as well as from the inferences they draw about other's attitudes. Thus, parents and teachers may tell a child that she is bright, but she may also infer this through role-taking, putting herself in their position and imputing to them an attitude toward herself.

Self-images are based upon the real or imagined responses of others, but their importance rests upon the fact that they focus on the qualities of the individual. Where identity informs the child (or the adult) how he or she is like others, self-image focuses upon the individual's unique characteristics, thus helping to differentiate self from others. To have an identity as female, Jewish, and a mother is to claim attachment to certain statuses and affiliation with particular groups. *Identity* thus represents attachment to and resemblance of others. To think of yourself as warm, nurturing, and capable is to claim personal qualities that are your own property. Self-image thus represents individuality.

Finally, society provides the basis for self-evaluations that constitute *self-esteem*. As individuals interact with others, they develop positive and negative feelings about themselves. From each act they derive some increment or decrement to self-esteem, adding to or subtracting from the stock of positive feelings about self. Self-esteem exists because the real and imagined judgments of others include an *evaluative* component. The child who is scolded for misbehavior not only learns that a particular kind of behavior is undesirable, but also that a particular kind of self is to be avoided.

The selves people develop—their identities, self-images, and self-esteem—emerge over time as individuals encounter socially structured activities. Before we can examine the contexts in which people develop selves, however, we need to examine more closely the links between self and conduct. In particular, how does socialization import society into the person, and how does the self figure in the control of behavior?

SELF AND THE CONTROL OF CONDUCT

The acquisition of self is the most important outcome of socialization, for the capacity to exert conscious control over behavior is a distinctive human characteristic. This capacity for self-control exists because people have the capacity to act toward themselves. Humans can examine their own conduct from the perspectives of others, anticipate reactions to alternative lines of conduct, and thus select an action that will yield the result they wish. In the following section we look more closely at how people control their conduct in this way.

"I" and "Me"

One way of conceiving the self is as a process in which there is an ongoing dialogue between "I" and "Me." Mead used these terms to refer to the two phases of the self process. In the "I" phase, the person reacts to a stimulus. When a telephone rings, for example, most people in our culture will immediately reach to answer it. This initial response is not something people consciously decide upon; it is impulsive and not subject to control at first. In the "Me" phase, the individual becomes aware of the direction of that conduct. For example, a woman sees herself answering the phone and checks to see that this is an appropriate action. If it is, she goes ahead and completes it. If it is not—if she is in someone else's home, for example, and it is their phone—she checks her impulse and waits for someone else to act. In checking her conduct in this way, the woman becomes an object to herself, a "Me" in her own eyes.

The "Me" phase of the act thus corresponds to the stage of *perception*, in which the person acts toward objects instead of simply responding to stimuli. To become a "Me" to herself, the woman must stand in some other place; she must take another role, whether that of a specific other person with whom she is interacting or of the generalized other. When a person takes the role of another, she makes an object of herself and her conduct. Only in this way does she gain control of conduct. If an act that has begun seems socially inappropriate or less advantageous than some alternative, it can be checked and another act substituted for it.

"I" and "Me" are phases of consciousness. At one moment in our conduct, we are alert to external stimuli and we respond to them. Almost immediately, we role-take, visualizing the direction of our conduct and the possible responses to it. In that moment our attention shifts to ourselves. "I" and "Me" do not have locations within the head (or elsewhere). They are not tangible structures; they are only names for the two phases of the self.

In some respects "I" and "Me" resemble Sigmund Freud's conception of *id* and *superego*. In his scheme, the former represents biological instinct, while the latter represents the influence of culture. Freud's theory also has a third element, *ego*, which mediates between id and superego. Both Freud and Mead were attempting to describe the process whereby individuals control their conduct or attempt to do so. And both theories are often misinterpreted so that "I," "Me," "id," and "superego" are seen as concrete entities rather than as aspects of process. In both schemes, the emphasis is upon process rather than the description of concrete entities located within the head.

Freud and Mead differ in one major respect. Where Freud saw the relationship between biology and culture as one of antagonism, Mead saw the relationship as more cooperative. For Freud, humans are affected by powerful biological drives, such as sexuality, which are controlled only at great effort by culture. The human being is thus a seething kettle of drives that are only partially and imperfectly constrained. Mead did not see this antagonistic relationship. Human drives or motivations, he felt, are largely the products of social experience. The "I" is thus not pitted against the "Me," but is helped and guided by it.

Symbolic interactionists do not see humans as perfectly socialized creatures. Society is brought within the person and exerts control, but not completely or perfectly. Human conduct contains the potential for novelty and change, for our impulsive responses to stimuli are not perfectly predictable. We are not so well or successfully conditioned that we learn an appropriate social response for each and every stimulus. Indeed, if we did learn our responses so well, and if there were a successful response to be learned for each situation, we would have no reason to be conscious of ourselves. We would simply respond impulsively to stimuli, as do other animals, and act without awareness of our actions.

But we do, in fact, encounter many problematic situations in which our initial, impulsive responses are not well-suited to circumstances. When traffic lights fail to turn from red to green when they should, we have to tell ourselves that they are probably broken. When infants cry when we are tired and irritable ourselves, we have to exert a self-conscious effort to deal with their problems and satisfy ourselves and others. We misjudge situations, responding to stimuli that are not the most relevant to our adjustment, so that we are forced to reconsider our lines of conduct. In short, human life is filled with many circumstances in which we must constantly control and modify our conduct.

Society in the Individual

There is something of a paradox in the way we humans control our behavior. On one hand, we can control ourselves because we have the capacity to become objects to ourselves and to respond to our own contemplated actions. On the other hand, this very capacity for self-objectification opens the door for social control. We can objectify ourselves because we have names given to us by others. When we act toward ourselves, we assume the perspective of others.

When we choose among lines of conduct, we choose from a limited set of alternatives taught to us by others. In short, when we acquire selfhood, we also acquire a susceptibility to social control. A main effect of socialization is thus to bring society and culture *within* the person. This is so in several distinct respects.

First, the dialogue that characterizes inner experience is a representation of actual or possible real *conversations*. Predictions of others' responses to intended acts frequently take the form of imaginary conversations in which the person acts and others speak their words of approval or disapproval. When this happens, social processes have been brought within the person's mind. The effect on behavior is the same as if a real conversation had taken place.

People learn their parts in such conversations in different contexts and different ways. In many types of routine behavior, lines are clearly provided, and people speak them ritually—as they have been taught. "Please" and "Thank you" have this character. Children hear the words and phrases used by those who occupy various positions, and when they themselves occupy these positions, they use these already written lines. And the creative and generative power of language permits people to say and to understand what they have never heard before.

Second, socialization imports *culture* into the person, and with it come values, norms, and knowledge of important objects. People are not, of course, passive victims of culture, forced to adhere rigidly to its norms and values, or limited only to established objects and definitions. As has been suggested, people can violate norms and disregard values, but not with impunity. When conduct does not accord with a norm, people must somehow square what they are doing with the norm, accounting for their departure from it. Thus culture places limits on what individuals can do, even if it does not rigidly prescribe their behavior.

People's actions are also limited by the social acts and objects they are capable of imagining. Culture does not provide an unlimited set of objects, but a finite set. In the course of socialization, humans learn a repertory of acts, and this set of familiar acts places some limits on what they can do or imagine themselves doing in specific situations. They are not, however, limited to doing only what they have seen or heard of others doing, since the creative qualities of language permit them to conceive of new ways of acting. If people can say what they have never heard before, putting words and phrases together in novel ways, they can also imagine what they have not previously imagined. They can create new meanings, new definitions of situations, new objects, and new acts. In short, they can *create culture*, but in doing so they must rely upon the culture they have already learned.

Third, socialization brings *social structure* within the person. One of the most important kinds of knowledge people acquire in socialization is knowledge about the social world. From infancy until death, humans busy themselves learning about the structure of their social world. In childhood, they learn the names of various family roles. As they encounter peers, schools, religious organizations, the world of work, politics, and every other arena of life, they learn about the roles they contain and the way people use these roles to coordinate their conduct. And, crucially, they learn where they fit within each of these spheres. They develop a mental map of each group, organization, and situation they encounter, and they use this map as a basis for understanding the actions of others as well as their relationships to them.

Several powerful expectations develop as a result of the incorporation of social structure within the person. People come to *expect* structure, to search for organized patterns of activity in each situation they encounter. And they expect to be able to locate themselves within the structures they identify. That is, they expect not only that they will be able to determine what is going on around them and how it is organized, but also be able to find a place for themselves in this activity.

Ordinarily, of course, the sense of social stucture and of the individual's place within it is not problematic. People learn many culturally given definitions of situations and how to associate standard definitions with real events. People learn the names and typifications of situations. They learn to look for the cues that enable them to identify a given situation as "a party" or "a baseball game."

Learning about situations occurs in several ways. Some learning is vicarious; that is, people learn about situations and the roles they contain by observation. Children learn about the structure of families, for example, by observing life within their own family and the families of their friends. Some of this learning occurs through direct experience; by going to parties, playing baseball, and being punished for stealing, people learn to recognize these situations and their roles. Learning also occurs in more formal and didactic ways. Teachers, parents, and peers teach about various situations and their definitions before the child actually experiences them. Then, when the child encounters and correctly defines a situation, it usually has enough knowledge to perceive its structure and find a place within it.

But socialization is not limited to routine and familiar situations. Children not only learn standard definitions of situations, but they also learn how to create definitions of situations and how to structure novel situations themselves. In this way they are not at a loss when they encounter the unfamiliar. This is possible because socialization teaches the fundamental lesson that social life is structured, that people should expect it to be organized, and that meaning and pattern can be found or created in every situation.

The Self and Motivation

How is the self implicated in the control of conduct? First, *identity* organizes and motivates the behavior of the individual (Foote, 1951). What people do depends heavily upon the identity they have in a specific situation. Second, conduct is usually geared to the enhancement or maintenance of *self-esteem*. Other

Winslow Homer, *Snap the Whip* (1872)
The Metropolitan Museum of Art, New York, Gift of Christian A. Zabriskie, 1950. (50.41)
Games are important because they convey to the child the idea that social life is structured. The child learns not only to play a given role in a game, but also learns that all human situations are organized by roles and that a role is requisite to the ability to interact with others.

things being equal, humans act so as to secure desirable identities and favorable self-images.

Identity Each act in which the person engages or contemplates engaging has implications for identity, both in the person's own eyes and in the eyes of others. Regardless of the situation, each person must have an identity in order to act, and once he or she has that identity, every act bears upon it in some way. An identity provides the person with a self that can and must be "presented" to others (Goffman, 1959).

Consider the example of a student consulting with a professor after class. In this situation, each has an identity (conferred on them by their respective roles as teacher and student) that governs individual conduct and the interpretation of the other's conduct. In her role-making, the professor strives to live up to the professor identity. She will attempt to say professorial things, to manifest the kind of serious, businesslike appearance she thinks this identity requires. So too, will the student attempt to present himself as a student, to say and do the things that will confirm this identity, to be respectful, inquiring, and solicitous. In general, most people behave in ways consistent with their roles in particular situations. Consequently, we expect persons who are teachers and students to interact with one another differently than they would if they were strangers, colleagues, or lovers.

Moreover, people ordinarily identify with their roles as they interact with one another, and so long as the roles in which they are engaged are culturally valued, people will seek to make these roles as best they can. The professor, for example, will seek to be everything that a professor should be, and the student will strive to be the best student he can be. By the same token, each will attempt to avoid actions that might discredit them. While the professor might wish to get rid of the student as quickly as possible, she recognizes that a rude dismissal would discredit her in the eyes of the student. It would not only constitute an inadequate performance of her role, but would reflect negatively on the student's image of her. Similarly, the student might wish to challenge the professor's treatment of a given topic, but realizes he must proceed cautiously. To be openly critical might discredit his desired identity as a good student.

Self-esteem As these examples suggest, action with reference to an identity is invariably colored by a process of *evaluation.* Role-making is not a neutral process in which we merely detect what is expected of us and do it. Rather, it is something in which *standards* of performance play an important part. This evaluative process has several aspects.

First, people derive their images of themselves from the actual and imagined appraisals of others. When they engage in social interaction, people know that others are evaluating them and that others will think well or ill of them depending upon how they make their roles. Sometimes the evaluative judgments of others are conveyed directly and overtly, as when professors tell students they have failed examinations. At other times, sentiments are imputed to others, as when people imagine that others view them positively or negatively. A professor faced with a bored and restless class might imagine that her students think she is a poor teacher.

Second, evaluative judgments have a *situational* and a *cumulative* impact. In any given situation people receive (or imagine that they receive) evaluations of their performances and use these evaluations to adjust their conduct. If they believe their actions are being negatively received, they may attempt to alter their behavior so as to get a more positive response. Positive evaluations, on the other hand, incline people to continue their established lines of conduct. In each situation, people succeed or fail in varying degrees to secure positive appraisals, and thus either add to or subtract from their overall positive feelings about themselves.

Third, as the previous discussion has hinted, people are motivated by a desire to improve and sustain self-esteem. Humans wish to think well of themselves, and within certain limits, they try to act in ways that will secure the approval and respect of others. Self-esteem is not the only motivation that affects behavior, to be sure, but it is a powerful one and is a major link between individual behavior and the social order. The desire for the approval of their fellow human beings makes people susceptible to social control. Individuals adjust their behavior to fit the expectations of others in large part to secure their approval. They try to adhere to cultural norms and values because, taking the role of the generalized other, people apply these standards to themselves and form positive or negative self-images based upon their conduct.

The process of socialization depends heavily upon these kinds of sensitivity to other human beings and their social and cultural standards. Every person responds to the direct and open evaluations provided by others, seeking to adjust his or her conduct so that others will find it worthy of approval. Perhaps more important, humans respond to their imaginations of other's judgments, adjusting their behavior to what they think others expect and will approve. Thus, what people learn about society and culture is shaped by the development and presentation of the self.

Although people exert strong influences upon one another, the socialization process is by no means perfect. People do not inevitably do what they are expected to do nor learn what they are supposed to learn. One basic reason is that although people seek the approval of others, they also have other goals. A student may wish to be thought bright and honest, but he may also want to get good grades. Since doing what parents and teachers expect—attending class and working hard—may not yield the desired result, an alternative means, such as cheating on examinations, may be considered. It would be absurd to suppose that people do only what specific or generalized others approve, since they sometimes ignore these others' opinions if they think they can get away with it. Approval is a powerful motivating force, but it can be overwhelmed by other objectives.

Moreover, changing behavior to secure the favorable opinion of others is not the only option open to people. The little boy who fails to live up to parental expectations has little choice but to change his behavior. He is likely to do so not only to secure parental approval, but also because parents and other adults hold power over him. But adults have a larger set of options. The opinions of those who disapprove can be considered insignificant; for example, the professor who is criticized by his students can decide that their ill-informed opinions are of little moment. The poorly performed identity can itself be defined as insignificant; the student who fails can decide that he is not a good student of sociology but that it doesn't matter, since he doesn't think much of sociology anyway. And, finally, people can seek new audiences that will approve of their performance; a professor who is not well-received by students can turn to fellow professors, who can commiserate with him and decry the poor qualifications of contemporary students.

Socialization and social control are thus powerful, but imperfect. Human beings are fully social, since everything they are is affected by their membership in society and their dependence upon culture. But they are never fully socialized, for against the forces of society and culture are arrayed the interests, strategies, imperfect learning, and creativity of individuals.

CONTEXTS OF SOCIALIZATION

The socialization processes just described do not occur in a vacuum, but in real places and social situations. Thus, to understand socialization fully, we must examine it in its concrete social contexts.

The contexts of socialization are enormously varied, particularly in a complex society. Socialization occurs in groups ranging from juvenile gangs to bridge games and from graduate seminars to nude encounter sessions. It occurs in organizations whose main social function is socialization, such as elementary schools, and in those, such as prisons and mental hospitals, whose purpose is to correct the defects of earlier socialization. It occurs in organizations where those in command hold enormous power over their charges, such as in the military, and in contexts where participation is organized along more voluntary lines, such as in the university. It is carried on by those whose roles are specialized for socialization: by drill sergeants and teachers, therapists and counselors. And it is conducted by others—parents, siblings, policemen, and entertainers—who have many duties in addition to socialization, and who may not even think of socialization as their responsibility.

Socialization in the Family

Most of all, and first of all, socialization takes place within the family. We speak of children as being born into society, but they are in fact born into families. This basic social unit—which varies in size, complexity, and organization from society to society—is the place where the child first encounters social structure. It is the place where the infant's needs are first met, but it is also the place where social controls are first applied.

The family—whether the simple nucleus of parents and children living in a household that characterizes the American family or the more complex and extended collection of kin of other societies—is the place where self first develops. The child is first an object to others within the family. This is where the child acquires language, and with it the capacity for role-taking upon which subsequent socialization depends.

Among the most fundamental lessons learned in early socialization is the fact that the world is divided into two sexes. The child learns that there are two kinds of people in the world, male and female, and that he or she is a member of one of these categories. Although the development of sex roles is so important that we will devote a chapter entirely to this topic, several points must be made here.

The discovery that there are patterns of behavior specific to each sex marks the child's earliest exposure to social roles and their expectations. From birth, the way parents treat a child is influenced by the child's sex. Every child is, to them as well as other adults and siblings, either a boy or a girl, and thus the object a child is depends upon its sex. This differential treatment helps establish the idea of role for the child, since it is one of the ways he or she first learns that there are different types of people who occupy different positions and who are expected to behave differently. Thus, not only does the child learn to be either a male or a female, but the basic acquisition of role-taking and role-making skills occurs in the context of sex-specific roles. It is not surprising that behavioral orientations related to gender are so deeply rooted in us, when we consider that it is in this context that we develop our initial behavioral skills and sense of self.

Early socialization into sex roles begins the process whereby the child acquires identity and self-image. The child "is" a boy or a girl; that is, he or she has an identity based upon sex that is established from the earliest period and will color nearly all subsequent role performances. Moreover, to have this identity is to have the qualities and attributes believed to be associated with it in the particular culture the child learns. Parents will treat the child as having qualities appropriate to its sex, and, as it acquires role-taking and role-making skills, the child will act as if it has these characteristics. If boys are thought to be active and girls passive, these ideas will color the way the child is regarded by others, and eventually they will color the child's view of himself or herself.

The family has enormous power over the child for several reasons. From the beginning, a child's needs are met within the family, and so the bonds developed there are especially intense. The perspectives of other family members—their roles as mother, father, brother, sister, and so forth—are the first from which the child may view itself as an object. Hence, identity is, from the first, founded within the family and based upon interaction within the family. Family members are the child's first significant others, and their responses, whether positive or negative, weigh heavily at first because they are the most frequent responses the child receives.

The family exerts power over the child in a more direct sense. Parents and other family members control resources that the child needs or wants. They are the source of life's necessities, of love and affection, of information. Consequently, the family is the place where the child first grasps the idea of *power*—the idea that others have control of necessary and desirable objects.

The development of role-taking ability is closely linked to the power parents exercise over children. From the vantage point of the children, adult expectations are frequently ambiguous. They quickly learn that rewards are to be had by behaving as parents expect, but doing so is not always easy. Although parents may have fairly precise ideas about how they expect their children to behave, they may not communicate these expectations clearly. And even when rules are clearly laid down, they may be inconsistently enforced, and conforming behavior may be inconsistently rewarded. Thus, children know that much depends upon their behavior but do not always know what to do.

Children are thus under considerable pressure to become accurate role-takers. They find it to their advantage to become as keenly sensitive as they can to the powerful perspectives from which their parents are acting. Because of this, role-taking ability becomes a power resource. By anticipating parental expectations and responses, children can better adjust their behavior and influence that of their parents. And by the same token, parents, because they control resources, have less need to be accurate role-takers. They can secure their will with less need for sensitive readings of their children's perspectives (Thomas, et al., 1972).

The child is socialized within the family, but not only by parents. Grandparents, aunts, and uncles may also have some impact, even in a society characterized by the nuclear family, by serving as sources of reward and as behavioral models. Older siblings are also important, for they can serve as readily visible models of conduct for the younger child. Brothers and sisters are also sources of information that cannot be obtained directly from parents. Like other peers, they provide information about sex that parents may not provide, and siblings of the opposite sex socialize one another into the perspectives of their respective genders. Finally, second and other later children are born into what amounts to a different family from that encountered by the firstborn. Whereas the firstborn child initially enjoys a virtual monopoly on parental attention and interacts only with them, younger children interact with their older siblings as well as with the adults in the family. One result is that the self-conceptions of firstborn children are more geared to identification with parents; those of younger children tend to be more peer oriented (Gecas, 1981:175).

While socialization is purposeful activity—much of what parents do is designed to achieve certain results—not every outcome of socialization results from parental plans. For one thing, parents have many responsibilities and interests in addition to the socialization of the young: earning a living, caring for a home, cooking meals, sexual activity, social interaction with other adults, and the like. Consequently, their attention is not continuously focused on how their actions will affect their children. In contrast, children are constantly engaged in the work of socialization, for every experience represents some potential for learning. For the child, every parental act is potentially meaningful, a source of information about self or society.

Moreover, socialization outcomes do not always reflect parental intentions. In an effort to secure compliance with their demands, some parents maintain an authoritarian, coercive atmosphere with little display of warmth toward the child. Although the parental goal is children who follow the parents' lead, the evidence is that such a style of socialization creates resentment, rebellion, and insecurity in the child. Those parents who maintain an authoritative climate characterized by explanations of their expectations and by positive affect seem more successful in getting their children to identify with them and with the adult world (Gecas, 1981: 173).

Although the family is the earliest and in many ways the most important context of socialization encountered by the child, there is reason to think the influence of parents may be declining as others, such as peers and especially the media, gain in impact (Bronfenbrenner, 1970). One reason for this possible decline in parental influence is the growing reliance upon child-care facilities outside the home as more and more women, including those with small children, enter the labor force. Whether in a single-parent family or a family in which both parents work, the results are the same: Mothers spend less time with their children than previously was the case.

Day-care facilities, other family members, peers, and television have begun to play larger roles in socialization. Although we do not yet know the specific effect of socialization by others, it is clear that no day-care staff can mirror parents' values, attitudes, and definitions of the situation. And peers' orientations are frequently at odds with those of the adult world. Yet both may be becoming more influential than parents. While the results are difficult to foresee, at a minimum it seems safe to say families will be less influential in the lives of their children than they once were.

Socialization in the School

In American society, children enter kindergarten at age five, although many will have had earlier experiences in nursery school or in a child-care program. When children enter school, they enter a new social world where new roles and new expectations await them. They spend more time than before with adults to whom they are not related, and they spend time with other children, but not in the previous context of play.

Entry into school entails a transition to a new phase of the life cycle and to a new social role. Previously, the child has been protected within the family circle, where its relationships with others have been highly personalized. The roles made within this family circle have been influenced by standard cultural definitions, to be sure, but they have been experienced by the child in a concrete way because they are embodied by particular persons—the child's own parents—over an extended period. Whatever the child's conception of mother, father, or self might be, those conceptions are derived from contact with a particular set of persons with whom he or she has had intimate contact.

In contrast, the school confronts children with impersonality. That is, they begin to encounter others who are primarily known by their social roles rather than as concrete human beings with whom they have a long-standing relationship of familiarity. In place of familiar faces, children encounter unknown people engaged in much less familiar roles. Teachers change from year to year, and a child may even deal with several teachers at one time. Each child

Joseph Pickett, *Manchester Valley* (1914–18)
Oil with sand on canvas, 45½ × 60⅝ inches. Collection, The Museum of Modern Art, New York. Gift of Abby Aldrich Rockefeller.

Schools loom large in American society, much as the schoolhouse seems to dominate this painting. The school is a major agency of socialization, and education is often seen as a powerful force for social change, as well as a major avenue to personal success and social mobility.

interacts with a larger number of other children, and relationships with many of them are similarly impersonal.

One consequence of this transition is that the school is a training ground for generalized role-taking and role-making skills. In the context of this organization, children develop the requisite capacity to interact with people whom they do not know. This is a major skill in a complex society, where social interaction with non-intimates is a pervasive feature of everyday life. In a simpler society, where family and community envelop the individual at every turn, these skills are less necessary and less developed.

Socialization for impersonal role-taking is a small part of a more encompassing process of *cognitive socialization* that is the major goal of the school. A variety of cognitive competencies are (at least in theory) fostered by schools, including knowledge of important facts and skills such as reading, writing, and calculating. Schools also intend to teach both the concrete skills requisite for life in the society and the more abstract and generalizable skills. Thus, schools teach both how to balance a checkbook and how to think analytically by using algebra.

But schools teach—or fail to teach—more than cognitive skills. For the child, they are important sources of information about norms and values, not all of which are in accord with what parents have taught. Moreover, schools are a major context where children learn the dominant ideologies of their society. Schools articulate a set of beliefs that underlie and support existing social institutions. Children learn not just how to balance a checkbook, but also learn a set of ideas about money and financial institutions, as well as societal values that support and rationalize the social definitions of money and its uses.

Some argue (Bowles and Gintis, 1976) that schooling in America exists primarily to perpetuate capitalist society, and that the skills taught in school are skills required by the industrial economy. In their view, the values and norms taught in school are those that facilitate the adjustment of the individual to the existing social order. Thus, schools teach people to be responsive to the demands of their employers, to value punctuality, and to believe in existing social and economic arrangements. Not only that, but the patterned relationships between teachers and students, which stress interaction on the basis of authority and submission, resemble relationships in the occupational world.

In broad terms, such an analysis is undoubtedly correct, for in any society it would not be surprising to find that schools reflect and support prevailing social arrangements. But too much should not be made of this perspective, for it is easy to exaggerate the extent to which schools intend to buttress the existing order and the degree of their success in doing so (Hurn, 1978: 202–204). First, ideologies that support and justify existing social arrangements are not so pervasive in schools that they are without competition from alternative belief systems. Teachers may be agents of the existing order, but they also may inculcate values that are at odds with existing arrangements. Thus, teachers may teach their students to be punctual and cooperative, while at the same time imparting contrary values that stress the importance of autonomy and independence.

Second, even if schools were overwhelmingly dedicated to the preservation of capitalist society (or, for that matter, socialist society), their probability of success should not be overestimated. Just as they often fail to teach basic cognitive skills, so they also often fail to convey ideology. The reasons for such failure include the fact that in a pluralistic society, children often enter school with established values that conflict with those of the school. And throughout their school careers, they continue to be exposed to the sometimes competing values of their family, friends, churches, and synagogues. Students are thus not blank slates on which schools can write at will, creating people who fit into the existing society.

There are, of course, conditions that foster the impact of schools upon their students and make them more effective in achieving their goal of influencing basic attitudes and values. People tend to be more susceptible to the influence of organizations upon which their identities depend. In order to influence the child, therefore, the school must somehow become an important part of the child's self-conception. Athletic competitions, assemblies, school songs, yearbooks, and similar activities are, in part, efforts to develop a sense of identification with the school and of loyalty to it and its purposes. Those who identify with the school through participation in such activities are more likely to try to meet its expectations of them and will be more influenced by it.

Christopher Hurn argues that the capacity of American schools to instill such identification is less than it was a century ago (1978: 212–213). School songs are sung less frequently and other rituals are less important; there is less school spirit, and the degree of student identification with schools has consequently diminished. Schools are places that harbor increasingly diverse values and opinions on the part of both students and teachers, and the curriculum of contemporary schools is more varied and more elective than in the past. The result is that schools are more heterogeneous and less solidified organizations that command less of their members' loyalty.

Others have suggested that contemporary students do not identify with schools and their values (Larkin, 1978). They perceive widespread student alienation, and a common attitude of both teachers and students is to get through the school day with as little involvement as possible. Where such conditions prevail, the effectiveness of schools as agencies of socialization, whether cognitive or normative, will be limited.

Peer Socialization

The family and the school are socialization contexts largely under the control of adults. Each has an authority structure and a distribution of resources that yields relatively little control to the child. In each, what power the young can exercise is apt to derive either from their role-taking skills, which permit them to anticipate the whims of adults, or from the last-resort capacity to exert power through rebellion. Indeed, the child's very participation in these contexts is involuntary, for we choose neither our parents nor our schools.

Childhood and adolescent peers provide contexts of socialization that differ sharply from school and family. Among others of approximately the same age (and often of the same sex), the young person is a status equal, with no one preordained as the leader. Instead, patterns of unequal power and authority emerge from interaction within the peer group. Moreover, the peer group is a voluntary association. Although peer groups exert a powerful influence over the young, and attachment to a group is usually a compelling interest, they can nevertheless be left at will.

In American society, peer groups are generally thought to be—and are—powerful contexts of socialization, often supplementing, but sometimes working directly counter to, socialization by adults. Children and adolescents spend considerable time with peers, and important kinds of socialization occur in their company. Why are peer groups so important, and what do the young learn within their boundaries?

Two factors seem particularly responsible for the existence of peer groups in American society. First, when children attend school they are removed from the immediate territory of the family. From ages five to eighteen, children spend seven or more hours away from home each day. Although much of this time is spent under the watchful eyes of teachers, children are still much more on their own at school than at home. They associate with one another on the way to school, at school (at lunch, during recess, before and after school), and on the way home. They are free to associate with one another to a degree and in ways that would not be possible if socialization took place exclusively at home.

Second, cultural definitions of the child and adolescent have an impact of their own. In contemporary American society, childhood and adolescence are considered to be distinct phases of the life cycle, and children and adolescents are thought to have special needs, characteristics, and dispositions that distinguish them from one another and from adults. Adolescents, for example, are thought to be especially susceptible to their emotions and to be preoccupied with establishing an identity. Even though the young are seen as becoming progressively more like adults as they mature, they are defined as different creatures who inhabit their own social world. Cultural definitions that treat them as different from adults and place them in their own social world thus help to give birth to the peer group.

In their own company, beyond the scrutiny of adults, peers have some capacity to create and transmit their own culture, rather than relying exclusively upon the culture received from adults. They can eschew the values of their parents and teachers, creating their own values to take their place. Sometimes the culture created within the adolescent peer group is directly opposed to that received from adults. Thus, where schools and parents stress obedience and hard work, the peer group may stress fun, kicks, rebellion, and even illegal activities.

Although peer groups thrive on a sense of contrast between themselves and the adult world, seldom do they generate seriously illegal activity. To do so requires exposure to adult models of crime, criminal opportunities, and a degree of alienation from conventional adults not characteristic of most adolescents. More typically, peer groups provide a context where, free of constant adult control and supervision, children and adolescents socialize one another in ways not provided for in their contacts with adults.

Viktor Gecas (1981) suggests that socialization in peer groups is particularly important in three areas. First, the peer group provides for the further development and elaboration of the self. The self developed in the family and school is heavily influenced by the authority structure of these contexts, where the child is someone to whom things are done and over whom control is exercised. The peer group is egalitarian—the child or adolescent is one among equals—and thus provides a new perspective from which to view the self. In the company of peers, the child can view itself as an autonomous, powerful individual, rather than as one in the thrall of others. Important and influential bonds are established between friends, but the friendship role is intrinsically less constraining than that of child or student. Friendship is an interpersonal role built out of the interaction of specific individuals, not a role rigidly shaped by cultural definitions. Hence, it permits more latitude for participants to experiment with their behavior and their personal styles.

Second, because of this greater behavioral tolerance, the peer group provides opportunities not available in school or at home for the development of interpersonal skills. As Gary Fine (1980) points out, the friendship bond permits mistakes to be made without fear of excessive condemnation. Friends can correct one another's mistakes of self-presentation, thus permitting the progressive refinement of the self presented to others. This can be done while avoiding the destruction of identity that might occur were mistakes made in the presence of adults. Outside of friendships, peers can be highly critical of one another. The adolescent girl who is sharply critical of the appearance or manners of another is herself engaging in a presentation of self, while at the same time displaying the norms of her group. Her target (for the most part) is protected from this criticism by her own friendship bonds and membership in some other peer group.

Third, peer groups provide for socialization unavailable from adults. Much sexual knowledge and lore, for example, is acquired neither from parents nor through sex education in the schools, but from peers. This is particularly true of the practice (as opposed to the theory) of sex. It is commonplace among adolescents to complain that classes in sex education never quite get to the point of revealing how people "do it." Generalities about "sperm traveling through the vagina" do not satisfy the curiosity of adolescents who are interested in the mechanics of lovemaking as well as in what it feels like and who initiates it. Peers, often older adolescents, provide this information.

Peer groups are potent socializing influences because the ratio of socializers to those socialized is very low. While a single teacher may deal with twenty to thirty students at a time, the typical peer group socialization experience is either one-on-one or many-on-one. The influence of the peer group is thus likely to be heavy simply because each individual is outnumbered.

It should not be supposed, however, that adolescent peer groups have a monolithic impact upon the values and beliefs of their members. Sometimes the powerful influence of peer groups is more the result of misperception than of the existence of widely shared group norms. Since teenagers value friendships and membership in their peer groups, they are reluctant to reveal their disagreement with one another or to depart too far from what they perceive to be the group's expectations. Thus what seems to them and to outsiders to be conformity with the group's norms may, in fact, be the result of the fear of sanctions rather than of positive commitment. There may, in fact, be no shared norms, but if individuals believe they exist and are fearful of being sanctioned for failing to live up to them, they will behave in accord with what they think the norms are.

Adult Contexts of Socialization

We asserted at the beginning of this chapter that socialization is not a finite process, but one that continues from birth until death. In a broad sense, learning never ceases. While an individual's basic values and orientations may emerge by early adulthood, they do not forever remain unchanged. Our images of ourselves are modified as we have contact with new people. The values we espouse are influenced by the opinions of those around us, so that as we change jobs or residences, we also change ourselves in both modest and major ways. As we mature, we are exposed to different expectations and experiences, and the skills necessary for coping must be learned as circumstances change. Life does not stand still.

What specifically do people learn as they move as adults throughout the stages of the life cycle? Among the earliest adult experiences is entry into a job or career, and this requires considerable learning. First, an occupation may require special skills that must be learned through prior training (as in medical school), on-the-job training (as in an apprenticeship), or some combination of the two. Some occupations are highly structured in their provisions for training and certification to practice the occupation. Physicians attend medical school, serve as interns and residents, and take examinations. In contrast, unskilled or semiskilled machine operators may have only brief instruction in the skills required for a job.

Second, people in an occupation learn about the career track of their line of work, then learn (or fail to learn) how to advance along it. Learning the career track of a business executive, for example, entails developing a set of expectations about the pace at which one should advance through the ranks. It also involves learning how to look for other jobs and how to use job-changing as a way of moving up. The individual must also learn about the reward structure of the occupation—which efforts are rewarded and which are not. Often junior executives must find a sponsor within the organization, someone who will promote their careers and lend a helping hand along the way. Such *mentors* are concrete models who, in addition to promoting a career, embody the values and norms of the profession or organization and thus socialize by example (Zuckerman, 1977: Ch. 4). In occupations, as in any activity, one must "learn the ropes" (Schein, 1968) in order to survive and succeed, and such mentors are key people in this process of learning.

Third, an important part of socialization in the occupational world is learning a realistic view of the occupation itself (Geer, 1972; Becker, et al., 1961). New members of professions or those who have just begun training are frequently very idealistic about the goals of the profession and how it should be practiced. Medical students, for example, have high hopes for their capacity to relieve human suffering and possess an idealized image of the physician. One effect of socialization in medical school is to replace these ideals with a more realistic view of the physician's capacities and character and to acclimate students to a world of work in which they must to some degree emotionally insulate themselves from their patients' suffering.

Fourth, members of any occupation learn to cope with failure. Particularly in societies where all are encouraged to advance as far as they can and to view failure to reach the top as a personal failure, adjustment to failure is a major problem. Since only a few will reach the top, most must lower their expectations and find ways of explaining and enjoying the success they do achieve. In Chapter 2, we described how musicians and baseball players deal with their inability to make it in the big leagues by redefining their goals, seeing their original effort to reach the top as not worth its cost in energy and time, and believing that there are more enjoyable ways to live their lives. This kind of learning also entails a redefinition of the self, for the success goals that were once central to the person's identity must now be moved out of center stage. Sometimes this self-redefinition requires a change of self-image. Many who hoped to excel at their occupations but who achieve modest success have to come to terms with the idea that they do not possess the ability or drive they once thought they had.

Arguing that adults pass through regular and identifiable stages of development, Levinson (1978) calls attention to a "mid-life transition," which occurs approximately between the ages of forty and forty-five. During these years, men (Levinson did not study women) ask themselves what they have done with their lives and whether they are getting from life what they really want. The transition is often a time of crisis, for a man must come to terms with his past by stripping away any illusions and false hopes on which his life has been based. It is at this time that he develops plans for a future, one based on a more realistic assessment of his whole life situation. Some men strike out in wholly new directions, trying a new career, for example, getting divorced, or experimenting with new life styles. The transition involves not only new activities and social involvements, but also a new self, a new identity. When people learn to act in new ways, they also learn new conceptions of themselves.

Although it is clear that people must learn to adjust their self-conceptions as they move through the life cycle, not everyone experiences a midlife crisis. Some researchers believe that most people experience little turmoil associated with these adjustments (Clausen, 1972). Curt Tausky and Robert Dubin (1965), for example, found that as men grow older, they tend to measure their accomplishments by comparing them with the social status from which they started, rather than with the top of their particular career ladder. Thus, a man who gained a higher occupational standing than did his father could feel satisfied, even if he did not make it as far as he had planned. Here, culture provides the symbolic materials for the reconstruction and protection of self-conception. Although upward social mobility is a value in American society, and people are thus urged to be as successful as they can be, it is permissible to use a relative standard of accomplishment and to emphasize the obstacles overcome rather than the distance traveled.

Adult socialization is not confined to the occupational world. Passage through the life cycle entails the continual acquisition of new roles and the shedding of old roles. People cease to be adolescents and become adults; they change from single to married, from being childless to being parents. As their children grow up, they become, successively, parents of infants, children, adolescents, and adult sons and daughters. Even when people become old, they still must learn new roles: as grandparents or as widows and widowers. Learning is involved in each role transition, for people must shed patterns of behavior associated with an old role and learn patterns appropriate to the new one. And wherever there are changes in key roles, there are also changes in identity and self-image. People learn to think of themselves as "parents" or as "old," and they learn to display the qualities associated with these roles.

Thus, for example, the new parent must learn skills not previously required in other roles. In addition to providing for the physical and psychological well-being of an infant, the new parent must learn to put off satisfaction of personal wants and needs in deference to those of the child. The new parent must learn about children: what they need, how they express their wants, and what to expect of them at various stages of development.

Socialization for parenthood occurs in a variety of contexts. One's own parents are not only role-models but also a source of information, just as one's own childhood memories provide some of the requisite information. Increasingly, as members of American society turn to experts to meet their everyday needs, experts in the care of children have begun to play a major role in parental socialization. Parents-to-be take courses in infant care, read books and magazine articles about children (Dr. Benjamin Spock has single-handedly socialized several generations of American parents), and watch television programs. Parents also learn from experience (which may be particularly tough on their firstborn children). Finally, parents socialize one another by sharing experiences and knowledge.

Like socialization in childhood, adult socialization is powerfully influenced by the development and enhancement of the self. Subject to many different contexts of socialization, children and adolescents frequently choose values, behavioral styles, and group membership and loyalty on the basis of their impact upon the self. Other things being equal, the young will value and be influenced by those social relationships that support or enhance their desired conceptions of themselves. It is no different for adults. They seek to define themselves as favorably as they can, to learn to act in ways that will secure the support of others for their self-conceptions, and to engage in those activities that confirm or enhance identities. Thus, the same drive for self-esteem that marks socialization during childhood also marks socialization during adulthood.

CONCLUSION

Socialization is the process that makes us human. If there is a single theme that characterizes the sociological view of socialization, it is the idea that this process is a constant in human life. People are never fully socialized, nor are they ever fully formed. They are always in a process of becoming, a process that is profoundly influenced by the structure of social life that surrounds them. People become what they are at any given point not because of innate developmental processes that simply unfold, but because of their interaction with other human beings, interaction that is shaped and influenced by social structure.

Although socialization makes people human and exposes them to the powerful influence of society, it does not make them mere putty in the hands of others. People are influenced by self-interest as well as by the expectations of others. Their drives to secure their own goals and enhance conceptions of themselves are powerful. And socialization, even though ceaseless, is never perfect; no one is the beneficiary or victim of a complete mastery of the culture and a complete mastering by the culture. Imperfect, self-interested, self-enhancing creatures that they are, people resist society, even as they rely upon it and take it within themselves.

SUGGESTED READINGS

ARIÈS, PHILLIPE. *Centuries of Childhood: A Social History of Family Life* (New York: Vintage, 1965).

BECKER, HOWARD S., et al. *Boys in White* (Chicago: University of Chicago Press, 1961).

DENZIN, NORMAN K. "Play, Games, and Interaction: The Contexts of Childhood Socialization," *Sociological Quarterly*, 16 (Autumn 1975), 458–478.

ERIKSON, ERIK H. *Childhood and Society*, rev. ed. (New York: Norton, 1964).

KOLLER, MARVIN R. and OSCAR W. RITCHIE. *Sociology of Childhood* (Englewood Cliffs: Prentice-Hall, 1978).

LEVINSON, DANIEL J. *The Seasons of a Man's Life* (New York: Knopf, 1978).

ROSE, PETER I., ed. *Socialization and the Life Cycle* (New York: St. Martin's, 1979).

SPIRO, MELFORD. *Children of the Kibbutz*, rev. ed. (Cambridge, Mass.: Harvard University Press, 1975).

7

Deviance and Society

In every human society there are people whose behavior elicits strong reactions from others. They steal, rape, assault, murder, lie, cheat, or engage in other acts that make people upset, resentful, angry, fearful, and determined to do something to stamp out this conduct and to punish the offender. Sometimes these same reactions are precipitated by people whose actions are not at fault but who belong to some stigmatized category. Homosexuals, cripples, blind persons, and the mentally ill, among others, behave like so-called "normal" people most of the time, yet they frequently engender distaste, revulsion, fear, avoidance, and efforts to control and punish when their identities become known to others.

Sociologists study these phenomena under the rubric of *deviance*. This chapter answers two essential questions about deviance: First, why do such forms of behavior exist? Why do some individuals act in ways that depart from social expectations? What forces produce these kinds of behavior? And second, what is the social significance of deviance? What impact do these forms of conduct have on society itself?

THE ESSENCE OF DEVIANCE

The kinds of persons and behavior encompassed by the sociologist's concept of deviance are so diverse that the nonspecialist is entitled to be suspicious of this category. After all, what do theft and mental illness have in common? What makes assault and homosexuality similar to one another? The armed robber violates the law by stealing other people's valuables, and people tend to see this as willful behavior that deserves swift and strong punishment. In contrast, although people may be upset by the behavior of the schizophrenic, particularly if the person is a friend or relative, this conduct is seen as a medical condition beyond the person's control. Assault inflicts direct harm upon someone, whereas homosexual acts between consenting adults do not. Yet to many people, the very idea of sexual acts between members of the same sex is far more upsetting than physical violence. Homosexuality is viewed as "unnatural," whereas violence may be regarded as an undesirable, but still a "normal" and "understandable" result of anger.

Deviance and Cultural Variations

From a sociological perspective, *behavior is deviant if it is so defined by the members of a given society*. People at various times and in different cultures look at deviance in a similar way, regardless of the specific content of the deviance. It is not the nature of a given act or category of persons that makes it or them intrinsically deviant, however, but a cultural framework of ideas and definitions. And the classification of a specific individual as deviant does not stem from the inherent nature of that person, but depends upon the application of such ideas and definitions.

Ideas about what constitutes deviant behavior vary markedly over time and from one culture to another. In American society, for example, both male and female homosexuality have been considered to be deviant by many people who regard sexual contact between members of the same sex as unnatural, disgusting, and possibly dangerous. Yet these attitudes have been changing in recent years, with more individuals "coming out" and living openly as gays. What was once clearly deviant is now less so, suggesting that it is social definition rather than anything intrinsic to homosexuals or their acts that makes homosexuality deviant.

A similar point can be made about the use of drugs as a form of deviance. The use of alcohol, marijuana, and other drugs, for example, has been, at various times, strongly condemned, tolerated, and even valued. From 1919 to 1938 in the United States (and from 1917 to 1919 in Canada), the production and sale of alcoholic beverages was prohibited as a result of a temperance campaign that began during the nineteenth century. Marijuana, the use of which had been legal until the 1930s, became the target of federal legislation, and during the heyday of the counterculture in the 1960s, prosecutions for the possession and sale of marijuana reached an all-time high. Later, during the 1970s, a movement to decriminalize the use of this drug began. In these instances, what was once socially acceptable behavior had become, for a time, a serious form of deviance.

These examples also illustrate another point. Even when an act is defined as deviant, a substantial portion of the population may continue to engage in it. Prohibition was widely ignored and marijuana continued in use even when vigorously controlled. The tendency to engage in proscribed conduct is not confined to a complex society such as ours. Among the Siriono, a hunting-and-gathering society of the tropical forest of eastern Bolivia, there are strong norms that emphasize that food should be shared. The Siriono live in extremely marginal circumstances where starvation is a constant threat. It is deviant to hoard food, yet people do. Indeed, it may be more common to hoard food than to share it with others. Sharing, it seems, is likely to occur only when food is abundant (Holmberg, 1969).

Behavior that is widely condemned in one society may be tolerated or even encouraged in another. Suicide provides a classic illustration of this point. Frowned upon generally in Western society, suicide is especially proscribed by the Roman Catholic Church. Suicide creates a social stigma for the survivors—it is something they have to "live down"—and the unsuccessful suicide finds his or her identity changed. The person becomes "suicidal," someone to be watched, someone whose behavior is an indication of mental illness.

In other cultures, however, there are circumstances in which suicide is permissible, if not mandatory. Among the Plains Indians of North America, for example, it was permissible for a warrior to commit suicide by staking himself on the battlefield so that he could not defend himself against the blows of his enemies. And among the Eskimos, an aging parent who felt himself a burden on the group and who wished to die could call upon his children to assist in his suicide by pushing him into the freezing waters or even plunging a knife into his heart (Weyer, 1924). This behavior strikes Americans as cruel and heartless, and we cannot imagine ourselves engaging in it. No doubt, it is not a pleasant or easy act for an Eskimo, yet it is one a parent could expect and a child could legitimately perform.

Certain kinds of behavior occur in most, perhaps all, societies and are also regarded universally as deviant. The taking of human life is considered deviant in all societies, but what constitutes murder is subject to cultural definition. In American society, for example, killing without intending to kill does not fall into the same legal category as a premeditated act of murder. The former is called *manslaughter*, and the latter, *homicide*.

Manslaughter usually receives mild punishment, if any, while homicide may call for severe penalties. Or to put it more directly, killing someone in an automobile accident is not the same as taking a gun and shooting him.

Theft is also a fairly universal form of behavior that is widely condemned. The same is true of violence. Yet even in these cases, societies differ in the way they define and deal with such conduct. Among the Mbuti Pygmies of the Ituri forest in Africa, stealing from one another is regarded with great horror. It is an unimaginable thing to do, but it nevertheless occurs. Yet the Pygmies think nothing of stealing from nearby Bantu villagers, whom they regard as animals. When one Pygmy does steal from another, the members of the group find it very hard to deal with, and they seem more interested in maintaining harmony and good interpersonal relationships than with administering justice (Turnbull, 1961).

As this example suggests, the fact that a form of behavior is considered deviant does not prevent it from occurring, nor does it mean that when such an act does occur, somebody will be charged and punished. All societies contain a great deal of unrecorded and unnoticed deviance. People do all kinds of things that violate law and custom and get away with it; that is, their behavior is not noted, and even if it is, they may escape the consequences. In a complex society such as ours, the capacity of an individual to escape the consequences of an act frequently depends upon that individual's social status. This is a matter we will consider in more detail later in this chapter.

Deviance is thus a complex phenomenon. What and who is deviant is a matter of cultural definition, not invariant reality. Yet there are some generalizations that can be made about the nature of deviance. There are three features that make these diverse forms of conduct and types of persons alike in the eyes of sociologists.

First, *deviance involves perceived threats to social order*. When people observe an act considered to be deviant or learn of its occurrence, they are apt to feel that their orderly and predictable social world is in some way under attack or endangered. Second, *deviance evokes efforts to control those whose behavior and/or persons are considered deviant.* The deviant is someone about whom people feel "something ought to be done." Third, *deviance brings discredit to the deviant.* People attribute a special negative essence to those who engage in deviant acts or fall into a deviant category. Deviants are variously regarded as bad, evil, sinful, deranged, amoral, or possessed by demons. Their deviance becomes their most important identity, one that controls their relationships with other people.

Deviance and Social Order

Deviance engenders a sense of threat. Sometimes this threat is immediate and very personal; when confronted with an assailant, we feel physically endangered. But, in a more fundamental sense, deviance threatens—or is perceived to threaten—not just the life or property of its victims, but also their ideas about society and what is orderly, predictable, and assured. The murderer, the thief, the homosexual, and the psychotic have in common the capacity to scare and upset people, to make them fearful, and to lead them to doubt the orderliness and predictability of the world in which they live.

People commonly talk about and define a given form of deviance by invoking norms. People think of murder as morally wrong as well as a violation of the law. Armed robbery is a crime. Homosexuality is viewed by some people as sin, a term that anchors normative definitions of conduct in religious beliefs. Whatever terms people use, however, deviance seems to involve behavior that departs from what people feel ought to be, or it involves people who do not seem to have the proper moral fiber or religious character. This is a normative way of viewing deviance.

Norms are an important part of our conception of social order. Thus, it is not surprising that people use norms to classify and define deviance. But when a deviant act is socially noticed, as when a murder is reported in the newspapers, it is not just a *particular* norm that is seen as being challenged. In a more fundamental sense, it is our expectation that people will behave in an orderly and normatively predictable way that is violated. Deviance threatens our expectation that people will behave predictably and do what they are supposed to do. Behavior that departs from what we wish it to be thus threatens our sense of what is. It is a challenge to our definition of social reality. When someone is murdered, we wonder "What is the world coming to?" We are apt to see society as falling apart, with chaos right around the corner.

Not all deviance, however, is conceived or discussed in terms of norms. In modern American society, people do not think of the mentally ill or the physically handicapped as willfully engaging in immoral or nonnormative conduct. The psychotic may hear nonexistent voices, the depressed person may be reclusive, and the deaf person may have speech that people think is difficult to understand, but the behavior of these persons is not conceived in normative terms. We do not classify their acts as wrong or sinful, nor do we hold them accountable for their conduct in the same way we do others.

Nevertheless, there is a sense in which these persons and their conduct are threatening to "normals" even when the normal individual recognizes such a reaction and tries to suppress it. People avoid the mentally ill and the physically deformed, almost as if contact with them might prove contaminating. Their presence is unsettling to many people, and interaction with them is thought to be difficult or impossible. They are representatives of abnormality, and as such they almost seem to challenge everyday conceptions of how people should look, talk, and act.

Deviance and Social Control

Sociologists use the term *social control* to designate social arrangements employed to keep the behavior of some people in line with the expectations of others. A frown or a sharp word reminds a child of a parent's expectations and serves as a signal that dire consequences may follow if the child does not get in line. Advice to a party guest to "stop being a wet blanket and have fun" serves notice that the individual should start behaving in accord with the proper definition of the situation. Similarly, when people try to excuse or justify such minor misdeeds and failings as being late for meetings or irritable and grouchy in their dealings with friends, they are responding to others' efforts to employ social controls.

In such everyday situations, people interacting with one another exert social control directly on behalf of themselves. Deviance, however, involves persons and activities thought to require *collective* attention. Because deviance is perceived as a threat to social order, it is viewed as a matter of concern to the society as a whole. A crime is not just of interest to its victim, but "belongs" to society. It is something about which people feel that society should do something. Thus, the proper response to murder in Western society is not revenge by the victim's kin, but the institution of formal procedures involving the police and courts. There are societies, of course, in which revenge by a victim or kin is viewed as the proper response to a serious crime. Even then, however, those who take revenge do so as agents of the society and do not act only in their own behalf.

The social control of deviance takes many different forms, depending upon the society, its prevailing forms of deviance, and its cultural definitions of proper ways to deal with deviants. The idea that punishment is the proper response to deviance is quite widespread, but punishment has taken many different forms throughout history, including death, torture, beating, mutilation, banishment, imprisonment, and enslavement. Punishment itself, however, is carried out only partly as a means of social control. In American society, we believe that criminals will be deterred from crime if punishment is swift and sure. (This may or may not be true, but it is still part of our system of cultural beliefs.) But punishment has other, less visible objectives. Since crime is a perceived threat to social order, punishment is a symbolic means of restoring that order. When a thief is imprisoned or a murderer hanged, it is as if the members of society collectively reassured one another that normality has been restored. As Durkheim (1893) suggested, crime outrages the "collective conscience," and punishment symbolizes that outrage as well as the reassertion of collective values and beliefs.

The social control of deviance also entails the *isolation* and *treatment* of the deviant person. Prisons punish; they also remove the offender from society, maintaining an orderly society and preventing the deviant from threatening it further, or so it is thought. Mental hospitals, as well as institutions for the retarded and handicapped, also serve this isolating function—keeping the deviant away from others who feel they might be injured or contaminated. Places such as prisons, mental hospitals, and custodial institutions are also conceived as places of treatment. Our contemporary ideas define the prison as a place of rehabilitation as well as of punishment. Criminals are supposed to learn the error of their past ways and develop attitudes and skills that will enable them to return to a productive life in society; the mental hospital is supposed to cure mental illness; and the institution for the retarded aims to teach these individuals the skills they are capable of learning.

We are not concerned here with the question of whether these institutions successfully accomplish their treatment goals. In all probability they are more successful in isolating deviants than in rehabilitating them. Nonetheless, in this and all societies, people invoke social controls on the basis of theories provided by their cultures. When deviance occurs or is noticed, these theories are brought into play. Social agencies and organizations spring into action to do their assigned work of social control. In the process, some kind of control is exerted over the person and activities of the deviant, and the collective conscience, having been outraged, is restored.

Deviance and Identity

The third defining attribute of deviance is that it provides the deviant with an identity—one that is negative, controlling, and "sticky." The person who is labeled, categorized, and denounced as a deviant acquires a social identity. In the eyes of others, that person *is* a murderer, thief, homosexual, or whatever. To acquire a deviant identity is to be differentiated from those who are "normal." Deviants become subject to *typifications* of their particular deviance category. People who murder, rob, have sexual intercourse with someone of the same sex, or are diagnosed as mentally ill come to be perceived through the framework of standard typifications. Their motives, actions, and character are perceived in typical ways. Thus, murderers may be "cold-blooded," homosexuals "perverts," and the mentally ill "dangerous."

The social identities of all kinds of deviants are similar because they are viewed negatively. Deviants acquire a *negative essence* when they acquire a deviant

Ben Shahn, ***Brothers*** **(1946)**
Tempera. 38$^{15}/_{16}$ × 25 $^{15}/_{16}$. Hirshhorn Museum and Sculpture Garden, Smithsonian Institution.

Deviant identities shape our perceptions of people and interpretations of their conduct. The title of this painting enables us to typify the actions of two men seen as brothers embracing. How different their activities and motives would seem if we identified these men as homosexuals!

identity (Katz, 1972). It is not only that people frown on the behavior of the murderer or the prostitute, but that they attribute a negative essence to the person. Deviant persons are symbols. People believe that not only through the behavior of deviants, but through their very being they *embody* what is frowned upon in a society. Conversely, the conduct and personal character of a few members of society are widely admired; war heroes, extraordinarily successful persons, saints, and the like do not merely live up to social standards, but exceed them. By doing so, their positive essence symbolizes good. Deviants, in like manner, do not merely fall short of societal standards, but negate them. Their negative essence symbolizes evil.

In their everyday lives, people make a great variety of social roles, and so have rather complex identities. A person has an identity determined by occupation at one moment and by family membership at another. Underlying various situated identities is a generalized sense of self as composed of many aspects. As a rule, people are accorded treatment that reflects this complexity. In a complex society, which requires people to assume different identities at different times, we recognize that people are simultaneously many things.

But deviant identities are controlling. When a person acquires a deviant identity, that individual comes to be viewed primarily, if not exclusively, in terms of that identity. Deviance becomes a paramount fact with which the person must deal and that others almost invariably take into account. Those who define homosexuality as deviance, for example, are apt to see this as the central fact of the homosexual's life. The person's other activities and involvements are seen as somehow revolving around the fact of homosexuality. The gay person, however, is apt to take a very different view. Although some gay men participate in a subculture in which sexual contact is a constant preoccupation, most homosexuals differ from heterosexuals only in sexual preference. In their attitudes, political affiliations, musical preferences, and appearance they are otherwise indistinguishable from other people (see Goode, 1984).

That others regard a deviant identity as all-important in governing their interaction with a deviant does not necessarily mean that deviants accept this view. Nevertheless, the way others treat us has a powerful effect on the way we see ourselves. The individual who is provided with an identity and a typification that goes with it is, in effect, provided with a ready-made social role. People expect homosexuals, murderers, psychotics, and thieves to be like their typifications, and they treat them as if they are their typifications.

This treatment provides deviants with cues as to how they ought to behave. Mentally disturbed persons, for example, are apt to be confused and to be highly receptive to cues they receive from others, particularly when they are first defined as ill (Scheff, 1966). Accordingly, they are likely to accept the deviant label and even to act as they think a mentally ill person would act. They make what they regard as an appropriate role. And even if typifications held by others do not themselves shape the conduct of the deviant, the deviant identity is apt to influence the deviant's view of self to some degree. To be labeled delinquent, mentally ill, homosexual, or otherwise deviant is to be given a place in the social world and a set of terms and ideas for conceiving of self.

For these and other reasons, deviant identities tend to be "sticky." Once attached, they may be difficult to remove. They are not completely indelible, of course, for this is something that varies according to the type of deviance and the seriousness with which it is viewed. The person convicted of premeditated murder, especially if it is committed for money, acquires an identity that is difficult to change. Other criminals tend to be viewed as capable of rehabilitating themselves. Although they may have the negative essence of a deviant identity, it is believed they can shed both the essence and the identity. Indeed, that is what is generally meant by *rehabilitation*; people lose their deviant character and so merit being treated as ordinary people.

THE CAUSES OF DEVIANCE

Although the forms and incidence of deviance vary markedly around the globe, no society is without some kinds of deviance. Theft and violent behavior, for example, are to be found everywhere, although societies define and react to them in different ways. People whose unusual behavior causes them to be treated as mentally ill in Western society are to be found everywhere, but their social classification and treatment varies considerably. They may be considered mad, held to be possessed by demons, or regarded as having special gifts.

How can we account for the universality of these forms of conduct and at the same time explain differences in the way they are culturally defined? Forms of conduct that are sometimes tolerated or approved—homosexuality and drug use are good examples—are later subject to condemnation. How can such changes be explained? Given a set of cultural definitions of what is deviant and what is not, some people are never touched by deviance, while others become deeply involved in one or more deviant activities. How can we explain who becomes deviant and who does not? And even when people engage in behavior that is defined as deviant and are noticed and apprehended, they may not necessarily be perceived as threatening, provoke strong efforts at social control, or have their identities transformed. How can we account for such variations in the application of cultural definitions of deviance?

The task of explaining deviance is made difficult by the diversity of the phenomenon. The concept of deviance embraces very different kinds of behavior that may ocur in a variety of situations and have diverse motives. This problem of explaining deviance can be seen in two examples: homosexuality and theft.

Aside from the fact that homosexuality is not everywhere defined as deviance, explaining its occurrence is complicated by several additional factors. First, there is not one kind of homosexual person, nor is there a single kind of homosexuality (see Goode, 1984: 361–371). The world of gay men differs from that of gay women. There are more male than female homosexuals, males have a larger number of sexual partners, and sex itself looms larger in their lives. Moreover, there are really several gay subcultures rather than one. Some gay men lead lives that are indistinguishable from those of heterosexuals and may hide their sexual preferences from their associates and their friends. Others, less numerous but more visible, lead more active lives as homosexuals, frequenting gay bars, baths, and other meeting places to find sexual partners. Even if we could confidently explain why some men develop a sexual preference for men (and social and behavioral scientists cannot yet do this) we still would have to account for these differences in life styles.

Moreover, the activities of homosexuals prove to be extraordinarily diverse. If we define homosexuality as genital contact involving members of the same sex, there is a seemingly limitless variety of contexts and meanings associated with such activity. Some men, typically married, make use of public restrooms and other locales as places in which to have impersonal sexual contacts (see Humphries, 1970). These restrooms (called "tearooms" by those involved) are frequented by homosexuals who perform oral sex upon these visitors, the "tearoom trade." The visitors, who are likely to stop by these places after a day at work before they go home to wives and children, do not fellate others, nor do they think of themselves as homosexuals. They are looking for impersonal sex and find this the cheapest and least-involving way of getting it. Homosexual contact also occurs in such contexts as prisons and the military, where men are isolated from women for long periods of time. In these places, too, men who engage in sexual contact with other men do not see themselves as homosexual. On release they go back to their heterosexual lives.

In explaining a complex phenomenon such as homosexuality, social scientists cannot rely on simple formulations. It is clear that some men develop strong sexual preferences for their own sex, but beyond that little is clear. Sexual preference is expressed in diverse ways. And what people consider to be homosexual may conceal diverse motives, situational definitions, and self-conceptions. The social scientist who seeks to explain homosexuality had best be careful!

The same is true of something as seemingly simple as theft, a form of conduct that is universally found and generally condemned. Theft in American society takes many forms, occurs in diverse situations, and has different meanings attached to it. Money and property get stolen in many different ways: homes are burglarized; people are mugged in the streets; banks are robbed; stores are subject to shoplifting. These are common and highly visible forms of theft—alike in the sense that they violate various laws against larceny, but different because they are dissimilar activities carried out by persons who are unlike one another in social background, motivation, and risks of apprehension. The suburban teenager who attempts to shoplift a tape for kicks in the local mall is engaged in an act that differs in some respects from that of the urban teenager who mugs for fun and profit. The burglar and the armed robber have different skills and outlooks; the former might well be unwilling to take the risks associated with the use of a weapon in the crimes committed by the latter.

Moreover, even though the American public is very aware of the crimes just mentioned because they are so frequently reported in the mass media and made the object of political campaigns, there are other, far less visible forms of larceny. The Internal Revenue Service reports that growing numbers of Americans are cheating on their income taxes by failing to report income, claiming deductions to which they are not entitled, or falsifying business records. Employees bring home office supplies and equipment, make personal use of company cars and telephones, and embezzle money from their employees. Corporate officials steal from the public by engaging in illegal price-fixing. The term applied by Sutherland (1949) to such behavior—white collar crime—itself underscores the fact that many people consider these forms of theft to be different from burglary and armed robbery.

These kinds of crime may not even be thought of as theft by those who engage in them. In theory, there is no difference between stealing $200 of office supplies and stealing a $200 watch. Yet, if caught, the burglar and the "honest" employee will probably be treated differently by the law, and they will define themselves differently as well. The burglar is less likely to get off; the employee is probably less likely to be prosecuted. The burglar may dispute his guilt in a particular charge but makes no bones about being what he is—a thief. The employee may admit a mistake but argue that he isn't really a thief and should not be punished. He has "suffered enough," he will say, just by being caught and exposed, and should not have to endure further punishment by going to jail or paying a fine.

The forms of deviance are thus so numerous, its varieties so diverse, and its complexities so great that deviance resists easy and straightforward explanation. We can suggest some general ideas that sociologists have developed, but we want to emphasize that none of these theories taken by itself is a complete explanation. We will first ask why some forms of behavior are defined as deviant and then consider why people engage in them.

Why Behavior Is Defined as Deviant

As we have suggested, what is considered deviance varies across societies and historical eras. Thus, the first task is to explain why a given society considers a form of conduct to be deviant, and how such conceptions change over time.

For some kinds of deviance, what must be explained is not why a specific form of conduct is prohibited, but rather the scope of the prohibition. For example, it would be difficult to find a human society in which violence or murder are categorically approved. Directed against the members of one's own family, group, or village, violence is undesirable and condemned. It seems to require no complicated explanation to understand why; people, we may assume, just naturally defend themselves and do not like to be physically harmed.

This is only partially correct. What constitutes violence is a matter of social and cultural definition rather than an absolute category. For a child raised in a culture in which spanking is an acceptable means of punishment, a thrashing may be painful and humiliating, but it does not fall within the child's conception of violence. It does not lead to the same response as an attempted beating by a peer because it is defined differently. Similarly, behavior that is considered violent in one context may be approved in another. Many human groups condemn any violent behavior when it is directed against their own group members, but tolerate it when it is directed against others. Neighboring tribal groups that speak different languages and have different cultures often regard one another as subhuman and find it quite acceptable to inflict atrocities on one another. The Nazi government's treatment and killing of Jews and Gypsies was tolerated by many Germans who accepted the "fact" that some people were not human.

As these examples point out, a form of conduct may be regarded as deviant in some contexts but not in others. Killing is ordinarily prohibited, but becomes a valued and encouraged act in wartime. People may condemn violence but nevertheless find many situations in which it is a useful and appropriate way to act. Some groups become targets of the hostility of others and are exempted from ordinary restrictions on behavior. And in many instances, a form of behavior may be condemned but at the same time delegated to others and therefore implicitly tolerated. During the Nazi era in Germany, the vast majority of German citizens claimed ignorance of Nazi crimes. The "dirty work" of the few was, supposedly, unknown to the many "good Germans." Some Germans were probably ignorant of the death camps; others probably pretended ignorance; and many others in all likelihood did their best to know as little as possible.

Within each culture there are conceptions of deviance that develop slowly over long periods. In societies without written languages, moral codes and restrictions are kept alive through myth and are passed orally from one generation to the next. They thus carry the weight of tradition and are slow to change. The individual who would engage in prohibited behavior must face not only his peers, but his ancestors as well. All stand together, as it were, prepared to ask why traditions should not be honored.

In literate, complex societies, many conceptions of deviance are enshrined in law. The legal definitions of voluntary and involuntary manslaughter, first and second degree murder, and other crimes, have developed in American society over centuries, ultimately deriving from English law. Conceptions of deviance that are embodied in the criminal law represent the more stable and widely accepted definitions of deviance.

Yet the law is open to change; legislatures can enact new laws and courts can make new interpretations of existing law. Customs and traditions continue to carry some weight in modern societies, but laws can be passed that may not reflect widespread popular sentiment. A particularly good example of the creation of a form of deviance by the passage of laws is provided in the history of marijuana as an illegal substance.

In 1937 the United States Congress passed the Marijuana Tax Act, which rigidly controlled marijuana through heavy taxation, making it likely that users and sellers would violate the law by attempting to avoid taxation. Subsequently, many states passed laws prohibiting the sale and possession of marijuana. Prior to this, few states had laws prohibiting marijuana and there was little public concern with the drug. Why then were such laws passed? The answer lies in an intense publicity campaign waged by the Federal Bureau of Narcotics, which publicized the supposed dangers of the drug. A dramatic picture was painted for Congress and the public of the horrors of "Reefer Madness," and the legislative response was to give the Bureau the laws it wanted, bringing marijuana under its jurisdiction.

Sociologist Howard Becker (1973) coined the phrase *moral entrepreneurship* to describe this activity. For a variety of reasons, including the desire of official agencies of social control to extend the scope of their authority and to increase the size of their budget, groups and organizations attempt to get certain activities defined as deviant. Their motives may not always be as patently self-interested as were those of the Bureau of Narcotics, which sought to expand its authority and increase its budget. In a society composed of many groups with diverse values and norms, it should not be surprising to find some groups seeking to extend their moral influence. People can be motivated by their norms, seeking to bring "truth" to the uninformed.

Moral entrepreneurs may also be moved by considerations of status and group position. The Temperance Movement of the nineteenth century, which dramatized the evils of drink and sought first to promote temperance and later achieved an outright ban on the consumption of alcohol, was largely Protestant in composition. Doubtless there were strains of Puritanism within this tradition that inclined temperance workers to see excessive drinking as a major evil. In addition, they were no doubt influenced by the damage wrought by drink on families. But, less visibly and more potently perhaps, these Protestants felt threatened by the arrival of European immigrants, most of them Roman Catholics, whose culture was sharply different from the native Protestants and who began to acquire increasing social status and political power. By the late nineteenth century the United States was fast becoming an urban society, a fact that also threatened the political power of these small-town and rural Protestants. Joseph Gusfield (1963) has interpreted the Temperance Movement as an effort on the part of the Protestants who supported it to regain their status in the society through coercive reform. By securing Prohibition, they sought to demonstrate at least their moral dominance over American society.

The passage of legislation at the behest of moral entrepreneurs is one way that new forms of deviance emerge. Not surprisingly, many of these new categories of deviance are taken more seriously by their creators than by other people. During Prohibition, for example, violation of the law was a national pastime. No one who wanted a drink had to go without one. Similarly, passage of laws against marijuana and vigorous enforcement efforts in later years failed to stamp out use of the drug.

Deviance is an important social category. People who are labeled as deviant are perceived through new eyes. Their activities and their persons become the legitimate targets of agencies of social control. Thus, it is not surprising that deviance also lends itself to political uses. By defining one group as a serious threat, other groups can alter the way members of that group are perceived and legitimize efforts to exert control over them. Moreover, by focusing attention on some forms of deviance, those who hold power can deflect attention away from themselves or from important problems that are not being dealt with.

During the United States' involvement in Vietnam in the 1960s and 1970s, for example, vociferous protests against the war, especially by students, were met by political leaders with allegations that amounted to a charge of political deviance. Protesters were labeled "bums," people who really wanted the

Ben Shahn, *The Passion of Sacco and Vanzetti* (1931–32)
From the Sacco and Vanzetti Series of 23 paintings. Tempera. 84½ × 48 inches. Collection of Whitney Museum of American Art. Gift of Edith and Milton Lowenthal in memory of Juliana Force. Acq#49.22

The case of Sacco and Vanzetti illustrates a political use of deviance. Tried, convicted, and executed for murder in the course of armed robbery, these Italian immigrants were political anarchists. Were they convicted on evidence? Or were criminal charges a convenient means of political persecution?

"enemy" to win, whose loyalties were not as they should be, who were not living up to the standard of conduct expected of "loyal" American men and women. These war protesters were, in effect, regarded as deviants. Their activities were portrayed as a threat to American society, its institutions, and its military effort. They were alleged to have bad motives and poor character. They were regarded not merely as dissidents, but as people who really did not deserve to be Americans.

Beginning under the administration of Lyndon Johnson and vigorously pursued by President Nixon, such efforts to have political protest defined as deviance were successful. Protesters came to be seen as un-American and as misfits. But as public sentiment against the war grew and a wider spectrum of people engaged in protesting it, the legitimacy of this deviance category waned. Especially after four students were killed on May 4, 1970, at Kent State University in Ohio, it became futile to associate protest with deviance, and the use of this tactic by those in power declined.

But for a time, it proved a useful means of deflecting criticism of the war and of the Johnson and Nixon administrations. Those who do not have the best interests of the nation at heart, it was alleged, who are "lazy bums" without enough courage to fight for their flag, should not be listened to. Moreover, they have to be watched, lest protest turn to violence and an effort to overthrow the government. On the basis of the creation of such a conception of political deviance and its application to war protesters, political officials were able to legitimize their efforts at surveillance and control.

War protesters themselves used similar tactics in an effort to discredit political leadership by referring to President Johnson as a "war criminal." Drawing a lesson from the Nuremberg war crimes trials after World War II, when many Nazis were tried and punished by the Allies for war crimes committed during the Hitler era, antiwar groups staged their own war crimes "trials." Political leaders were charged, "tried" in absentia, and found guilty. The portrayal of political leaders as war criminals was, in effect, an effort to turn the politics of deviance against those who had employed it. By de-legitimizing leaders, antiwar activities sought to enhance their own legitimacy and that of their cause.

At the same time, crime became a major public issue, with political candidates vying with one another in opposing crime and promising to make the streets safe. During the 1960s and 1970s crime rates did increase in the United States, although not as much as alleged by some politicians, nor in proportion to the hysteria they attempted to generate. Crime, it seems, was an important symbolic issue, a means of fanning partisan flames and winning political support.

Why People Engage in Deviance

It is difficult to explain why people engage in acts that are defined as deviant. Some individuals find others of the same sex appealing; others believe a war is wrong and try to protest it; still others steal, cheat, and lie because they perceive it to be for their benefit. These are clearly forms of conduct that cannot be encompassed in a single explanation. They resemble one another in the ways they are defined by people, but not in the motives or social conditions that produce them. What follows, then, is a discussion of several different explanations of deviance, none of them fully satisfactory.

Motivation and Deviance One way of explaining why people engage in deviant behavior is to focus on the concept of motivation. Human behavior is goal oriented. People do not merely behave aimlessly or habitually, but do what they do in order to secure certain goals for themselves. Perhaps deviants have goals that are different from those of ordinary people, or perhaps they have the same goals but use illegitimate means to pursue them.

One of the classic sociological theories of deviance focuses on this very issue. Robert Merton (1957) argued that all societies encourage their members to pursue certain goals and at the same time prescribe means for attaining them. In American society, Merton said, success is inculcated as a major goal, and money is perhaps its most important and visible criterion. The acquisition of wealth and the goods and services it purchases are measures of an individual's success and, ultimately, of his or her worth. At the same time, the society erects barriers to the pursuit of success. Everyone is encouraged to believe that success is important and attainable, but not everyone can or will succeed. Access to education and jobs, for example, is not equally available to all. And in a race for success, as in any race, some people will lose—indeed, some must lose so that the others can declare themselves winners. Consequently, some people are doomed to failure from the start.

In Merton's theory, the conformer is the person who accepts and continues to pursue the goals that are stressed, using the socially approved means of working hard to achieve success at school or on the job. Deviance arises among those who develop one of four possible deviant adaptations to failure. *Ritualism* entails "going through the motions," meaning that the person has lost any hope of success or belief in its importance, but ritualistically puts in time at work—a conformist in outward appearance. In *retreatism* the individual drops out, ceasing to value success or to make any effort to attain it. People can drop out or retreat by using drugs, becoming drifters, and otherwise failing to live up to ordinary responsibilities. In *rebellion* people reject both the definition of success and the means of attaining it. They can rebel politically or by becoming attached to different life styles, some of which may entail deviant activities. Finally, in *innovation* people continue to pursue success, but employ illicit means to secure it. Crime is the result of this mode of adaptation; people climb a ladder of success provided by various forms of criminal activity.

Merton's theory contains some useful ideas, although like many theories it is sometimes overgeneralized. People do, in fact, attempt to use illegitimate means to acquire what they cannot acquire legitimately. They do retreat from social involvements. They do create new life styles that depart from and resist conventional roles. And motivation is important; people behave in order to secure certain ends.

But this theory cannot explain everything. Although many people find their aspirations for success thwarted, only some become deviant. And although success does seem to be a goal that is strongly emphasized in American society, it is doubtful whether it is as narrowly defined in material terms by everyone as the theory supposes. This theory does help explain why those who define themselves and their circumstances in the ways predicted become deviant. But not all people define themselves in these ways. They continue to conform and to hope for success against the odds, they define success in different ways, or they act on the basis of motives not encompassed by the theory.

It is important to stress that Merton's theory, like other sociological theories, is not meant to explain the deviance of any particular individual. Unlike the psychologist, who might seek to unravel the complex and unique chain of circumstances that lead a particular criminal to become deviant, the sociologist is interested in *typical* motivations and circumstances. The sociologist is not interested in the complex psychodynamics of the individual retreatist, for example, but in the social conditions that make retreatism one of several possible orientations and in the kinds of retreatist activities that are possible in a given society.

Deviant Subcultures Another explanatory theory of deviance emphasizes the fact that deviants often seem to live in their own world, adhering to their own distinctive life styles. In this view, deviant subcultures come into existence and foster deviant conduct. These subcultures contain values, norms, and definitions of social reality that substitute for those of the dominant culture and provide members of a deviant social world with definitions of situations, social roles, and valued identities.

The subcultural theory has been used to explain the activities of lower-class, urban male adolescent gangs (Cohen, 1955). Faced with a school system that dooms them to failure, such boys band together and form gangs whose values are the reverse of conventional society's. These gang values emphasize fighting and stealing, thus providing the boys with an avenue to success and at the same time providing a way for them to thumb their noses at conventional middle-class society. Cloward and Ohlin (1960) modified and extended this explanation, pointing out that different kinds of gangs emerge in urban settings. Some gangs are primarily oriented to fighting with other gangs, others engage primarily in robbery and theft, and still others center upon drug use. The kind of gang a boy joined depended on several factors. Where adult criminal activity was present and recruited boys, theft-oriented gangs would predominate. Where there was no such adult crime, conflict gangs would be the norm. And those boys who could not succeed in theft or conflict gangs would end up in retreatist gangs focusing on drug use.

Subcultural theories such as these emphasize the idea that specifically deviant norms and values develop and encourage deviant activity. This is sometimes true and sometimes not. Studies of gangs, for example, do not show the values of delinquents to be simply opposed to those of middle-class society. Delinquent boys often support conventional rules even while breaking them. At the same time, those who engage in activities defined as deviant and who regularly associate with one another do develop more or less distinctive values, codes of conduct, and ways of looking at the world. Participants in organized crime, for example, define their activities as legitimate, enforce rules governing members' conduct, derive status and self-esteem from their activities, and use a vocabulary of motives appropriate to their social world.

Part of the experience of becoming deviant involves recruitment and socialization into a deviant subculture. Thus, for example, young men learning that their sexual preference is for men discover other gay men and the places where they meet, learn the cultural lore of the gay world, and come to share views of the nature and meaning of homosexuality that prevail within the gay community. We can therefore say that becoming a homosexual involves becoming a part of a social world and its subculture. But in the case of homosexuality, the existence of the subculture does not explain the existence of the behavior. Men do not develop homosexual preferences because they are recruited to the social world of gay men; instead, this subculture provides a vehicle through which their preferences can be understood and expressed.

Deviance and Control The presence or absence of social control also plays a role in explaining deviance. In his statement of this approach, Travis Hirschi (1969) suggests that deviance is apt to occur when the individual's links to society are weakened or broken. People are tied to society in several ways. They are attached to others by bonds of kinship, friendship, affection, and respect, and thus care about others' opinions. In the course of their lives people invest considerable time and effort in, and thus develop commitment to, many things—careers, reputations, and material possessions. People become involved; they become busy with the people to whom they are attached and devote time to the things to which they are committed. Finally, people come to believe in the norms and values of their society; they think it is right to do certain things.

The probability of deviance increases as these links between individual and society are weakened. If people are not attached to others, then they do not care about their opinions. Crime thus becomes "thinkable," for there is no reason to avoid it in order to maintain the respect of others. Similarly, if the person has no commitments, there is nothing to lose by deviant activity. If the person has no involvements, then there is time for the contemplation of deviance. And if belief in the norms is weak, then these norms do not stand in the way of the individual contemplating a deviant act. In short, this approach explains deviance by looking for situations where social controls are weakened.

As with other explanations, there is some value in control theory. Many people, perhaps most people, have impulses from time to time that might get them into trouble. People perceive opportunities to cheat in business or on their income taxes. Married people are sexually attracted to persons other than their spouses. An adolescent perceives a chance to steal a record from a store or to have fun by getting drunk with friends. Under most circumstances, people control these impulses themselves; they hold them in check, engage in role-taking, and decide that the activity is not worth the risk. But some people are less able to do this, and so engage in deviant activity.

On the other hand, control theory seems to assume that people will commit deviant acts unless otherwise checked. It thus takes a jaundiced view of human nature, regarding the impulse to be deviant as something that does not have to be explained. This perspective overstates people's disposition to engage in deviance. And although it may fit some kinds of deviance, such as delinquency and crime, it does not help as much with other kinds of deviance, such as homosexuality.

Labeling Theory Symbolic interactionists take a different approach in trying to explain why people engage in conduct that is socially defined as deviant. Their approach, generally called *labeling theory*, rests on several premises.

First, the interactionist perspective emphasizes that deviance is meaningful behavior, just like any other behavior in this respect. Deviants form their conduct as they interact with others, using the basic processes of role-making and role-taking. Their individual and social acts are meaningful. Deviants, just like others, engage in conduct so as to pursue their goals and coordinate their acts with those of others. They form their conduct in concrete situations, and the things they do both stem from and shape their identities.

An important result of looking at deviance in this way is that the sociologist abandons the search for very simple explanations. Just as we cannot explain the rich diversity of conforming behavior on the basis of theories that stress single factors such as motivation, social control, or subcultural affiliation, so we cannot explain deviance in this way. Instead, we must look at deviant activity in the settings in which it occurs and discover its meaning in the eyes of those who engage in it.

Second, labeling theory holds that explaining why people *begin* to engage in some form of deviant behavior is not the same as explaining why they *continue* to engage in it. The other explanations we have discussed would treat an adolescent's first minor brush with the law in the same way as his tenth serious encounter. They assume that whatever explains the youth's first troublesome conduct can equally well explain the latest. These approaches take the view that deviance, especially crime, can be explained by a single theory.

These are unrealistic assumptions. Adolescents can get into trouble the first time for quite diverse reasons. Perhaps one boy steals a watch from another on a whim, without having thought about the consequences of his act or even what he will do with the stolen goods. Another boy may be in the wrong place at the wrong time and get caught with other boys who are in trouble with the police. Another may find himself forced to defend himself in a fight. Still another may quite consciously and deliberately plot a crime. A great variety of circumstances may attend a youth's first experiences with violating the law.

Moreover, the meanings associated with these experiences are likely to be very different. The youth inadvertently caught with others will probably feel a little dumb or unlucky because he was in the wrong place. Perhaps he will be angry with himself for getting into trouble. The boy who plots a theft and is discovered in the act will also likely be angry with himself—for getting caught. The kid who fights to defend himself may regret the fact that he got himself into a situation where he had to fight.

The third premise of labeling theory is that social reactions *transform* deviance and the meaning of deviant conduct. The youth who steals on impulse may attribute little significance to this act until caught. At that point, the reactions of others—police, parents, social workers, and the courts—begin to give his conduct meaning. People find him troublesome, perhaps even threatening. What was to him a lark is now something in which the law has the right to intervene, and he becomes the object of social control. Theft becomes a fact about himself that others take into account as they interact with him; it becomes a key to his identity, which is now in some danger of being viewed negatively by others.

The person's early involvements with deviant conduct are termed *primary deviance* (Lemert, 1951). Labeling theory takes the view that these primary activities may have diverse meanings and arise from many different factors. At this stage, individuals do not think of themselves in terms of deviance. The boy in our previous example does not say, "I am a thief" or "I am a delinquent." But as soon as a primary act is noticed by others, processes are set in motion that may lead to additional involvement in deviance and that will affect the nature and meaning of subsequent acts. These later acts are termed *secondary deviance*, and from the perspective of labeling theory, they can be explained only by taking into account the way others react to the primary acts.

Let us imagine some alternative scenarios. In one, our whimsical thief is caught, charged with being a juvenile delinquent by reason of theft, found guilty by a judge, and placed on probation. His old friends avoid him; he has acquired a "bad reputation" and their parents forbid association with him. He finds that his parents now treat him somewhat differently as well. They are more suspicious about what he does with his time and what he buys. He begins to feel that he is under a cloud. Gradually his attachments to parents and their expectations weaken, and he is drawn into association with other boys who have also been in trouble. In their company he finds some self-esteem, but he also gets into trouble repeatedly.

In another scenario, the boy is also caught, but his reception by others is more sympathetic. Instead of being charged with delinquency, he is permitted to return the watch to its owner. Few people find out that he has been in trouble. He is taken to a therapist for a few sessions, where he talks about himself and learns some techniques for controlling his sometimes errant impulses. He is reassured that getting into trouble once does not brand him as a criminal for life. He keeps his old friends, and although not exactly angelic, he gets into no further trouble.

There is yet another scenario that might occur. Here the thief is not caught. He gets away with the theft of a watch because no one would ever suspect him of stealing. Nevertheless, he worries a great deal about what he has done. He feels guilty and imagines how disappointed his parents would be were he discovered. He throws the watch into the river where it will never be found, and he vows never again to do anything so stupid and so unlike himself. He stays out of trouble, and only years later does he tell anyone about his brush with "crime."

In the first of these scenarios, additional deviance eventually follows the reactions of others to the initial troublesome conduct. Primary deviance in this instance leads to secondary deviance. In the latter two scenarios, however, a single episode of deviance occurs, but no subsequent activity takes place. What differentiates the first scenario from the second and third?

The first youth meets an essentially negative response. He is treated as a troublesome kid, someone who has stolen before and who is apt to do so again. People watch him, avoid him, and in general put him under a cloud. He is isolated from former friends and drawn toward others who themselves engage in troublesome activities. It would appear that several things have happened. The individual is treated *as a deviant*—a thief—on the basis of this initial involvement. He is thus put under some pressure to think of himself as a thief, to wonder if there is not some defect of character that has led him to steal. He is led to doubt his previous self-conception and to substitute a new one in its place. And, isolated from the company of other conforming youth, he is made ready for participation in a social circle that will support a new self-conception and socialize him into new patterns of activity.

In contrast, the boys in the second two scenarios show no changes in self-conception. They remain attached to familiar people and take their opinions and reactions seriously. Although the act of the second boy is discovered, it does not lead to the classification of that boy as a thief, and so does not have a marked effect on his self-conception or identity in the eyes of others. The third boy is not discovered, but is able to define his act as something wrong, something not in keeping with his self-conception.

We can summarize by saying that the transformation of primary deviance into secondary deviance depends on the responses of others and their impact upon self-conception. If others begin to define an individual as deviant, they also begin to exert pressure on that person to think of himself or herself as deviant. Conceptions of self depend upon the way others act toward the person. Thus, if people act toward a person as if he or she were a hopeless delinquent, this might begin to figure in that individual's self-conception.

Self-concepts and images people form of themselves are important for several reasons. First, people are drawn toward others who will act toward them in a positive way and thus help provide a positive self-image and enhance self-esteem. Because of this, the person labeled as a deviant may be drawn toward other deviants who will provide support for the self, or at least not attack it. The boy in our first scenario thus finds that other troublesome boys are less hostile and more supportive than adults. Second, people act in terms of their self-conceptions. We are able to organize our conduct in everyday life on the basis of identities. We know what to do because we think of ourselves as students, employees, sons, or daughters. The person who is labeled as a deviant is supplied with an identity in terms of which he or she can act. Thus, the boy in our example is assigned an identity, a fact that encourages him to carve out a role for himself as a delinquent in the company of other boys.

With labeling theory, as with the others, there is always a danger of attempting to make the theory explain everything. But labeling theory does not explain all deviance. Primary deviance may stem from a variety of sources, and labeling theory in itself has little to say about its causes. Labeling theory stresses that no single theory can account for all primary deviance; there are simply too many circumstances that can precipitate troublesome, norm-violating conduct.

Once primary deviance does occur, labeling theory stresses the effects of social responses on the subsequent conduct of the individual. But even here, the theory does not maintain that the attachment of labels will inevitably lead to more deviance. People can resist labels as well as accept them. Indeed, if we assume that people do their best to think well of themselves, then we have to assume that they will try to resist negative identities. Moreover, people are not just labeled by others; they label themselves as well. Thus, the boy in our third scenario recognizes the possible implications of theft on the way others think of him and, having successfully avoided discovery, is able to resolve not to do it again, and so to preserve a positive identity.

Labeling theory leads to an additional insight into explaining why some people become seriously involved in deviance while others do not. If we focus on juvenile crime as an example of deviance, it is clear that a great many youths at one time or another do things that could potentially get them into trouble with the law. Studies based on the reports of adolescents reveal that such conduct is very widely distributed. There are, for example, few significant differences between lower-class, working-class, or middle-class youth in self-reported delinquency. But it also seems to be the case that those youths who repeatedly get into trouble with the police, who get involved in more serious forms of deviance, and whose conduct is taken very seriously by police and courts are less likely to be middle-class and more likely to be lower-class or working-class. Why should this be so?

One explanation is that formal agencies of social control respond to troublesome behavior partly on the basis of the social class of the youth involved. (Such agencies of social control include schools, police, courts, social-work agencies, and probation officials.) If the kids are middle-class and come from "respectable" families, they may be less likely to be processed officially through the courts and less likely to be regarded as essentially bad. On the other hand, lower-class minority kids may find themselves subject to the gamut of formal controls and under intensive labeling pressure.

This kind of situation is mirrored in the way adult crimes are defined and regarded. The adult who holds up a liquor store will likely have the book thrown at him if caught. More often than not, this individual will be someone of lower-class or working-class background. The middle-class person who embezzles funds from an employer will be handled more gently. The latter is more likely to be let off with a warning and less likely either to go to jail or to experience any change in self-conception or public identity. White-collar criminals do not think of themselves as criminals. They are apt to think they have made mistakes, that they are not really bad, and that they should not be punished.

The causes of deviance are clearly diverse and complex. Conduct that is deviant in one society or at one time is not considered deviant elsewhere or at other times. No single theory can explain everything. No single motive is common to all forms of deviance, nor even to all instances of a given kind of deviance. Yet, as we suggested earlier, the diverse forms of deviance are similar in the social reactions they generate. All precipitate fear for the social order, provoke social control agencies, and have consequences for the identities of those who break the rules. As we shall see in the concluding section of this chapter, deviance also has consequences for society—some of which may prove surprising.

THE SIGNIFICANCE OF DEVIANCE

The preceding pages have barely scratched the surface of the vast body of sociological ideas about deviance. Nevertheless, it is time for a summing up: What have we learned about the nature and causes of deviance? And what is the significance of deviance for society? The answer to the first question can be found in four principles of deviance that summarize and extend our major points. And the answer to the second question is that deviance is an inevitable, and perhaps even necessary, aspect of society.

It is impossible to summarize neatly what sociologists have learned about deviance. Nevertheless, there are four points that are especially important. Each of these principles expresses a variation on a major theme, namely that the forms of conduct considered deviant by members of a given society result from the same social processes that produce conduct not considered deviant. (1) Like all behavior, deviance is meaningful activity. It is constructed by people engaged in defining situations, making and taking roles, and interpreting one another's acts. (2) Like all conduct, deviance has diverse motives. There are no specifically "deviant" motives, for people do things considered deviant for the same variety of reasons that they engage in socially approved conduct. (3) Like all conduct, deviance occurs in defined situations. A particular form of deviance cannot be explained without examining the circumstances in which people form their conduct. And finally, (4) the self is implicated in deviance, just as it is implicated in all forms of conduct. Deviant acts, like all others, are shaped in a process in which people assume identities, respond to the opinions others have of them, and attempt to enhance and protect the self.

Deviance Is Meaningful Activity

People's everyday conceptions of deviance incline them to regard such conduct and the people who engage in it as very different from themselves and their conduct. The armed robber, the prostitute, and the junkie seem to live in

Henri de Toulouse-Lautrec, *Rue des Moulins* (1894)
Cardboard mounted on wood, 32⅞ × 24⅛ inches. The National Gallery of Art, Washington. Chester Dale Collection.

In this painting, Parisian prostitutes await a required medical examination. Perceived as deviant and thus socially outcast, their lives are nevertheless interwined with conventional society, which regulates their activities and uses them to help define the limits of appropriate conduct.

a strange and distant social world that operates on different principles from theirs. This is not surprising, for everyday conceptions of deviants themselves tend to create this sense of difference. Deviance is threatening to people's conceptions of reality; deviants are threatening and so have to be isolated and punished; they have a negative essence, a form of being that is the opposite of what is admired and valued.

Yet in many respects the distance between conformity and deviance is less than is supposed. A prostitute, for example, is engaged in a social role every bit as much as the banker. The role is not valued in the same way, to be sure, but its performance requires skills and knowledge just the same. Like all occupations, prostitution requires the acquisition of esoteric knowledge—what sexual activities customers prefer, how to detect a potentially violent or abusive customer, how to simulate interesting conversation and sexual pleasure. And the prostitute, no less than the banker, uses this occupational knowledge to construct a role performance—to look and act the way the customer expects, to lead the customer through a standard sequence of activities, to handle various problems that arise along the way.

Deviance is meaningful activity in other respects as well. A banker has a fairly well-developed ideology that explains the social value of this enterprise. The banker is apt to view the granting of loans as a valuable service, making it possible for people to purchase homes, expand businesses, and in other ways contribute to the community. The occupation itself is explained by the banker in terms that add significance to the activity and also turn attention away from less popular facets of the business, such as foreclosing on mortgages. Similarly, the prostitute is apt to regard her calling as a legitimate service that provides certain men with a sexual outlet they can find nowhere else. More expensive call girls, who charge more for their services and cater to a more affluent group of men, may cultivate a knowledge of art, good food, and conversation, viewing themselves as professionals and businesswomen. Both bankers and prostitutes, it would seem, explain their occupations in terms that make them socially meaningful.

There is, of course, one major difference between the meaning of deviance and that of other kinds of conduct. Deviant conduct is *assigned* a different meaning by the members of society. It is conduct whose meaning for most people is that it is wrong, undesirable, something to be controlled. In many instances, of course, deviance gets this meaning not because of anything that is intrinsic to the activity in question, but because of the way that activity comes to be defined. Thus, activity whose meaning is ordinary at one time may later acquire a deviant meaning.

Deviance Has Diverse Motives

Most everyday images of particular forms of deviance are formed out of typifications. Because most people have little contact with these social worlds, they rely upon what they see and hear from the media. Thus, the typical gangster is a member of the Mafia, wears conservative gray suits and dark glasses, drives a black Cadillac, and is of Italian origin. The male homosexual is typified as an effeminate, limp-wristed, lisping creature whose sexual preference is clearly visible to all.

Our typifications of deviant persons incline us toward a distorted view of their motivations. "Common sense" tells us that deviants are moved by very different motives than ordinary people; they are evil, crazy, or, at the very least, different from us. And the same "common sense" tells us that deviant activity is the sole preoccupation of the deviant. Thus, the juvenile delinquent is viewed as motivationally very different from nondelinquent adolescents. The delinquent is viewed as a sociopath, perhaps, or as someone engaged in a quest to get revenge on a society that has been unfair. And lastly, "common sense" says that the delinquent is an individual engaged in a perpetual search for opportunities to engage in delinquency.

But it is not so, at least not to the degree imagined. As was suggested earlier, adolescents may get into trouble due to circumstances that have very little to do with motivation. And, even on the road to a delinquent career, their brushes with the law may occupy a small fraction of their waking hours—small islands of time in a sea of conventionality. Similarly, the prostitute has goals and aspirations that differ little from those of ordinary people—a desire for security, for some measure of respect, for a decent life.

Deviance, like normal conduct, has its origins in quite diverse motives. One prostitute may be driven to this occupation by economic need, another by pathological masochism, and still another by a quest for thrills. One delinquent boy may be drawn into illegal activities by his peers but wish desperately to escape their influence, while another cheerfully participates as his gang rapes, pillages, and murders. The same is true of most people in their everyday lives. One banker throws himself into a passionate love affair with money, while another secretly longs to be a poet. Diverse motives underlie our participation in social life.

Deviance Is Situated Activity

Symbolic interactionists emphasize that conduct cannot be explained without specifying the situations in which it occurs. People pursue their goals, make and take roles, and explain their actions to themselves and others in concrete situations.

This principle is no less true of deviance than of other forms of conduct. One form of juvenile delinquency, for example, is that of the violent street gang whose members engage in fights with other gangs and sometimes also direct their violence against other members of the community, child and adult. It is tempting to see this activity merely as a result of violent personalities or as caused by the glorification of violence in television and films. Such explanations, however frequently they may be repeated, are scientifically inadequate because they neglect the real, concrete circumstances in which violence occurs. Violent adolescents do not prowl the streets looking for opportunities to express their supposedly violent personalities, nor are they engaged in conduct that is essentially imitative of what they have seen in the media. Violent conduct is more complex. It requires a situation in which a group of people can engage in violence and perceive either a gain in doing so or think there is no alternative. It often requires a precipitating event, such as an attack by a rival gang. And even where violence is directed against adults, as when derelicts are senselessly killed, it requires a definition of these homeless men as legitimate targets of violence and a situation defined as an appropriate one for such violence to be expressed.

None of this is said in order to excuse or explain away deviance. There are many forms of conduct whose definition as deviant seems highly arbitrary, in the sense that the social reaction to them seems far out of proportion to their significance. It is hard to see why homosexuality, for example, should be so threatening. Yet there are also forms of deviance that are harmful to society and its members. Our point here is not to excuse or justify any of these activities, but to point out that the popular explanations of many of them are frequently quite erroneous. To explain social behavior, we have to examine the social contexts in which it actually occurs, as well as the meanings it acquires and the motives of participants.

The Self Is Implicated in Deviance

Humans are creatures with selves, and this fact is as central to an understanding of deviance as of any form of conduct. The deviant is not merely someone whom society has programmed erroneously, any more than the conforming person is merely someone successfully programmed. All of us form our acts in the same way, through a process of reflection in which we take into account the implications of our conduct for our identities, for our self-esteem, and for the way it will appear to others.

It is the importance of the self that leads symbolic interactionists to emphasize the role of labeling. We live in a world of named objects, one of which is the self. We act toward these objects partly on the basis of their names. Thus, to attach a label to a person as a "homosexual" or a "criminal" is to imbue that person with a reality—to attribute a set of characteristics, motives, skills, and problems. A label attached is something with which the individual must contend. It is something to be denied or resisted, a source of doubt about one's future, but also a way of organizing one's self-conception and conduct. The woman who has a few experiences engaging in sex for money is apt at some point to label herself and be labeled by others as a prostitute. Although this label is negative in its implications in conventional society, it also has positive features. It provides a way of conceiving the self, just as the occupation provides a place in the world. It may even provide the basis for self-esteem based on association with like-minded individuals who do not share the widespread condemnation of this activity.

CONCLUSION

These four principles of deviance tend to diminish our sense of difference between deviant and conforming activity. All human behavior is meaningful, diverse with respect to motivation, occurs in defined situations, and implicates the self. Yet some forms of conduct, as well as the people who engage in them, are treated as very different, and an effort is made to create a sharp contrast between "them" and "us," between deviant and normal behavior. Why is this the case?

To understand the significance of deviance, it is necessary to grasp the fact that not all of its social consequences are immediately visible. The effects of violent crime, such as rape or murder, are in one sense perfectly obvious: people are hurt. Robbery and vandalism have economic costs, as do white-collar crimes. The effects of homosexuality are more difficult to pinpoint; after all, the human race has not yet failed to reproduce because of insufficient heterosexual activity, nor is it likely to do so. Yet, at least from the perspective of those who detest homosexuals, there is some kind of threat involved, difficult though it may be for others to perceive.

Deviance has effects and ramifications that extend far beyond what is immediately visible and obvious. All of them cannot be discussed here, but a few basic points can be made.

First, if deviant activity is perceived as a threat to social order, it also provides one of the ways social order is maintained. Recall that one of the defining attributes of deviance is that people perceive it as a threat to their conceptions of social reality. Deviant activity seems to undermine the normal, orderly world. It is threatening not just because it is sometimes physically injurious, but also because it is a challenge to people's definitions of reality.

Behavior that threatens common-sense understandings also serves to bring those understandings into view and remind people of them. Those who seem different, whose motives and purposes seem foreign to us, remind us of the motives and purposes we consider normal. Conduct that violates norms reminds us of the norms. Deviance, therefore, is a social boundary-maintaining activity. The deviance of some reminds others of socially defined limits on behavior. Deviance, in the metaphor of sociologist Kai Erikson (1964), highlights the "normative contours" of society.

It would be silly to argue on this basis that deviants perform a useful social function, that without them we would not know right from wrong, normal from abnormal. It would be equally absurd to try to convince a victim of rape that her humiliation served the function of throwing light on the permissible boundaries of sexual conduct. Deviants clearly do not do their work *for* society, and society could clearly do without their activities.

Yet these forms of deviance do dramatize right and wrong and exercise our conceptions of good and evil. The human world is symbolic, and thus in many ways abstract and intangible. Deviance concretizes our symbolic world by providing examples of wrong and evil conduct. These examples help define what is good and right, and they do so perhaps more powerfully than positive statements of values and norms.

The existence of so many forms of deviance whose threat to social order is not obvious raises the possibility that at least some deviance categories are manufactured. When a new category of deviance is created, new forms and mechanisms of social control are required to enforce new moral boundaries. These definitions of morality and normality may in many instances be quite arbitrary and reflect the interest of particular groups rather than that of society as a whole. Thus, shoulder-length hair on young men in the late 1960s was deviant in the eyes of their middle-aged parents. No threat to society, their appearance and the behavior and attitudes it symbolized nevertheless aroused an effort to bring their conduct under control. Long hair symbolized an attack on the prevailing social order.

A second and closely related conclusion is that deviance frequently becomes an issue when an established vision of society is challenged by a new vision, or when new groups threaten the power of old ones. As we suggested earlier, the Temperance Movement was a form of symbolic politics in which a declining group, rural and small-town Protestants, fought a battle against the ascending power and influence of urban dwellers, many of whom were Catholics and foreigners. Drink became a deviance category, a symbol of one's place in society. The same may be true of abortion at present. For many Americans, permissive laws on abortion symbolize a woman's right to control her body. For others, abortion symbolizes a threat to a whole set of values and beliefs about the family, sexuality, and proper conduct.

In these instances, deviance categories are used as weapons as groups struggle with one another. This is another reminder that deviance is fundamentally about social reality. It is not just that some kinds of conduct are viewed as harmful, but that they are part of a social struggle about what society should be.

Finally, the social response to deviance is an occasion on which social solidarity is expressed and reinforced. As we suggested earlier, punishment is a common response to deviant behavior. Although it may sometimes be argued that the purpose of punishment is to reform the deviant, there is a more basic reason for its use. Punishment expresses outrage against the activities of the deviant. It is a means used by those who are not deviant to stand shoulder to shoulder against those who are. It reaffirms not just the norms and values that people believe, but also their collective dedication to one another in the struggle to preserve such norms. In punishing deviance, society reaffirms its existence and its rights.

These features of deviance make it likely that any society will have at least some forms of deviant conduct. Even where men and women do not inflict violence on one another, have no conception of theft, and never cheat or lie, it seems likely that they would create distinctions between appropriate and deviant conduct, find examples of the latter, and create social arrangements for its prevention and control.

SUGGESTED READINGS

BECKER, HOWARD S. *Outsiders*, rev. ed. (New York: Free Press, 1973).

CONKLIN, JOHN E. *Illegal But Not Criminal: Business Crime in America* (Englewood Cliffs: Prentice-Hall, 1977).

ERIKSON, KAI T. *Wayward Puritans: A Study in the Sociology of Deviance* (New York: Wiley, 1966).

GOFFMAN, ERVING. *Stigma: Notes on the Management of Spoiled Identity* (Englewood Cliffs: Prentice-Hall, 1963).

GOODE, ERICH. *Deviant Behavior: An Interactionist Approach*, rev. ed. (Englewood Cliffs: Prentice-Hall, 1984).

ROTHMAN, DAVID. *The Discovery of the Asylum* (Boston: Little Brown, 1971).

SCHUR, EDWIN. *Crimes Without Victims* (Englewood Cliffs: Prentice-Hall, 1965).

8

Collective Behavior and Social Change

Most of the time everyday life seems ordinary and routine to the members of a society. They interact with familiar people in familiar places, relying upon accustomed roles and definitions of situations. On the job or at home, people know what to expect of one another, and they become oriented to doing things in accustomed ways. They encounter problems they have faced before and come up with well-worn solutions to them. Life seems predictable and uneventful.

But it is clearly not always so. People sometimes find themselves in unfamiliar situations, facing problems for which they have no ready-made solutions. Natural and human-caused disasters disrupt the flow of everyday events, destroying lives and property. People become caught up in the enthusiasm of a political rally or a religious revival. Fans riot at an international soccer match. And sometimes people wish strongly to change society, to alter the way things are routinely done, and devote their energies to bringing about social change of one kind or another. Sometimes, life seems filled with unexpected events and seems anything but ordinary and routine.

Collective behavior is a term used by sociologists to designate such extraordinary and nonroutine social occurrences. The term covers much ground, including diverse situations and forms of conduct: the collective excitement found at mass gatherings such as sports events and rock concerts; changing fashions in clothing or music; behavior in response to floods, earthquakes, and other disasters; panic when the exits of a theater or other space become overloaded as too many people attempt to leave at the same time, often resulting in injury or death; sudden, inexplicable outbreaks of disease symptoms for which no physical cause can be found and which usually disappear in short order; social movements of many different kinds, ranging from the creation of new religious groups to the pursuit of social justice and equality by the Women's Movement or the Civil Rights Movement.

What do these diverse forms of behavior have in common? This chapter will answer this question as well as several others: What are the differences between collective behavior and routine behavior? When and why does collective behavior occur, and how does it work? What is the impact of collective behavior on society? Does it change society? Although an effort to answer these questions necessarily emphasizes the differences between ordinary behavior and collective behavior, they are not as dramatically different as they may seem. We will see that people experience collective behavior as extraordinary. Yet it rests upon the same basic processes of social interaction and conduct formation as the most ordinary and organized situations in everyday life. Just as organized conduct depends on definitions of the situation, role-making, and role-taking, so does collective behavior. And although collective behavior may involve the pursuit of social change or represent an excited departure from the mundane, it is still intimately connected to everyday routines, for it occurs within established organizations and takes existing society as its point of departure.

THE NATURE OF COLLECTIVE BEHAVIOR

Collective behavior has several features that help distinguish it from ordinary behavior. Not every form of collective behavior is characterized to the same degree by each of these features, but taken together they define the concept. After discussing these features and comparing collective and ordinary behavior, we will take a closer look at a few examples of collective behavior.

Features of Collective Behavior

Problematic Situations The first identifying mark of collective behavior is that it usually involves a problematic situation of some kind. A problematic situation is one in which there is some obstacle to routine conduct, something that makes it impossible for people to conduct "business as usual" and to act as if nothing unusual is happening. Situations may be problematic in many different ways, but what they have in common is that ordinary, customary forms of behavior do not work.

In a flood, for example, many problematic situations may occur. People's homes may be destroyed or uninhabitable, so that emergency housing has to be found. Water supplies may be contaminated and transportation disrupted. The routines of work and school have to be put aside until normal conditions can be restored. Damage has to be repaired, debris cleared away, and survivors cared for while the dead are buried. In a disaster, coping with such problems takes priority over everyday routines.

Not all problematic situations involve the material disruptions of a disaster. Participants in a religious revival meeting, for example, may come to feel they can no longer carry on their lives as before. They may feel that their worldly success is futile and their possessions unsatisfying, and that they must change their ways and "get right with Jesus" if their lives are to be satisfying. In this instance, the problematic situation exists because people perceive a condition of the soul or spirit that makes it necessary for them to change their lives.

Similarly, the antiabortion movement that emerged after the U.S. Supreme Court legalized abortions in 1972 exemplifies a form of collective behavior in which the problematic situation is a matter of social definition. For those opposed to abortion under any conditions, each destroyed fetus represents another human life needlessly taken—a case of murder. For them, abortion seems so problematic that it cannot be ignored, for to carry on life as usual would be to accept legally sanctioned murder. For those who support a woman's unconditional right to abortion, just the opposite seems true. Any interference with abortion is an unwarranted limitation on a woman's right to control her own body. On either side, the situation seems so problematic that extraordinary action is called for. Thus, individuals on both sides suspend other activities and make the campaign the focus of their lives. Demonstrations are mounted, political pressure groups formed, pamphlets written, and other activities undertaken in order to resolve the problematic situation.

Not all problematic situations are as drastic or obvious as those we have mentioned, but nevertheless provide an occasion for collective behavior. An automobile accident, for example, is a problematic situation. Motorists passing the scene of an accident will frequently stop and try to help—directing traffic, going to call for police or an ambulance, giving first aid to the victims. Here, people assemble to deal with a situation that has temporarily disrupted their routine. When authorities arrive, passersby can go on their way and return to their routines.

Although a problematic condition is generally found in episodes of collective behavior, some situations have other earmarks of collective behavior but do not involve much that is problematic. Sporting events often generate an involved, excited crowd that cheers every gain or bemoans every defeat. People feel caught up in the excitement of the moment. Yet—unless the behavior of the crowd gets out of hand—these events are problematic only for those who do not become caught up in the excitement.

The Collectivity A second feature of collective behavior is that it occurs in a distinct form of organization known as a *collectivity*. Although there are many types of collectivities, some of which will be described later, all differ in important ways from established social groups and organizations.

Collectivities are not guided in fixed or routine ways by stable social roles and familiar definitions of situations. An established group, whether a particular family, a circle of friends, or a work group within a larger organization, usually has routines that are fairly stable and predictable. Families, for example, keep mostly within familiar cultural definitions of what families should be. Although each family has customs and traditions of its own, even these form a part of its accustomed ways of doing things and are taken for granted as normal by its members.

Collectivities are more fluid, for they *create* responses to problematic situations and so must invent new ways of doing things. They spring into existence in order to deal with certain problematic situations, and their rules of procedure and allocation of responsibility are geared to these situations. They have leaders, but these emerge in response to the situation and are usually not chosen by any established process. They have members, but the criteria for inclusion in a collectivity are loose. Sociologists Ralph Turner and Lewis Killian put it this way:

> The members are those who happen to be participating, and the leaders are those who are being followed by the members. (1972:5)

Collectivities are, therefore, often capable of very rapid change as conditions change. Some members drift away, while new participants are recruited. New

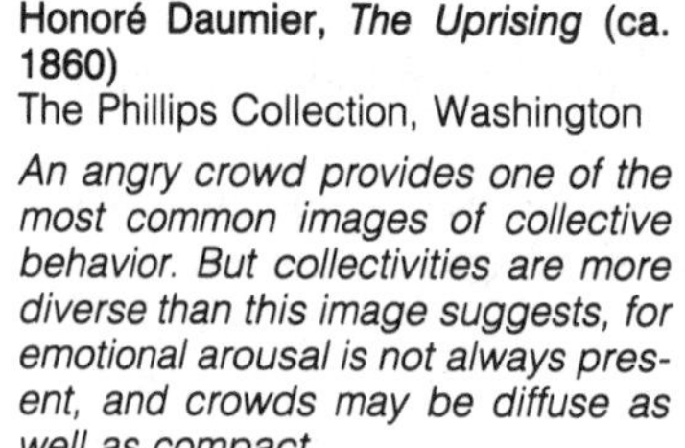

Honoré Daumier, *The Uprising* (ca. 1860)
The Phillips Collection, Washington
An angry crowd provides one of the most common images of collective behavior. But collectivities are more diverse than this image suggests, for emotional arousal is not always present, and crowds may be diffuse as well as compact.

leaders emerge from the collectivity and take the place of those whose leadership is no longer accepted by members.

The *crowd* is perhaps the most visible and widely known form of collectivity. An angry mob confronting an individual suspected of having committed some heinous crime is a crowd, as are the following: an audience that flees a theater in panic when a fire breaks out; shoppers who break down the doors of a department store to be the first to get to a sale; spectators who gather around the scene of a fire; rioters in the streets; a widely scattered but large number of people who suddenly begin to participate in the latest fad or craze; college students who converge on Daytona Beach or Fort Lauderdale, Florida, during spring break.

Crowds vary along many dimensions, but three are especially important (Turner and Killian, 1972: Part II). The first is the extent to which a crowd develops its own division of labor. In a *solidaristic crowd*, such as the kind that develops in a riot, the objectives of the crowd could not be accomplished by individuals acting alone, but require coordination. Thus, a division of labor emerges as the crowd forms and solidifies its goals; people begin to find a role for themselves in the crowd's activities. By contrast, in the *individualistic crowd*, such as an audience that flees a theater in panic, the behavior of individuals is uncoordinated. People behave in a parallel fashion without regard for one another, and there is little or no division of labor.

The second dimension along which crowds may be classified is the physical distribution of crowd members. Some crowds, such as a lynch mob or audience, are *compact*; people behave in close physical proximity to one another and communicate directly. The opposite of compact crowds are *diffuse* crowds. The latter, exemplified by followers of fads and crazes, are spread over vast distances and communicate indirectly, relying especially upon the mass media.

Thus, people learn that the Beatles, Pac Man, or Cabbage Patch Dolls are "the latest thing" and rush out to buy or participate.

The third important distinction is between *acting* and *expressive* crowds. The acting crowd tries to accomplish some objective, such as taking revenge on the police for arresting a member of the community or lynching a suspected criminal. The expressive crowd is more preoccupied with creating and sustaining a mood or feeling, as when a religious gathering is moved to ecstasy or college students revel during spring break.

Some examples of collective behavior mentioned earlier illustrate the nature of crowds. Those individuals who first arrive at the scene of an accident are selected by chance. They have no history of interaction with one another and no predefined leaders and followers. Yet, at the scene of the accident, a division of labor will develop. Some will direct traffic, while others administer first aid; some will take charge of the situation as a whole, while others follow their lead. When police and medical officials arrive on the scene, the collectivity is apt to drift away as these organizations take charge. Men and women who for a brief interval have created a collectivity that has dealt with a problem go on their way and may never see one another again.

In disasters, as in accidents, there are groups and organizations whose task it is to cope with unexpected and tragic events. Yet collectivities nevertheless play a role in the social response to disaster. People generally do not wait passively for authorities to act but help themselves—organizing rescue teams, volunteering to fill and place sandbags in time of flood, providing food and shelter when people are forced to leave their homes. Although guided by a felt obligation to help those in need, such collectivities are not preestablished but emerge and change as circumstances dictate.

Social movements are another kind of collectivity and exemplify the fluidity of collectivities, and especially the nature of their leadership. The Consumer Movement in the United States for many years was personified by Ralph Nader, whose book on the automobile industry, *Unsafe at Any Speed,* sparked the movement for safer cars. No one "appointed" Nader to be a watchdog for consumers, but he and the organizations he founded nevertheless performed this role. Nader helped create the very movement he led; he played a leadership role because so many people followed him that others, notably federal and state officials, had to take his movement seriously.

Emergence A third characteristic of collective behavior is the prevalence of *emergent* norms and situational definitions (see Turner and Killian, 1972, Chapter 2). In their everyday routines, people rely upon familiar definitions of situations. In each situation where people interact, they know what to do and what to expect of one another because they share a definition of the situation. Entering a restaurant, people know the kinds of activities that are permissible and those that are not. They can identify the main participants and correctly predict their conduct. They know what will happen, more or less, and when the need arises they can exert social control over others. People who make too much noise or dress inappropriately will thus be subject to disapproving stares. The situation and its norms are clear and reasonably stable.

In collective behavior it is otherwise. Situations involving collective behavior have definitions, but these usually have to be constructed and reconstructed as events occur. Situational definitions are relatively emergent rather than relatively stable. And although normative pressure is exerted upon people in such situations, the norms themselves are emergent rather than fixed in advance. In many situations involving collective behavior, people become acutely aware that they are expected to behave in certain ways. But these expectations are a product of the situation rather than being predetermined.

The first task of people in a disaster, for example, is to determine the seriousness of the threat. It is no small thing to abandon one's home and possessions and flee with only what can be carried. People want some assurance that evacuation is really necessary, which may explain why people often resist evacuation until the last possible moment. A disaster, in other words, is not simply defined by the warnings delivered by authorities. People make their own definition of the situation, perhaps saying that things aren't as serious as they seem, or that there is still time before they have to leave.

As a situation becomes defined, those present act on the basis of the emergent definition. The definition is a powerful constraining force, just as it is in routine situations. Yet there is an important difference. In everyday life, we can verify our definitions of situations not only by observing the behavior of others, but also by drawing on our previous experience. Often we have interacted in similar situations or even with the same people. We know what is typical of those persons and of the situation. But in a disaster people are usually unfamiliar with what is going on around them. They have no previous experience on which they can rely. Thus, people may convince one another that they are secure when in fact they are in great danger.

People exert strong influences on one another in collective behavior situations. Faced with unfamiliar events, people need information and interpretation, so they are likely to be receptive to what others say. *Rumor* (defined as the process in which information is developed, transmitted, and modified in collective behavior) is a potent force. People hear bits of information, augment them, fit them to existing definitions of the situation, and pass them on to others. In the absence of contrary evidence and with no fund of experience, people are more apt to believe information regardless of its truth.

Participants in collective-behavior situations communicate normative expectations as well as information. Not only do norms emerge that define appropriate behavior, but social controls are brought to bear so that at least outward conformity with these norms is assured. Although there is no overt verbalization of norms, participants nevertheless sense what is expected of them and feel considerable pressure to conform.

These processes can be seen in operation during musical concerts. Sometimes a performance will be so well received that the audience gives the performers a standing ovation at the end, frequently prolonging their applause in an effort to encourage an encore. No one announces to the audience that the performance deserves such an enthusiastic response; this definition of the situation emerges out of the individual reactions of a considerable segment of the audience. Once people begin to stand, however, they communicate to others both the definition of the situation and the idea that they, too, should stand up and cheer. As more people do stand, it becomes increasingly difficult for others to remain seated. They feel a kind of social pressure to accept this definition of the situation and to behave accordingly. The performer also is subject to this pressure. The emergent definition of the situation calls for an encore, perhaps for several, and it may be impossible to resist.

The Sense of Novelty Finally, collective-behavior situations are viewed by participants as extraordinary events. Part of the definition of the situation in any episode of collective behavior is the idea that unusual, exciting, or novel things are happening. A concert audience enthusiastically cheering a performer feels that they have witnessed an unusually excellent performance. Victims of a disaster regard it as an event that they will remember for a long time. Participants in a religious or political movement sense an opportunity to make real improvements in the society and feel that what they are doing is something special and uniquely important.

To put this another way, in collective behavior, people put aside ordinary routines and invest time and energy in an extraordinary situation. As a result, there is often a generalized sense of excitement and energy associated with collective behavior. In an enthusiastic audience, for example, the attention of many people becomes riveted on the event itself and their participation in it. Their excitement reflects the fact that they are totally invested in this activity. That is, the individual has an identity as an audience member and acts wholeheartedly on this identity. The person's energies are fully mobilized by this event. Similarly, individuals who throw themselves into filling sandbags during a flood have identities conferred by this activity. Full identification with such a role permits people's energies to be completely dedicated to it, and people often find they are capable of feats of strength, endurance, or leadership they could not have imagined.

Although collective behavior does involve a sense of engagement and excitement, there is one reservation to be noted. Not all participants in collective behavior share in the excitement, nor do all accept the prevailing definition of the situation. In a concert audience, for example, there are likely to be some who rise and applaud in an effort to conform to the definition of the situation but who have not particularly enjoyed the concert and who do not share a sense of excitement. Some individuals doubtless lend their hands during a disaster not because they are involved and committed, but because they cannot resist the social pressures to do so. Their public actions do not necessarily mirror their private attitudes and feelings.

Turner and Killian (1972: 21-24) point out that there is often an "illusion of unanimity" surrounding collective behavior. That is, an observer might conclude from witnessing an episode of collective behavior that participants all felt the same way about it. Typically, however, the motives of people are diverse, even when their behavior seems to conform outwardly. Accordingly, Turner and Killian propose a five-fold typology of participation in collective behavior (1972: 27-29).

First, some participants in an emergency or other kind of collective behavior situation are *committed* individuals who feel they have a special obligation to do something and who feel strongly that something must be done. Perhaps they were first on the scene, have a special relationship to those affected, or feel that they have special skills that are needed by others. A second type classified by Turner and Killian are the *concerned*. These people feel a sense of involvement, but are less likely to suggest lines of activity themselves and may be most responsive to suggestions made by others, participating as the definition of the situation emerges. A third type—to whom Turner and Killian give no special name but who may be termed the *excited*—derive a sense of excitement from participation in collective behavior and are motivated not by a desire to help or by a concern with the specific problem but simply by a desire to be there and to be a part of things. Also likely to be present in many episodes of collective behavior are *spectators* and *exploiters*, who watch or attempt to realize personal gain from the event taking place. Spectators may take no action, but are an important part of the crowd because they form an audience that may be drawn into activities as they develop. Exploiters are detached from the concerns of the crowd but are motivated by the desire to use the crowd as a cover for criminal acts, such as looting during a disaster.

FORMS OF COLLECTIVE BEHAVIOR

Collective behavior occurs under such diverse conditions that it can only be sampled here. In the following pages we will try to convey some of this diversity and discuss the kinds of collectivities that emerge and the conditions under which they do so.

Behavior in Disasters

Human responses to disasters are among the most extensively studied forms of collective behavior. The reasons are mostly practical. Whatever our technological prowess, we are still prey to earthquakes, fire, floods, and volcanos.

John Steuart Curry, *Tornado* (1932)
Lithograph. Edition: 25. 9⁵⁄₁₆ × 14 ¹⁄₁₆ (composition); 11¼ × 15¾ (sheet). Collection of Whitney Museum of American Art. Purchase. Acq#32.97.

Collective behavior is common in disaster situations. In some areas of the American midwest, tornados are commonplace. Hence, the farm family in this lithograph is about to enter a storm cellar prepared specifically for shelter from the tornado.

Such disasters cause human suffering and damage to property, and in some instances they disrupt whole communities and the lives of their members.

One of the most interesting findings about disasters is that the actual behavior of people confronted by them does not match many common-sense predictions of what people will do (see Wenger, et al., 1976). Disasters are often portrayed in the mass media (in such films as *Earthquake* and *The Towering Inferno*) as evoking maladaptive, disorganized, and even antisocial behavior. Several myths about disasters are especially prevalent. People are thought to panic in the face of disaster and to flee without regard to their obligations to one another. Looting is thought to be commonplace, with hordes of looters converging on the scene and taking the property of victims. The imposition of martial law is thought to be frequently required in response to disasters. Rates of crime are believed to increase, along with antisocial behavior in general. Evacuation is believed to be a frequent necessity, with victims willingly cooperating in their rescue. Victims are thought to experience shock in the aftermath of disasters and to be so numbed that they can scarcely care for themselves. And, finally, the common image of many disasters is one in which the Red Cross and other agencies provide shelter for those displaced from their homes.

These commonplace images are fascinating because they are so far from the truth (see Quarantelli and Dynes, 1972). Panic, for example, is an infrequent result of disaster situations. It develops under specific conditions that can occur in quite ordinary circumstances. In closed spaces, such as theaters or nightclubs, panic is likely to develop only if certain conditions are met. If people feel an urgent need to leave a place because of some threat (such as a fire or a threatened explosion), if exits are limited in number so that people are partially entrapped, if the escape route becomes blocked or overloaded by too many people, and if those far from the blocked exit do not learn that it is blocked, then it is likely that those most distant from the exits will continue to press forward. Under such conditions people become frightened, competitive, and frustrated, and some individuals may be killed or injured by the behavior of others (Turner and Killian, 1972: 84). But the general response to disaster is not such fearful, panic-stricken behavior. Indeed, such conduct is quite rare.

Similarly, other images of disaster behavior are myths, not reality. Looting is an infrequent phenomenon in disasters, although reports of looting are frequent. Martial law has never been declared in a disaster situation in the United States. Crime rates have been found to decline after a disaster, partly because the whole system of social activities is altered, but also because the police turn their attention away from misdemeanors in order to focus on problems associated with the disaster itself. People are frequently reluctant to evacuate a disaster area, and it can be a major problem for officials to get people to move. Shock is not a generalized initial response to disaster; people are not so numbed that they cannot act. Indeed, much of the initial adaptation to a disaster, such as finding people, caring for the injured, and providing essential services, is accomplished by the victims themselves. Finally, most disaster victims find refuge with friends and relatives and do not utilize official shelters. And although the Red Cross is generally there, it is often perceived as a cold and excessively bureaucratic organization by disaster victims, many of whom feel considerable hostility toward this organization.

Why should typifications persist if they are so patently false? And why don't disaster victims act on these typifications and behave the way we expect them to? These questions are not difficult to answer. Newspaper, radio, and television news reports play a part in perpetuating these myths, as do films. Panic, looting, and shock are newsworthy and tend to be reported when they do occur or when they are rumored to have occurred. But the absence of these phenomena is *not* newsworthy. Consequently, popular images of disaster are shaped by what gets reported rather than by what actually occurs. Disaster victims themselves, in the face of a flood or tornado, must grapple with the immediate situation. They are guided by their practical knowledge and the need to apply it to a concrete situation, and they make their roles in accordance with these requirements, not in line with popular typifications.

Urban Riots

Beginning in the summer of 1965 and for several successive summers, a number of black ghettos in American cities were the scene of rioting. Los Angeles, Chicago, Newark, Detroit, Cleveland, and other cities experienced turbulent periods during which sizable crowds assembled, stores were burned and looted, battles with police occurred, rocks and Molotov cocktails were thrown, and snipers fired on bystanders as well as police and firefighters. Some of these disturbances lasted for days, and they became a major topic of news reports and political discussion. Whites living in urban areas were alarmed, even though the violence was confined to black areas and more blacks than whites were injured. A Presidential Commission was formed to study the riots, identify their causes, and to make recommendations on how they might be prevented and controlled. Why did these events take place? What factors precipitated them? How did they develop once underway?

Many sociologists studied the riots, their dynamics, and their causes. The Presidential Commission—the Kerner Commission, named after Otto Kerner, its chair and a former governor of Illinois—produced a lengthy report after extensive study. Diverse interpretations of the riots were produced and their causes continue to be discussed. Our analysis is based on the work of James R. Hundley, Jr., a sociologist at Michigan State University who, with three other researchers, conducted one hundred and fifty interviews with informants who had witnessed the riots in several cities. Hundley identified five major preconditions for such urban riots, each of which must be present before a riot can occur.

First, potential crowd members must believe that a crisis exists. For blacks living in ghettos, such a perception was easy. Historic patterns of discrimination against blacks, unemployment, poor education, and other problems easily produced a strong sense of injustice. Blacks saw themselves—and still do—as unjustly having less than whites.

Second, participants must perceive that legitimate channels of protest and change are closed. Again, blacks generally believed that it would do little good to work through established political channels, which were dominated by whites. These two conditions create a problematic situation for ghetto residents.

Third, participants must believe that a riot will somehow lead to changes in existing conditions. Hundley found that those he interviewed thought ghetto residents were "at the end of their rope" and that, perhaps, "Whitey" would respond to a riot, if not to peaceful protest and political activity.

Fourth, a riot requires people in close proximity to one another. The urban riots of the 1960s tended to occur on warm evenings and weekends when people were in the streets and could rapidly communicate an emerging definition of a situation.

And finally, a riot requires a breakdown in accepted relationships between police and community members. One of the persistent complaints of blacks in cities is the violent and discriminatory practices of the police, who were almost exclusively white at the time the riots took place. In black ghettos, police were and are regarded with suspicion and hostility.

These preconditions set the stage for the urban riots. People believed a crisis existed. Their frustrations were growing, as was their sense of inequality and injustice in relation to the black community. And the belief grew that violence might accomplish what other tactics had not.

Hundley also identified four developments that are responsible for producing a riot at a specific place and time. First, a riot requires the creation of rumors that a riot or "something" is going to take place. Prior to a riot, members of the ghetto community talk more about their frustrations, about the police, and about the possibility of getting out of hand and "blowing the place up." Second, the initiation of a riot requires some precipitating incident, an event that typifies the grievances of the community. An arrest of a community member in which brutality was alleged often provided such an incident. The resulting open hostility against police required the particular incident in order to get started, but was directed at a history of suppression and not just this event. A third factor is the convergence of large numbers of people around the precipitating event. A crowd assembles for a variety of reasons: some people are nearby; others hear of the incident and come for a look; some come with the idea of rioting; and others come to exploit the situation by engaging in ordinary forms of deviance, such as theft. Finally, the riot gets going when those assembled create and communicate a definition of the situation: a wrong has been committed and something has to be done about it immediately.

Once a riot begins, ideas about what courses of action to take come from a variety of quarters. The crowd picks up some ideas and discards others. These ideas come from *keynoters*, especially visible or vocal individuals whose suggestions are acted upon by the crowd. Efforts by police to control rioters often produce further incidents and lead to intensified activity. As specific patterns of crowd activity emerge and are repeated—patterns such as breaking windows, looting white-owned stores, or setting fire to abandoned dwellings—they become normative; that is, engaging in these activities becomes a normal, expected form of riot participation. Eventually, the riot runs its course. Intervention by outside agencies such as the National Guard, coupled with the withdrawal of many participants and curious bystanders, leads to the eventual diminution of riot activities.

Hundley's analysis emphasizes the importance of situational definitions in the formation of riots. People riot in part because they are angry and frustrated with social conditions, but there is more involved. In order for a riot to occur, the situation must be defined in such a way that a riot seems to be a useful and inevitable event. Riots also illustrate the important fact that crowds are not unanimous in their motives. Some rioters act on the basis of a protest definition of the situation. Others take advantage of this definition and engage in activities that benefit themselves. Looting, for example, enriches the looter, whose sole motive for participation is the thought of gain. Like other forms of collective behavior, riots assemble diverse people whose goals can be pursued within the situation that is defined and created.

Hysterical Contagion

Occasionally we read newspaper accounts of the sudden appearance and rapid spread of disease symptoms for which there is no medical explanation. Workers in a factory may experience dizziness, skin irritations, or headaches. School students may begin fainting or experiencing nausea for no apparent reason. Although medical conditions can never be completely ruled out in such incidents, there is often evidence that the diseases and their symptoms are imaginary. Such episodes of *hysterical contagion*, as it has come to be called, have long fascinated students of collective behavior.

A classic study of hysterical contagion, the so-called "June Bug" episode, was conducted in a southern textile factory (Kerckhoff et al., 1965; Kerckhoff and Back, 1968). During a week-long period in the summer of 1962, sixty-two persons received medical treatment for what seemed to be insect bites. The symptoms included fainting, pain, nausea, and feelings of disorientation. The victims were nearly all white women who worked on one shift located in a single area of the plant. Investigators from the Communicable Disease Center in Atlanta, a federal agency that investigates such health problems, could find no evidence of insects or toxic agents that could have caused the symptoms and concluded that their origins were psychogenic.

Such episodes of behavior are frequently explained by citing various forms of stress in the lives of the victims. The pressure of examinations in school, for example, or the threat of layoffs in a factory may produce psychosomatic symptoms in some people. Yet even under conditions of strain, not all who are affected by the conditions develop the symptoms, either initially or after they have seen others display them. Thus it would appear that social factors are at work that influence the spread of the "symptoms."

The social scientists who studied the "June Bug" episode interviewed 185 women, 58 of whom had been affected by the "bug." They sought to determine the relationships among affected women and to learn if the "bug" was concentrated among women who knew one another well, confined to those who were socially isolated, or equally distributed among all. They were guided by the idea that the development of such symptoms, thought to be psychogenic in origin, is not merely an individual phenomenon but is socially patterned.

They found that at the beginning of the epidemic, when a few people first exhibited symptoms, those most likely to follow their lead were socially isolated women, those less integrated into a friendship network with other women in the plant. Such networks provide definitions of reality and of appropriate conduct, and at the beginning they insulated their members from involvement. Without such a network, a woman was more likely to respond to those first showing the symptoms by interpreting her own bodily sensations in symptomatic terms. Later, as more women developed the symptoms, they became more credible to socially affiliated women. When women within a friendship network began showing the symptoms, a chain reaction was initiated. Women within the group began to expect to experience the symptoms, and those displaying the symptoms became more legitimate. Finally, as the number of women reporting the symptoms grew, everyone believed that the "bug" existed, and cases appeared in the factory without regard to networks of friendship and interaction. The epidemic ended when it became less legitimate to report symptoms; exterminators were called in to "kill the bugs," and so reports of symptoms declined in credibility.

This study shows that definitions of situations are important, and that their creation and dissemination is influenced by existing patterns of association. The collectivity, in this instance, developed within the boundaries of an existing organization and was partly shaped by its existing formal and informal structure. The behavior of one or two isolates was initially not a credible model for the behavior of others, especially those who were part of established friendship circles. But as the numbers of affected women grew, other, more socially integrated women also reported symptoms, and then their friends were also likely to be affected. At a certain point, the phenomenon was so widespread that a majority believed in it, feared it, and expected to experience it. In some instances, perhaps, existing physical symptoms were reinterpreted in terms of the spreading belief in the "bug." In the case of other women, the phenomenon itself generated sufficient anxiety to produce the symptoms. And, it should be noted, where powerful expectations existed, it took very little for them to be confirmed.

Social Movements

Social movements are perhaps the most durable and extensive of the several forms of collective behavior. At times in history they have been highly visible to the members of a society and a major factor in the changes it experiences. Turner and Killian define social movements succinctly:

> A social movement is a collectivity acting with some continuity to promote or resist a change in the society or group of which it is a part. (1972: 246)

Examples of social movements in recent American history abound: The Civil Rights Movement, the Antiwar Movement, the Nuclear Freeze Movement, the Women's Movement, the Environmental Movement.

The fact that we write about these movements in capital letters (and think about them that way as well) says something very important about them.

John Sloan, *She's Got the Point* (1913)
Mead Art Gallery, Amherst College

Social movements are an integral part of American history. The "WSP" in this drawing may refer either to the Women's Suffrage Party or the Workers Socialist Party. The artist was involved with both of these movements in the early part of this century.

Movements are more lasting forms of collective behavior and, in American society, very important forms. The lifetimes of the typical readers of this book and of its authors have spanned the rise of several major social movements. Without the activities of the Civil Rights Movement in the period after World War II, relationships between blacks and whites in American society would be very different from what they now are. The Antiwar Movement changed the attitudes of Americans toward the United States' involvement in Southeast Asia and toward subsequent foreign involvements as well.

Why do social movements arise? When do they succeed? What shapes the tactics they choose to pursue their goals? The way sociologists answer these questions can be seen by examining a single social movement: the Environmental Movement, which attained the status of a movement around the turn of the century with President Theodore Roosevelt and the Conservationists. Its contemporary efforts have led to the passage of significant legislation and the formation of agencies such as the Environmental Protection Agency. Why did this movement come into existence? Why was it successful? What tactics did it use?

Turner and Killian (1972: 247) point out that our common-sense explanations of social movements view them as the result of growing frustration with some problematic condition. The discontented band together, develop a plan to deal with their frustrations, and undertake a series of actions that will accomplish their goals. But, as is often the case, common-sense explanations overlook or misinterpret important facts. The limitations of such an explanation can be seen in a cursory analysis of the Environmental Movement.

First, although social movements do stem from discontents of various kinds, those who are most deprived are not necessarily the most likely to initiate or support a social movement. One of the goals of environmentalists, for example, has been to improve the quality of air and water by reducing the impact of industrial pollutants, untreated sewage, and automobile exhausts. Those who are most affected by poor air quality are frequently residents of cities who live closest to factories and major highways. But the Environmental Movement did not initially get its strongest support from these individuals, but from more affluent suburbanites whose own environments were less polluted. Indeed, many blue-collar workers in cities were and are very skeptical of environmentalists (out of fear that environmental legislation would lead to the closing of industries and the loss of jobs). And reports come from all regions of the country that communities often choose continuing pollution if stopping the polluter means decreased employment.

A second limitation of the common-sense approach to social movements is that the goals of a movement may be quite unrelated to the source of discontent. The Temperance Movement, discussed in the chapter on deviance, is an example of a movement in which the goals—prohibition of alcohol—are not directly related to the source of people's discontent—a changing social order and personal loss of status. It has been suggested that many participants in the Temperance Movement were propelled as much by a quest to regain social status as they were by any horror of alcohol. Beneath the announced goals of any social movement are more complex motivations.

Preserving and protecting wilderness and wildlife is another goal of the Environmental Movement. Although this goal is important in its own right and reflects a serious concern that wild creatures and places are endangered, there are additional sources of discontent. For example, many environmentalists are critical of urban, industrial society. They point out that its pace seldom allows people an opportunity for reflection, and that it encourages excessive faith in the power of human technology to solve all problems. These individuals often talk about wilderness as a refuge of the spirit and as the embodiment of values that contrast with those of industrial society. Thus, the Environmental Movement's advocates are not only concerned with the protection of wilderness, but they also are discontented with modern urban, industrial society.

A third problem with the common-sense approach is that it overemphasizes the importance of emotion as a driving force in movement activities. The idea that movement participants perceive a problematic condition and that their wish to change it is fueled by their frustration and discontent is an inadequate explanation. Usually it is effective organization rather than discontent that keeps a movement in existence and enables it to achieve some of its objectives.

During the late 1960s, for example, there was a rising tide of public discontent with environmental pollution. Events such as a dramatic oil spill in the Santa Barbara channel off the California coast focused attention on the potential for destruction and hazards to human and animal life. The high-water mark was the celebration of Earth Day on April 22, 1970, when perhaps twenty million Americans demonstrated against the degradation of the environment. Songs were sung, automobiles were smashed, and there was an outpouring of fervent commitment to environmental quality.

Important as this emotion was, the significant achievements of the Environmental Movement derived mainly from the efforts of many organizations that existed both before and after Earth Day. The day-to-day organizational activities of groups such as the Audubon Society, the Sierra Club, and Public Interest Research Groups—testifying in court, lobbying Congress, and focusing public attention on polluting industries—translated the movement's fervent support for goals into concrete accomplishments.

Finally, the common-sense explanation of social movements does not give enough emphasis to the role of established groups in furthering movement objectives. Social movements need support wherever they can find it, not only from their members, who lend energy and money to the cause, but also from groups who already hold power and who can be effective allies.

Some of the success of the Environmental Movement in the 1960s was due to the existence of such groups as the National Audubon Society, Sierra Club, and the National Wildlife Federation. Although their goals were not identical with the movement's, they were compatible. The Audubon Society easily extended its interest to issues other than birds, and the National Wildlife Federation began to lobby not only for the rights of wildlife, but also for preservation of the environment. Moreover, these organizations, which had been founded decades before and whose main concerns were with the preservation of wilderness and wildlife, had already established public credibility and a presence in Washington. They had national memberships that could be mobilized to exert pressure on public officials. Thus, those who became concerned in the 1960s with the pollution of the human environment found ready allies in existing organizations. And in the final analysis, the success of any social movement lies in its ability to change the ideas, beliefs, and decisions of those who hold power. This most often occurs when persons, groups, and organizations that have power accept all or part of a movement's program and make it their own.

THE EFFECTS OF COLLECTIVE BEHAVIOR

Collective behavior occurs in a variety of forms. Some, such as episodes of hysterical contagion, are very short-lived and appear as brief interruptions of the ordinary, workaday lives of the people they affect. Others, like the rioting crowd, seem to be the antithesis of organized social behavior, for they appear to threaten the very idea of a peaceful society. Social movements seek changes in society as it exists. But they may endure for decades and, in some instances, become intertwined with the very organizations and social institutions they seek to alter.

What are the social consequences of these diverse kinds of collective behavior? There are as many answers to this question as there are forms of collective behavior. We can provide a few illustrations in the following pages.

The Effects of Disaster

In a great many instances, natural and human-caused disasters have little impact upon the society, although they may be tragic for those immediately affected. After the immediate destruction of earthquake or flood has been cleaned up, communities rebuild. Infusions of federal disaster relief help communities reestablish homes and businesses. In many cases, rebuilding occurs on the same vulnerable locations as before—on flood plains, for example, where high waters are likely to recur. Even though individuals and families may be killed, injured, or displaced, the community reorganizes along much the same lines as before. The disaster evokes solidarity among community members, who draw closer together during the crisis and try to recreate their lives.

This is not always the case, however. In February of 1972, muddy flood waters suddenly burst through an illegal dam built by a coal-mining company and devastated the community of Buffalo Creek in West Virginia. The dam—an unsafe pile of coal mine refuse behind which waters were impounded for use in preparing coal for market—simply collapsed after several days of wet weather. One hundred and twenty-five people were killed in the flood. The community—several villages and settlements strung along the length of the narrow mountain hollow—was utterly destroyed.

In this, as in most major disasters, people first reacted with shock to the events, responding not only to the physical destruction itself, but to the almost unimaginable destruction of their way of life. Not just buildings, but the terrain itself was altered. It was impossible even to determine exactly where some buildings were once located. In a response unlike that which occurs in most disasters, however, the people of Buffalo Creek did not quickly recover their spirits and set about the task of recovery. They were individually traumatized, suffering from anxiety, depression, apathy, and similar reactions. But they were collectively traumatized as well. Their community was gone.

In his moving portrayal of the Buffalo Creek flood, sociologist Kai Erikson (1976) points out that in most disasters, victims are surrounded by and outnumbered by nonvictims. Although individuals and families suffer terribly, there is a surrounding community that can absorb them, organize self-help for recovery, and serve as the basis on which the community is rebuilt. In Buffalo Creek, however, the community as a whole was a victim. Consequently, most of the organization and work after the flood was performed by outsiders. The survivors of the flood were eventually housed in trailers, but this was done without regard for former locations of their neighborhoods. As a result, they remained apathetic and disoriented; the flood devastated their lives as well as their homes and businesses.

Riots and their Aftermath

Nearly two decades have passed since the urban riots of the middle and late 1960s. Although for several summers urban dwellers feared the renewal of violence and destruction, outbreaks have been infrequent since that time. What effects did these events have on the society? Did riots cease to occur because they led to major improvements in the condition of blacks or changes in relations between blacks and whites?

A case can be made that violent protest was instrumental in directing attention to the social and economic condition of black Americans and in serving notice on whites that these conditions could no longer be ignored. No doubt the riots did contribute to white awareness of black inequality and to the perceived urgency of attending to it. It is important to note, however, that the riots could have had such an effect only if they were defined as protest activities. Although the violence and destruction associated with the riots was widely deplored by blacks and whites, there was also a majority consensus that they would not have taken place except for the social and economic suffering of urban blacks. Hence, they were viewed as an understandable, if not quite legitimate, form of protest.

It should also be noted that some efforts to remedy the condition of blacks, such as the social legislation of the War on Poverty, had begun before the outbreaks of violence. It is thus possible that the riots were partly an effect of earlier changes as much as a cause of subsequent ones. Because of previous activities of the Civil Rights Movement and the passage of legislation, the hopes and aspirations of black Americans increased. Not uncommonly, frustration with unjust conditions is greatest not when injustice is greatest but when changes begin but do not proceed rapidly enough.

It would be difficult to argue that urban blacks ceased to riot because their condition drastically improved. In many areas of the country, urban blacks may be little better off now than two decades ago. And in a few cities, confrontations between blacks and other social groups, as well as the police, have sporadically recurred. In Miami, for example, several episodes of rioting have taken place, often focused as much on hostilities between blacks and Cuban-Americans as between blacks and whites.

The explanation for the declining frequency of riots can perhaps be found in changing perceptions of the social and political tactics that can achieve change. Talk in ghetto communities of the 1960s focused on the need to dramatize inequality, galvanize the black community, and teach "Whitey" a lesson. As Hundley's analysis suggests, such talk helped define the situation in which riots could occur. But talk in the 1980s focuses on the registration of voters, running black candidates for political office (including the presidency), and demonstrating the political clout of blacks, who are a majority in many northern industrial cities. Riots have declined, it appears, in part because the definition of the situation has been transformed.

The Functions of Hysteria

It is difficult on first glance to see how outbreaks of hysterical contagion could have any significant impact on the society. They are short-lived phenomena that seem to involve brief disruptions of routine, and participants have no particular interest in pursuing social change.

Such phenomena do not change society, but they may nevertheless have social consequences. In their everyday lives—interacting with one another, working, facing a variety of problems and events—people accumulate anxieties and frustrations. They become tired, angry with one another, tense, bored with their routines, restless, and in other ways receptive to activities that might bring relief to these feelings. Although people do not consciously seek to develop physical symptoms in order to have a change of pace, they may still be receptive to the definition of the situation offered by an episode of hysterical contagion. It is easy enough to concretize vague feelings by interpreting and intensifying them in terms of an illness said to be sweeping through a town, school, or factory. And it is not difficult for tired or bored people to be aroused by the excitement of such an event.

In this sense, hysterical contagion may provide a kind of social safety valve. Although people do not consciously catch such illnesses in order to reduce tensions or escape boredom and monotony, they may still have this effect. The products of collective behavior, such epidemics are nevertheless socially structured occasions on which routine is disrupted, tensions reduced, or boredom relieved. It would be too much to say that such occurrences are socially necessary to have these functions served. It would be closer to the truth to say that they seem to be almost inevitable occurrences that have this effect.

The Results of Social Movements

Social movements are specifically oriented to achieving change and have the greatest potential for producing it. But their capacity to effect change depends upon a number of factors, and change itself may be measured in different ways.

First, social movements can achieve change only if they have measurable criteria of success. Frequently, movements will enunciate very specific goals that they wish to attain in a finite period of time. For example, black leaders might seek to extract a commitment from white businessmen to create a specific number of new jobs that would go to unemployed urban black youth. A specific goal of this kind provides an easily measured success criterion. At the same time, such specific objectives do not meet all of the needs of a movement and its organizations. Social movements need a broad base of public support, and this requires them to mobilize the energy and emotions of potential adherents. Frequently this requires them to engage in a variety of actions, such as public protest demonstrations, that may have little direct effect but that are necessary in order to attract and keep followers.

Not all social movements formulate goals very clearly. The so-called Human Potential Movement was a loose amalgam of humanistic psychologists, therapists, sensitivity group advocates, and others that began during the 1960s. It is an example of a social movement whose goals were somewhat vague. Although its members wished to create a more humane society and shared many of the goals of the Women's Movement, the Antiwar Movement, and the Civil Rights Movement, their approach was very different. Human potential advocates sought to change society by changing the individual, by making the person more open, honest, psychologically secure, and capable of achieving his or her potential. But their criteria for the self-actualizing person, to use the term popularized by the psychologist Carl Rogers, were necessarily somewhat vague. Presumably only the person can know when self-actualization has been achieved. Thus, their criteria for social change were also vague; "peace, love, and understanding" are objectives many people might support, but it is harder to know when they have been attained than when two hundred new jobs have been created.

Another condition that affects the success of contemporary social movements is professionalization. Increasingly, social movements rely on large organizations whose funding comes from member support but whose day-to-day activities are conducted by a paid professional staff. Environmental movement organizations exemplify this trend. For example, the National Audubon Society employs many individuals who work full-time lobbying Congress, testifying before committees, keeping watch on the Environmental Protection Agency and other federal bureaucracies whose activities have an impact on the environment. Few movements can succeed without mobilizing this kind of effort. To a growing extent, achieving social change means passing legislation or convincing the courts to interpret existing legislation in desired ways. Such results require full-time professionals with the skills necessary to convince legislators and judges.

Although movements seem to require professionals, they also require members, people who are uninvolved in the day-to-day work of the movement but whose opinions, votes, and dollars keep things moving. There is, therefore, some degree of competition among various social movements for these resources. Movements vie with one another and with charitable organizations for memberships and contributions. They are aided in this quest by the fact that movement participation can provide a relatively inexpensive identity for members. For the price of a membership, people can become part of, say, an environmental organization, acquire a sticker for their car that proclaims their support of the organization, receive a slick magazine, and almost certainly achieve a sense of participating in something important. Indeed, involvement in various social movements may tap energies and provide for personal identity in a way that conventional political organizations and activities can no longer do in American society.

CONCLUSION

Collective behavior is an important social phenomenon. It is not simply an erratic departure from routine, but is linked to the ordinary situations of life. Disasters and emergencies challenge this routine and mobilize men and women to try to reconstruct a familiar physical and social world. Violent forms of protest arise in response to the way people define existing social conditions and their chances of improving them. Social movements are likewise oriented to change, but persist over longer periods of time and may become stable features of the social and political landscape. And even such phenomena as hysterical contagion may play a role in managing the stresses and strains of everyday life.

When sociologists study collective behavior, much of their attention is focused on social change. In this connection, it should be noted that a collective-behavior perspective cannot answer all questions about social change and how and when it occurs. This is so for at least two reasons.

First, although violence, social protest, and social movements are usually oriented to social change, not all change stems from such purposive social action. Both social and technological innovations may produce changes that were not anticipated by their creators. The introduction of the automobile in the early twentieth century, for example, led to a series of unplanned social changes that had a major impact upon American society. Young people attained a freedom and mobility they did not enjoy in horse-and-buggy days. They could get farther away from home, and they found in the car a privacy they enjoyed nowhere else. The mass production of cheap cars provided a form of personal transportation that gave the average citizen an unprecedented degree of mobility. Businesses, homes, and factories could be built without regard to their location near rail or water. Public transportation fell into disuse outside a few urban centers. The whole urban and suburban landscape was transformed by the automobile.

Second, the study of social movements tends to focus attention on the purposes and intentions of men and women within a relatively short span of time and can lead us to neglect developments over longer periods. Over the broad sweep of human history, for example, humankind seems to have been evolving a culture that is more technologically sophisticated and capable of increasing mastery over the environment. We have become a dominant species, using larger quantities of energy, transforming the whole landscape with our cities, farms, and factories. Attention to relatively short-lived social movements draws our attention away from this cultural evolution.

As an approach to the explanation of social change, a focus on collective behavior does have one major advantage. The character of human society—whether it remains relatively stable or changes rapidly—has to be explained by examining what people actually do. Neither social stability nor social change are automatic processes or caused by mysterious forces. Society changes because people, for various reasons, begin to act differently to solve old problems in new ways, or to define conditions they once accepted as new problems to be solved.

SUGGESTED READINGS

ERIKSON, KAI T. *Everything in Its Path* (New York: Simon and Schuster, 1976).

GURR, TED ROBERT. *Why Men Rebel* (Princeton: Princeton University Press, 1971).

PIVEN, FRANCES FOX and RICHARD A. CLOWARD. *Poor People's Movements: Why they Succeed; How they Fail* (New York: Vintage, 1979).

ROSNOW, RALPH and GARY A. FINE. *Rumor and Gossip: The Social Psychology of Hearsay* (New York: Elsevier, 1976).

SHIBUTANI, TAMOTSU. *Improvised News* (Indianapolis: Bobbs-Merrill, 1966).

SMELSER, NEIL J. *A Theory of Collective Behavior* (New York: Free Press, 1963).

TURNER, RALPH H. and LEWIS M. KILLIAN. *Collective Behavior*, 2nd ed. (Englewood Cliffs: Prentice-Hall, 1972).

9

Male and Female

When a child is born, its sex is a matter of enormous interest to everyone. "It's a boy" or "It's a girl" are apt to be the first words spoken about the newborn. This bit of information, which is based simply on external genitals, becomes the basis for profoundly different treatment over the course of the child's life. In virtually every society, sex is a major dividing line. The dichotomy between men and women is seen as natural, and the differences between them are often perceived to be great. This chapter will look at this dichotomy, explore its biological basis, examine how people are socialized to live up to cultural definitions of the nature of men and women, and see some of the ways in which the roles of the sexes differ and are made to remain different.

THE NATURE OF SEX DIFFERENCES

Biology

A newborn child is ascribed a sex on the basis of external sexual organs. There are, however, a number of factors in addition to genitals that differentiate males and females. These include internal organs, hormones, and chromosomes.

Every human being begins life when a sperm and egg, each bearing twenty-three chromosomes, unite to form an embryo from which the infant ultimately develops. Two of the forty-six chromosomes (which normally occur in pairs) determine the sex of the child. In males, these two chromosomes are designated X and Y; in females, both are designated X. Each sperm and egg carries half of each pair of chromosomes. The egg carries only X chromosomes; the sperm carries either an X or a Y chromosome. Therefore, the sex of the embryo depends upon the sperm that successfully fertilizes an egg. If the chromosomes are an XX pair, the child is a female; if they are an XY pair, it is a male.

Until an embryo is about six weeks old, its sex can be determined only by analyzing chromosomes; all embryos are born morphologically female. In these first weeks, each embryo has tissue that ultimately becomes either testes (male gonads) or ovaries (female gonads). The gonads manufacture hormones, including androgens (of which testosterone is the most potent), estrogens, and progesterone. All three hormones are found in both sexes, but in varying levels. In embryos with the XY pair, the gonads produce fetal androgen predominantly and block the formation of female gonads, thus allowing male reproductive organs to develop; in embryos with the XX pair, less fetal androgen is produced and female reproductive organs develop. Later, during sexual maturation, these hormones are also important in producing *secondary sex characteristics*, such as facial and pubic hair, breast growth, and voice changes.

The gonadal, genital, chromosomal, and hormonal aspects of sex are normally consistent within the individual. That is, most males are chromosomally XY; they develop testes and a penis; and testosterone is the predominant hormone. Similarly, most females are chromosomally XX; they develop ovaries, a vagina, and a uterus; and estrogen and progesterone are their dominant hormones. In rare cases, there are discrepancies. For example, a genetic female may lack a uterus, or a male's production of testosterone might be insufficient to produce normal male secondary sex characteristics. For the vast majority, however, the sex of the individual is unequivocal. One is either a male or a female.

From a hormonal standpoint, sex is a matter of degree, since both male and female hormones are present in everyone. Yet almost everyone treats sex not as a continuum but as a dichotomy. This is because it is the *social* rather than the *biological* definition of sex that is important to humans. From the moment of birth, human young are treated as either male or female, and it is this treatment on the basis of cultural definitions of maleness and femaleness that affects the way in which they grow up and the behavior they learn.

The imposition of sex-related characteristics on infants was well demonstrated in a study in which investigators interviewed the parents of newborns within twenty-four hours of birth. Although the infants were similar in size and other features, the parents did not choose the same words to describe their child's behavior. The parents were given a list of words in pairs. From each pair, they were asked to choose the word that best described their child. Parents of daughters responded with words like softer, finer-featured, littler, and less attentive. Parents of sons described them as firm, larger-featured, better-coordinated, more alert, and stronger. Apparently even at the beginning of life, sex organizes our perceptions of our children (Rubin, Provenzano, and Luria, 1974).

Sex as a Role

From a sociological standpoint, sex is a role; that is, being identified as male or female imposes upon a person a set of duties, obligations, and rights that are commonly associated with that sex by the members of the society. The sexual dichotomy is thus a major way that social life is organized. It affects what an individual can and cannot do—for example, holding a particular job or engaging in certain team sports. Unlike most other roles, sex is a role one occupies simultaneously with other roles. The identity it confers sticks with the person from one situation to the next. In many situations, expectations associated with sex pertain to conduct, even if an occupational role is at that moment controlling behavior. Thus, women may be expected to act differently from men regardless of the specific situation. For example, executives are often expected to be aggressive, but women executives may also be expected to satisfy the female role demand and be nonaggressive. Where there have been changes in social organization—as when women begin to do work formerly reserved for men—such role conflicts become more common. In general, however, sex roles complement rather than conflict with other social roles.

Sex roles have a powerful effect on the way people actually behave. Knowledge of behavior appropriate to one's sex becomes crucial in role-taking as well as role-making. To interact with a member of the same or the opposite sex, you must be able to occupy that person's sex role in your imagination and thus anticipate the other's response to your own conduct. And finally, the existence of sex roles implies the development of differing self-conceptions by males and females. Not only are people faced with differing role requirements that shape their role-making and role-taking, but they come to think of themselves as males and females. They make sex an important part of their identity, have images of themselves that are founded in part upon sex roles, and base their self-esteem in part upon the extent to which they live up to those roles.

Considering sex as a social role leads to two important groups of questions. First, how has it come to be that males and females are assigned certain rights and obligations on the basis of sex? Why is it that some societies exclude women from certain occupational positions that command power and influence? Why do some societies define a woman's place to be in the home taking care of children, while in other societies, women share in the production of goods on which the family's livelihood depends? Why are the women in many, but not all, societies felt to be weaker and more emotional than men? Why are certain personality traits viewed as masculine or feminine?

Second, how are sex roles learned? How do boys and girls learn behavior appropriate to their roles? How do their self-conceptions come to mirror the cultural definitions of male and female?

WHY SEX ROLES?

Why are sex roles important in the coordination of social life? No matter where we look among historical and contemporary societies, sex is a relevant dimension of the human experience, shaping individual perceptions, influencing what people do, constraining careers. Why should human societies have developed such different ways of treating men and women, and why does differential treatment persist even in the face of attempts to alter it?

Biological facts clearly play some role in an explanation of the sexual division of labor, although just how significant they are is a matter of considerable dispute. The most obvious difference between the sexes is that women can become pregnant, bear children, and nurse them, and that men cannot. We might expect that this difference would have at least some consequences for sex roles. Pregnancy and lactation, while not as incapacitating as they have sometimes been thought to be, are still not insignificant events. Pregnancy imposes special requirements on the body, which has to divert its resources to the developing fetus; the later stages of pregnancy may restrict bodily movement somewhat; and lactation requires that a woman be oriented to the needs of an infant who regularly and insistently demands food.

But what should be made of these biological facts? One line of reasoning would be that the biological difference is sufficient by itself to account for sex-role differences. A woman's role, in this view, is "naturally" a domestic one, centered around childbearing and child raising, and women are equipped with "natural" talents, drives, and instincts to enable them to meet their maternal responsibilities. Thus, social role definitions merely recognize what is natural and obvious: anatomy is destiny.

There are numerous reasons to reject this simplistic view. The most important evidence is the existence of considerable historical and cultural variation in the roles of men and women, much more than can be explained by strict biological determinism. In simple hunting and gathering societies, for example, there is a characteristic division of responsibility between men and women. Men tend to range more widely and to do the hunting; women are more concentrated around the home base and engage in gathering activities while supervising young children. But although there is a division of labor in the performance of necessary tasks, it should be noted that both men and women engage in productive work. Women in such societies are not simply creatures of home and hearth.

As human societies evolved, they developed the capacity for settled agriculture, a system that relies upon the domestication of plants and animals rather than on the tapping of nature's bounty through hunting and gathering. As this occurred, men began to devote more of their time to agricultural activities and less to hunting. Although women continued to bear the greater share of domestic responsibilities for home and children, they also worked alongside their husbands in the fields. In an agricultural society, as in the hunting and gathering society, the family itself was a productive economic unit, and women as well as children shared in productive activity.

It is in industrial societies that we see some of the sharpest differences between the roles of men and women. As production moved out of the family unit and into the factory, women and children continued to work alongside their husbands and fathers. In the sweatshops of the late nineteenth and early twentieth centuries, for example, women and children were exploited, as were men, working long hours for low wages. However, with the gradual passage of legislation protecting woman and children and with the growing productivity of the industrial economy, work became increasingly defined as an activity for men. Women were relegated to the roles of wives and mothers, and children were given more time before they were permitted to enter the work force.

For much of the twentieth century, women have not been an important part of the labor force, with certain exceptions. During World War II, for example, women took over many factory jobs previously reserved for men because men were serving in the armed forces. Despite their adequate performance in "male jobs" on assembly lines and such, few continued at those tasks after the war ended and the men returned. Rosy the Riveter was expected to return to home and hearth, and generally speaking she did.

Women in the labor force have typically been relegated to occupations thought to be especially suited to their talents and capabilities. Thus, for example, women have been thought competent to be teachers, nurses, and librarians, but not engineers. Ideas about "women's work" have not remained historically constant, however, for work that at one time was thought to be too demanding for women, such as using typewriters, later became defined as work beneath the dignity of men but for which women were suited. And even within those occupations where women are numerically in the majority, positions of authority tend to be filled by males. Thus principals and library directors are more likely to be men, while rank-and-file teachers and librarians are more likely to be women.

As long as women were willing to view their employment as a secondary role to home and family, such inequities could prevail. But in recent years, two developments have begun to transform the nature of women's participation in work. First, demands for a rising standard of living have clashed with inflation, leading many women into the work force as a means of supplementing the family income. Many contemporary working families find it difficult to survive or to live as they would like on a single income. Second, economic forces have combined with an emerging ideology of equal participation in society to bring about major changes in sex-role definitions. Although women are still paid less than men, even for the same jobs, there is a decreasing acceptance of this fact and a growing readiness on the part of women to define themselves as entitled to equal pay and equal career opportunities.

Cultural diversity and historical changes make it clear that women can do and have done what men do when the need or the opportunity has arisen. Whether they were sharing agricultural work or entering the industrial labor force because of national need or economic necessity, women have arranged for child care and have done the work that needed to be done. And while men and women alike have at times felt strongly that children need the exclusive and devoted attention of their mothers, these attitudes have not been difficult to put aside when circumstances dictate. Clearly, there are no "natural" barriers to women's participation in the work place. In short, the biological facts are not as powerful as they might appear at first glance. Around the globe and throughout history, men and women have created social and cultural arrangements sharply different from those of our recent past.

In spite of considerable variation in what men and women actually do, in the way the capabilities and limitations of the sexes are defined, or in the way culture shapes the temperament of men and women, one important fact remains: on the whole, men have had more power over women than women have had over men. Political leaders in human history have been predominantly male. Laws governing property have generally accorded more rights to men than to women, and the law in Western society has frequently treated women in the same category as property. Women's access to jobs and to such civil rights as voting or owning property has been controlled by men. Even in societies where descent is reckoned through the woman (matrilineal societies) or where a newly married couple takes up residence in the locality of the mother (matrilocal societies), men have been the effective centers of power. And perhaps most important of all, it is the activities of men—in work, in science, in the arts, in religion—that have been defined as truly important. What women do is "women's work," and while it must be done, it is not important enough for men to do.

Perhaps the simplest explanation of male dominance is to attribute it to a conspiracy. Men hold power, it may be argued, because they view themselves as a class whose interest lies in subjugating women. Thus, from this perspective, at every point in history, men have conspired to wrest power from women. The tools with which they have done so are numerous. By gaining control of the state and its force, men have supplemented their natural superiority of strength with control over the legal institutions of a society. By gaining control over the religious apparatus, men have been able to build an ideology in which the subjugation of women is given religious sanction. By gaining control over the industrial mode of production, men have been able to exploit women as a part of the labor force to be used or disposed of as needed.

There is little doubt that men have controlled these major institutions. This control probably originated in the greater strength and size of men—about 15 percent greater than women, on the average. But explaining the persistent subjugation of women as a conspiracy to hold power assumes much more male consciousness of kind than the evidence supports. The exploitation of women in the labor force can be explained as part of a general tendency in a capitalist economic system to secure labor at the lowest possible cost and to engage in whatever exploitative activities are necessary to do so. No appeal to a male conspiracy is needed; in fact, men are exploited along with women. Many male religious leaders may not want to lose their control of religious functions, but it is likely that *tradition* rather than conspiracy keeps men in the more important positions. The religious ideologies of both Judaism and Christianity include beliefs that have given special rights, duties, and privileges to men. Regardless of the obligations incumbent on women, both religious traditions have accorded men a more honored and powerful place than women. These beliefs were consistent with the culture of the Middle Eastern societies of biblical times where Judaism and Christianity first developed. Today, even though social conditions are different, many women and men oppose change because they are committed to their religions and consider the social order encouraged by their religious beliefs to be the only proper one.

It is likely that the inertia of cultural tradition provides a better explanation of continuing male dominance and of the persistence of inequalities in sex roles than does a conspiracy theory. Once established, cultural beliefs and social practices tend to persist unless there is reason or pressure to change them. As the United States industrialized during the second half of the nineteenth century, for example, the roles of men and women became more rigidly separated. There developed conceptions of differences between men and women that were in many ways more pronounced than in the earlier agrarian America, a society in which men and women often labored side by side in farm and home.

Pablo Picasso, *Woman Ironing* (1904) Oil on canvas, 45¾ × 28¾ inches. Solomon R. Guggenheim Museum, New York. Gift, Justin K. Thannhauser. Photo: Robert E. Mates.

Although contemporary women participate widely in the labor force and aspire to a variety of careers other than housework, old typifications die hard. Thus, women who pursue careers may still be expected to do all those household tasks, such as laundry, that have traditionally been defined as "women's work."

The home became defined as the province of the wife and mother, a haven of virtue and comfort in a cruel and competitive world of affairs.

These definitions of the roles of men and women have persisted, even though the circumstances that brought them about have changed. People pass on to children their conceptions of the "proper" roles of men and women, and these conceptions do not necessarily reflect the current needs of the society nor even what men and women actually do. As we mentioned earlier, today husband and wife may both feel they must be employed in order to maintain an adequate standard of living. Consequently, traditional familial roles of the husband/father and wife/mother often cannot be met, yet many parents continue to pass on the traditional definitions of sex roles. For example, in many homes only female children are expected to do household tasks like cooking, sewing, washing dishes, dry, and child care; and only male children learn how to change an 'just a carburetor, or rewire a lamp.

SOCIALIZATION

Sex roles are transmitted through sex-role socialization, that process through which we learn appropriate role behavior and come to view ourselves as members of one sex or the other. Several psychological explanations have been advanced to account for this process of socialization, and we will review them briefly before developing a sociological view. Each of these theories identifies an important aspect of the process of sex-role socialization.

One important set of theories, of which Freudian psychoanalytic theory is the best known, emphasizes the concept of *identification* as being the basis for learning culturally appropriate sex roles (see Becker, 1971, for a discussion of Freudian theory from a perspective not unlike that of symbolic interactionism). In this view, children learn appropriate sex-role behavior because they identify with the parent of the same sex. Boys model themselves after their fathers and girls model themselves after their mothers. Each parent by his or her own behavior sets up standards that the child strives to meet. The wish of the child to be like the parent is explained by identification, by the development of a close emotional bond with the parent. This bond is not without tensions and complications. In Freud's view, children have a strong sexual interest in their parents. Thus, boys enter into a sexual rivalry with their fathers and fear castration as a punishment for their efforts to be close to their mothers. This castration anxiety leads them to identify with the possible aggressor—their father. The explanation of why girls identify with their mothers is a bit more complex, involving penis envy, the initial selection of the father as a love object, and the eventual decision to identify with the mother out of fear that continued attachment to the father will result in the loss of the mother's affections.

A second theory, known as *social learning theory*, takes a somewhat different path (see Bandura, 1969). Its main emphasis is upon the reinforcement of discrete items of behavior. Each time the child acts, its conduct is met with either approval or disapproval, depending in part upon whether the conduct is sex appropriate. Thus a girl who gives an imaginary tea party is praised, while a boy doing the same thing might be punished or at least receive a neutral response. Bit by bit, the theory seems to suggest, children learn what to do. Because they are rewarded for appropriate behavior, it remains in their repertory, while inappropriate behavior is dropped. Social learning theory also leaves room for imitation, similar to the theory of identification. In this view, children select their acts not simply on some random basis, but by imitating the behavior of significant figures such as the same-sex parent. Thus a child's learning is often not the consequence of trial and error, but is a rather efficient imitative process.

Finally, *cognitive developmental theories*, associated with the Swiss psychologist Jean Piaget and with the American psychologist Lawrence Kohlberg, suggest that individuals develop a firm and absolute sex categorization early in their lives. In Kohlberg's theory (1966, 1969), each person learns he is male or she is female, and this knowledge becomes the basis for many inferences made about conduct. Children select their behavior on the basis of their cognitions of what their behavior should be in terms of their sex identification. In this theory, behavior is not simply responding to rewards and punishments. In other words, a young male child thinks: "I am a boy, therefore I should act like a boy." As children mature and their cognitive powers develop and mature, the inferences are more powerful and refined, and the model of what is appropriately male or female is more abstract. Still, whatever the child's age, there is always a model of male or female that serves as the basis for inferences about how to behave.

Of these three theories, Kohlberg's is most consistent with a symbolic interactionist perspective and seems sociologically most useful. For symbolic interactionists, a role is not just a set of behaviors or a catalogue of duties and responsibilities. When people engage in successful role-making in everyday life, they do not, as has already been said, merely select a particular bit of behavior for the role they are playing. Nor, in many circumstances, does the role give detailed guidance about what to do. Life is so complex and situations are so varied that people must rely upon general principles and ideas rather than on detailed specific rules. A role is better conceived as a fairly abstract model of conduct, useful in making guesses about what to do in specific instances, but not always providing literal directions.

A symbolic interactionist would say that children use their self-categorizations as the basis for making inferences about how to behave in various circumstances. The boy who has just fallen and hurt himself, for example, will feel a strong impulse to cry. Up to a certain age, he will do so. But at a certain point, he will begin to inhibit this impulse, making the correct inference that "big boys don't cry." He has recognized that his behavior may meet with disapproval if he does cry. Thus, a process of inference (deciding that behaving like a boy requires him to avoid crying) is accompanied by a process of role-taking (imagining the responses of others to his act).

It is the self-conception that organizes this process of inference. Conceptions of "boy behavior" and "girl behavior" depend upon the recognition of consistencies in the behavior of boys and girls. Individuals are led to make inferences about their own conduct because sex differences become a crucial part of identity. We know that we are of one sex or the other; we think of ourselves as having the characteristics of one sex or the other; and our self-evaluations come to depend upon maintaining those self-images. To maintain the image of ourselves as malelike or femalelike, we must take our inferences about male and female behavior and convert them into actual conduct. Thus we infer what a male would do or what a female would do, and then we actually do it, depending on whether we are male or female. If we did not, we could no longer claim an identity that is important to us, nor could we feel positively about ourselves.

As this account suggests, it is the identification of self with a social category (male or female) that seems particularly important in shaping conduct. Individuals identify with the category male or female and on that basis make behavioral choices. Yet identification with same-sex parents and behavioral reinforcement also play some role in shaping behavior, and the theories that emphasize these processes cannot be lightly dismissed.

It is, for example, difficult to dispute that identification with a parent is a crucial aspect of sex-role socialization. While one can take very serious issue with Freud's views, particularly his emphasis upon castration anxiety and penis envy, the notion that a close and complex emotional bond develops between boys and fathers and girls and mothers seems quite accurate in Western society. Fathers and mothers provide the most immediate and powerful models for conduct and the most powerful sources of information about maleness and femaleness to the child.

The foregoing explanation of socialization emphasizes the inferences children make about male and female conduct. However, it is important to recognize that all behavior is not consciously or intentionally selected. Particularly at the earlier stages of socialization, the child's capacity for self-consciousness is limited, and much that is learned is best explained in terms of simple reinforcement. At later points, the capacity for inference is limited, partly by the child's stage of cognitive development and partly by limited social experience. At the stage of socialization Mead (1934) called the *play stage*, much of what children do is imitative in a very simple sense. Children do what they have seen important adults do, imitating adult actions and words by playing "house" or "work," but their play is not governed by an organized sense of what the adult world is like. Girls may imitate their mothers, not because at this stage they understand the female role, but simply because their experience and cognitive ability limits them to imitation. Later, at the *game stage*, children engage in more highly organized play. Indeed, their conduct generally is more highly organized. At this stage, children develop and refine the capacity for role-taking, for cooperative interaction with each other as well as with adults. When this happens, children begin to make more elaborate and accurate inferences about male and female roles as well as other roles they play. They begin to have a sense of where male and female fit in the scheme of things. They begin to have a sense of how society is structured and how their own activities are expected to fit within this structure.

To summarize, symbolic interactionists would say that children gradually acquire the capacity to make male and female roles. Their capacity depends at the earliest stages upon reinforcement and imitation. Gradually, more of their ability to behave in an appropriate sex role hinges upon their overall grasp of the sexual division of labor and their capacity to make correct inferences about sex-appropriate behavior. In this learning process, the child identifies with both

Emile Renouf, *The Helping Hand* (1881)
The Corcoran Gallery, Washington

What kind of sex-role socialization is taking place in this painting of a young girl and an older man? Is the girl learning that a female can pull an oar just as well as a man? Or is she learning from the smiles of those watching this "cute" scene that a girl can "help" but never really do "a man's job"?

the sex role itself and with parents and other significant others who represent the sex role.

LANGUAGE AND SEXUAL IDENTITY

How We Talk about the Sexes

Language is a powerful clue to people's perceptions of the world and can help us understand their behavior. As we have said, language is a repository of culture; its words label the diverse objects that exist for a people and which are important in their lives. Hence, in examining the way men and women talk and the way they are talked about, it is possible to learn more about the nature of sex differences. Numerous studies indicate that there are significant differences in language related to sex.

As indicated earlier, the sexual dichotomy is an important element in the division of labor. Men and women perform different jobs in society. Consequently, it is not surprising that many occupational titles pertain more to one sex than to another. Many job titles carry with them a strong implication that incumbents are members of one sex, even if in theory members of the opposite sex could hold the position. Mention of a nurse leads the listener to think of a woman, even though men can be and are nurses. The assumption that nurses are women is so entrenched in our society that men who are nurses generally have to be identified explicitly as "male nurses." To put this another way, the cultural typification of "nurse" includes the attribute "female," so that when we think of the former we automatically think of the latter.

The association of a job title with gender has led feminists to be especially conscious of the way language shapes our perceptions of occupational opportunity. Such titles as policemen, firemen, and the like, by referring explicitly to the male gender, seem to carry the implication that only men can hold such jobs. Thus, there have been efforts to change usage to reflect less gender bias, for example, police officer or firefighter, terms that contain no explicit reference to gender.

In the town where the authors live, the local governing body is called the Board of Selectmen, a traditional New England term for that group of "select" men who were responsible for local governance. In recent years, many verbal battles have been fought over the issue of whether the traditional term should be abandoned in favor of a Board of Selectpeople or Select Board. The theory underlying such efforts is that the typification of certain positions or occupations as exclusively male is supported by terms that mention only the male gender. Although this is undeniably so, it does not follow that changing the terms of address automatically opens up these positions to women. As occupations such as nurse suggest, a title can be closely associated with the female sex, even if it contains no explicit reference to gender. By the same token, it is possible for typifications of positions to change, even if their titles continue to have a gender reference. Thus, even though the attempt to officially change our town's Board of Selectmen to a Board of Selectpeople has been defeated several times, it does not mean that the community thinks the board can be composed only of men. It is commonly understood that women as well as men can hold the office. Indeed, four of the last five chairmen of the Board of Selectmen have been women, and three of the five selectmen are women.

In short, the typification associated with a word is more important than the literal meaning of the word. Gender-loaded terms may persist even when the typifications change; hence, people can easily think of female selectmen. And terms may be changed to eliminate sexist bias without altering the typification; hence, even though the official title is firefighters, most people probably think of them as men.

Terms of address—whether people use titles in addressing one another or adopt a more informal style of using first names—are good clues to relative status and power in any human relationship. Those with more power have greater freedom in addressing their subordinates. Not surprisingly, therefore, differences exist in the way men and women are addressed.

On the whole, women are addressed by more familiar terms than are men in similar positions. Even when two persons are of equivalent social status, the female is more likely to be addressed in familiar terms. Often women will be called by their first names in circumstances where men are called by their last names. In a university, for example, male professors will refer to one another by last name ("See Hewitt about that"). But rarely will they use this form to refer to a female colleague. She will be referred to by first name ("Did you ask Myrna?") or by last name preceded by title ("Ask Dr. Hewitt," or "Professor Hewitt" or even "Mrs. Hewitt").

These differences in the way we habitually refer to men and women reflect profound differences in their position in the social world and in their identities. Not only are men more powerful than women, holding most of the important occupational and political positions, but the identities of men and women are founded on very different grounds. A man's identity—his own sense of who he is in the world and others' views of who and what he is—is ordinarily founded on a conception of himself as an autonomous, independent, acting being. In contrast, a woman's identity is much more likely to be founded on her relationships with others, particularly men. As Robin Lakoff suggests, a man is known by what he does; a woman is known by the men with whom she is associated (1973: 65).

This fact is illustrated by the way men and women are treated in newspaper and magazine articles. Most men about whom articles are written are individuals who are noteworthy because of some action or achievement. Whether they are politicians, athletes, actors, business leaders, or scientists, virtually every male discussed in the media got there on his own. Not so for females. Despite an ever-growing number of women who have achieved positions comparable to men and who similarly are the subjects of magazine articles, studies have shown that most articles about women are concerned with the wives, mothers, or daughters of prominent men. This clearly emerges in the annual list of "most admired women," which consistently includes the wife of the president of the United States and other famous men's wives.

There are also differences in the style and content of articles about men and women. It has often been recognized that females are more likely than males to be described in terms of their physical attributes ("a striking blond" or "a plain woman in her forties") or by their familial status ("the mother of three," "a divorcee," or "wife of local businessman, Sam Wilson"). Rarely do the media describe a man as a "tall blond with a receding hairline" or as "Tom White, husband of Jane White, local realtor."

One other language difference in articles about men and women is the way that the sexes are identified by name. Just as was discussed above, men are more often referred to by their full name, their last name alone, or their last name with a title. Rarely will they be identified by their first name alone. Women, however, are often identified by their full name at the beginning of the article and then by their first name. Rarely will they be called only by their last name.

Sex Differences in Speech

The speech of men and women differs in three important ways: in content (what they talk about), in style (how they use the language to express themselves), and in vocalization (the way their voices sound). These differences both reflect and help to sustain the unequal positions of men and women in society.

The adult male and female voices do not sound alike. Some of the deeper and more resonant qualities of the adult male voice can be attributed to shorter and thicker vocal cords. But cultural definitions of how men and women should sound also play an important part, because in speech, as in other forms of behavior, we learn to conform to social expectations. Just as it is assumed that men and women sound different, it is also a common assumption that boys and girls sound alike. Recent linguistic studies have shown this is not the case. Researchers have shown that listeners can identify the sex of a child simply by hearing recorded voices (Sachs, 1975). Even when boys and girls of similar size and weight (and therefore with the same size vocal tracts) were compared, judges were able to identify correctly the sex of the speaker. Although the basic frequencies of boys' and girls' voices were the same, subtle changes could be made by children to make their voices fit the appropriate adult gender speech patterns. Thus, it is culture and not simply anatomy that differentiates male and female voices.

Like other aspects of gender-appropriate behavior, children learn correct linguistic styles and carry them into their adult lives. Confronted with the same situation, for example, men and women are apt to express their reactions differently. Faced with a stolen car, a woman might say, "Oh my! My car is gone!" A man in the same situation might say, "Damn it! Where in the hell is my car?" These differing reactions reflect the observation that men, on the whole, use stronger expletives than women. Similarly, adjectives such as "lovely" or "adorable" are more likely to be used by women than men.

However, style is not just a matter of using different expressions or words. Males have been found often to have a more empirical style of speech than females. Eakins and Eakins (1978) looked at how male and female students gave directions. One individual was shown a line drawing of a series of boxes and asked to tell the rest of the class how to reproduce it. Men were more analytical and literal in their directions. For example, a male student said, "The left side of the square intersects the midpoint of the top side of the square below it at about a 45-degree angle." Women seemed more casual in their approach. Their description was, "It is a box standing on its end touching the middle of the box below it." Also, male students repeated the instructions more frequently than did female students.

Similarly, when men and women were asked to describe a photograph their linguistic styles differed. Men objectively described the photographs of people in various settings, whereas women interpreted them. For example, a male would describe a photograph literally:

> The eyebrows intersect to form a v-shape in the center. The eyes are narrowed and elliptical, the mouth droops a centimeter at each corner and parallels a shadow line on the face. (Eakins and Eakins, 1978: 28)

The female's interpretive style is exemplified in the following description:

> He has a distasteful look and he might be posing as skeptical of what he hears. (Eakins and Eakins, 1978: 28)

The foregoing examples show how men and women establish different styles of speech by using different vocabularies. These vocabulary differences between the sexes will be discussed in more detail in the general discussion of the content of speech.

Some stylistic differences between male and female speech are so great that scholars have written about women's language. Such a language includes the use of intensive adjectives and adverbs (such a, terribly, adorable); qualifiers (I guess, perhaps, it seems to me); and fillers (um humm, umm). Among the most studied features of women's language is the *tag question*, which is neither a statement nor a question, but falls in between. "It's time for lunch, isn't it?" softens the straightforward assertion that "It's time for lunch," but at the same time it is not really an inquiry.

Robin Lakoff (1975), in her study of women's language, argues that the use of the tag question by women is a way of avoiding strong statements. There are times, of course, when the use of a tag question is a legitimate, logical device to convey meaning. If there is a possibility that someone has misinterpreted something another speaker has said, for example, a person may properly use the tag question for confirmation: "You said you were coming, didn't you?" Tag questions are frequently used in small talk at parties. The speaker knows the answer but uses the tag question to initiate a conversation: "This is a great party, isn't it?" Finally, people sometimes use tag questions to get confirmation of something they hope will happen: "You are going to clean your room before you go out, aren't you?"

Tag questions are particularly important in a woman's speech because they are employed as a means of avoiding strong assertions. When a woman says "That's a great idea, isn't it?" she is making it easy for someone to disagree with her. Sometimes the use of this form is an intentional means of avoiding confrontation; by lessening the assertiveness of a statement, it is easier to disavow it if others disagree. But regardless of intent, frequent use of the tag question causes the speaker to be seen as weak and indecisive.

The use of lengthy, roundabout ways of making requests is another way in which women devalue their positions. One way of getting someone to do something is to make a direct request: "On your way home, please pick up a loaf of bread at the market." But this is not the only way of making the request. Some women say, "If you don't mind, would you pick up a loaf of bread on your way home?" This both lengthens the request and reduces its force. Indeed, some women cushion their requests to seem hardly like a request at all: "I know you're busy, but if it's not too much trouble, would it be possible for you to stop on your way home and buy a loaf of bread? If you can, I would really appreciate it." While any of the foregoing ways of making a request might produce a loaf of bread, which mother would you be most apt to listen to?

The stylistic differences between men's and women's speech are not only interesting in themselves, but they also have real consequences for the relationships between men and women. As we have seen, tag questions and the lengthening of requests weaken a woman's position. Similarly, the use of intensifiers and sex-stereotyped qualifiers tend to trivialize her statements. Thus the very style of women's speech tends to put them at a disadvantage in their interaction with men, and in doing so, helps to perpetuate a social structure in which men and women have unequal positions.

Given their different positions in the division of labor, it is not surprising that the content of men's and women's speech differs markedly. Differing occupation and life experiences call for different vocabularies. For example, men are more likely to know what an Allen wrench is, while women will know how to sauté something. What people talk about and the words they employ reflect their activities. Hence, to the extent that the roles of men and women differ, their language will reflect this fact.

In any complex society, distinctive categories of people have specialized vocabularies. People use words and assume that others will understand what they mean. If a word has a common meaning that differs from that of the group, there can be difficulties in understanding. In addition, some words have distinctive meanings in different groups. For example, the word "crop" means something harvested to a farmer, a way of trimming a print to a photographer, and a short whip to an equestrian. Since most people know the appropriate vocabulary of any group to which they belong, problems rarely arise and such distinctive vocabularies are of little consequence in everyday life. However, if male vocabularies are important in many occupations—for example, if a successful sales-person must know about football or politics—and a woman has learned only female vocabularies, she will be at a disadvantage regardless of academic training and ability. To put it another way, as long as women's speech is different from that of men, and as long as women's language is less important, women will be at a disadvantage.

Semantic Derogation

There is yet another way by which language impacts upon gender. Schulz (1975) has called this "the semantic derogation of women." By this, she refers to the fact that many words used with specific reference to women are derogatory, trivialized, debased, or otherwise devalued, while similar terms with reference to men carry no such derogatory connotation. Consider, for example, the two terms used to indicate unmarried persons, bachelor and spinster. What did you picture as you read those two words? If you were like many Americans, you saw the bachelor as virile, relatively young, and perhaps something of a man-about-town or swinger. But the spinster is not the bachelor's female counterpart. You probably pictured her as older, gray-haired, up-tight, prim, and proper.

Even more indicative of the impact of language on society's view of men and women are the changes that have taken place in the English language over the past several centuries. In her study, Schulz looks at titles used for men and women and how these have developed differing meanings. For example, the word "Lord" continues to be used in its original sense, referring to a particular class of English noblemen; "Lady" is the female version of the word. However, while lord has remained restricted to those of noble birth, any female is likely to have the term lady applied to her. Similarly, the word "governor" usually refers to someone who has authority in a state or territory. The feminine version of the word, "governess," is not a woman in control of a state; she is a nursemaid, and her domain is that of children.

An even better example of the changing meanings of words are the terms "master," "madam," and "mistress." Originally all three referred to the head of a household. Such is not the case today. The masculine form, master, has no derogatory referent, and even if the man does not use the word himself, he is not likely to find fault with someone who calls him the master of his household. But what of the woman who is called either a madam or a mistress? The former has come to be a person who oversees a household of prostitutes, and the latter is a woman kept by a male for sexual purposes. The tendency for words used in reference to women to carry with them definite sexual connotations is one of the more telling findings in Schulz's study. Words that refer to men are much less likely to have such meanings.

CONCLUSION

Modern society confronts men and women with different expectations and presents them with unequal opportunities. It exerts powerful pressures on both sexes to adopt self-conceptions that reflect cultural definitions of sex differences, to seek entry only into those social roles thought to be open to members of one sex or the other, and to behave in sex-appropriate ways in all spheres of life.

Men should think of themselves as men, fill masculine jobs and other male roles, and act like men. Likewise for women.

As we have seen, the cultural definitions of men and women are embedded in the very language we speak. Our words tend to mirror, and thus reinforce, the social structure. Not only do men and women speak differently and address each other differently, but even occupational titles often carry implications about the sex of the incumbent. Each speech act can be seen as a reaffirmation of culture, a realization of the society's beliefs about men and women, and thus a force maintaining the inertia of cultural tradition. By their words and deeds, people give life to culture and help sustain the social structure of inequality between men and women.

Yet, powerful as they are, culture and social structure do not totally control our actions. Since the 1960s the Women's Movement has mounted effective resistance to many traditional beliefs and accepted practices. While women still lag behind men in employment opportunities and compensation, some barriers have begun to break down. There is somewhat more recognition of the capabilities of women and acceptance of their role in occupations outside the home.

What of the future? How far will equality between the sexes progress? How far can it progress?

These questions cannot be answered with any certainty. For some radical feminists, the goals of the Women's Movement will not be attained until every vestige of sex differentiation and sex inequality is removed; men and women would be indistinguishable in attitudes, in the opportunities open to them, and in the tasks they perform. For others, the Women's Movement has already been too successful in undermining what they perceive to be the natural and just arrangement of relationships betwen the sexes. They are likely to continue to mount resistance to movement goals. Therefore, it may be that the years ahead will see continuing social conflict over the proper roles of and relationships between men and women.

One issue that will be important in this conflict is the extent to which it is possible to have a society in which the tasks of men and women are completely undifferentiated and in which there is total equality between the sexes. Many feminists believe that full equality is possible, that personality differences between the sexes, as well as differences in interest and strength, are completely the result of socialization. If this is so, they argue, then it is at least theoretically possible to structure a society in which future generations are taught norms of sexual equality and in which sex differences will disappear. In this view, even the special reproductive role of women as childbearers need not imply tremendous sex differences in other spheres of life, since men can be taught to take on their share of parental responsibilities. Control over reproduction, through contraception and abortion, is also seen as contributing to an eventual equality between the sexes.

Others are not so sure. While firmly committed to equality and sharing of parental and other household responsibilities, some feminists believe that biology cannot be completely overlooked. Discoveries in the field of neuroendocrinology have led sociologist Alice Rossi to conclude (1977) that there may well be inherent differences in the ease with which men and women learn certain tasks. This injects a new perspective into the study of sex-role socialization, for it indicates that while culture plays a powerful role in governing what we learn, biology influences the propensity of each sex to learn certain kinds of roles. Consequently, women may more naturally and easily learn tasks associated with childbearing and childrearing than do men. If this is true, it will not be easy to resocialize men so that their commitment to parenting has the same intensity as that of women. But, as Rossi points out, saying that something is difficult does not make it impossible. Biology may constrain, but it need not dictate.

While the exact nature of the influence of hormonal factors upon learning remains to be worked out, one fact now seems clear. Humans have evolved biologically to a point where culture is the dominant force influencing our behavior. But we are not yet disembodied spirits whose physiology and biochemistry are irrelevant. Without discounting the tremendous influence of culture, it seems unlikely that differences between men and women are due to cultural factors operating alone. In the years ahead, as we seek to reconstruct our culture to provide for more humane and equitable definitions of the roles of men and women, careful research into the way that culture molds and shapes our basic biology will be an important task.

SUGGESTED READINGS

EAKINS, BARBARA W. and R. GENE EAKINS. *Sex Differences in Human Communications* (Boston: Houghton Mifflin, 1978).

LAKOFF, ROBIN. *Language and Women's Place* (New York: Harper & Row, Pubs., 1975).

LAWS, JUDITH LONG and PEPPER SCHWARTZ. *Sexual Scripts: The Social Construction of Female Sexuality* (Hinsdale, Ill.: Dryden Press, 1977).

OAKLEY, ANN. *The Sociology of Housework* (New York: Pantheon, 1975).

ROSSI, ALICE. "A Biosocial Perspective on Parenting," *Daedalus* 106 (1977): 1–31.

THORNE, BARRIE and NANCY HANLEY, eds. *Language and Sex: Difference and Dominance* (Rowley, Mass.: Newbury House, 1975).

TUCHMAN, GAYE, ARLENE KAPLAN DANIELS, and JAMES BENET, eds. *Hearth and Home: Images of Women in the Mass Media* (New York: Oxford University Press, 1978).

10

Social Inequality

In every society, people are unequal. Even in the simplest hunting and gathering societies, some individuals and families manage to collect more food or build more secure dwellings. In more sophisticated agricultural societies and in modern industrial societies, inequality is a more important and persistent fact of life. Some people own large tracts of land, while others have a small plot or none at all. Some people have more money than they will ever need, while others have scarcely enough to enable them to survive, much less maintain a decent standard of living. Some individuals are highly respected for the important work they do, while others perform menial tasks and are viewed as inferior. Some people have positive images of themselves, while others regard themselves as worthless. In most societies, these forms of inequality are not simply the result of individual differences in effort or initiative but are part of the social order.

What different forms does social inequality take? Why does it exist? What are its consequences for individuals and for society as a whole? Is inequality inevitable? This chapter attempts to answer these questions. It will look at the nature of social inequality as sociologists conceive it and at the forms of inequality in contemporary society.

THE NATURE OF INEQUALITY

People can be unequal in many ways, for anything that can be possessed in varying quantities can be distributed unequally. Land, food, money, houses, tools, physical strength, knowledge, intelligence, beauty, honor, and self-respect are among the things that one person or group may possess more or less of than some other person or group. Whatever things are defined as important by the members of a given society, it is likely that some people will have more of them than others, that those who have more will try to keep what they have, and that those who have less will want to get more of what is valued.

Power, Prestige, and Wealth

Two major intellectual figures—Karl Marx and Max Weber—strongly influenced the way contemporary sociologists look at social inequality. For Marx, economic inequality was of prime importance in shaping both the history of a society and individuals' experiences in it (see Bendix and Lipset, 1966). Marx argued that it is not simply inequality of wealth that is important, but rather the way wealth is produced and socially organized. From his point of view, whoever controls the means of production controls society. Marx argued that over time, societies become divided into two competing social classes. One class is composed of people who own and control the means of production (land, tools, factories); thus, they determine what is produced and how much of it is distributed and to whom. The other class is composed of all those who are dependent on the controlling class; they till the land or work in the factories.

Peggy Bacon, *The Social Graces* (1935)
Drypoint. 10⅞ × 7⅜ inches. Collection of Whitney Museum of American Art. Purchase. Acq#36.42.

Social classes differ greatly in their conceptions of etiquette, use of leisure time, and styles of informal socializing. "The social graces" are thus an aspect of life style—one that serves to identify members of the same class to one another and to make outsiders instantly visible.

Weber shared Marx's belief that economic factors were important in understanding society (see Gerth and Mills, 1958: 180–195). He agreed that a class was composed of people with a similar economic position, but he did not think that economic factors simply determined a society's social stratification. He tried to balance the economic determination of Marx and his followers by distinguishing between class and status. For Weber, both dimensions of inequality are important. *Class* groups are composed of people whose relationship to the means of producing goods and services is similar and who may or may not consciously band together to pursue their common interests. Factory owners are a class in this sense, as are shopkeepers or factory workers. *Status* groups are composed of people at a comparable level of respect, prestige, or honor. Whereas class is based upon economic considerations, status is based upon the amount of respect claimed by and accorded to particular social groups—the nobility, the upper crust, working people.

Social classes are unequal in *life chances*, a concept Weber introduced to refer to the individual's present and future likelihood of success. Life chances include the probability that an infant will be healthy and survive; the amount and quality of education the individual can attain; the quality of available food, housing, and medical care; in short, the person's prospects for economic success in life. In Weber's analysis (a view shared by contemporary sociologists), class membership determines life chances. That is, the extent to which you acquire any of the things valued in your society is dependent to a great extent on where you start in the class system.

People with similar *life styles*—customs, attitudes, and values—form status groups. Such people are conscious of their position in a hierarchy of such groups. The members of a status group, such as the English nobility or the members of the Social Register in an American city, think of themselves as "better" than other people. Working people who have modest occupations and incomes are apt to look down on the "lazy" and "irresponsible" poor, but at the same time to feel that they count for less than the more successful and wealthier middle class. A status group is a community of people who, although they may be widely dispersed geographically, share a sense of similarity and common fate.

In the long run, economic considerations govern the formation of status groups. Class groups are likely to develop common life styles and to perceive their similarities and common interests. But as Weber emphasized, the social hierarchies of class and status do not always correspond closely. Those who are the richest in a society may not comprise its highest status group. Many American families whose wealth and social position have been passed on for generations have much less money but higher social standing than more recently successful families. As the owners of old wealth, they are the status group to which the more recently successful aspire to belong. Similarly, a skilled blue-collar worker might earn more than an office worker, but white-collar jobs are generally evaluated as more desirable and higher in prestige in industrial societies.

One idea especially differentiates Weber's ideas from those of Marx. Marx thought that the members of the *proletariat* (the worker class in industrial capitalism) would ultimately become conscious of themselves as a class with common interests; they would then band together and overthrow the capitalist class. They would do so, he felt, because they had real common interests that could not be forever ignored. Although they might for a time refuse to recognize the interests that bound them together, workers were exploited and would eventually recognize that they must overthrow their masters.

Unlike Marx, who saw society always becoming a two-class system, Weber argued that many class groups can form. Weber not only thought the development of *class-consciousness* to be precarious, but he also felt Marx's concept of objective class interest to be shaky. Members of a society, he wrote, can define their interests in a variety of ways and perceive a variety of alliances. Those who are at a given level of wealth and economic position do not necessarily recognize their similarities, band together, or seek to pursue common ends. They may do so under some conditions, but not inevitably.

Weber also felt that status considerations could undermine consciousness of class position. Poor Southern white farmers, for example, share a class position with poor black farmers, but the two have historically formed different status communities. Whites, who looked down upon blacks as inferior, could not imagine banding together with them to pursue common economic interests. Their status position as "white" has greater import in their lives than does their class position of "poor." In this, Weber's analysis is close to that of symbolic interactionists: people act on the basis of their definition of situations. There is no simple objective reality shaping people's lives; conduct is shaped by people's perceptions of reality. Thus, those in differing status groups may believe that this difference is more important than their "real" shared class.

Following Weber's lead, sociologists emphasize factors in addition to economic differences in their analysis of social inequality. These many ways of determining inequality can be concentrated into three categories: wealth, prestige, and power.

Wealth Although social inequality is based on various factors, one of the most significant is wealth. This term refers to economic assets and takes many different forms, the most frequent being property and money. But whatever its form and source, wealth is something that can be held, used, and transmitted to others.

Property—in the form of land, houses, factories, ships, trucks, slaves, and a host of other things—is a key form of wealth and is based upon a cultural idea referring to the *right of ownership*. In simplest terms, to "own" property is to have the right to do with it as one wishes—to grow crops of one's choosing, to destroy or improve a building, or to sell the property to someone else.

Anything can be property, including people (in societies that practice slavery), material objects, and ideas. Who can own what is determined by a society's culture. For example, in contemporary Western society, individuals may own land as well as objects, but the Plains Indians of North America did not think of themselves as "owning" the land on which they lived and hunted. Each group had a conception of the territory over which it customarily roamed in search of buffalo, but these people had a very limited conception of their "rights" to the land. They did not conceive of it as something they could sell or give to someone else. The land simply "was." Yet even in such societies, differences in wealth occur. Whether measured by horses, blankets, robes, or beads, some people had more wealth than others.

In contemporary societies, property is an important legal concept. The various forms of property are usually defined and protected in laws and by legal agreements between individuals. Rights to land, for example, are governed by law and conveyed in deeds. Thus, local zoning ordinances usually place some restrictions on what can be done with land, such as making it illegal to build

factories on land zoned for residences. And a deed is a legal document symbolizing the transfer of rights to a piece of land from one individual to another. Ideas are a form of property governed by patent and copyright law. By patenting an invention or copyrighting a book, the person prevents others from using his or her ideas for their own benefit. How one acquires and disposes of property varies. In contemporary society, it is often closely tied to another form of wealth—money.

Unlike property, the value of which is often determined by intrinsic qualities of the object, the value of money is symbolic and exists solely because the members of a society agree that certain forms of metal, paper, or whatever have value. And where money is used to determine wealth, a different dimension is added to exchange. People are not limited to *barter* (trading discrete items of property) but can trade goods or labor for money. Money is a generalized medium of exchange that is especially important in complex agrarian and industrial societies. People work for wages and are paid in objects that are physically worthless but symbolically valuable. A dollar bill, as we all know, has little value in itself; its worth (like that of other things, such as gold or silver) depends upon its definition as valuable and upon the fact that people act on the basis of this definition. Money is thus a symbolic, but also a very important, form of wealth.

Money is the usual form of personal wealth in industrial societies, in which most people work for others and earn a weekly or monthly income. Comparatively few people inherit large sums of money or leave large sums to their heirs. And although many people accumulate savings, they are largely savings from earned income. In other societies, wealth may take different forms. In an agricultural society, for example, people may have relatively little cash and purchase very little of what they need; their wealth takes the form of land, livestock, tools, and stored food. Whatever form it takes, wealth is likely to be unequally distributed in the society.

Power Power may be defined as the capacity of some people to get others to do what they want them to do, even if the others resist their efforts to control them. Employers have the power to compel their employees to follow company rules while at work, and the employees risk losing their jobs if they do not comply. The state has the power to compel parents to send their children to school, and parents risk fines if they do not comply.

Power rests upon a variety of resources. The possession of superior force through physical strength or having a monopoly on violent weapons is one power resource. The thief compels a victim to hand over money because of the possession of superior force, just as the police use force to subdue the criminal. Wealth is another resource of power. The employer who owns factories and tools controls the distribution of money to workers, just as the owner of a medieval estate controlled land, and thus controlled the capacity of peasants to scratch out a meager living from the soil. Knowledge is also an important power resource. Those who control computer technology in the contemporary world, for example, have power because what they have is something very much wanted by others—the capacity to produce goods and services and to organize and control information more efficiently.

Power rests upon the fact that resources are scarce; they do not exist in unlimited quantities. In some cases, scarcity occurs naturally. There is, for example, only a finite amount of land available for human use. But some kinds of scarcity are artificially contrived, as in the case of knowledge. Any number of people can know a given fact—for example, how to make an efficient automobile or a supercomputer. Knowledge becomes scarce when it is prevented from flowing freely, so that many do not learn what a few know. Knowledge may be made scarce in a variety of ways: religious leaders may keep certain rituals secret; professionals, such as physicians and lawyers, may use esoteric language that is not widely or easily understood; corporations may maintain trade secrets or take out patents that restrict the use of inventions.

Whatever the resource on which it is based, power is rarely absolute or unequivocal, but emerges as individuals and social groups contend and negotiate with each other (see Strauss, 1978). The person or group in possession of power has to be willing to commit resources to secure desired ends. School officials, for example, have to be willing to take families to court to enforce truancy regulations. Companies have to be ready to fire workers who do not comply with their demands. Usually there are costs associated with the use of power, even when the power rests upon an absolute command of a resource. A company that ruthlessly exploits its workers and fires all who resist it may find that it has strengthened their resolve to resist. The cost of its exercise of power is the workers' increased militancy, which may lead them to contemplate using resources they had previously refused to use. In the years before organized labor won the right to strike and bargain collectively, for example, unyielding companies sometimes found their plants sabotaged by angered workers.

The unequal power possessed by individuals, groups, and collectivities in a society is not an abstract social force, but a reality created and recreated in everyday life. As people seek to pursue their goals, they are apt to define certain situations as permitting or requiring the use of power. Power is likely to be exercised, for example, when individuals or groups pursue goals that conflict with those of others and when they perceive its use as likely to yield results. The corporation seeking to keep its employees' wages low, for example, is seeking to advance its own interests, and it will use the power it has if its leaders believe they will be successful. Power rests partly upon the resources possessed by people or groups, but also upon others' perceptions of how significant these resources are and how likely it is that they will be used. Thus, if workers think that a company's economic condition is precarious and that it will be unable to find other workers to replace them, they are likely to conclude that a strike will benefit them, that the company will make wage or other concessions in order to avoid a long strike.

Prestige Prestige is more elusive and more difficult to define than power, but it is an important aspect of social life nevertheless. In any society or community, some groups and individuals are valued more highly than others. They are thought, by themselves and often by others, to be somehow "better"—to be worthy of respect and emulation, or to exemplify what an admirable and successful person should be like. A person with prestige is one whom others think worthy of their respect and admiration, someone they would urge their children to emulate. In American society, a physician is generally valued and respected because of his or her occupation. A manual laborer may be an equally fine or moral person, but will not command respect because of occupation.

Who has more prestige and who has less depends in part on the values emphasized in a society. Whatever human beings are capable of valuing—knowledge, strength, the accumulation of property, or power—they can make the basis for according or not according prestige. Where power is the chief goal for which people strive—as, for example, some would argue is true in the federal government and its various branches and agencies—power confers prestige. In Washington, D.C., it is said, people are respected in proportion to the power they have or appear to have. Where people define education as an important goal, those who are educated will be honored. Jewish communities, for example, have traditionally emphasized learning, and the poor scholar who was deeply learned in the Torah and Talmud was an honored person in the Eastern European Jewish villages before World War II. Poor he might be, but he was nevertheless sought after as a potential husband for more well-to-do brides.

Sometimes prestige depends upon lineage. Old and respected families can be found in almost every American community. The sons and daughters of these families, whose social position reflects the acquisition of wealth and power at some time in the past, claim some measure of respect simply on the basis of family membership. The Lodges of Massachusetts, the Rockefellers of New York, or the Hearsts of California exemplify such families. They claim respect not only on the basis of wealth, but on the basis of lineage—the fact that they are descendants of wealthy and powerful ancestors.

In industrial societies, occupation and education are the primary bases for according people prestige (see Nock and Rossi, 1979). The worth of a man or woman is often measured by their occupation. Moreover, research has shown that the ranking of occupational prestige is remarkably similar among industrial societies (Treiman, 1977). In general, occupations that earn higher incomes and whose members have attained more years of education confer higher prestige. Because occupational success is valued and defined largely in terms of money and training, its attainment confers prestige on the individual. In addition to occupation, however, contemporary societies also evaluate people on the basis of race, religion, gender, and other ascribed and achieved social statuses.

Typifications play a part in the attribution of prestige to individuals. Part of the typification of an occupation has to do with the skills, personality characteristics, and even moral attributes of people engaged in it. Supreme Court justices are thought to be learned, wise, and honest. Used-car salesmen are typified as dishonest and aggressive. Typifications of members of racial, ethnic, or religious groups also operate. The racist stereotype of the "lazy black" or the antisemitic portrait of the "greedy Jew" affect the process whereby individuals gain or lose prestige. Such typifications provide a lens through which the attributes and motives of individuals are perceived and interpreted, and respect is either accorded them or expected from them.

However defined in a given society, prestige usually entails *deference behavior*. People defer to those higher in prestige; that is, they overtly demonstrate attitudes of respect, admiration, or in some cases even veneration. Deference can be observed in a variety of ways. Terms of address provide one clue to the prestige ranking of interacting individuals. Physicians and college teachers, for example, are often addressed as "Dr." or "Professor," but are likely to call their patients or students by their first names. A similar pattern was part of the traditional norms of race relations in the American South. Blacks addressed whites as "Mr." or "Sir," but whites were free to address blacks by their first names.

Deference can also be expressed in somewhat more subtle fashion. Imagine a department-store clerk approached simultaneously by two customers, one in work clothes, the other in the designer-labeled uniform of a suburban housewife. It is likely that the clerk would first offer to help the better dressed woman and only then turn to the other woman. Doing so might not even reflect a conscious decision; habituated as we are to showing deference based on prestige, we often are unaware of doing so.

Deferential behavior does not necessarily reflect underlying deferential attitudes. The department-store clerk and her working-class customer may well resent the suburban housewife, even while they are showing deference. A patient may resent the casual way the physician addresses her by her first name and attribute this to the arrogance of male physicians. In Colonial America the elderly had very high prestige—the proper attitude toward them was one of veneration—but there is evidence that the young often resented the old and the power they held.

Groups of people similar in prestige—Weber's status groups—do not necessarily agree with the judgments of others about their standing. Working-class people, for example, may feel looked down on by middle-class people, who live in better houses, dress more expensively, drive newer cars, and seem to avoid them socially. But feeling denigrated by others does not mean that members of the working class accept these evaluations. The life styles of people who are better off may be desirable, but members of lower status groups need not, and usually do not, simply accept the notion that they are less worthy, less moral, or less deserving of respect. Yet, as we will see later in this chapter, the fact that people are unequally valued does have some influence on the way they see themselves. Unequal evaluation is a social fact with which those who are poor and working class must contend.

Why Does Inequality Exist?

Inequality is a ubiquitous and persistent feature of social life. Wealth, power, and prestige are unequally distributed in every society of any complexity, and such inequalities seem to persist even when people abhor social inequality and try to reduce its amount and lessen its impact. Why does inequality exist?

People have always sought to explain why some own property and others do not, why some people are viewed as more worthy or admirable, and why some have the capacity to control the lives of others. Not surprisingly, the answers people have found have quite often reflected their position in the order of things. The successful American businessman believes his wealth and social position are the result of his dedication and skill, and that anyone willing to do a little hard work can accomplish just as much as he. The West Virginia coal miner sees his fortunes rise and fall with the demand for coal and reckons that the union provides at least some protection from the power and greed of the mine owners. The corporate woman senses that many opportunities are closed to her because of gender, and the Southern mill worker knows she is paid too little but sees no way to combat her exploitation.

Sociologists have been as fascinated by this question as has humankind generally. Many efforts have been made to explain inequality, but no explanation is accepted as valid by all sociologists. Conflict theorists and functionalists (whose views were discussed briefly in Chapter 1) have created competing explanations of inequality, but symbolic interactionists have had relatively little to say about this topic. In fact, symbolic interactionists have been justly criticized for paying too little attention to conflict and inequality and too much to cooperation. Partly the neglect of inequality stems from their emphasis on studying face-to-face interaction and the dynamics of conduct formation. Here, as well as elsewhere in this book, we will attempt to show that symbolic interactionism has something to say about such matters. Our interpretation of inequality draws upon ideas from several perspectives and tries to put them together in a way that is consistent with symbolic interactionism.

We can begin by distinguishing three things that have to be explained: the *possibility* of inequality, the *existence* of inequality, and the *persistence* of inequality. It is one thing to explain why inequality is possible, to describe the conditions under which it may come about. It is a different matter to explain why inequality actually does come into existence or to explain why it endures. Yet each question is important, and ideas that help us answer one of them may not help answer the others.

The possibility of social inequality depends upon the existence of a surplus of production. As Marx and others have emphasized, the first task of human beings is to survive, to provide themselves with food, shelter, and protection from predators and the weather. Many modern people are far removed from these basic activities and lose sight of the fact that life ultimately depends upon work that provides adequate food and shelter. For much of human history, people have been able to produce just enough to subsist. The technology of simple hunting and gathering peoples permits them to acquire what they need from nature, but not much more. Working cooperatively, the members of each family or village produce the food and shelter they require, perhaps storing some provisions for the future but never acquiring much more than they actually require.

Significant inequality becomes possible only when people acquire the capacity to produce much more than they need (see Lenski, 1966). How much surplus production is possible depends upon the technology available to a society. The technology of hunting and gathering peoples is relatively simple; it permits them to kill game or catch fish, to gather such food as grows naturally, and to make the tools and implements necessary for hunting, gathering, food collection and storage, and shelter and clothing. At a more advanced level of technological development, horticulture is practiced. Using relatively simple tools, people domesticate plants and animals and grow a significant part of their food supplies. Surpluses become even larger with the development of more powerful agricultural technology; the farmer with an ox-drawn plow is capable of cultivating more land than one with a digging stick and hoe. Finally, the development of industrial technology leads to even greater surpluses.

Surpluses make it possible for people to acquire wealth: a larger and longer-lasting supply of food, a better house, a supply of extra tools or weapons, more cultivated land. Inequality begins with *accumulation*; that is, individuals, families, and groups acquire and keep control over various forms of wealth. At first, inequalities of wealth reflect superior individual talent or initiative. Some people are more adept at farming—perhaps they just work harder at it—and manage to cultivate more land and grow more bountiful crops. Perhaps a successful family can permit one of its members to concentrate on something he or she does especially well, such as making new or better tools.

Inequality becomes more extensive when those who have accumulated wealth use it as a power resource, when accumulated wealth becomes the basis for exerting control over the activities of others. The family that has accumulated a surplus of food is in a position to feed people who do not have enough to eat, and it thus gains the capacity to influence their behavior. In subsistence societies there may be powerful norms of sharing, yet, as we discovered in our discussion of deviance, such norms are still violated. And as societies develop larger surpluses, such norms seem to decline in significance. Thus, a family that accumulates cultivated land and food may begin to hire the labor of those who have been less successful. When this occurs, the family with land and food has the power to shape what happens to those without wealth: to determine how much they will be compensated for their work, what share of the crop they will receive, how many hours they will work, and where they will live.

Why does the accumulation of wealth lead to its use as a resource of power? Why do beliefs in sharing give way to the exploitation of labor? Does the possibility of inequality make its existence inevitable?

These questions are not easy to answer. One could appeal to "human nature," arguing that human beings are naturally disposed to maximize their personal rewards and will readily do so at the expense of others. Yet, as was pointed out in Chapter 5, human nature provides a poor explanation of conduct. It is in the nature of human beings to be symbolic creatures, but the meanings by which they organize their lives are variable. It is likely that the tendency of contemporary people to see acquisitiveness as an inherent part of human nature simply reflects their own stock of cultural ideas and explanations.

Yet inequality *is* ubiquitous; wherever the capacity to accumulate wealth has developed, there have been people willing to use it as a resource of power with which to exploit others. Perhaps this can be explained by another point made in Chapter 5, namely that human beings have the capacity to choose between acting on the basis of self-interest or acting in the interest of the community as a whole. Not governed by instinct, humans can perceive alternative lines of conduct: sharing an extra bit of food or consuming it privately, contributing the extra production to the community food supply or forcing those in need to work for it. Because this possibility of choice exists, it seems likely that some people will choose exploitation, whatever the norms and values emphasized in their society.

If even a few people choose to use their wealth as a power resource, the existence of inequality is virtually guaranteed. Others may try to assert the cultural value of sharing, but this may well not be sufficient to overcome the determination of the wealthy to assert their power. Conflict is not inherent in human nature, nor do all human beings seek to exploit their fellows whenever they can. But the accumulation of wealth makes it likely that some people will perceive the possibility of exploiting others and act on this perception. When they do, conflict over resources occurs, and those with power have the upper hand.

In order to explain fully the existence of inequality, it is necessary to explain its persistence. Technology makes possible the accumulation of wealth, and the perception of advantage makes it likely that some people will exploit others. But the full flowering of social inequality rests upon the fact that exploitation is not just an individual matter. Human beings organize for many purposes, including efforts to protect what they have accumulated and to accumulate more if they can.

The family is a crucial group as people organize to protect what they have. The family that acquires land is able to exploit the labor of other families and thus can accumulate even more wealth and power. It must then protect its wealth and power, taking steps to ensure that its goods will not be stolen or that the exploited will not rebel. Its members seek to extend their power, to accumulate weapons as well as land and goods, and to induce others to do their fighting for them. They are likely to band together with other wealthy families with whom they feel they have interests in common.

A key problem in the protection of wealth and power, whether in the form of land or factories, is to maintain control from one generation to the next.

If the members of a family acquire great wealth, who their sons and daughters marry becomes crucial, for they will seek to keep wealth within the family rather than having it dispersed. One result is that the wealthy associate with and marry the wealthy, for in that way even greater wealth and power may be acquired, and property may be passed down safely from one generation to the next. Wealth and power thus encourage the formation of groups of families who perceive a common interest in joining together to conserve and increase their wealth.

There is one additional feature of inequality to be discussed: prestige. The accumulation of wealth seems to set the stage for exploitation and the creation of even more inequality. But, as we have shown, human beings also assign one another unequal value. One person shows deference while another accepts it. One category of people feel themselves to be especially honorable and noteworthy and assign the rest of humanity to the status of inferiors. How is it possible to explain the development of prestige as an important dimension of inequality?

Part of the answer lies in the fact that as inequality develops and persists, those with wealth and power seek to justify their social positions. Human beings are creatures attuned to the meaning of situations and events. It seems unlikely that those who were first exploited by their fellows responded meekly to their situation. Instead, they probably resisted by whatever means they could, using what limited power resources they had, including appeals to cultural values of sharing and equality. Thus, from the beginning, those who have exploited their fellow human beings have had to justify their actions, putting themselves and their activities into the most favorable light.

Inequalities in prestige thus stem partly from the efforts of the powerful to define their superior wealth and power as *legitimate*; to argue, for example, that their wealth is a sign of God's preference for them or an indication of their higher morality. One way that powerful groups attempt to do this is by seeking to monopolize not only the material resources of power, but also those resources dependent upon cultural ideas and values. Those who control land, food, and other resources also seek to control symbols, to determine who is taught what about society, human nature, and why wealth and power are distributed as they are. "The ideas of the ruling class," Marx wrote, "are, in every age, the ruling ideas" (Bottomore and Rubel, 1964: 78). Those families and groups who control the production of goods also manage to exert considerable control over culture —over religious ideas, what is taught in schools, and what is printed in books. Ultimately, those with economic power attain great influence over culture.

Ideas about social, moral, and religious worth are thus one source of inequalities in prestige. Those with power have invented an astonishing variety of ideas with which to justify themselves. The idea that kings have a "divine right" to rule, that God has ordained the positions people attain in life, or that the Bible says that black people are inferior to whites are among the more obvious examples. And in contemporary society, as in the past, men and women rely on ideas to justify social inequality. Americans who have achieved success may thus like to attribute it to their own efforts and believe that the poor deserve their fate because they are shiftless and lazy.

It would be misleading to suggest that the rich and powerful in any society attain absolute control over ideas and symbols, for it is apparent that they do not. Religious bodies and doctrines, for example, frequently serve to justify and support the position of the wealthy. But when Marx observed that religion is the "opiate of the masses," he was only partly correct. True, religious leaders can encourage the exploited to believe that they are loved by God, who has ordained their suffering as preparation for a good life to come in the next world. Yet religious groups and their ideas are never fully dominated by those with economic power. Religious ideas have been used to justify exploitation, but they have also been the source of resistance to it.

The relationship between ideas and exploitation is thus complex. Those in power seek to define themselves as good and worthy, and they tend to favor religious and other beliefs that justify their social position. Yet those who are without power do not always naively accept what they are taught. The deprived may comfort themselves that God will reward them for their suffering, but they do not define their suffering as right, and under some conditions their religious faith may encourage them to rebel.

In seeking to explain the possibility, emergence, and persistence of social inequality, we want to emphasize that there are no mysterious biological or historical forces at work. People are not unequal because inequality is biologically ordained; conflict over resources and their distribution does not result from any natural human inclination to selfishness or aggressiveness; and class and status groups do not result from the hidden operation of historical "laws." Things happen in human affairs because people encounter conditions, perceive opportunities, and act on the basis of their definitions of situations. History is a product of human activities.

Thus, conflict is an important part of social inequality because some people perceive the opportunity to exploit others and act on the basis of their perceptions, and because people differ in their definitions of what is just. Inequality is transmitted from one generation to the next because people seek to protect their assets and investments and to pass them on to their children. And whether people accept their positions with resignation or resentment or seek to acquire a better life for themselves depends upon whether they define their situation as inevitable, as hopeless, or as susceptible to change. Just as much as any other aspect of society, inequality is created and sustained as people interact, define situations, and make and take roles.

From Inequality to Stratification

When we look at a specific society, we do not just see individuals and families who are unequal in wealth, power, and prestige. As social inequality develops and persists from one generation to the next, some form of social stratification usually develops. *Social stratification* refers to the solidification of social inequality so that it becomes an important influence on the coordination of social life and a key part of the social construction of reality. Stratification entails a number of developments. Groups of families coalesce into social classes and status groups. People who share similar positions in the social division of labor develop similar life styles and some degree of consciousness of themselves as sharing similar life chances. Social arrangements develop that regulate relationships between members of different strata and restrict movement from one social level to another. And people's perceptions of the society as a whole and their place and opportunities within it take into account its layers of wealth, power, and prestige.

Many varieties of social stratification exist. They vary according to the number of strata that can be found, the extent to which people in each stratum are conscious of themselves as members of a class or status group, and the possibility of movement from one stratum to another.

Sociologists use a number of terms to describe stratification. As we have already pointed out, *class* refers to position in the economic division of labor, while *status* refers to social honor or prestige. Sociologists sometimes also talk about *socioeconomic status*, a term that refers to the person's social standing as defined by a composite of such dimensions as income, education, and prestige. Those who are similar in socioeconomic status do not necessarily constitute a class or status group. Socioeconomic status is an objective category in the sociologist's scheme of classification and may be variously defined, whereas class and status groups exist only when people think of themselves as belonging to such groups.

Sociologists generally distinguish between two major kinds of stratification systems—caste and class. In a *caste* system (of which traditional India is the classic example) there are a number of layers, each composed of families and individuals with a very sharply crystallized sense of group membership. A specific life style is associated with each caste group, and life chances are closely tied to caste membership. In India, for example, many occupations were traditionally associated with specific castes. A person born into the lowest caste, the Sudra, is destined to serve others. In caste societies, the system of class and status rankings is exact and rigid. Each caste has an exact prestige ranking relative to other castes, and major caste groups are often divided into subgroups, each of which is ranked. Membership in a caste and subcaste is hereditary; one's caste membership, prestige, occupation, and life style are fixed at birth and cannot be changed.

In a *class* system, such as that found in the United States, Canada, and other industrial societies, there are several strata, each composed of families and individuals with some degree of similarity in life style and life chances and some consciousness of themselves as members of a class or status group who share a common fate. In a class system there are no legal barriers to *social mobility*; an individual can attempt to move from one stratum to another without any legal

Reginald Marsh, *Why Not Use the "L"?* (1930)
Egg tempera. 36 × 48 inches. Collection of Whitney Museum of American Art. Acq#31.293.

Stratification systems can mix class and caste. These subway riders presumably fall in the bottom half of the class structure, but they are further divided by a caste line between black and white. Caste barriers are less rigid now than previously in American society, but they have yet to disappear completely.

restrictions. At the same time, there may be extralegal restrictions on mobility. To move upward in the system of stratification may require attaining a level of education, for example, that is financially beyond the reach of many individuals.

The amount of homogeneity of life style and class- or status-consciousness in class societies varies from one society to another. A more clearly working-class life style can be found in Britain than in the United States, and class-consciousness is sharper in the former than the latter. Britons have a sharper sense of social divisions and usually agree about the dividing lines between one group and another in their society. Even the way a British person speaks reveals class membership, as the musical *My Fair Lady* made clear in an amusing way. The major task in transforming Eliza Doolittle into a "proper gentlewoman" was getting rid of her working-class Cockney accent. And Britons are often franker about admitting class differences than are Americans; there is a more open attitude toward the fact of social class, though not necessarily agreement with it.

The American system of classes, as will soon be discussed in more detail, differs from the British model. There is less agreement in American society about which social classes exist, and there is a corresponding ambiguity about the life styles associated with class. There is a working class, to be sure, but distinctions between how working-class people dress or speak are more difficult to define than they are in England. Life chances are linked to social class, but the American belief in equality often obscures this fact. Instead of the frank admission that social class matters, Americans are more apt to believe that personal qualities and accomplishments are what matter in the evaluation of the person. Yet the social standing of one's parents and the prestige and wealth of one's occupation *do* matter in American society.

American stratification is also made complex by racial and ethnic inequalities, a topic to be taken up in Chapter 11. Although American society is a class society, relationships between blacks and whites for much of its history were caste relationships. Membership in each group was hereditary, intermarriage between racial groups was prohibited by law, blacks and whites did not enjoy equal access to education and occupations, and dominant whites ranked blacks as socially and biologically inferior. Caste stratification between blacks and whites has been giving way to class stratification, but the transformation is not yet complete (Wilson, 1980). Ethnic differences have been somewhat less caste-like than race, but the fact that the American population is composed of diverse ethnic groups has complicated the class structure. Ethnic groups rank one another in terms of prestige, and they create distinctive life styles that can partially supersede class differences.

In a class society, social mobility is theoretically always possible. Whether measured by the social standing of parents (intergenerational) or by the person's career (intragenerational), mobility is something individuals aspire to and sometimes achieve. In caste societies, in which legal barriers prevent individual movement from one group to another, social mobility occurs when whole groups acquire higher prestige and rank, gaining the right to enter occupations from which they were previously barred. A caste system judges individuals on the basis of group membership, so the fate of the group is the fate of the individual as well. Class societies are more likely to emphasize individual achievement and to tolerate or even encourage individuals' efforts to move into higher-ranked groups.

INEQUALITY IN CONTEMPORARY SOCIETY

How much and what kinds of inequality exist in contemporary industrial societies? Do people have opportunities to improve their social and economic position? What are the effects of inequalities on the way people think, feel, and act? These questions do not have simple answers. Sociologists have studied inequality and stratification endlessly, but the topic is complex, and scholars frequently make conflicting interpretations of the same data. The goal here is to acquaint you with some of the major issues in the field and to identify at least a few areas on which there is agreement.

The Distribution of Wealth, Prestige, and Power

Income and Wealth It is not difficult to describe the distribution of income in a country like the United States. The usual approach is to rank income-earning individuals and families from low to high. By dividing the resulting array into categories containing equal numbers of persons—into fifths, for example—it is possible to calculate the share of total income received by the lowest fifth, next lowest fifth, and so on. Using this approach, it is clear that substantial income inequalities exist in the United States (see Table 10-1).

Interpretation of Table 10-1 is simple and straightforward. In 1980 the poorest fifth of individuals and families in the United States received only 5.1 percent of the income generated in the society, whereas the richest fifth got 41.6 percent of the income. Each category—the lowest fifth and the highest fifth—contains roughly the same number of people. But the "pie" that is sliced up and distributed is eight times larger for the richest fifth than for the poorest fifth. Furthermore, there has been little change in this distribution over two decades.

Income distribution does not provide a complete picture, of course, for some kinds of benefits do not show up as income. Food stamps, for example, do not count as income in the statistics presented in Table 10-1. Those in the lowest category are probably eligible to purchase government food stamps, which increases the purchasing power of their income. At the same time, however, welfare benefits such as food stamps that aid the poor are outweighed by other government benefits that aid those who are better off.

The income-tax system, for example, provides an abundance of loopholes and special provisions that benefit those with higher incomes. Income from capital gains, realized when stocks and bonds are sold at a profit, is taxed at a lower rate than ordinary earned income. Since one has to have a relatively high

Table 10-1 Shares of Income Received by Fifths of Families and Individuals, 1960–1980

	Percent Share		
	1960	*1970*	*1980*
Lowest fifth	4.8	5.4	5.1
Second fifth	12.2	12.2	11.6
Third fifth	17.8	17.6	17.5
Fourth fifth	24.0	23.8	24.3
Richest fifth	41.3	40.9	41.6

SOURCE: U.S. Bureau of the Census, *Money Income of Families and Persons in the United States: 1980 Current Population Reports*, P-60, no. 132 (1982), p. 58.

income in order to realize such profits, this feature of the tax laws provides a kind of "welfare benefit" to those who are better off. The same is true of the provision in the tax codes that permits a deduction for interest paid on a home mortgage. Since income tax rates are progressive—rates get higher as income rises—a deduction of two or three thousand dollars is worth more to a high-income taxpayer than to one who earns less. In effect, the federal government subsidizes mortgage interest payments, but it gives wealthier taxpayers a larger subsidy than poorer ones.

The various provisions of the tax codes are sometimes called "tax expenditures." In granting exemptions, deductions, or lower rates to some taxpayers, the federal government is giving up income it would otherwise receive. This can be viewed as a form of expenditure, for every dollar not collected because of a tax deduction is a dollar that cannot be spent by the government. It is a dollar that has been spent, effectively, on those to whom the special provisions apply. Yet these expenditures are hidden—they do not show up in government budgets—and many people are simply unaware of their existence. They are important in that they help conceal the nature and extent of social inequality. They are, in effect, a way in which people's perceptions of the social world may be made to be sharply at variance with objective reality. The average taxpayer who owns a modest house, for example, is very happy to deduct mortgage interest from taxable income and just does not see that the wealthy owner of a fancier house is being more heavily subsidized by Uncle Sam. Moreover, the middle-class individual may well decry the direct expediture of public funds on welfare benefits but fail to see that such tax expenditures are a form of middle-class welfare.

Income inequality is only a part of the total picture of inequality in American society. Wealth—the accumulated money, land, stock certificates, and other income-producing assets possessed by families and individuals—is also important, and the evidence suggests that inequalities of wealth are even greater than those of income. The distribution of wealth can be shown in the same way as the distribution of income (see Table 10-2).

Table 10-2 Wealth Shares Held by Fifths of Consumer Units

	Percent Share
Lowest fifth	0.2
Second fifth	2.1
Third fifth	6.2
Fourth fifth	15.5
Richest fifth	76.0

SOURCE: U.S. Office of Management and Budget, *Social Indicators, 1973* (Washington, D.C.: U.S. Government Printing Office, 1973), p. 182.

The vast majority of Americans, as well as members of all industrial societies, subsist on income derived from their occupations. But as people climb the economic ladder, more of their income is generated by accumulated assets—interest and dividends from investments, rental of land, capital gains, and the like. In 1980, for example, of the aggregate of income earned by families with incomes under $25,000, 4.2 percent came from dividends, interest, rental income, trusts, and the like; the corresponding figure for families with incomes over $25,000 was 6.29 percent. For those with incomes over $75,000, fully 16.3 percent of aggregate income came from such sources. As the saying goes, "It takes money to make money," and those who have accumulated wealth and pass it from one generation to the next are at a distinct advantage. Not only do they have larger incomes, but more reliable incomes as well. Economic troubles are less harmful for those with substantial assets than for those with few or none. The wealthy family can absorb even major financial setbacks. The working couple with only a small nest egg of house and savings is able to absorb some losses (such as those caused by a temporary layoff or the expense of illness), but it cannot endure for very long. The poor family is at the mercy of each fluctuation in the economy.

Poverty What is poverty? Who are the poor and how many of them are there? Have efforts to reduce poverty succeeded?

There is no absolute definition of poverty. In this, as in other aspects of inequality, social constructions of reality play almost as large a role as objective circumstances. The standard of living of many Americans classified as poor would seem luxurious to starving citizens of less developed countries in Asia and Africa. Indeed, even the definition of poverty held by Americans has changed as the overall standard of living has improved. Conditions that might once have been considered normal for an urban working-class family now may be deemed unacceptable, because expectations about what constitutes a minimum acceptable living standard have increased. And the definition of poverty is also a political matter. Since the War on Poverty initiated by the Johnson administration in the early 1960s, politicians, social scientists, and the poor have disagreed over what constitutes poverty. Obviously, how poverty is defined—at what income level the poverty line is set—influences the claims political leaders are able to make about progress toward the elimination of poverty.

In 1963, based on a series of studies of the resources people need to maintain themselves at a minimum level, the federal government announced an official poverty line of $3,130 for a nonfarm family of four. This figure was based on a "market basket" of food and other goods and services calculated to maintain people temporarily while experiencing unemployment or other hardship. Each year since then, the figure has been adjusted for increases in the cost of living, and rose to $9,862 in 1982. Using this objective standard, the percentage of the population living below the official poverty line declined from 20 percent of the population in 1963 to 15 percent in 1982 (*Statistical Abstract of the United States, 1984*).

But during the same period, the general standard of living rose; the income of Americans increased at a faster rate than the cost of living. In 1963 the poverty line of $3,130 was about half of the median family income of $6,250. By 1978, however, the median family income had risen to $17,640, an increase larger than would have been caused by inflation alone. But the 1978 poverty line of $6,662 was calculated on the basis of the 1963 rate plus inflation, with no allowance for an improved standard of living. Thus, by 1978 the poverty line was only 38 percent of median income. In other words, although the poverty line had kept pace with inflation, it had not kept pace with general expectations about the standard of living.

As Gilbert and Kahl (1982:314) point out, the official governmental definition of poverty began to depart from the definition used informally by most Americans. When asked what level of income is needed to get by, Americans have tended to estimate a figure that is about half the median family income. Government and popular estimates of the poverty line thus corresponded closely in 1963. But as the standard of living rose, the market basket deemed adequate for the poor did not change, even though that purchasable by others expanded considerably. Even though the absolute location of the poverty line (adjusted for inflation) remained the same, its relative location declined. A family defined as poor in 1978 was relatively worse off than one defined as poor in 1963.

Not all of the poor are permanently poor, of course, although there are conflicting estimates of the percentage who are. At least 10 percent of Americans are poor in any given year; perhaps another 25 percent live on the margins of poverty and fall into the category some years and not others; and perhaps 3 percent of Americans are permanently poor. Whether temporary or permanent, most poor people are of working age (or are children of such parents) and either do not have jobs or do not get paid enough to raise them above the poverty line. Although most poor people are white, a higher percentage of nonwhite families are poor. Families headed by blacks are more than two times more likely to be poor than those headed by whites. And families headed by women are five times more likely to fall below the poverty line.

Prestige Inequalities of prestige are perhaps less obvious than material inequalities, but they exist nevertheless. Even in American society, whose members hold strong egalitarian beliefs, some people command more respect than others. They are admired, held up as models of success, and deferred to. And in spite of the importance of the individual in American cultural values, prestige seems to be more a result of social position than of individual effort or achievement.

Among the various social positions that affect prestige, occupation has a commanding place. There is a well-defined prestige hierarchy in industrial societies that remains constant over time. The classic study of occupational prestige was conducted by the National Opinion Research Center (NORC) in 1947; its findings were confirmed in a major replication in 1963. The NORC study asked respondents to rate the standings of ninety occupations: excellent, good,

Table 10-3 Prestige of Representative Occupations

	NORC Score (1963)
U.S. Supreme Court Justice	94
Physician	93
College professor	90
Banker	85
Public school teacher	81
Electrician	76
Undertaker	74
Policeman	72
Insurance agent	69
Carpenter	68
Plumber	65
Machine operator in a factory	63
Truck driver	59
Clerk in a store	56
Restaurant cook	55
Janitor	48
Garbage collector	39

SOURCE: Robert W. Hodge, et al., "Occupational Prestige in the United States, 1925–1963," *American Journal of Sociology*, 70 (November 1964):286–302.

average, somewhat below average, or poor. By averaging the ratings given by all respondents to each occupation, the researchers constructed a ranked list of the occupations by prestige. Table 10-3 lists a few representative occupations.

What does occupational prestige mean? Occupational prestige rankings summarize the views of many people about the comparative worth of occupations. They give us insight into the kind of cognitive map of the society carried by people and used as a basis for making judgements of one another. Although people tend to agree about the overall rankings, they also tend to place their own occupations higher than do others. And when it comes to individual rather than occupational prestige, many other factors enter into social judgements of worth. Family background, ethnicity, race, education, and individual performance affect the prestige accorded to individuals.

Power There is little dispute that power is unequally distributed in contemporary society. If only because of the unequal distribution of income and wealth, some individuals and families have far more resources than others. There has been considerable controversy among social scientists, however, about the degree to which this power is politically concentrated. *Elite theorists* have taken the view that power is concentrated in the hands of a few, at both local and national levels, and have generally argued that economic elites control major social and politicial decisions. *Pluralist theorists* have taken a contrary position, holding that there are so many groups contending for power that none can dominate. An extreme pluralist position would hold that no one holds power, that competing groups effectively cancel out one another's influence over decisions, so that often decisions are simply not made.

The relationship between political and economic power will be discussed in more detail in Chapter 15; here we want to focus on two facts about power inequalities that affect people's lives.

First, the evidence from many studies of community power indicates that people who make decisions at a local level are drawn primarily from the upper and upper-middle classes, with an especially heavy concentration of business leaders. People who own businesses or who are educated and skilled professionals and who are connected with one another by social and family ties tend to have most influence over decisions that affect everyday life: whether a highway will be built, old housing torn down to make way for office buildings, or tax advantages offered to attract new industry. Those who are working-class or poor have relatively little impact upon community decisions because they command few resources that would give them a say in such decisions. This is true even when working-class and poor people influence the election of public officials. Mayors and city council members, regardless of their political orientations and debts to their constituencies, have to take the views of economic and social elites into account.

Second, the evidence also indicates that local decisions are powerfully shaped by national decisions, particularly by those made by a corporate elite. More and more Americans are employed by corporations whose base of economic activity and power is national or international in scope. General Motors, IBM, and other corporate giants exert a profound influence, not just over national governments and international affairs, but also over individual lives and local events. The careers of many people are oriented to the corporation rather than to the local community; they go where the corporation bids. Before locating in a community, a corporation may secure tax concessions, getting reduced real estate taxes for a period of years, for example, as an inducement to locate in the community. If local decisions are not to its liking, the corporation can move elsewhere and find the conditions it wants.

Do Social Classes Exist?

Social inequality is a demonstrable fact of American life. But is this a class society? Are there clearly demarcated class and status groups with distinctive economic positions and life styles whose members are conscious of themselves as members of a class?

From the sociologist's vantage point, it is not difficult to outline the class structure of American society. Since class is dependent upon economic position, the class structure can be portrayed by examining the way economic activity is arranged and controlled. Describing the organization of status groups is more difficult, and coping with the question of class consciousness—the extent to which people think of themselves as members of a group with common interests—presents even more problems. A bit of history will help in portraying how these things fit together.

Prior to the 1830s, America was a bustling agricultural society, with much of its economic activity centered in farming and the production of raw materials. There was manufacturing and trade, to be sure, but industrialization was just getting underway and did not occur on a grand scale until after the Civil War. The majority of people were small farmers, artisans, mechanics, craftsmen, and small merchants. Only a few were rich; the society believed powerfully in equality (except in matters of race and sex). America was egalitarian not only in outlook but also to some degree in fact. Great differences in wealth would not develop until later.

It was industrialization that laid the foundations for the class and status structure we know today. The economic expansion of the late nineteenth century created a capitalist class—a small but powerful group of industrial entrepreneurs who developed railroads and other basic industries and services like steel, coal, oil, banking, and retailing. The names associated with this class are well known to Americans: Rockefeller, Vanderbilt, Carnegie, Woolworth, and others. These families acquired their wealth during a period of unprecedented economic expansion. They formed a class in the straightforward economic sense: they engaged in capitalist activity that built a variety of industrial enterprises, and they clearly thought of themselves as men with common interests and values. Many of them were imbued with the Protestant ethic of hard work and led ascetic lives, leaving to their families and descendants the conspicuous display of wealth in lavish life styles.

Their common interests and perspectives led these industrial capitalists to become a status group as well as a class group. They (and their descendants even more so) held similar values, thought alike, and tended to confine their social relations to their own circles. The tendency to form and maintain social circles that exclude others is perhaps the clearest mark of the existence of a status group. During the late nineteenth century this new capitalist upper class overtook, became merged with, and gradually supplanted an already existing upper class. The economic successes of men like Cornelius Vanderbilt were at first greeted with disdain by the existing American upper class—families such as the Lodges of Massachusetts and the Astors of New York. Gradually, however, the social circles of the old and the new upper classes merged and, in the process, something new was born: a national upper class. Prior to industrialization, American upper classes were regional; afterwards, there came to be one national upper class, essentially a class (and status group) composed of wealthy capitalists and their descendants.

The same process of industrialization that produced a new upper class also produced a working class in American society. Industrialization required vast numbers of new workers to lay railroad track, construct buildings, and run the machines. Much of the supply of labor was provided through immigration, a topic discussed in Chapter 11. From the late nineteenth century to just before World War I, vast numbers of immigrants arrived from Europe and, to a lesser extent, Asia. Their men laid the rails, carried the mortar, shoveled the coal, and operated the machinery, while their women and children worked long hours at low wages in the sweatshops of New York, Boston, and Chicago. They were a working class in the classic Marxist sense; they had nothing to offer but their labor, and they were ruthlessly exploited by their capitalist masters. Gaining a foothold in the new country was difficult, and their struggle to win better working conditions (and the right to bargain collectively about these conditions and the price of their labor) was long and bitter.

For a time during the late nineteenth and early twentieth centuries it appeared that the conditions for proletarian revolution specified by Marx were developing in the United States. There was increasing polarization and bitter strife between capitalists and workers. In such episodes as the Homestead strike in 1893, violence erupted between workers and capitalists, with the state usually intervening on the side of the owners. For several reasons, however, class polarization did not continue to develop as Marx predicted, and the American working class did not develop the same kind of consciousness of itself as did the upper class.

One reason a very distinctive working class with a high degree of self-consciousness did not develop was that American workers did win some concessions. They gained the right to bargain, and legislation gradually eliminated some of the oppressive working conditions under which they had labored. Moreover, the fact that American workers were drawn from diverse ethnic backgrounds meant that there were always differences in outlook among them. These men and women felt pride in their national origins and felt loyal to their *ethnic groups*—that is, status groups based on nationality. Finally, America was perceived as the land of opportunity by many immigrants. They had not journeyed to these shores to become a part of a working class, but to make their fortunes, to make a new life in a new world. They wanted to become a part of a developing middle class, whose emergence we will shortly discuss.

These factors inhibited the workers' development of an identity based on social class. Men and women identified with ethnic groups as much or more than with the working class. They saw themselves as Poles, Italians, and Jews, and did not readily respond to appeals to view themselves simply as members of the proletariat. Most of all, they identified with the future; they saw themselves and their children becoming successful, middle-class Americans who did not have to endure hardship and work with their hands. They based their identities on the society and its opportunities, rather than on a vision of the classless society envisioned by Marx.

A sizable middle class was an important feature of nineteenth-century America. Farmers, small merchants, and self-employed professionals such as physicians and lawyers were a large part of the population and were a major influence on the society. But industrialization and the accompanying growth of cities at the expense of rural areas and small towns eventually led to a major change in the nature and composition of the middle class. The *old* middle class of nineteenth-century America, as the sociologist C. Wright Mills (1951) called it, has been replaced by a *new* middle class whose members have somewhat different occupations, social origins, and outlooks.

What is the new middle class? Instead of relying for a living on their own tools, property, and knowledge, like the business people and professionals of the old middle class, the members of the new middle class are mainly employees of larger organizations. They are bank managers, store clerks, salespeople, office workers, teachers, welfare caseworkers, and others whose jobs require some skill and education and require little manual labor. Their careers and futures are tied to the success or failure of the organizations for which they work. They live predominantly in urban (or suburban) places. And many of them are the children, grandchildren, or great-grandchildren of immigrants.

What is the significance of the middle class, and does it constitute a status group in Weber's use of the term? The answer with respect to the old middle class is clear. Businessmen, farmers, and professionals were a powerful and self-conscious social group within the context of a preindustrial nineteenth-century society. The new middle class presents a more complex picture. As American society industrialized, the new middle class greatly increased in size (the economy needed clerks, typists, and hosts of managers), and membership in this class was a source of prestige. White-collar jobs were much sought-after prizes, and those who won them felt they had accomplished something. But continuing changes in the nature of the economy have transformed the middle class and the way it is seen by its own members as well as by others.

America is now generally considered to have entered a postindustrial phase of development. Its economy is less and less tied to such basic, heavy manufacturing industries as steel or automobiles and is increasingly dependent upon high technology and upon jobs in the service sector. There are fewer steel and automobile workers and more clerks entering data at computer terminals or serving as welfare caseworkers. The number of blue-collar workers has shrunk, while the number of low-level white-collar workers has vastly increased. At the same time, educational differences between blue-collar and white-collar workers have narrowed; nearly everybody now graduates from high school, and a considerable proportion go on to college. With the entry of immigrants and their descendants into white-collar jobs, the social origins of the new middle class are now not much different from those of the working class.

The result of these changes is the declining significance of membership in the middle class and the blurring of distinctions between middle-class and working-class Americans. Holding a white-collar job does not define a person as being of the middle class as clearly as it once did, nor does it confer the same prestige. Blue-collar workers are as well educated and earn as much and sometimes more than white-collar workers. They have the same ethnic and religious backgrounds. And, as some observers have pointed out, their jobs are becoming less and less different. The clerk who enters data at a computer terminal does not engage in manual work, but neither does the job require very sophisticated skills.

It is thus not clear just what kind of a class structure is emerging or what kinds of consciousness of class will develop. Americans still aspire to be middle class, and a majority of people consider themselves to belong to this class. But it is a category whose boundaries are difficult to describe and whose members themselves do not seem to have either a clear conception of membership or sharply defined life styles. It is an ambiguous middle that challenges the perceptions of the sociologist as much as the lay person.

The perceptions of people are important in describing the class structure of any society. We can take Marx's view of class as a starting point of analysis. A class exists when its members have a similar position in the economic realm. But the existence of a class also depends upon its members' definitions of themselves as such. When it comes to the national upper class, there is little doubt that a class exists. People in the corporate stratosphere, along with those who have inherited great wealth and social position, travel in their own circles, have a clear conception of their class interest, and do their best to preserve and extend their privileged position. But as we move downward in the system, each successive layer is more difficult to describe with clarity, and only at the bottom of the social order do we again find highly crystallized class and status groups. Thus, upper-middle-class professionals and managers have some sense of themselves as a class and of where they fit in the scheme of things. But for the ambiguous middle, social perceptions and life styles are more variable and more vaguely defined. At the bottom—among those who do manual work or who are temporarily or permanently poor—social class begins to crystallize once again. Thus, we can talk about a working class whose core membership is composed of blue-collar workers; a class of working poor; and perhaps a permanent underclass, those who are permanently out of the labor force and below the poverty line.

Part of the difficulty in identifying distinct social classes stems from the fact that Americans are not strongly inclined to think in class terms. Inequalities of condition exist alongside strong beliefs in equality of opportunity, that people can better themselves if only they will try. And along with this emphasis on equality there is a lack of a vocabulary with which to talk about and perceive social class. Given a choice between upper class, middle class, and lower class, a majority of Americans will call themselves middle class. If working class is added to the choices, then a majority will call themselves working class. When asked about class membership in an open-ended manner, slightly more people call themselves working class than middle class. And there is, overall, a reluctance to attach class labels.

Even in a Marxist approach to social class, it is difficult to predict precisely how people will identify with a social class. In Marxist theory, a class is defined by the relations to production. The working class consists of those who have only their labor to sell and are therefore controlled by the bourgeoisie, who own and control the means of production. But some positions, which Erik O. Wright (1979: Ch. 2) calls *contradictory class locations,* are intermediate between the two major classes. Factory foremen, for example, are close to the working class, but do exercise some measure of control over workers. Thus, their identification with the working class may be attenuated by their position of marginal superiority. Similarly, top corporate managers have only limited participation in the ownership of the corporation, but may have considerable control over how the organization is run. Middle-level managers are in the most intensely contradictory position, for while they exercise control over parts of the organization, they are themselves controlled by others. Such contradictory locations clearly diminish the propensity of individuals to identify with one side or the other.

We cannot, then, conclude that America is (or is not) a society with social classes. Depending upon the stratum in question, there are varying degrees of class consciousness and class identification. In one sense, this means that people's images of the society as a whole depend upon their position in its array of inequalities. To be born into the national upper class is to be very conscious of one's position in a stratified society. The same may be said of those born into the lower class or working class. For them, images of the society may well be strongly influenced by the facts of inequality and the perception of themselves as on the bottom. For members of intermediate strata, the society is less likely to be perceived as organized along class lines. Their focus is more apt to be on individual effort and accomplishment, with a vaguer conception of social classes and their interrelationships, and with a keener appreciation of the ways in which classes control and are controlled by others.

Life Styles and Self-conceptions

Do social classes and status groups, to the extent they can be identified, differ in the way their members think, feel, and act? That is, are there differences among classes in the way married couples interact or raise their children, in how people spend their leisure time, or in their general attitudes toward life? And does membership in a social class or status group have an effect on the way people see themselves?

The same ambiguities that exist in the identification of social classes also make it difficult to portray life styles. There are some clear differences in the way people live at the top and the bottom of the social hierarchy. Some of the differences are merely the result of unequal wealth and income, but many reflect differences in social perspectives, values, and self-conceptions. In the strata between top and bottom, however, it is difficult to find sharply contrasting life styles, just as it is impossible to find clearly drawn class lines. The life styles of the upper middle class and the working class are different, but people in the ambiguous middle tend to have life styles that resemble one level or the other roughly in proportion to how close they are to it in income and prestige.

A series of studies that portrays an important class difference in life styles, and that also helps explain how such differences come about and are perpetuated, was conducted by Melvin Kohn (1969). The focus of his work was the origins and consequences of social class differences in socialization, particularly in the values parents attempt to instill in their children. Stated simply, Kohn found that parents at different class levels tend to prefer different characteristics in their children. Those at higher class levels want their children to be capable of *self-direction* and empathic understanding, whereas those at lower levels favor behavioral *conformity*. Kohn found that members of the higher-class groups favored curiosity, responsibility, self-control, and the consideration of other people as characteristics they wanted their children to have. In contrast, members of lower-ranked groups favored obedience, honesty, good manners, and neatness. The former seemed to be interested in the child's psyche, in the internal motives and dispositions developed by the person, whereas the latter were interested in fixed and external standards of behavior.

Why should there be such class differences in the attributes parents seek to instill in their children? Why do upper-class parents value self-direction and downplay conformity? Although Kohn did not work from a symbolic interactionist perspective, he theorized about the origins of such differences in a way that is quite consistent with this perspective. He took the position that occupation is a key aspect of social class, and that people's value orientations, which they seek to transmit to their children, are influenced by their occupational experiences. The higher one ascends in the class hierarchy, the more one finds occupations in which people have to make their own decisions, work independently, use initiative, and in other ways exercise self-direction. The lower one descends, the more one finds occupations in which work is highly routinized, closely supervised, and affords little opportunity for self-direction. Professional and managerial jobs require self-direction, but blue-collar jobs usually demand conformity.

The values people develop for themselves and seek to inculcate in their children thus seem to originate in appraisals of their own situations and of the strategies that promote adjustment to them. The working-class person recognizes what it takes to get along in the world of work: not brains or initiative, but the capacity to do what others tell you to do. The upper-middle-class person knows that success depends on the capacity for self-direction. People act on the basis of their appraisals and come to repeat the strategies that prove effective. Over time, these strategies become stabilized and become values people hold for themselves and pass on to their children.

Kohn's work has two major implications that may not be immediately obvious. First, to the degree that parents socialize their children to hold certain values, they help to perpetuate their children's position in the class system. Children who learn that conformity is important to future success are not only learning a value but are also developing a self-conception that will influence their future occupational identity. Obeying teachers is practice for obeying employers later in life, but it is also practice for self-concept and identity. Children learn to think of themselves as obedient, as persons who can be counted on to follow directions. And, just as important, children learn a generalized way to relate to others of higher rank or power. They learn to assume an obedient and dutiful identity, to *be* the obedient person in a variety of role relations. There is good evidence that the self-concepts people develop influence their future choice of occupations, that people choose occupations that require attributes they think they have (Rosenberg, 1981:615).

The second implication concerns the class system itself. Not only does socialization tend to give people self-images that keep them in their class positions, but it tends to reinforce a set of expectations and definitions that preserve the system. To be upper class or upper middle class is not simply to value self-direction, but to feel efficacious, to feel that you are in control of your fate and can make decisions that affect your own life. To be working class is not just to value conformity, but to feel controlled by "forces and people beyond one's control, often, beyond one's understanding" (Kohn, 1969: 189). To think of yourself as belonging in a certain place in the social world—as being working class or upper class—is to solidify and maintain that social world by keeping alive a certain image of it. Social inequality is sustained not just by sheer power and exploitation, but also by the images of self and society it fosters.

There is a good deal of evidence that shows that social class does affect the way people see themselves (see Rosenberg and Pearlin, 1978; and Sennett and Cobb, 1972). Among adults, self-esteem, which is a measure of the respect and admiration people accord themselves, varies with social class. The higher the person's social standing, the higher his or her self-esteem. Those in occupations that confer higher prestige and incomes can compare themselves favorably with those lower in the class hierarchy. They see the deference they are accorded and they tend to attribute their success to their own qualities and efforts. Their jobs, homes, and material possessions are badges of accomplishment. The result is that they feel better about themselves. Those in poorly paid and low-prestige occupations tend to feel demeaned. They feel that they do not count, that there is nothing of particular value about them. Their low incomes and occupational prestige are badges of insignificant ability and accomplishment.

CONCLUSION

Social inequality is a complex social reality. The objective inequalities of wealth, power, and prestige perceived by the sociologist do not necessarily correspond to the way people perceive themselves and society. Social inequalities are not fixed and eternal but result from the concrete actions of real human beings as they seek to make a living and protect what they have acquired. And inequality has symbolic as well as material significance, with implications for the psyche as well as the body.

SUGGESTED READINGS

DOMHOFF, G. WILLIAM. *Who Rules America?* (Englewood Cliffs: Prentice-Hall, 1967).

DOMHOFF, G. WILLIAM. *Who Really Rules?* (New Brunswick, N.J.: Transaction Books, 1978).

GANS, HERBERT. *More Equality* (New York: Pantheon, 1973).

HARRINGTON, MICHAEL. *The Other America* (New York: Macmillan, 1962).

JENCKS, CHRISTOPHER, et al. *Who Gets Ahead?* (New York: Basic Books, 1979).

LEWIS, MICHAEL. *The Culture of Inequality* (Amherst, Mass.: University of Massachusetts Press, 1978).

SENNETT, RICHARD and JONATHAN COBB. *The Hidden Injuries of Class* (New York: Vintage, 1972).

11

Race and Ethnicity

The members of any society are joined together by a shared culture and language and by their dependence upon one another in the division of labor. But, as we have seen, people are also differentiated from one another by a host of factors. The division of labor, whether along lines of sex or occupation, separates people on the basis of experiences and social perspectives, even as it unifies them into a web of interdependent people. And inequalities of power, prestige, and property further differentiate people, making their experiences and life styles different and creating grounds for them to be conscious of their differences.

Among the factors that differentiate some members of a society from others, two have been of special importance in American society and have received considerable attention from sociologists. These are the related factors of race and ethnicity. In simplest terms, a *race* can be defined as a category of people labeled and treated as alike because of some particular physical attribute or attributes. An *ethnic group* is a collectivity whose members are usually assumed to share a common ancestry and culture. Yet as we will see, subtle variations and overlapping influences of ethnicity and race make these simple definitions incomplete.

In this chapter we examine the origins and nature of racial and ethnic divisions in American society. Two general ideas will guide the analysis. First, race and ethnicity must be placed in a historical context if they are to be understood. Racial and ethnic groups are a historical product of their society, and thus their contemporary culture and relationships to the society can be traced to their historical experience. And second, racial and ethnic relations have been profoundly influenced by ideas. Race and ethnicity are matters of public debate and intellectual study, and their contemporary realities are the product of what people, including social scientists, have thought about them.

ETHNIC ORIGINS

How do members of a society get to be differentiated along racial and ethnic lines? Historically, geographical and/or linguistic boundaries have served as barriers that kept groups apart and enabled them to develop and preserve distinctive societies and cultures. Exploration, conquest, and mass migration have been the vehicles throughout human history by which differing groups have been brought into contact with one another. As often as not, such contact has meant conflict. It has also resulted in the creation of nation-states that are racially and ethnically diverse. North America provides excellent examples of these processes and their consequences.

Beginning with extensive exploration by European nations in the sixteenth and seventeenth centuries, the native populations of North America were conquered and overwhelmed by successive waves of immigration. From the start, there was conflict between the European settlers and the existing Indian population. The growing numbers of Europeans and their quest to settle the land

Currier and Ives, ***Across the Continent***
Colored lithograph. Yale University Art Gallery. The Mabel Brady Garvan Collection.

Just a century ago, as the major westward expansion depicted in this classic Currier and Ives print was ending, new waves of immigration were beginning. Contemporary racial and ethnic relations were powerfully affected by such historical patterns of settlement and economic development.

pushed Indians relentlessly out of any land desired by whites. In addition, Indians were the victims of European ideology that viewed them as less than human, as savages who could and should be displaced to make way for white civilization. If a tribe was destroyed, few white settlers were concerned. And in addition to the many killed in armed conflict, others were decimated by diseases introduced by Europeans.

After four centuries of conflict between Indians and whites, the native population of the Americas was greatly reduced. In the area north of Mexico at the time of the first European-Indian contact, the native population has been estimated to be about one million. This had decreased to about 240,000—a decline of 75 percent—by 1900. Similar declines occurred in Mexico, the West Indies, and Central America. A recent analysis of Spanish records indicates that there may have been a native population in Mexico alone of eleven to fifteen million. By 1600 the Mexican Indian population had been reduced to two million.

European settlers in the Americas affected more than the numbers of native peoples. Trade, sharing of ideas, and intermarriage quickly led to changes in Indian culture and in most instances to its decline. The introduction of the horse, guns, manufactured cloth, and beads into Indian culture meant changes in native life. Indians were often pushed out of their ancestral lands, to which their cultures had become adapted, and onto reservations that could scarcely support them in their traditional way of life.

If the lives of Native Americans were changed by the European settlement of North America, so too were the lives of the immigrant settlers changed by the colonial experience. Immigrants to what would become the United States came from many nations in Europe, but most were English. And from the beginning, in the overwhelmingly English colonies, there were pressures for non-English-speaking residents to learn and speak English and thus demonstrate their allegiance to England. Later, after the American Revolution, there were even stronger pressures to speak English and thus demonstrate a commitment to the new nation. Thus began a pattern of *Anglo-conformity* that has persisted into the twentieth century.

During the nineteenth and early twentieth centuries there were successive waves of immigration. The immigrants first came from northern and western Europe and later from eastern and southern Europe. When the early waves of immigrants arrived, there was enough open land to allow anyone to stake a claim for a farm on the frontier. Into the upper midwest (especially Minnesota and the Dakotas) went Norwegians, Swedes, and Finns. Into Illinois, Iowa, and Texas moved large numbers of Germans. When later immigrants from Greece, Italy, Russia, and Poland arrived, free land was rarely available. For them, opportunity was greatest in the rapidly industrializing cities of the east coast and midwest.

Different patterns emerged on the Pacific coast where, in addition to Indians, there was a large Spanish population from the southwest and Mexico. Consequently, westward-migrating Americans found two indigenous groups that were later joined by Japanese and Chinese immigrants from Asia.

From earliest times, some Americans felt there should be no new immigrants, but during the late nineteenth century the need of a rapidly developing society for workers outweighed the fears of Americans who sought to maintain a social order which was "American" (meaning English-speaking). Immigration was thus encouraged by many industrialists. It was not discouraged by national policy, and the number of immigrants entering the United States from 1880 to 1910 was larger than the number of Americans already citizens. In this environment, many Americans, particularly in California, were concerned that immigrants would "corrupt" American culture. This fear of foreigners is called *xenophobia*. It has always been present in the United States, and it underlies such policies as the Chinese Exclusion Act of 1892 and the restrictive immigration legislation of the 1920s.

The restrictions to immigration came too late, however. By the twentieth century, America was irreversibly a multiracial, multiethnic nation. People with different cultures from every continent made up the American population. And as we shall see, their traditional ways of life did not disappear. The ethnic group became part of American culture.

Slavery

Much of this immigration was essentially voluntary. Economic, political, and religious conditions in the lands of their origin led people to move to the United States (and other places). For one segment of the American population, however, migration was not voluntary.

In 1619, twenty black slaves landed and were sold in Jamestown, Virginia, thus making the American colonies (and later the states) active participants in the slave trade. Until 1808, when it was outlawed in the United States, hundreds of thousands of black Africans endured the torture and degradation of the "middle passage" across the Atlantic in the holds of slave ships, only to be sold into perpetual servitude. All told, the trade brought an estimated ten million blacks to the New World, of whom fewer than 10 percent came to the United States.

The economic advantages of slavery were greatest in the South, where labor-intensive plantation crops of sugar, cotton, tobacco, and rice were dominant. Slavery became a particularly important institution after the invention of the cotton gin in 1793, a development which created an increased demand for raw cotton. While less than 5 percent of Southerners owned slaves, most Southerners were convinced of the necessity of slavery for the region's well-being. This was not the case in the Northern states, where, by 1805, slavery was outlawed.

Not all blacks residing in the United States before the Civil War were slaves. In 1860 just over 10 percent of blacks were free. Some had been *manumitted*—that is, freed by their owners. Others were the children of free blacks, and some had escaped. Some blacks had been free for many generations because their ancestors came at a time when the institution of perpetual servitude was not clearly established. These blacks lived much like white indentured servants.

But the status of the free black was not the same as the status of the free white. Restrictions limited the opportunities of blacks in almost all areas of life. Most states restricted the kinds of work that a black could do. Courts did not accept testimony from free blacks if the case involved a white person. Although free blacks briefly had the right to vote in some Northern states and even in one Southern state (Tennessee), by the late 1830s voting rights for blacks had been abolished. Even churches refused to admit free blacks or required them to sit in special sections. And in those communities where blacks could be educated, separate schools were established.

The Civil War, the Emancipation Proclamation, and the passage of the 14th Amendment to the Constitution brought an end to chattel slavery. But the economic and social subjugation of blacks continued. Most blacks in the South continued to be agricultural workers, either receiving very low wages or serving as sharecroppers. Under the sharecrop system, workers received a share of the crop in return for their labor on an owner's land. Under this system, the tenant was charged for food, shelter, and fuel by the white plantation owner. As often as not, the tenant's share of the crop was not sufficient to cover these charges. Hence, many blacks were in perpetual debt, and even though they were no longer slaves they remained under the economic thumb of the plantation owner.

The social system that developed in the South after the Civil War persisted essentially unchanged well into the twentieth century and is best described as a caste system. In the American South, the caste division was based on the color line. Not only did the mores establish rigid lines between the races, but legislation (popularly known as the Jim Crow laws) was passed to reinforce custom. For example, custom dictated that blacks show proper deference to whites by not speaking to a white unless first spoken to. There also was the established practice in which even the most accomplished black professional had to be addressed by his or her first name, while at the same time a black physician or minister was required to address all whites, whatever their occupation or social status, as Mr. or Mrs.

The Jim Crow laws in all Southern (and some Northern) states reinforced the differences between races by establishing strict patterns of segregation in transportation and public accommodation. Blacks rode in Jim Crow cars on trains, attended separate schools (where schools were provided), sat in separate sections of buses and theaters, and drank from "colored" water fountains. Vending machines would be marked "white" and "colored," and in most cities blacks were not served in "white" restaurants. This segregation extended to almost every aspect of life. When the authors of this book began camping in the mid-1960s, campground guides still listed some state parks as "colored."

But racism was not directed solely against blacks, nor was it confined to the South. While the North was the source of considerable sentiment for the abolition of slavery before the Civil War, blacks did not fare much better there than they did in the South. They were the victims of hostile attitudes and actions in many Northern cities, where they were feared as potential competitors by white laborers. Meanwhile, in the West, new forms of racial prejudice and discrimination emerged as Chinese and Japanese entered the country in large numbers.

Asian Immigration

The Chinese first came to the United States during the second half of the nineteenth century. They were primarily laborers, recruited to work on the transcontinental railroads. In 1852 there were about 25,000 Chinese in California, and that number doubled during the next decade. By the 1870s they constituted about 10 percent of the population of California. The Japanese, who arrived later, numbered only about 10,000 in 1900, a small fraction of the total California population of 1.5 million. And even by 1920, the Japanese population was just over 70,000.

Although the size of the Chinese and Japanese populations in the entire country was not very large in proportion to the total population, there developed a virulent form of anti-Asian racism that focused on the so-called "Yellow Peril." The 1877 California Constitution, for example, outlawed the employment of Chinese workers by any business in the state. There also were vigorous attempts to discourage the entry of Asians into the state and the nation. Legislation was passed restricting the purchase of land in California by Asians. The Chinese Exclusion Act of 1882 prohibited Chinese immigration. Later all Asian immigrants were prohibited from applying for and being granted citizenship. The overwhelmingly anti-Chinese and, later, anti-Japanese attitudes of the West Coast culminated after Pearl Harbor in an executive order authorizing the relocation of 112,000 Japanese and Japanese-Americans in 1942 to concentration camps in Utah and Nevada.

European Immigrants

In the years after the Civil War, great changes were occurring in the United States, and many of these changes involved the composition of the population and relationships between subgroups. In the South, blacks were briefly able to participate in government during Reconstruction, but the development of a caste system between blacks and whites was of more lasting consequence. In the West, Japanese and Chinese immigrants endured bitter racism from whites, while the indigenous Indians and the Spanish-speaking populations gave ground before the westward movement of English-speaking Americans.

However, it was in the East and North that some of the most profound changes took place. Industrialization, already underway before the Civil War, was accelerating, and the nation was becoming increasingly urban. This economic and population growth was sustained, in part, by waves of immigration that dwarfed anything experienced either before or since that time. These immigrants were European, at first from the north and west of Europe, and later from the east and south. Their numbers were immense, and their eventual impact upon the society was considerable.

The Irish were the first of the large waves of non-English and non-Protestant immigrants. Just as the Chinese were building the railroads of the West, the Irish were providing cheap labor for the railroads of the East, the mills of New England, and the coal mines of Pennsylvania. Between 1820 and 1920, more than four million people came from Ireland to the United States. Although they were white and almost all spoke English, they were Roman Catholics, and their unfamiliar customs marked them as strangers. Anti-Irish riots occurred in northern cities; the Know-Nothing Party was formed specifically to oppose the Irish; in such urban centers as Boston, the legend "No Irish Need Apply" was commonplace in employment notices.

The United States accepted even more immigrants from Germany than from Ireland. Over six million Germans came to the United States in the century beginning in 1830. Unlike the Irish, who settled primarily in the cities of the Northeast, the Germans scattered more widely over the country. While many settled in cities such as Milwaukee and Cincinnati, many more became farmers throughout the midwest. In general, the German immigrants were a more varied group than the Irish. The Irish emigration was heavily economic in motivation (many Irish left because of the Irish potato famine of the 1840s and its consequences), but Germans emigrated for more diverse reasons. Some entire religious communities migrated from Germany to seek freedom of worship in the United States. Other Germans fled the aftermath of the unsuccessful Revolution of 1848. Still others immigrated, like the Irish, because the opportunity for economic success was greater in the United States than in Germany.

In the last two decades of the nineteenth century, a major change took place in the sources of American immigration. As fewer people arrived from Great Britain, Germany, Scandinavia, and the Low Countries, more people were immigrating from southern and eastern Europe. Except for the Irish, the "old" immigrants were overwhelmingly Protestant, and they had assimilated rather easily to the English culture of the United States. The "new" immigrants from Poland, Hungary, Russia, Italy, Greece, and other nations in eastern Europe and around the Mediterranean were overwhelmingly Catholic and Jewish, and in cultural terms very dissimilar from the English.

These new immigrants were viewed with fear and hostility by those already here. Recruited to the developing industries of the northeast, the migrants settled in concentrated numbers in the cities, where they formed highly visible ethnic enclaves. Often they lived in what can only be described as crowded slums where their strange customs and large numbers intensified their differences from English-speaking Protestant Americans.

The new immigrants—non-Protestant peasants living in urban industrial environments—came to be perceived as a threat to the social status of the dominant rural and Protestant groups in American society. Any immigration has a disturbing effect on the arrangement of status groups in a society. But the immigration of the late nineteenth and early twentieth centuries was so large and was viewed as so foreign that it was especially threatening. Moreover, the sense that the immigrants were different was heightened by a general American distrust of foreigners, widely held despite the active recruitment of newcomers to meet the demands of rapid industrialization.

Concerns about the growing heterogeneity of the American population led to basic policy decisions and legislation intended to regain the cultural and social homogeneity assumed to have existed in earlier times. We have already mentioned the Chinese Exclusion Act of 1882, later made a permanent feature of the United States immigration laws in 1902. Considerable public and private money was poured into schools and social agencies whose purpose was to change foreigners into Americans. Not only were immigrants taught English and given facts about American government, but they were put under considerable pressure to adopt an American way of life and to put aside their native culture in favor of American culture. In other words, they were pushed to assimilate.

Not trusting the success of such programs of Americanization, the pressures of nativist sentiment led in 1924 to the National Origins Act. This law established an annual ceiling for the number of immigrants who could enter the United States and established national quotas limiting the number of immigrants who could come from each country. These quotas severely limited the number of immigrants from lands outside of northern and western Europe. Few immigrants were accepted from China, Japan, Australia, Greece, Turkey, Poland, or Russia, while many were allowed from England, Ireland, France, and the Low Countries. As a result, in some countries people would have to wait years before they could immigrate to the United States, while in others the quotas went unfilled. These restrictions on American immigration would remain in force for more than forty years.

UNDERSTANDING ETHNIC RELATIONS

From this brief historical account, we now turn to the interplay between ideas and realities in racial and ethnic relations. We will begin by looking at the way early sociologists analyzed the social problems of race and ethnicity. They, like other intellectuals of the time, were profoundly affected by the developments just described. In their attempts to make sense out of the changing social order, they also tried to ascertain what happens when people of different cultures and races come into contact.

The Belief in Assimilation

Of all ideas about race and ethnic relations, none has had greater impact upon sociology (and perhaps on American thought as a whole) than the belief in the ultimate *assimilation* of immigrant groups. Assimilation was first analyzed as a process by Robert E. Park, a sociologist at the University of Chicago, in his discussion of the *race relations cycle* (1926). The cycle, he said, begins when two dissimilar cultures come into contact. Competition and conflict over the scarce resources of the society then follow. Over time, the two groups work out patterns of accommodation, developing systematic relationships that regulate the conflict between them. These patterns may include caste relationships and segregation, as was the case with black and white relations in the United States. As time passes, primary relationships develop between members of the two groups; they intermarry and join the same organizations. Ultimately, assimilation takes place.

Assimilation has two everyday meanings, both of which seem to capture the essence of what Park had in mind. First, to assimilate can mean "to become like," so that immigrants assimilate by becoming culturally like people in the dominant group (those Americans already settled in the country). But assimilation can also mean "to take up into." This second and related meaning suggests that immigrant groups are absorbed into American society. Thus they merge into the dominant group as well as behaving like it.

George Catlin, *Assiniboin Chief, before and after Civilization* (1857–69).
15⅝ × 21¾ inches, oval. The National Gallery of Art, Washington. Paul Mellon Collection.

Pressure to assimilate was applied to Native Americans just as to immigrants from other countries. The popular belief, depicted in this painting, was that the Indian could move from "savagery" to "civilization" if he or she abandoned traditional religion, culture, and clothing.

During much of the twentieth century, assimilation was a prevailing social belief as well as a sociological concept. After massive immigration ceased in the 1920s, the country's attention turned to other matters: the Great Depression and World War II. During this period, the eventual assimilation of immigrant groups was simply taken for granted by the general public and by sociologists.

Prejudice and Discrimination

During the 1930s and 1940s sociologists and other social scientists sought to determine what was retarding the assimilation of ethnic and racial groups. For many, the answer lay in the related concepts of prejudice and discrimination. *Prejudice* refers to the attitudes and feelings, generally negative, that an individual holds toward other groups and their members. These attitudes are not based upon experience of the other group; they are founded upon prevailing stereotypes of those groups. A *stereotype* is a simplified portrait of the members of a particular racial or ethnic group, emphasizing many negative characteristics of the group, but often a few positive ones as well. It is a particular kind of typification (see the discussion of typification in Chapter 3). Stereotypes do not describe the actual behavior of the members of a group, nor do they admit the possibility that the members of a group may not all be alike in their behavior or attributes. Rather, the stereotype exaggerates some aspect of commonly observed behavior and applies it uncritically to the group being stereotyped.

Whereas prejudice refers to beliefs and attitudes held by individuals, *discrimination* refers to their behavior toward the members of a racial or ethnic group. Prejudice and discrimination frequently operate together, each supporting the other. For example, black Americans have been the victims of discrimination in education. Until the 1954 Supreme Court decision (*Brown* vs. *Board of Education of Topeka, Kansas*), blacks attended schools that were segregated by law. Even after segregated schools were declared illegal, blacks continued to receive an inferior education in many school systems, and segregation persisted. This discrimination, resulting in part from prejudicial views of blacks as intellectually inferior, led to their receiving an inferior education—which could then be used to justify the assertion that they were genetically "inferior."

The concepts of prejudice and discrimination heavily emphasized the role of the individual. Research focused on the personality structure of prejudiced people—for example, in the well-known studies of the authoritarian personality (Adorno, et al.: 1950)—and sought to explain the origins and persistence of prejudice in psychological terms. Allport (1954) followed this approach in his analysis of the prejudiced person. Others looked at the effects of discrimination and prejudice on the personality of the individuals who were their object. Examples of this are Stanley Elkins's (1959) study of the "Sambo" personality of American slaves and Kardiner and Ovesey's (1951) study of the personality of Southern blacks. Both argued that major personality adjustments and damage resulted from life in an environment of prejudice and discrimination.

This pronounced emphasis on the individual as the source of prejudice and discrimination reflected the prevailing belief in assimilation as well as the assumption that discrimination was generally caused by prejudice. Because it was generally held that racial and ethnic groups would and should assimilate, scholars tried to determine why some people resisted this process. The result was an overemphasis on individual and psychological factors and a relative neglect of societal conditions. Attention was paid to the individual mind and behavior rather than to group organization. Attitudes and aspirations of members of various ethnic and racial groups were generally ignored, as were the relationships of groups to one another or to the society as a whole.

Types of Assimilation

More recently, sociologists have turned their attention away from individual attitudes and have focused instead on the often complex relationships between ethnic groups and the society as a whole. They noticed that racial and ethnic groups were not disappearing as easily or as fully as had been anticipated. Some concluded that this situation could be partially attributed to the fact that assimilation was a more complex process than had been imagined.

One sociologist, Milton Gordon (1964), looked at the relationships that exist between a dominant host society and migrating minorities and argued that the members of a minority group could adopt the culture of a host society and yet remain apart from it in other respects. For example, blacks, Jews, and other ethnic groups maintain a strong consciousness of themselves as groups, try to get their members to marry within the group, and develop institutions such as clubs, religious bodies, and schools that are parallel to those of the society as a whole. But at the same time, these groups share parts of the host society's culture; they know and use its language and share many of its customs.

Gordon discusses seven types of assimilation, each a separate aspect of the general process. He called the first form of assimilation *cultural assimilation*. This refers to a minority group's changing its cultural patterns to those of the host society—learning its language, for example, or adopting its religion. After cultural assimilation occurs, Gordon says there can then be *structural assimilation*, the large-scale entrance as equals of members of a minority group into the cliques, clubs, and institutions of the host society on the level of primary, face-to-face interaction. So long as there are country clubs, fraternities, veterans organizations, and similar social groups that are composed only or predominantly of the members of particular races or ethnic groups, structural assimilation has not taken place.

According to Gordon, cultural and structural assimilation must take place before the process can be completed. Later stages of assimilation include widespread intermarriage; the development of identification with the host society; the absence of prejudice and discrimination against members of a minority group by the host society; and the absence of value and power conflict between the minority and host groups.

Gordon's analysis makes it clear that assimilation is not a simple event but rather a complex process with many distinct subprocesses. Consequently, assimilation ought not be considered as a single step taken by a group as it moves from being a minority to becoming part of the majority. In most cases, assimilation occurs in some areas of life but not all. For example, members of a minority group will often adopt the dominant culture but remain structurally separate. In addition, when there is prejudice or discrimination by the host society, the minority group often cannot assimilate. Nowhere is this more clearly seen than in the case of black Americans.

Racism

Early in the twentieth century many observers assumed that black Americans were the most assimilated of all immigrant groups. It was argued that blacks had, after all, ceased to speak their native languages; they no longer followed their native African religions; and their traditional social institutions had been abandoned. Those who saw blacks as examples of successful assimilation pointed to the fact that blacks spoke English and generally belonged to Protestant churches. That this state of events had been achieved through *force* and that blacks were held to an economically and politically inferior position did not alter the perception that blacks were an assimilated group.

Using Gordon's approach to assimilation, we can see that blacks were culturally but not structurally assimilated, for they neither entered primary relations nor participated in the institutional life of the society on an equal footing with whites. Until the 1950s it was impossible in most parts of the country for blacks and whites to eat in the same restaurant or attend the same school or church. In the South, where the majority of blacks lived, there were even greater restrictions. Schools, buses, and trains were segregated. Blacks and whites could not sit together in theaters, could not drink from the same water fountain, and in some communities were even required to use separate vending machines. Considering such restrictions, blacks had just barely begun the process of assimilation.

Gradually, as a result of the Civil Rights Movement of the 1950s and 1960s, the legal bases for such restrictions were removed. Federal legislation, combined with Supreme Court decisions, removed the legitimacy of most *de jure* (legal) discrimination. Yet, despite this, many forms of *de facto* discrimination persist. Education provides a striking example. When school boards could legally assign students to schools on the basis of race, there was *de jure* segregation. When students are assigned to schools on the basis of the neighborhoods in which they reside, and these neighborhoods are predominantly of one race or the other, *de facto* segregation exists.

Another consequence of the Civil Rights Movement was the recognition that not only individual attitudes and behavior and legal restrictions limit black participation in society, but that institutions practice racism as well. *Institutional racism* refers to the fact that prejudice does not invariably underlie discrimination. Institutions may discriminate against blacks by prescribing that people behave in certain ways, even though no intent to discriminate underlies their behavior. The practice of "red-lining" followed by some banks is a good example. Under this practice, banks identify certain areas in cities where mortgages for homes will not be issued because, they say, the declining value of the property in the area creates too much risk. Since blacks are most likely to be living in these red-lined areas, they face greater difficulty in obtaining mortgages and purchasing homes—not because the bank overtly refuses to deal with blacks, but because its general policies fall especially heavily upon blacks. In fact, the individual banker who rejects a mortgage application from a black in a red-lined area may not have any prejudice against blacks. Indeed, he or she could be black.

Institutional racism may also be expressed in employment policies. Until recently, few blacks were police officers, firefighters, or civil servants. Only after civil rights legislation opened up the hiring process were blacks and other minorities able to obtain many jobs in the public sector. And in the private sector, it has taken governmental pressure and court action to force employers and unions to recruit minority workers. Such pressure often takes the form of a requirement that employers develop *affirmative action* plans to recruit minority members, with the threat of legal sanction if they do not.

As long as the economy is healthy and there are plenty of jobs available, affirmative action policies can and do create more heterogeneous work forces. However, when the economy declines and workers are laid off, many businesses and governments follow a traditional policy of "last hired, first fired." Such a policy often means that blacks are disproportionately fired since they usually have been the last hired. Personnel officers may not harbor any prejudice against blacks, and yet, because of institutional factors, a type of racism emerges. But some have charged that another form of racism emerges if the institution fires whites rather than blacks in order to protect the last hired.

Another consequence of the Civil Rights Movement was the recognition that, regardless of the considerable cultural assimilation of black Americans, there was nevertheless a distinct and important black culture. Blacks, it was recognized, were not simply Protestant Americans with dark skins. Rather, like other ethnic groups, they had developed and maintained distinct patterns of behavior, attitude, and language. Earlier scholars had noted differences between whites and blacks but interpreted such differences in terms of individual or cultural pathology. Thus, by behaving in ways that were culturally black, some individuals were judged to have developed emotional disturbances. This interpretation can be found in such books as Kardiner and Ovesey's analysis of Southern blacks, and they were not alone. Many psychologists, psychiatrists, and social scientists interpreted differences between blacks and whites so that blacks were seen as falling short of white culture and were called "culturally deprived." More recently, most scholars have come to believe that the black experience in America has produced a culture that has served blacks well in their adjusting to a hostile and degrading environment. Far from being deprived, blacks have a rich culture adapted to the particular demands of their environment.

Cultural Pluralism

By the late 1960s, scholars were not only discovering that there was more to black culture than pathology; they were also coming to grips with what was being perceived as a resurgence of ethnic group loyalty among other Americans. Sociologists began to discover what the members of such groups had known all along—that ethnic traditions remain strong in the United States. While early generations of American immigrants learned English and became American citizens, they abandoned neither their sense of identification with their ancestors nor many of their cultural patterns. Consequently, many would argue that the 1960s were marked not by a resurgence of ethnicity but rather by a rediscovery of ethnicity by social scientists. This increased attention to ethnicity was, in part, the consequence of the growing aggressiveness of blacks and the attention paid them by social scientist and others.

Out of the increased discussion by ethnic group members and social scientists emerged the concept of *cultural pluralism.* The theory of assimilation, as we have seen, assumes that minority groups eventually will adopt the dominant culture of the host society and in time will disappear as separate groups. But where cultural pluralism exists, each group maintains its distinct culture and retains its group identity.

Cultural pluralism is not a new idea. Even before the great wave of the "new immigration" had ceased, some scholars took issue with assimilation, both as a prediction of what would take place and as a prescription for what should happen. These critics of assimilation felt that immigrant groups would not and should not lose their distinct cultures and become indistinguishable from those in the host society. Therefore, at the same time that popular opinion was calling for the rapid Americanization of immigrants, others recognized that complete Americanization was not necessary. They saw no conflict between the retention of traditional cultural practices and full participation in the economic and political life of the society. In fact, it could be argued that pluralism is much more in accord with American democratic values than is enforced assimilation.

Neither assimilation nor pluralism completely describes what has taken place in American society. The assimilation perspective correctly grasps that immigrant groups have adopted many aspects of American culture, but it fails to understand that immigrant groups have had an important role in shaping what we now define as American culture. The immigrants of the late nineteenth and early twentieth centuries confronted an American culture that was not simply a continuation of the English culture that dominated the colonies. Rather, American culture had been shaped continuously by successive waves of immigrants and the cultures they brought with them. Thus, the cultural practices that Italians and Poles found when they arrived in the early twentieth century had been shaped in part by the culture of the Germans who had arrived a half-century earlier. For example, Sundays in the 1920s were not the somber and dark religious days of the New England Puritan; they more closely resembled the more relaxed and joyous day of the German immigrants.

The analysis that focuses on pluralism correctly emphasizes that American immigrants have retained significant aspects of their original cultures and have sustained a sense of group identity. But, like other theories, it has an oversimplified view of what the culture of immigrant groups is like and from where it derives. It is accurate to say that immigrant groups adopted many aspects of American culture while retaining some traditional patterns. But this statement does not go far enough. Immigrant groups maintained traditions, but they also developed new cultural patterns after they had been in this country for a time. These new patterns were neither carryovers from the old world nor American dominant cultural patterns, but rather specific creations of the migrant group in the American context.

Ethnogenesis

The concept of *ethnogenesis* refers to the fact that an ethnic group and its culture are created within a host society and are not merely transplanted from the old country. Blacks, for example, lost most of their native culture through slavery. Yet at the same time, generations of experience in slavery and after created a new specifically black American culture.

The same process, although different in degree, was experienced by other ethnic groups. Jews, for example, came from various areas of Europe where centuries of living had produced not a single Jewish culture but several distinctive cultures. Several generations of life in the United States have yielded a single ethnic group of which almost all Jews feel a part. At the turn of the century, this single group did not exist; Jews of German origin distinguished themselves from those of eastern European background and felt their own success threatened by the arrival of large numbers of "uncultured" and "foreign" newcomers.

The process of ethnogenesis takes place over several generations and cannot be said to ever reach a final or conclusive state. Each group changes over time as conditions change. This reflects the fact that culture is not a static thing that gives unchanging guidance to individual and group conduct. The ideas, beliefs, norms, and values that shape our behavior do not persist unchanged forever, but are continually being reshaped as we interact and seek to meet the circumstances that confront us.

Thus, for example, Jews at the turn of the century were highly conscious of the differences between German and eastern European Jews. Their religious observances, social customs, and occupations were markedly different. The events of the 1930s and 1940s had a profound impact upon the nature of Jews as an ethnic group. The Holocaust and, later, the founding of Israel were events of transcending importance, not only in sustaining a sense of Jewish identity, but also in creating a group identity that made earlier internal differences seem unimportant. As this example suggests, international events are a part of the environment that shapes ethnogenesis in a particular society. One might similarly point to the Soviet domination over the Ukraine as an example of an international event that has affected the attitudes and group loyalties of American ethnic groups. For Ukrainians in America, the status of the Ukraine as a captive nation is an important issue, and as such it provides a focal point in their own group identity.

The process of ethnogenesis is also affected by the way newly arriving groups are perceived by the host society. Part of a group's consciousness of itself is derived from how it is treated by others. If the dominant group perceives the members of a minority as a single group, it is likely that minority group members will see themselves in similar terms. For example, there were significant differences between northern and southern Italians, as there were between German and eastern European Jews, but those already present in the United States often

Thomas Hart Benton, *Field Workers*. (1945).
Oil on parchment. 8¾ × 18½ inches. Hirshhorn Museum and Sculpture Garden, Smithsonian Institution.

In the fields of the South, black Americans forged a new culture and a sense of peoplehood from their experience of oppression under slavery and afterward.

did not perceive these differences. For members of the existing American society, there were just "Jews" or "Italians" arriving in great numbers. And while northern Italians may have felt themselves very different from Sicilians or Neapolitans, in the eyes of members of the host society, they were all members of a single group; they were simply "Italians." This social definition contributed to the group's emerging conception of themselves as Italian-Americans.

As the foregoing discussion implies, in order for an ethnic group to exist, its members must develop a *consciousness of kind*; that is, they must feel that they are like one another and different from outsiders. These similarities and differences can have many bases. For example, some groups feel bound together because of their color, others because of their religion, some because of a shared language, and most because of a common ancestry. Regardless of the basis of such group identity, members of an ethnic group are able to distinguish themselves from others who have a different color, religion, language, or national origin. They know who are "we" and who are "they."

Knowledge of who constitutes a particular ethnic group is almost always well defined by members of the group itself. Those who are members of different groups may frequently lump together others into groups that would not be thought of as a single group by their own members. For example, when white settlers came into contact with Native Americans, they rarely distinguished members of one tribe from another. Thus, while the Iroquois and the Shawnee had distinct societies with different cultures, they and the still more different Sioux, Navajo, and Cheyenne were, for most white Americans, simply Indians. Indeed, so little awareness of differences among Native Americans was exhibited by whites that rarely did anyone comment on the government's policy of taking children from different, and often hostile, societies and placing them in a single Indian boarding school.

After three centuries of being defined as Indians and not as members of specific tribes, Native Americans today find themselves members of a single ethnic group. They continue to see themselves as Sioux, Cherokee, or Hopi, but they also see themselves as Indian, and as such they can join together with others who are tribally different into pan-Indian organizations. It is not important whether the name given to this ethnicity is "Indian" or "Native American." Regardless of name, a new, more inclusive group identity has been created. This new consciousness of kind in part accepts the view of others and in part reflects events over the past three centuries.

Closely related to the impact of others' definitions of who constitutes the group is the effect of government policy and regulations. We have already mentioned the policy of the Bureau of Indian Affairs (BIA) of sending Indian children to schools without regard to their tribal membership. Recent affirmative action programs designed to increase the number of minority persons in education, occupation, and housing have had a similar effect. In order to ascertain minority participation, the government must be able to determine who are members of ethnic groups. Rather than count Cuban, Puerto Rican, Mexican-American, Spanish-American, and other Spanish-speaking individuals as members of different ethnic groups (they each have distinct cultures and histories), the United States government has established a new category—Hispanic—which is determined by such designators as "Spanish-surname" and/or "Spanish-speaking." As a consequence, members of quite dissimilar groups (indigenous Spanish Americans of New Mexico and Cuban refugees in South Florida) find themselves drawn together. For their individual group benefit, they now need to work with one another. And as time goes by, it is likely that they, like the Indians, will begin to identify with one another.

Types of Minority Responses

The discussion of ethnogenesis suggests that the interaction between an ethnic group and the rest of the society creates the ethnic group and shapes its character. The characteristics of the ethnic group and the way it fits into society thus depend partly upon the way the group is defined and treated by the host society.

Some ethnic groups may be termed minority groups. Louis Wirth defined a minority as

> a group of people who, because of their physical or cultural characteristics, are singled out from others in the society in which they live for differential and unequal treatment and who therefore regard themselves as objects of collective discrimination. (Wirth, 1945: 348)

Not every ethnic group is, therefore, a minority group, for an ethnic group may be the dominant group in the society (for example, English Canadians). Similarly, a minority group need not be the smallest group in the society, nor must it be smaller than the dominant one. In South Africa, for example, the relatively small segment of the national population who are Afrikaners (whites of Dutch descent) is the dominant group, and the numerically larger group of black Africans is the minority.

Wirth correctly pointed out that a minority group may orient itself to dominant groups in several different ways. Which one it chooses depends to some extent upon how the dominant group treats it. Thus, under some conditions the minority may seek to assimilate to the dominant group, while in other circumstances it may seek to attain tolerance of its distinctive culture under some form of cultural pluralism. If it makes such attempts and is rebuffed, the minority may choose to secede from the dominant society, either by removing itself physically (as did the Mormons in moving from the midwest in the nineteenth century) or by becoming politically independent (as many French Canadians in Quebec are attempting today). Another choice open to the minority is militance. It may strive to stand up and fight for its rights against the dominant group or, under some conditions, even fight to make itself the dominant group. Frequently, there are disagreements within the minority group over which stance to adopt; some urge assimilation or pluralism, while others opt for secession or militance. The position taken depends as much upon the dominant group's wishes as upon minority preferences. This can be seen in the experience of Mexican Americans in three southwestern states.

Although they share a common native land and similar culture, Mexican-American relationships with Anglos differ in Texas, New Mexico, and California. Each of these states contains a large concentration of Mexican Americans. In each, however, the group received somewhat different treatment at the hands of Anglos, and as a result, different patterns of interethnic relationships emerged.

Joan W. Moore (1970) found such different patterns to be particularly clear in the political arena. She found that there was substantial political participation of Mexican Americans in New Mexico, but considerably less in Texas and California. Why, she asked, did Mexican Americans make up a third of the New Mexico state legislature (at the time she wrote) and provide one of the two United States senators, while at the same time in Los Angeles County (with over a million Mexican Americans) there was not a single Mexican American county supervisor or city councilor? The answer to this question, she argued, lies in the differing history of the group in each state.

Mexican Americans in New Mexico were the established and dominant group when the area became a territory of the United States after the Mexican War in 1850. There was an established social structure, with a landed upper class and a peasantry. This elite continued to play an important role in New Mexican politics throughout the territorial period. In fact, the state constitution of 1912 guaranteed the rights of Spanish-speaking people, and sessions of the New Mexican state legislature were at first conducted in both English and Spanish. Throughout much of this period, there was an alliance between wealthy Spanish landowners and Anglo ranching and railroad interests. In this respect, New Mexico resembled a classic colonial situation, where an indigenous elite does not suffer particularly at the hands of the colonizing power, but joins with it in controlling an area. After statehood, many immigrants arrived, including a large number of new Mexican immigrants in the 1920s. At that point, a distinction developed between the "old" New Mexicans, who began to refer to themselves as Spanish-Americans, and the "new" Mexican immigrants, referred to simply as Mexicans. The growing influx of Anglos and their increasing economic power slowly pushed out the old elite landowners after statehood. But in spite of this, Mexican-American participation in politics remained higher in the state than elsewhere in the southwest.

There has been far less participation of Mexican Americans in Texas politics. Even though Mexicans fought for Texan independence alongside Americans at the Battle of the Alamo, the relationship between Mexicans and Anglos in Texas has been one of conflict. At the time of annexation, most Mexicans lived in the Rio Grande river valley, where they still are numerically the largest group. In most of Texas, however, Mexican landowners were soon replaced by Anglos. Cattle and later cotton became the main industries, with Mexicans providing the bulk of the work force. Both near the border and elsewhere, the Texas Rangers were employed to keep Mexicans in inferior positions. This domination by Anglos tended to reduce the chances for Mexican participation in the political arena, and even in those areas in which Mexican Americans were numerically strong (such as the Rio Grande river valley), Anglos filled positions of political power.

In California there was yet a different pattern of interethnic relations. There was an indigenous Mexican population in California at statehood, but it was relatively small. Many Mexicans owned large ranches and farms. Here, unlike New Mexico, the workers were Indians rather than other Mexicans. It was not until this century that large numbers of Mexicans were recruited to work in the fields and industries of California. And later, when economic conditions worsened, it was from California that many Mexicans were forcibly returned to Mexico. Such economic exploitation of an immigrant group is unique in American history. Mexicans are the only group who have been rounded up en masse and returned to their homeland. Yet the demands for labor and the opportunities of the area have outweighed any other pressures. Consequently, the number of Mexican Americans has continued to grow as people continue to come north in search of opportunity. The legacy of the exploitation of Mexicans and Mexican Americans remains in southern California; despite their large population, few have actively participated in the political structure. Since the formation of the United Farm Workers by Cesar Chavez and the accompanying sense of membership in La Raza, this participation has been slowly increasing. (Literally, *La Raza* means "the race," but the term is used by Mexican Americans to convey a sense of peoplehood and community.)

The population of the United States is comprised of many different ethnic groups whose members have arrived in this country voluntarily and involuntarily. They have come in great numbers from some lands and in smaller numbers from others. Some groups are concentrated in particular regions, while others are scattered throughout the country. Some were met with hostility, while others were warmly welcomed. In addition, quite varied economic and social conditions prevailed at the time each group arrived. Today, each group is part of American society. And yet the collective sense of identity of each group has been shaped by its individual history: by the reasons its members came to the United States, the welcome they received, the prejudice and discrimination they suffered, the stereotypes developed about the group, and the economic, political, and social opportunities available to its members.

ETHNIC STRATIFICATION

As we discussed in Chapter 10, social stratification entails the unequal distribution of power, prestige, and property. Not surprisingly, in the United States social stratification is intertwined with ethnic group membership, as it is in most pluralistic nations. Ethnic groups are not equal in power, political participation, prestige, or social status, nor are their members equally successful in the occupational realm.

For several years, one of the authors of this book has used the following classroom exercise to illustrate the close relationship between ethnicity and social stratification. Introductory sociology students are asked to rank individuals by social class or social standing. The only information they are given is an alphabetical list of distinctively ethnic-sounding names. Although some students argue that they cannot do such a ranking without additional information, over several years the lists constructed have been remarkably similar. Almost everyone lists "John Adams" and "David Goldberg" at the top. "Stanley Smolinski" is at the bottom, along with "Juan Gonzales." It is significant that the students who do these rankings attend a university that draws heavily from some, but not all, of the ethnic groups listed. The rankings thus reflect the students' evaluations of their own groups, as well as their evaluations of other groups, including some with which they may have had little contact. It is interesting that the German name (a group that is not common in New England) is ranked higher by the students, many of whom are Italian and Irish, than are their own ethnic groups.

These rankings reflect subjective perceptions of American ethnic groups. A more objective analysis would examine income, educational levels, and occupational distribution of various ethnic groups. Unfortunately, such data are difficult to find. The United States Census, which enumerates the American population every ten years, does not have a good measure of ethnicity. Its questions about foreign birth do not catch those whose immigrant origins are several generations back. In addition, in order to sustain the separation of church and state, the Census does not ask questions regarding individuals' religious preference. This means it is impossible to identify some ethnic groups accurately. The Census does not, for example, ask whether Germans or Russians are Christians or Jews. This distinction is crucial in understanding ethnicity, since Jews from Germany and Russia usually identify themselves as Jews and not as Germans or Russians. Similar ethnic distinctions based on religion are true of the Irish; whether an Irish person is Protestant or Catholic is not a minor distinction.

Because Census data are not available, objective studies of ethnicity must rely upon surveys of samples of the American population. These surveys do not try to question everyone in the country, as does the Census, but they do question a sample of Americans chosen to be as representative as possible of the total United States population. In addition, the private corporations who conduct these surveys need not concern themselves about the separation of church and state and therefore can ask questions regarding religion. In general, these surveys are an excellent source of data regarding American ethnic group membership.

Table 11-1 is based upon surveys conducted from 1963 to 1972 by the National Opinion Research Center (NORC) of the University of Chicago. It shows differences among ethnic groups in years of education completed, percentage holding white-collar jobs, and average income. The table indicates that some of the perceptions held by students seem to be accurate. Jews, for example, have the highest number of years of education, the highest average income, and the largest percentage employed in white-collar jobs. On the other hand, while student perceptions imply that Irish Catholics earn less and have less education than the English, the data show the opposite. British Protestants have a higher percentage of their group in white-collar jobs, but they also have less education and earn less than do Irish Catholics. Such objective data clearly indicate the problems of subjective analysis.

One fact that emerges from both survey and Census data is that on every dimension of stratification, blacks and Hispanics are at the bottom. Their educational opportunities are the most restricted, their incomes the lowest, and their chance for occupational advancement the poorest. These conditions are directly attributable to the continuing effects of discrimination. Yet the last two decades have seen many attempts to improve the lot of these groups, and such efforts have not been without results.

Table 11-1 Demographic Characteristics of American Religio-ethnic Groups, Based on Seven NORC Surveys

Group	*Years of Education*	*Percent White Collar*	*Family Income*	*Percent of Population*
Protestants				
British	11.9	53	8309	13.6
German	11.0	40	7858	12.6
Irish	10.6	38	7022	5.5
Catholics				
Irish	12.2	49	9255	3.4
German	11.3	45	8903	3.6
Italian	10.7	39	7979	3.6
Polish	10.0	34	7940	1.4
Slavic	10.4	31	7693	2.5
French	10.4	25	7478	1.6
Spanish	9.3	24	3145	1.3
Jews				
German	12.9	57	9326	.3
Eastern European	13.8	79	11,114	1.7
Other	13.3	73	11,218	.5
Blacks	9.7	18	5425	13.4
Orientals	11.6	35	7918	.2

SOURCE: Adapted from Andrew M. Greeley and William C. McCready, *Ethnicity in the United States: A Preliminary Reconnaissance* (New York: John Wiley & Sons, 1974), pp. 42–43.

Federal and state equal employment legislation and affirmative action programs seem to have had a substantial impact upon the educational, occupational, and income opportunities of many blacks. Prior to the passage of equal employment legislation, there were no barriers to outright and overt discrimination. With the passage of such laws and the pressures on private and public employers to provide affirmative action, conditions have improved.

Yet, it has been argued that such efforts have not improved life chances for all blacks, but only for a certain category of blacks. William J. Wilson (1980) believes that employment legislation and affirmative action have helped blacks with access to education to secure jobs demanding high levels of skill. Legislation, working hand in hand with a growing demand for educated employees, has significantly helped blacks who could get the requisite training. But at the same time, many blacks without access to education have remained poor and unemployed. These conditions are true for others in the society as well. Hispanics and Asians, like blacks, have members who are able to move up the economic ladder because of their skill and training, but at the same time, both groups continue to have many who remain behind.

CONCLUSION

What is the role of ethnicity in contemporary American society, and what are the prospects for the future? It is clear that ethnic group membership continues to be an important force in people's lives. This is so in a number of respects.

First, one's position in the social hierarchy is shaped by race and ethnicity. Despite the national belief in equality of opportunity, both individual and institutional prejudice and discrimination still work to produce unequal incomes and life chances for members of different ethnic and racial groups. In contrast to explicit ideologies that emphasize the equal value of differing cultural traditions in a pluralistic society, patterns of hostility and differential evaluation persist between various groups. Therefore, whatever one's individual values or beliefs, it makes a difference whether one is Irish or German, oriental or black, a Polish Catholic or a Polish Jew.

Second, these negative aspects of race and ethnicity show little propensity to disappear. Not only do individual discrimination and prejudice continue, but institutional racism has proven to be incredibly long-lived. After three decades of effort, the racial integration of such basic social institutions as the public school remains problematic. And where the opportunities for equal education remain differentially distributed in the society according to race or ethnicity, other opportunities also continue to be unequally distributed.

Ethnicity and race continue to be important for another reason. Modern Western nations are often called mass societies—that is, they are characterized by a complex division of labor, by impersonality, and by social forces that keep people in isolation from one another even while they are lumped together in an anonymous mass. In such societies, membership in an ethnic group is a way for the individual to develop and sustain a sense of belonging. The person who maintains an ethnic membership is not alone in the world. There are others beyond the family with whom he or she can feel at one.

Ethnicity, then, fills the space between the family and the society as a whole. Once people lived in small social groups that provided comfort and stability; today's large, complex modern societies cannot do so. It seems that only in times of national crisis do members of a large society feel at one. At other times, many people identify with an ethnic group not only because it gives them a sense of who they are—it is part of their self-concept—but also because it gives them a sense of togetherness with others. When ethnic identity is not infused with negative connotations and does not bring with it unequal opportunities and life chances, it makes life in modern society less alienating.

SUGGESTED READINGS

GENOVESE, EUGENE D. *Roll, Jordan, Roll: The World the Slaves Made* (New York: Vintage, 1976).

GLAZER, NATHAN and DANIEL PATRICK MOYNIHAN, eds. *Ethnicity: Theory and Experience* (Cambridge, Mass.: Harvard University Press, 1975).

GOSSETT, THOMAS F. *Race: The History of an Idea in America* (New York: Schocken, 1965).

GREELEY, ANDREW M. and WILLIAM C. MCCREADY. *Ethnicity in the United States: A Preliminary Reconnaissance* (New York: Wiley, 1974).

GUTMAN, HERBERT D. *The Black Family in Slavery and Freedom: 1750–1925* (New York: Vintage, 1977).

KILLIAN, LEWIS M. *The Impossible Revolution: Phase II* (New York: Random House, 1975).

KITANO, HARRY H. L. *Race Relations*, 3rd ed. (Englewood Cliffs: Prentice-Hall, 1985).

WILSON, WILLIAM J. *The Declining Significance of Race*, 2nd ed. (Chicago: University of Chicago Press, 1980).

12

The World of the Family

Few social institutions get as much attention in American society as the family. Social critics, journalists, government officials, psychiatrists, and other figures proclaim their alarm, concern, or confidence about its condition: "The family is dying." "In our impersonal world, the family is more important than ever." "The government has taken over more and more of the functions of the family." "Popular culture is undermining the family."

Much of what is written in popular magazines and spoken on television about the family comes to contradictory conclusions about it. In the eyes of many people, the family is an endangered institution on the verge of destruction by massive and undesired social changes. Equality of men and women, sexual promiscuity, the availability of abortion, and the decline of parental authority over children are, for them, evidence of disorganization and moral decay of what they consider the most important of all social institutions. In their eyes, the family must be saved if society is to survive.

For others, the family is an oppressive institution that must change. Some critics feel that the family confines women to the household and consigns them to an inferior social position. Consequently, they would free women of their exclusive responsibility for childrearing by placing more responsibility on the community as a whole. Others believe the family places too many restraints on the individual. Since they feel the American ideal of lifelong marriage and sexual fidelity is simply unattainable, they believe remaining single and childless is preferable to getting married and having children.

Social scientists also hold similar contradictory opinions about the condition of the American family. Some scholars consider the family to be in considerable disarray and point to rising divorce rates and declining marriage rates as evidence. Others consider the family to be viable and point out that most people get married, and that the vast majority of those who divorce get remarried. Like other people, social scientists sometimes see what their beliefs lead them to expect, and this is nowhere more true than with respect to a sphere of life such as the family, about which people have passionate convictions.

After reading this chapter, you will see that the family, like most of the social world, is complex. Although there are identifiable patterns of interaction in the family, it is a rich and developing social reality that defies simple description. Like other groups, a family is constantly being shaped and reshaped by the ideas as well as the activities of its members at any given moment. Families provide a context in which people coordinate many important activities—sexual activity, bearing and raising children, producing and consuming goods and services, eating and sleeping. But its reality is not just the sum of these activities, for the reality of the family is also shaped by people's ideas about what it is and what it should be.

WHAT IS A FAMILY?

If someone asks you, "Do you live with your family?" how do you answer? Do you say, "No, I live in a dorm, not with my parents," or "Yes, I live at home"? However you respond, you are defining the family as a group of people closely bound together by marriage and birth. Thus, if you are not married, you probably consider your parents, brothers, and sisters as your family. But if you are married, then your spouse and children are likely to be the family with which you live. But at the same time, you have probably not stopped thinking of your parents and siblings as family.

Most Americans consider a family to be "a legally united couple living together in their own household and raising their children together" (Skolnick and Skolnick, 1977: 4). This is the ideal definition of a family shared by members of this society: a father, a mother, and their children. Yet this definition does not deal fully with the realities of modern American family life. What about

Richard Norris Brooke, *A Pastoral Visit* (1881)
The Corcoran Gallery of Art, Washington

The nuclear family has historically been at the center of Americans' conceptions of ideal family life. Smaller today than it once was because fewer children are born per couple, the family unit has also lost considerable responsibility for socialization. But it remains an important center of life activities.

children from prior marriages; how do they fit into such a family? Similarly, do a person's mother or father cease to be family if they are no longer living together in a household? What if there is only one parent? Do a divorced (or widowed) mother and her children constitute a family? And what about a lesbian couple who adopt a child? Are they a family?

We can begin to deal with such questions by pointing out the obvious: Regardless of the complications of family life, most people, like you, can readily answer such questions. People have a common-sense conception of what a family is. Their ideas, derived from culture, are also influenced by the realities they see around them. Thus, in most cases, people think of the family as parents, siblings, spouse, and children. Yet they have room in their conception of what a family is for single-parent families, the inclusion of grandparents or other adult relatives, adopted as well as natural children, married couples without children, and other variations.

Important as common-sense conceptions of families are (for, after all, these conceptions provide us with our grasp of social reality), they are also misleading. Americans, like the members of any society, are inclined to be ethnocentric in their view of the family, seeing their own institutions as inevitable and natural. But the family is an institution that takes many different forms in different societies and at different times. To understand the social forces that play upon and within the family, therefore, a more encompassing view is required.

Family Activities

A useful way of looking at family life is to examine the kinds of activities that commonly occur in families and at the way these activities are coordinated. Several different kinds of activity can be associated with or performed in families. Not all of these activities are equally important in the family system of a given society, and some may simply be absent in one society or another. Nevertheless, they are activities that are commonly centered in family life.

First, *people bear and raise children* within families. Because human beings bear helpless young, they are faced with the practical problem of caring for and socializing their children. Humans do not, as a rule, heap this task upon the individual mother, but find a variety of ways to share the responsibilities of childrearing. Typically, such responsibilities are shared by other adults who are related to the mother either through blood or marriage—her own mother, her sisters, perhaps her husband or his kinfolk. The range of variation in who shares responsibility for childrearing is quite broad, but it is universally a social activity occurring in some kind of family group.

The traditional culture of the Hopi Indians in northern Arizona exemplifies care by kin. The Hopi are *matrilineal*; that is, they reckon descent through the mother's line, so that it is the mother who provides the child with his or her social location. They are also *matrilocal*, meaning that when a couple marry they live in the woman's house. This *extended household* typically consists of a woman and her married and unmarried daughters, together with their husbands and children. The infant is nursed by its mother, but many of the responsibilities of child care and socialization are assumed by all members of the household, and the child is raised in the household of the grandmother (Dozier, 1966).

Such patterns of childrearing contrast sharply with those patterns developed in the United States during the nineteenth century and that persist in many families today. In this case, the care of the young child and much of the burden of socialization prior to the school years is the exclusive domain of the mother. Because American families are often geographically mobile, families are often widely dispersed. The mother is isolated with the child in the house and may have no extended network of kin to whom she can readily turn for aid. Grandparents, aunts, uncles, and siblings cannot easily share child care.

Contemporary American child-care arrangements have generated considerable discussion. Many people criticize the allocation of child-care responsibilities exclusively to the individual nuclear family. The heavier share of responsibility borne by women, they feel, reinforces their unequal position in society. Some would prefer that child care be provided by extended families, where emotional and physical burdens can be shared by kin. Others look to government and private institutions to create facilities that can provide day care so that mothers can work outside the home.

One of the more drastic efforts to reshape the organization of childrearing is that of the Israeli agricultural settlement, the *kibbutz*. There, children live in their own dormitories rather than with their parents, and child care is performed in nurseries and schools by specialists. Peers are also important in the care and socialization of the young. Parents are freed of the constant responsibilities of caring for the child, but parents and their children nevertheless do develop special and affectionate relationships (Spiro, 1965).

A second activity of families is closely related to the bearing and socialization of the young: Families provide a *social location* for the newborn child. They give it not only a home and food, but, just as important, they give the child *legitimacy*, that is, status as a legal, recognized member of the society. Frequently, but by no means invariably, legitimacy is established by a marriage bond between the biological father and the mother. *Marriage* can be defined as "a socially recognized, durable, although not necessarily lifelong relationship between individual men and women" (Gough, 1977: 24). In American society, for example, a child is legitimate if the mother is married to its biological father. Typically, the mother's husband is presumed to be the child's father unless there is some specific reason not to make this assumption. A child can also gain legitimacy by being adopted.

Not all societies, however, care about the child's biological father, nor do they make this a test of legitimacy. Among the Nayar, a pre-nineteenth century military caste in India, two forms of marriage existed. In the first form, a young woman prior to puberty was "married" to several men of her caste. One of these, a representative called the *tali* husband, spent several nights with her after the wedding. He might or might not continue to have sexual relations with her afterwards; regardless, any of her children by men of her own caste were legitimate because the *tali* husband was their symbolic father. The second form of marriage was the *sambandham,* which involved a "visiting husband." A woman would have as many such husbands as she desired if they were members of the same or a higher caste. Only if they were of a lower caste than she were the offspring they fathered considered to be illegitimate (Gough, 1955).

Social location and legitimacy are thus social and not biological matters. The American conception of marriage as a lifelong union of a man and woman who live together is not universal, nor is it dictated by biology. Our conception of a family as a nuclear unit of husband, wife, and legitimate children is, as we have shown, not universal, nor is it a product of our biological makeup. And the terms we use to designate various forms and degrees of kinship are also matters of social definition.

In the American kinship system, *mother* is a term applied by an individual to one person, his or her biological mother. In many societies, however, people call their biological mother and her sisters by the same term, and likewise refer to their biological father and the father's brothers by the same term. In such systems of kinship terminology, the important distinctions are between the several people called *father* (the biological father and his brothers) and the mother's brother, a male who has a special relationship with and particular responsibilities for the child and is called by a special term.

Third, families are *residence units.* People live, eat, sleep, and find basic social companionship in family units. The American family, now and historically, has been composed of a husband, wife, and children dwelling together as a nuclear family. At various times, this unit may also have included aged parents, other relatives, or even boarders, but the nuclear unit has historically been the American ideal. In the United States the number of people living together in a household has decreased from colonial days. In 1790, more than a third of all households had seven or more members, while in 1980, 2.2 percent did. And while half of all households in 1980 have one or two members, in 1790, only 10 percent were this small. In colonial days the family was larger mainly because there were more children.

There is also great cultural variation in the social and geographical location of the family residence unit. American families are typically *neolocal*; that is, the newly married couple establish a residence of their own rather than moving into the household of their parents. (There are obvious exceptions to this rule, for economic problems or housing shortages may sometimes make it difficult to establish an independent residence.) Among matrilocal groups such as the Hopi, the husband is the one who moves to the wife's residence. Among other groups, residence is *patrilocal*; that is, the household unit is established in the residence or the vicinity of the husband's family. In many societies, the family that dwells together is larger and may contain more than one married couple. Multigenerational families are much more common in other societies than in the United States.

Regardless of size and location, the family unit is a place where people coordinate some of the most fundamental activities of social life. Among these activities is one with great significance: Families are *economic units*. Here, again, families in different societies function economically in different ways, but in all societies the family has some economic role. Among the farm families of colonial America and other agricultural societies, the family was a major producing organization. Men, women, and children of the family labored side by side to produce the grains, meats, vegetables, produce, and other products upon which their subsistence depended. This remains true today of such groups as the Amish, a religiously oriented set of communities found in eastern Pennsylvania, Ohio, and Indiana. Relying on traditional farming methods, the family remains the center of economic life.

But most contemporary Americans experience a sharp segregation of work and family. Few families engage in any productive activity themselves. The family has become an organization whose economic activity centers on *consumption*. Families decide what goods and services they will purchase, but do not themselves produce them. Where the farm family of the eighteenth century produced its food, the contemporary family purchases food in a grocery store with income earned from a job. Moreover, consumption is an important family activity. In a relatively wealthy society such as the United States, a great deal of time seems to be spent shopping, making purchases, and (presumably) enjoying the great many consumer goods available.

Typically, the economic activities of families have been based upon a division of labor between men and women. The scope of this separation of activities varies widely, but in no society is it completely absent. (In Chapter 7 we discussed the issue of sex roles in considerable detail. Later in this chapter we will examine some changes in sex roles in the American family since colonial times.)

Finally, *families regulate sexual activity*. In American society, sexual intercourse is regarded as an activity in which married couples can rightfully engage. Although premarital and extramarital intercourse are more widely tolerated now than several decades ago, marital intercourse remains the ideal. In other cultures this close association of sexual activity and the husband-wife family bond does not exist. Among the Nayars, for example, women were free to have sexual intercourse with any man so long as he was a member of their caste or a higher caste. Undoubtedly this attitude had something to do with the fact that the men of this group were frequently absent from their homes because of their military activities. Among other groups, as well, sexual activity is not regarded as something confined exclusively to the married pair. Hospitality among traditional Eskimos often involved a man's sharing his wife with a visitor, for example, and many cultures have more permissive attitudes toward sex than our own.

Notwithstanding such variations in how closely sexual activity is confined to marriage, family systems invariably entail rules that forbid sexual relations and marriage between close kin. The *incest taboo*—the prohibition of sexual relationships between such close relatives as mother and son and, with rare exceptions, between siblings and between father and daughter—is universal. There is more variation in the regulation of sexual contact and marriage between other relatives. In American society, marriage between cousins is forbidden by law in many states; in other societies, the ideal mate is a cousin. Among the Arunta, a hunting and gathering people of Australia, for example, a young man was normally expected to choose a wife from among his mother's mother's brother's daughter's daughters (Spencer and Gillen, 1927).

Childbearing and childrearing, the establishment of social legitimacy, living within defined households, economic activity, and sexual behavior are the major areas of human activity associated with the family. The range of variation in the way people organize these activities is enormous. The members of each society take for granted their own established definitions of reality and see what they do as normal.

In many societies, family and kinship provide the sole basis for social life. Every social activity is organized on the basis of family, and kinship provides the only map people have or need. In these societies, such as the Arunta of Australia, the role relationships between any two people are always governed by kinship. Individual identity is always established by a kin relation to the other with whom the person interacts. Important norms that affect social interaction are based upon kinship, so that one is polite, familiar, or even avoidant with another depending upon the kinship relationship. In economic, religious, political, and all areas of life, family is everything.

In Western societies, of course, kinship provides only a part of the social map. Some activities are organized along the lines of family and kinship, but not very many. The nuclear family is in many respects a small social world unto itself, and much of what people do in their everyday lives is done outside the context of the family. Moreover, the family has a very different meaning in contemporary American life. It is not viewed as the seat of economic activity, but often as a place of emotional refuge for the individual beset by the pressures and anxieties of the world. Although it continues to provide social legitimacy for the child and to be the place where early childrearing occurs, many of the activities that characterized the family in the past have been transferred to other social organizations, such as schools, welfare agencies, physicians, and the like. The family's views of sexual activity seem to have changed, and some would argue that the cultural definition of marriage as a lifelong commitment has also changed.

How has the contemporary family come to be as it is? In the following section we will attempt to answer this question, describing the nature and the historical development of the contemporary American family.

THE FAMILY IN HISTORICAL PERSPECTIVE

Members of a society ordinarily experience institutions such as the family as fixed and inevitable. They share typifications that provide images of what family life should be. Their language provides terms for various kin and thus also gives them ready-made categories for thinking about these people. Norms and values help people determine what is normal and usual in family life. There are definitions of whom the individual can and cannot marry and approved procedures for courtship. Young parents know to whom they can turn for advice or assistance in childrearing. Some kinds of sexual activity are thought to be normal, and people share ideas about how often they should have intercourse and how much they should enjoy it. As a result, people have a set of guidelines available to them as they move through the life cycle.

Yet matters are rarely as clear-cut as typifications of family life make them seem. Typifications are rarely complete, and they cannot cover every contingency or problematic situation that may arise. Some are widely shared and learned well, but others are not. For example, most Americans are clear who grandparents are; they are the parents of one's parents. But fewer people can identify their second cousins or define this kinship category. Moreover, the role obligations of various kin to one another may be ambiguously defined. What rights and responsibilities does a grandmother have toward her grandchildren? And people may hold beliefs about family life but not be very confident about them. Is it acceptable to marry someone for a reason other than romantic love? Is extramarital intercourse really socially disapproved? Can people really be happy married to one another for life?

Some people see discrepancies between the theory and reality of family life as evidence that the American family is either changing or declining. If people are uncertain about what they can, should, or must do, perhaps it is a reflection of the failure of culture to provide them with adequate guidance. If they are not as contented as they think they should be, this may reflect the inability of current family arrangements to provide the satisfactions required. Perhaps the family has deteriorated from its once proud, stable, and healthy condition.

Without denying that real changes have occurred and are occurring in the American family, we can suggest that this way of looking at things can be misleading. The conclusion that the contemporary family is falling apart often rests upon a romanticized vision of the family in the past. In this view, the family was once a stable institution that accomplished all of the tasks heaped upon it. People got married, lived and loved happily, raised their children successfully, never experienced conflict or thought of divorce, and grew old in the bosom of a warm and supportive extended family.

Television and movies have helped to convey this image of traditional family life. During the 1970s, one of the most popular programs on television was "The Waltons," which described a family's struggle for survival during the depression years of the 1930s. The family included a husband and wife, their six children, and the man's mother and father. Together they lived in a house in the mountains of Virginia. The show portrayed the many virtues of multigenerational family life: The mother could turn to the grandmother for assistance, the children did not have to wait for a special visit to interact with grandparents, and the father, grandfather, and sons could work side by side. It was implied that this "old fashioned" family type was preferable to contemporary families living in suburban isolation.

The image is appealing but largely mythical. In spite of the frequently repeated assertion that our ancestors lived in multigeneration extended families where grandparents and other relatives shared in the work of the family, it seems likely that the nuclear family was then, as it is now, the preferred family unit (Demos, 1979: 47). And people, then as now, faced problems in living up to their ideals of what family life should be. Perhaps they had fewer illusions about happiness—in life generally as well as in the sphere of the family—but what illusions they had were frequently dashed. Our ancestors experienced conflict and disillusionment in their marriages, just as we do. Divorce rates were lower, to be sure, but families still broke up for a variety of reasons, including the relatively early deaths of one or both spouses. And, it is worth noting, the rising divorce rate about which there is great contemporary concern has, in fact, been rising for over a century.

In short, there was no golden age of the American family from which the institution has declined. Major changes have occurred, to be sure. But the transformation of the family from what it was to what it is cannot be explained in terms of decay. To grasp these changes, we have to examine the way society itself has changed over the past two centuries and see how people tried to adjust to these changes.

The Early American Family

The typical American family during the colonial period and the early years of the nation was in many respects not unlike the modern family. It was a nuclear unit of husband, wife, and children, joined occasionally by an aged grandparent, by servants, or perhaps even by a criminal assigned by the state to its care and supervision. Men and women, then as now, assumed that they would start a new household when they married. And, contrary to the belief that marriages were arranged by parents solely for economic reasons, affection was an important condition for marriage. Although economic considerations were significant, and the families of bride and groom often bargained hard before they provided the goods and resources necessary to get a married couple started, it was affection that came first. A couple courted and became interested in one another before practical matters were introduced (Demos, 1977: 63).

John Singleton Copley, *The Copley Family* (1776–77)
Canvas, 72½ × 90⅜ inches. The National Gallery of Art, Washington. Andrew M. Mellon Fund.

Although the family shown here is white and of higher economic standing than the black family portrayed in Brooke's "A Pastoral Visit," both works emphasize and to some extent idealize family life. Modern people have no trouble recognizing the strong family sentiment evident in both pictures.

And, it is likely that colonial men and women, like those of other times and places, loved their children, took pride in their accomplishments, and were saddened by their suffering.

And suffer they did, parents and children alike. Mortality rates for infants and for women in childbirth were very high. Death rates varied sharply from one year to the next as epidemic diseases took their toll. Life expectancy in the colonies was short by contemporary standards; few men and women lived long enough to see their grandchildren grow up. Old people were held in high esteem, but there were not very many of them. Life was hard and often short, if not nasty and brutish.

Changes in mortality rates and life expectancy are part of the difference between early and contemporary families. Today, people live longer, the death rate is more predictable from year to year, and fewer families are disrupted by the death of a spouse. But there are additional sharp differences between the colonial and the modern family. To begin, the household was a major economic unit, indeed, the primary unit in which goods and services were produced. Modern social arrangements lead people to expect that they will work outside the home in factories, offices, and stores. But America through the early part of the nineteenth century was a preindustrial society. Men, women, and children of this earlier era worked side by side growing food, tending animals, and producing clothing, barrel staves, shoes, wagons, and whatever else they required to survive.

The economic centrality of the family had a number of consequences. The family was the chief agency of socialization, and young men and women learned from their parents the skills they would use later in life. The worlds of adults and children were more closely joined than at present. The young worked under the supervision of their elders and were regarded not as a species apart, but as members of the community with responsibilities. Similarly, the social worlds of men and women were closer together than they have become. To be sure, women were regarded as inferior—as weaker and untrustworthy—and were to be subservient to their husbands. But men and women shared a way of life and a common outlook to a degree contemporary people would probably find surprising. Even as they divided the labor of the household, colonial men and women shared in its tasks, helped one another overcome obstacles, and shared a world view.

Finally, the family in early America was an integral part of a community. People thought of the family as the basic unit of society. Indeed, they often thought of society as a kind of family, viewing political leaders as akin to fathers in their jurisdictions. And the family head was regarded as an agent of the state. Far from being an isolated and autonomous group, the family was a unit in which the community as a whole took an interest. The state could intervene if a man treated his children or wife harshly. And so important was the family as a unit of society that people looked with suspicion on those who lived alone. Frequently courts would direct such individuals to find a family with which to affiliate themselves. There were few "cracks" in colonial society in which an autonomous individual could hide.

From the very beginning, the American family (many of whose ideals were first imported by Puritans from England) was subjected to forces not experienced in the Old World. Unlike the Old World, America was a land of immense spaces. The settlement patterns of the Old World quickly began to change in the face of opportunities provided in the new. Sons did not have to await a father's death to obtain land. As soon as they became old enough to marry and establish their own households, men and women often found they could do better by moving to unsettled land than by accepting a portion of land in the village where they had been born and raised. And whereas the young in the Old World had to cross an ocean to find opportunity, American youth merely had to move further west. And as the young moved on, leaving their elders and their native villages behind them, they began to change the shape of the American family.

One effect of this ability to move was to strengthen the position of the young and to undermine the authority of elders in the family. A young man who disagreed with a parental decision could seek his fortune elsewhere, or threaten to do so and thus gain leverage within the family. This independence led to transformations of both communities and families. The individual became more important, and family and community less important. In addition, with geographical mobility came less allegiance to the authority of family and community. Men and women became more free to do what they wanted without the interference of families and without regard to the opinion of the community.

These were not automatic or mysterious developments caused by unseen social forces. Individual men and women sensed that better opportunities lay elsewhere, and they acted accordingly. As the descendants of people who had already broken with their parents in moving across the ocean, American youth were continuing a tradition of seeking a better life. If they defined their situation such that movement seemed to offer the best prospects, they acted upon it. Even if they did not actually move, many young people realized that the threat to do so meant greater power in negotiating arrangements with their parents and community leaders. Not surprisingly, along with such attitudes went the tendency for the young to identify less with family and community and to become more individualistic. Individuals' identities came to depend more upon their own efforts and less upon their attachments to their families or to the places where they were born and raised.

The Effects of Industrialization

As the nineteenth century progressed, the pace of change accelerated. A new nation was being formed, a continent tamed. From the standpoint of generations of European settlers, it was empty—the presence of a native population of Indians notwithstanding. The mood of the nineteenth century was expansive. Opportunity was in the air. Not only were there new places for people to go; there were new jobs to do. The young man and woman in colonial times could look forward to a life that would resemble that led by their parents. But nineteenth-century America was industrializing. New factories and industries were springing up, and there were new opportunities for commercial success.

One consequence of the rise of factories and of the intensification of economic activity during the nineteenth century was the separation of the spheres of men and women, as well as family and work, to a degree previously unheard of. Home became defined as a sanctuary from the harsh realities of business and industry. Instead of the place where the work of life took place, home became a refuge from that work and its sometimes heavy toll on physical and emotional health. At the same time, it became the man's role to work, to pursue the "main chance" and to grasp whatever opportunities he could for the benefit of his family. And it became the wife's duty to guard the home, to raise the children, and above all, to embody all those virtues of tenderness and kindness that were ruled out of order in the world of commerce.

One interpretation of this change is that people perceived their old community and family values to be threatened (Demos, 1977: 67). People liked having new opportunities; they wanted to get ahead, to achieve as much success as possible. But they also sensed that their traditions and values were being lost. In their relentless quest to improve their lot, people were uprooted from their parents and the communities in which they were born. They left familiar landscapes behind and entered new and unmapped social and geographical domains.

Hearth and home, and above all woman, became defined as the place and person where traditional values and ideals were enshrined. As people were torn from familiar communities, the family became a more valued social unit. And women became primarily wives and mothers, nourishing the souls of husband and children alike and defending compassion, tenderness, and concern in the bastion of the home. The rigid division of labor between the sexes and the relegation of women to home and child care, experienced by twentieth-century women as oppressive, stem from the efforts of our nineteenth-century ancestors to preserve something of their social traditions, and perhaps also their sanity.

The status of children also changed during this period. Formerly thought of as a miniature adult who could work side by side with elders on the farm, the child during the nineteenth century became divorced from the world of work. Relegated to home and mother, the child knew little or nothing of the world of the office or the factory (except, of course, for those children of working-class and immigrant families who were exploited in the mills and factories of the industrializing society). The child began to be seen as a special and different creature. At the same time, as the links between families and communities weakened, families were increasingly thrown upon their own resources to care for children. Thus, there began during the nineteenth century the vast literature on child-care advice that has continued to this day.

One of the long-term consequences of industrialization was the removal of many activities from the control of the family. Parents during the nineteenth century began to feel responsible for the development of their children and for launching them into a new and exciting—but also dangerous—world. But anxiety over the process of childrearing led to increasing dependence upon experts. Schools assumed more of the tasks of socialization, because parents could not be expected to teach their children all the skills required for life. In most instances they did not know what to teach the young, and, employed in offices and factories, they scarcely had the time to do so. As new generations of immigrants arrived, it became a major social priority to Americanize them, to teach them not only the English language and the skills and attitudes needed to fit into an industrial society, but also the customs of their new society.

One way of summarizing these developments is by saying that the practical activities associated with socializing the young were increasingly removed from the family. At the same time, the affective side of family life became more important. The family became the bosom where the developing individual was to be nourished, where the emotional needs of people were to be satisfied in a way that could not be met elsewhere.

There was another, perhaps less visible change. Our eighteenth-century ancestors valued the family highly and saw it as a model for other spheres of activity. But the family was not something problematic for them; they were not self-conscious about their participation in family life nor about the importance of the family. But beginning in the nineteenth century, self-consciousness about family matters began to grow. People focused more on the family, talked about it, and saw it as problematic. This is not surprising, in view of the many social changes that were having an impact upon family life. But it is instructive for people in the twentieth century who are apt to view the problems of the contemporary family as unique. Both the way we look at the family and many of the difficulties of family life are not recent, but have their origins in the nineteenth century.

THE CONTEMPORARY AMERICAN FAMILY

The condition of the contemporary family cannot be easily or briefly summarized. We will focus on three major aspects of family life here. First, we will look briefly at the demography of the family. How many children are born, when they are born, and how long they live are demographic conditions that significantly affect the way people live and their images of family life. Second, we will examine the family life cycle, focusing on people's expectations about the occurrence of significant life events. And third, we will look at the family as a socially constructed reality. How do contemporary Americans perceive the family and how do their perceptions affect their activities?

Demography and Family Life

Demography is the study of the size and composition of population. Demographers are interested in such matters as *fertility* (how many children are born), *mortality* (the rate at which people die at various ages), and *migration* (the movement of people between and within countries). These aspects of population influence the way people interact with one another as well as their attitudes, values, and images of social life.

The feature that most visibly distinguishes the contemporary family from that of even a century ago is its size. People today have fewer children and prefer fewer children than did their grandparents and great-grandparents. Married couples today generally express the desire to have only enough children to yield *zero population growth*. In practice, this means two children, for the mortality rates of infants have declined so much over the past century that most parents can assume that all of their children will survive to become adults.

The preference for smaller families probably reflects several factors. When children contributed their labor to the family farm or business (and even when they worked as child laborers in mills and factories), they were an economic asset. Their products and wages were often felt to be necessary to the family's survival. For the most part this is no longer true. Children, who are usually prevented by child-labor laws from performing any significant work except in family farms until their late teens, represent a drain on a family's resources. They must be fed, clothed, given medical care, and educated—requirements that cost money and toward which the child makes only a modest contribution, if any.

Moreover, nowadays children are thought to require a great investment of parental time. Modern American definitions of parenting emphasize that childrearing requires a great deal of effort and commitment. Children must be nourished emotionally as well as physically, and they are believed to require a great deal of time and attention. Such definitions of childhood, and the heavy emphasis on the responsibilities of parents to launch their children successfully in the world, encourage smaller numbers of children.

One result of this tendency toward smaller nuclear families is that people now and in the future will have smaller kinship networks. Fewer children mean fewer siblings and cousins, and ultimately fewer aunts and uncles. The parents of many contemporary college students were born in the 1930s and 1940s, and many of them had several siblings and a host of cousins, aunts, and uncles. Today's students themselves are likely to have a smaller number of siblings and cousins, and their children and grandchildren will perhaps have even fewer. Thus, a child born in 1940 may have had five or six aunts and uncles on each side of the family, with perhaps two or three cousins from each married pair. A child born in 1970 is more likely to have one aunt or uncle on each side and perhaps four or five cousins in all.

Smaller households and fewer relatives do not imply, however, that the family is less important in contemporary life. People continue to maintain contact with relatives and engage in many different activities: helping one another with childrearing and other household tasks, exchanging gifts, engaging in recreational activities, and just visiting with relatives. The fact that many people establish households at some distance from their kin may make some of these activities less frequent or more difficult. A grandparent who lives several hundred miles away cannot drop by to babysit or just visit. Still, people consider it important to maintain contact with their relatives, and they feel that family can be counted on when help is needed.

The Life Cycle

Demographic factors are important for several reasons, not the least because they help define what is "normal" in the eyes of most people. People tend to take it for granted that the world they have experienced is normal. An individual growing up in a large, lively family with frequent interaction among a large group of kin will regard this kind of family as normal. The individual from a two-child family with few aunts, uncles, and cousins and little interaction based on kinship will have a different idea about the nature of family life.

For much of the twentieth century, typifications of the family have increasingly centered on the kind of nuclear family unit discussed above. A man and woman marry in their early twenties; they establish their own household and have two children; by the time the couple have reached their fifties, the children have gone off to college or established families of their own. Such typifications are important in the social coordination of many important activities. As we pointed out in Chapter 5, time is an important organizing principle in social life. People develop expectations about when certain things will happen to them—in this case, when they will leave school, marry, have children of their own, and grow old together as a couple.

The sociological concept of the *life cycle* or *life course* is an attempt to capture this sense of life as movement through several stages. The life cycle consists of a series of identities people expect to have at various points in their lives. As people go through their lives, they assume and shed identities based upon age. For example, in American society they are infants, children, adolescents, middle-aged, and elderly. Other societies make different distinctions. Adolescence, for example, is a creation of modern society, not a universal age category. Whatever age categories are recognized, membership in one of them affects the person's sense of self and of behavioral possibilities. Each category is subject to typification, so that people think of themselves in terms of capacities and characteristics associated with that age. The American adolescent expects to do things a younger child cannot do, such as driving a car and staying out late. The elderly may find that the young dislike seeing any evidence of sexual interest or activity in them because sex is somehow not appropriate for old people.

The life cycle and its identities are tied to a sense of development and change. At each point, people not only define themselves in terms of their present identity but also look forward to the next one. Children look forward to the physical and social changes they are told will come when they become teenagers. Adolescents look forward to new rights as they become adults. Men and women in middle age are at the peak of social activity, but also look ahead to what will happen to them as they grow older: decreasing parental obligations, retirement, and old age.

Age-related identities are closely associated with the family, for as people achieve certain ages there are expectations associated with family life. For example, being married is an identity that a majority of people plan to assume at some point in their adult lives. To be sure, permissible alternatives to marriage have become more easily available in the twentieth century. It is easier to get divorced (and more people do); remaining single is a possibility for both men and women; more couples live together before marriage; and homosexual unions are more open and more tolerated. Nevertheless, the fact remains that the vast majority (better than 90 percent) of all men and women expect to marry and will in fact marry at least once.

Among those who marry, the vast majority (again over 90 percent) expect that they will have children. Notwithstanding the time and expense associated with raising children—as well as the fact that it is more permissible than ever not to have them— children remain a very salient part of American's typification of what will happen to them in their lives. Fewer children are desired, but still they are wanted by most men and women.

For the individuals involved, marriage and children mean major identity changes. The marriage ceremony formalizes an identity that had been paramount since courtship began: *couplehood.* It imposes upon the pair the roles of husband and wife. In addition, they are legally and socially a couple; they are a social unit in the eyes of their family and of society at large. They think of themselves as a couple and organize their activities on the basis of this identity.

This is not to say, however, that there is a single kind of interpersonal relationship that typifies American married couples. In a study of marriage, Cuber and Harroff (1965) discerned five types of marriage based on the kind of interpersonal relationship a married couple had evolved. In the *conflict-habituated* marriage, tension, conflict, and incompatibility permeate the relationship, which nevertheless endures over many years. The relationship of conflict becomes a constant reference point for husband and wife and a basis for their identities. In the *devitalized* marriage, the emotional closeness and mutual enjoyment of the early years disappear, and the relationship becomes a "habit cage" in which there is little feeling or investment of self. In the *passive-congenial* marriage, there has never been a great deal of self-investment in the marriage; the couple do what is expected of married couples but attach little significance to the relationship as compared with other involvements, such as work. In the two remaining marriage types—the vital and the total—individual identities are heavily dependent upon marriage. In the *vital* marriage, husband and wife are psychologically close in their important life involvements, and in the *total* marriage this mutual identification is nearly all-encompassing.

The advent of children is associated with even more significant changes in identity. When children arrive, the couple become mother and father as well as husband and wife. Their economic and social responsibilities become larger; their concerns shift from an exclusive interest in each other to the welfare of a child. In their own eyes and in the eyes of others, life takes on a new seriousness. Suddenly they are responsible for the care of an infant, a task for which they have probably had only minimal preparation. They have to feed, clothe, and see to its many and varied demands, often without having had much chance to learn how to do so.

Americans tend to view the parents as responsible not just for the physical care of the child, but also for the kind of person the child becomes. They are even less well equipped to meet this responsibility. No one knows just what socialization techniques will yield happy and successful adults. Parents are thus

Pablo Picasso, *First Steps* (1943)
Oil on canvas. 51¼ × 38¼ inches. Yale University Art Gallery. Gift of Stephen C. Clark, B.A. 1903.

Baby's first steps, like other milestones in the child's life, are also important steps for other family members. As the child's identity is transformed, so are the concerns—and the identities—of parents and siblings, who must adapt to changing demands upon them.

caught in a difficult situation. Tradition carries little weight in this society; people turn to experts as much or more than the experiences of their parents for guidance. Yet the experts give confusing advice, so that it becomes difficult for parents to know how well they are meeting their role responsibilities as parents. As a result, parenthood can be a difficult and stressful identity.

Moreover, the identities of both man and woman are changed by the arrival of a baby. In spite of some movement toward more egalitarian patterns of child care, in attitude if not always in practice, the child is still a more constant focus of the woman's attention than of her husband's. For many women, their working careers will be interrupted by the birth of a child, although increasing numbers of mothers work even while their children are young. For most women, identity becomes heavily invested in the activities of caring for the child. When she nurses the infant or pushes the baby carriage down the street, her social identity becomes that of mother. And, from the perspective of her husband, she may also become more identified by child care than by her role as wife. Particularly in a culture such as ours, where the care of children is conducted within the nuclear family unit by the mother, husbands may feel themselves in competition with infants for the woman's attention.

Once children arrive, family life is in many ways shaped by the sequential passage of children through several age grades. Talking and walking, toilet training, starting school, entering puberty, graduating from high school, and starting work or college mark the acquisition and loss of various identities by the child. In addition, family activities are in many ways geared to the identities of its children. How people spend their money, where they go on vacation, what leisure activities they prefer, and similar matters are affected by the ages of their children. Parents' time schedules are influenced by the need to drive their children to day care or school or to compete with adolescents for the use of the family car. Mothers' activities and social contacts are influenced by the ages of their children; in many cases, women's contact with other women is based upon the ages of their children.

Events in the child's life cycle are also markers of the life cycle of the family as a unit and of the identities of husband and wife. The identities of parents are influenced not just by their chronological age or progress through a career, but also by the identities of their children. When a child departs for college, marries, or has a child of its own, the parents as well as the child experience a change of identity. They are apt to think of themselves as entering a new phase of their own lives, with new possibilities as well as responsibilities ahead.

Demographic changes have markedly affected identity in middle age and beyond. People now live much longer than they did a century ago, with life expectancies well into the seventies for men and women. This fact, coupled with a preference for fewer children, means that men and women complete child-rearing sooner than was once the case, and they have more years to spend together as a couple once the children are grown. A hundred and fifty years ago, a woman might begin bearing children in her early twenties and not stop until her late thirties or forties. Coupled with a shorter life expectancy, this meant that frequently one parent had died before all of the children were grown and living independently. Today, children are often reared and have left home by the time a woman is fifty. Thus, she and her husband have more years to spend together as a couple.

This transformation has a number of implications. Women who have spent the childbearing years at home and have not worked often find themselves with little to do and with a disrupted sense of identity. With children gone and husbands at work, they have no *place*. Although they are still mothers with an interest in and sense of responsibility for their children, there is little for them to do when their children are hundreds of miles distant. Moreover, the couple with an "empty nest" must learn to cope with a new situation: interacting with one another as a couple without the presence of children. This is something they have not done since the earliest years of their marriage.

Usually, people become grandparents at some point in their lives. In earlier times, many people became grandparents soon after they ceased having their own children. Today, it usually takes longer for children to start their own families after they leave home. Those whose children attend college before marrying may have to wait a while before they become grandparents. Whenever it occurs, the advent of grandparenthood marks an identity transformation; it is a signal that the person has entered a new phase of the life cycle. Even though contemporary grandparents are active and in good health, many will remember their own grandparents as seeming very old. Thus, becoming a grandparent is a step toward developing a conception of self as old.

In contemporary America there is one other major influence on family roles associated with age: retirement. For most people, the age of sixty-five is a major event and identity change because it marks the end of their active working career. Many men have spent over forty years working. Their responsibilities, obligations, and sense of self have been rooted in their jobs. With retirement comes a return to the family as a more significant source of identity. Just as the departure of the last child profoundly affects the woman's identity and puts her into greater contact with her husband, retirement of either spouse means the couple has more time to spend together.

The social meaning of old age and the identities of the elderly are very different from what they once were. Shorn of authority and responsibility, the old are free to live life as they see fit, provided they have the financial resources with which to do so. Moreover, health care has improved, and people not only live longer but in most cases they remain healthier.

Yet old age may also be problematic, for in many ways it is an identity without a role. Increasingly, it appears, the social role of the elderly is to enjoy their "golden years." Marked by their chronological age in the eyes of others, the old themselves may feel little different from when they were younger. But with no particular duties and responsibilities other than to enjoy life, it can be difficult for people to have a sense of meaningful participation in social life. People acquire meaningful identities by *doing*, and not just by being located in a social category by self or others. Thus, many old people are irritated that the young often think they cannot do anything useful. And they may as a result sometimes feel socially useless themselves.

Family and the Perception of Reality

The family is a pivotal group because it provides the social context within which people find many important identities and engage in important activities. But the family is important for another reason; as an institution that receives considerable attention in this society, the family is a focal point of people's perceptions of social life. It figures centrally in the social construction of reality—in the images people have of themselves, their prospects in life, and of society as a whole.

As was pointed out earlier, the social meaning of the family has changed with the passage of time. Pre-Revolutionary Americans thought of community and society as being like families, with leaders exerting paternalistic influence and authority over their brood. Later, during the nineteenth century, the family came to be viewed as a refuge, a "haven in a heartless world," as the historian Christopher Lasch (1977) referred to it in a book by the same title. The contemporary family also looms large in social perceptions, and often does so as a symbol of conflict, social problems, and social change.

One of the major concerns of many contemporary Americans is the divorce rate, which is perceived as approaching record and disastrous levels. It is true that divorce rates in the United States are among the highest in the world, although the rise in rates dates back to the Civil War and is not the recent phenomenon some suppose. But it is also true that other societies have historically had very high divorce rates. The divorce rate in Japan was among the highest in the world in the 1890s, but then fell until about 1970. Moreover, it is by no means clear that high divorce rates are as significant a social problem as some people believe.

Common sense suggests that a rising divorce rate is the result of increasing marital conflict, and that its long-term result will be the destruction of family life. But there is not much evidence to support either of these suppositions. Conflict is probably inherent within marriage, which is an intense and intimate interpersonal relationship in which many opportunities for disharmony are apt to arise. There is no reason to assume that marital conflict has increased in proportion to the divorce rate, for men and women of previous eras also disagreed over the upbringing of children or felt restricted by demands for marital fidelity. Indeed, the number of accusations of adultery brought by Puritans suggests that even then the marital bond was not all it was supposed to be!

Some things have changed, however, that have made for rising divorce rates. First, as William Goode suggests, disapproval of divorce has been declining (1982: 154ff). Although not positively valued, divorce is a more thinkable act now than it was in the past, one that carries far less social stigma for men *and* women.

Second, divorce is not only more thinkable, but it is also legally easier to obtain. Until the 1960s, legal grounds for divorce were limited. In many states, infidelity was the only basis on which a spouse could sue for divorce. Only in Nevada were divorces easy to obtain, and divorce was a thriving industry there. Elsewhere, even if it was possible to obtain a divorce, it was an expensive and time-consuming process. Today, divorce is legally much simpler, with many more legal grounds on which a court can grant it. And the development of *no fault divorce*—in which neither party is judged to be at fault and the divorce is essentially a matter of agreement—means lower legal fees and quicker, simpler divorces.

Third, marriage is no longer the only available living arrangement, a change that has particularly affected women. It is socially permissible for women to live and to earn a living on their own, something that was far less true even a century ago.

Fourth, contemporary Americans have taken very much to heart the argument that people have the inalienable right to the pursuit of happiness. People are supposed to be happy, Americans believe, and marriage is a relationship that is supposed to make them so. Thus, being unhappy is today a legitimate excuse for ending a marriage—an excuse that would not have been acceptable a century ago.

Changing social definitions and expectations have thus made it easier for men and women to divorce. Any given marital situation may be defined by either party as one in which a divorce is a relevant solution. And, of course, as more divorces occur, divorce becomes a more accepted part of reality. It becomes a normal and typical response to a difficult marital situation.

The fact that divorce has become more common does not necessarily mean that the family is endangered. Divorced people generally remarry, forming new families as they do. Divorced men and women may bring children from previous marriages to such new *blended families*. The fact that people do remarry and form new families suggests that they continue to think of marriage and family as important and desirable.

Although rising divorce rates do not necessarily indicate social disintegration, there is considerable alarm regarding the prospect that many marriages will end in divorce, partly because the family is widely regarded as important, and partly because of the slowness with which expectations catch up to reality. The family seems central to the way Americans have viewed the world; marriage and parenthood have been taken for granted as identities that nearly everyone will acquire. And Americans have attributed to the family and its socialization practices an immense capacity to influence the child's development and eventual success. It is not surprising, therefore, that as family patterns change, critics view these changes with alarm.

Another aspect of family life that has become a major focus of concern is *family violence*. Spouse, child, and parent abuse, marital rape, and the sexual abuse of children have received considerable attention from journalists, social welfare professionals, medical personnel, and law-enforcement agencies. People increasingly perceive family violence as a problem and feel that social intervention is required.

Without disputing the seriousness of these kinds of behavior, which violate most Americans' deeply held convictions about how human beings should treat one another, it is probably an error to think of such behavior as an epidemic that has recently emerged in our society. Increased concern with and discussion of a social phenomenon does not necessarily indicate increasing prevalence. Indeed, as Richard Gelles (1976) has argued, the idea that child abuse is a growing social problem is a myth. There certainly has been more attention to child abuse, but there is no convincing evidence that it is more prevalent. It is likely that there have long been parents who have abused their children. What is new today is the fact that professionals concerned with child welfare are more willing to fight it.

Prior to the 1970s, child abuse was largely missing from criminal statistics, not because such behavior did not occur, but because teachers, physicians, neighbors, and social workers were less likely to bring it to the attention of police. Similarly, spouse abuse has probably not increased significantly in recent years. But changing conceptions of the rights of women and the willingness of women to assert them have probably led to an increasing tendency of women to fight back—to leave husbands who abuse them, to file complaints with the police, and to institute divorce proceedings. Clearly, the underside of family life, an unmistakably serious social problem, has come increasingly to light in recent years.

The perception of a dramatic increase in family violence, even if erroneous, clearly affects perceptions of social life in general. Confronted with reports of the sexual abuse of children in nursery schools, rape, wife beating, and the abuse of children by their parents, we are tempted to conclude that social morality is declining. Yet this is a misleading image, for it is arguable that these forms of violence and exploitation are inherent in American culture, that they stem from basic social arrangements rather than from recent social changes.

It seems likely, of course, that the family will become a focus of concern in a period of social change. Many people see the changing family as an institution besieged, with family life seen as undermined by a host of changes taking place. More permissive sexual norms, the growing visibility of and acceptance of homosexuality, a perceived explosion of premarital and extramarital sexual activity, and the legal and social acceptance of abortion seem to represent an attack on views of normal and typical life cherished by many people. In this context, family violence provides an additional bit of confirming evidence.

It thus seems inevitable that the family is a potent symbol for political figures and social movements with diverse ideologies and goals, and that it will remain so. An image of disorganization and decline provides a potent political symbol for conservatives who wish to lay the blame at the feet of their liberal opposition. Abortion opponents point to such developments as evidence that the practice of abortion lends sanction to a more pervasive disregard for human life. The Women's Movement can point to sexual abuse as evidence of underlying sexist attitudes that justify and encourage the abuse of women in general. The family, it seems, is not only the setting for some major social problems, but a symbolic battleground on which diverse issues are fought.

THE FUTURE OF THE FAMILY

Social scientists have not yet developed the ability to predict the future, and it is unlikely that they will ever do so. Even if they could grasp all of the immense complexity of social life, they would still have to reckon with the capacity of human beings to act in novel and creative ways. Because people are symbolic creatures, their thoughts and intentions often remain unseen. The sociologist may try to understand how people view the world and predict what they are likely to do, only to find that they act in unexpected ways.

Still, we can make some educated guesses about what family life in the future is apt to be like. Such predictions are based on the way people seem to define family life at present, and on the assumption that such definitions will continue to prevail. But if people begin to define their situations differently, they will act in ways we cannot now foresee.

It seems very likely that alternatives to marriage and family will continue to expand, but unlikely that they will replace the family as the ideal. In the past, marriage was not simply preferred by most people; it was essential. Women were virtually without a place in society if they were not married. But a woman's identity no longer depends so crucially upon marriage. Men and women can choose to remain single, for example. Although they may still encounter parental resistance to such a choice, neither parents nor the community now exert sufficient social control to prevent them from making it. The same is true of childlessness; more married couples in the future will probably choose not to have children.

Perhaps the most visible alternative to marriage is *cohabitation*—living together without becoming legally married. In the 1960s, when this practice began to be more commonplace, it was very controversial and led to considerable friction within families. Since then, however, it has become not only widely practiced but also tacitly accepted. Families that would have recoiled in horror at the thought of a son or daughter living with someone without being married now often quietly accept this as a fact of modern life. They may not approve of such arrangements but recognize they are powerless to do anything about them.

The very acceptance of such trends is one reason to expect that they will continue. Young people today may simply define a few years of singlehood or a childless marriage as a normal part of life. Indeed, cohabitation may even become a regularized part of the life cycle. With contraceptives and abortion readily available, sexual relations outside of marriage have become increasingly accepted. Cohabitation may thus be a new social invention, a way of regularizing social and sexual relationships not only for the young, but perhaps the elderly as well. One sign of the regularization of cohabitation is that courts have begun to work out the legal obligations of such partners to one another. The recent well-publicized spate of palimony lawsuits and settlements are an indication that this regularization is now well underway.

Another contemporary trend that seems destined to continue is the growing participation of women in the labor force. More women, including women with young children, are working, and there is no reason to expect this trend to stop until the percentages of working women and men become similar. There are several reasons for this expectation.

First, for many women, working is either a real or a perceived economic necessity. Some women work because they are heads of households solely responsible for supporting themselves and their children. At any given time, a third of black families and 10 percent of white families are headed by women (Goode, 1982: 70). Such women have no choice but to become part of the labor force. Other women work to supplement their husbands' incomes, either because they must in order to maintain a decent standard of living, or because they choose to do so in order to improve their standard.

Second, working is becoming an increasingly valued and perhaps even necessary part of a woman's identity. Careers once closed are gradually opening up to women, and the idea that women can have careers has gained widespread acceptance. Women's liberation has done a great deal to teach women not only that they can work outside the home, but also that they must. The battle against restricting women to home and children has to some extent denigrated these traditional roles. Many women, particularly those with more years of education and from middle-class backgrounds, feel uneasy about remaining at home as wives and mothers. To gain a sense of self, they feel that they must have a paying job outside the home.

The growing tendency for women to work outside the home will not be without impact upon life within the family. For example, we have seen how the care of children has been one of the most central tasks of the family. As more and more women become employed, child care may gradually come to be more equally shared between husband and wife, and it may also be conducted outside the home in child-care centers.

The evidence suggests that most working women continue to be burdened with the larger share of household tasks. Yet it seems likely that this will gradually change. Women who are making an economic contribution to the family are likely to have a stronger voice as they negotiate with husbands and children about responsibilities for housework. Although men will probably resist—housework is not a great deal of fun for either sex—they will, as Goode suggests, adjust.

This adjustment can take two forms. One will be to have housework become the responsibility of both spouses. Although housework has remained primarily the woman's role, more and more husbands cook, wash, clean, and care for children. The other adaptation is for both men and women to develop new standards for the "well-kept" house. Neatly made beds, highly polished floors, and shining silver may no longer be considered important. In a family where the wife works outside the home, the man may have to accept the idea that a house can be less neat and clean that the one in which he was raised.

Divorce is also likely to be a continuing part of the family scene. No one can predict with any confidence whether rates will continue to increase, to increase more slowly, or even to decline, although the second of these possibilities seems most likely. Based on present rates, it has been estimated that 40 percent of current marriages will end in divorce.

Divorce will continue to occur for several reasons. Even if marriages become more egalitarian, they will not necessarily be happier. Individual happiness is very highly valued in American society, and it is unlikely that any relationship can provide the degree of freedom and satisfaction that people in this society expect. Given the expectation of happiness from marriage and the acceptance of divorce as a solution, it appears likely that individual men and women will continue to define their partners as the source of their misery and divorce as an escape.

One result of continuing high divorce rates is that the single-parent household may become a common feature of the social landscape. If 40 percent of marriages do end in divorce, many children will be socialized either by one parent or within a new family when the parent remarries. In this as in many other aspects of social life, patterns that become widespread also come to be viewed as normal. In the future, people may regard a single-parent household as something entirely ordinary, fully as acceptable if not as common as a conventional family. And when such patterns become routine, they also become more likely. The fact that people routinely get divorced and live as single parents makes it easier for others to perceive these adjustments as solutions they can use themselves. What is extraordinary for one generation may seem ordinary to the next, and perhaps even typical for generations to follow.

CONCLUSION

To varying degrees, all of the trends in family life that we have noted are related to the great emphasis placed in American society—and perhaps increasingly in the modern world—upon the individual. Men and women of times past had little opportunity to think of themselves except in the larger context of the family or community. The individual was not then the center of the universe, and people expected to yield to the interests of the community as a whole. Thus, an unhappily married man or woman would be forced to accept personal unhappiness in the interests of the children. A dissatisfied child would nevertheless yield to parental directives.

Today it is different. Individuals think of themselves, to paraphrase Edgar Lee Masters's poem, as captains of themselves and masters of their future. And when happiness and satisfaction are judged, the individual is likely to be the standard. Altruistic concern for others is not dead, of course, nor is community totally absent, but their importance has declined relative to the emphasis placed on the individual. This individualism has had its effects in many aspects of social life, and the family is among them. That husbands and wives are more independent of one another and children are less controlled by their families is but one aspect of modern American society.

Such predictions as these depend, of course, on people continuing to define situations as they have been defining them and to act as they have been acting. There is nothing magical in such social trends, however, and so one should be cautious about predicting the future. Demographers in the 1930s thought that fertility would continue to decline. Yet after World War II, birth rates shot up and the age of marriage decreased somewhat, conditions that did not reverse until the 1960s. Historic demographic trends have now resumed, but decisions made by married couples in the 1940s and 1950s, which increased the population of the United States well above what was expected, had effects that will ripple through the society for years to come. People have a way of doing the unexpected!

SUGGESTED READINGS

GELLES, RICHARD. *Family Violence* (Beverly Hills, Cal.: Sage, 1979).

GOODE, WILLIAM J. *The Family*, 2nd ed. (Englewood Cliffs: Prentice-Hall, 1982).

GORDON, MICHAEL, ed. *The American Family in Social-Historical Perspective*, 2nd ed. (New York: St. Martin's, 1978).

HAREVEN, TAMARA, ed. *Family and Kin in Urban Communities, 1700–1930* (New York: New Viewpoints, 1978).

RUBIN, LILLIAN. *Worlds of Pain* (New York: Basic Books, 1976).

SHORTER, EDWARD. *The Making of the Modern Family* (New York: Basic Books, 1975).

STEIN, PETER J., ed. *Single Life: Unmarried Adults in Social Context* (New York: St. Martin's, 1981).

TUFTE, VIRGINIA and BARBARA MEYERHOFF. *Changing Images of the Family* (New Haven: Yale University Press, 1979).

13

The World of Religion

If you are like most Americans, when you see the word *religion*, you think of churches and synagogues and the activities that take place in them. Usually we think of religion in terms of membership in some particular group or organization, participation in its ritual activities, and the adoption of its beliefs regarding the meaning and purpose of life and the nature of the world, including conceptions of the supernatural. An Easter sunrise service, a wedding, a bar mitzvah, a prayer meeting, and Friday night, Saturday, or Sunday morning services are some of the situations and social acts associated with religion in our society. Thus, for many people, religion means belonging to a church, attending its services, believing in that church's conception of God, subscribing to its ethics and ideals, and celebrating the holy days and life-cycle events its prescribes.

WHAT IS RELIGION?

Religion is all of these things, but it is also more. The American view of religion is rooted in the culture of the West, and consequently it has been shaped by Judaism and Christianity. Other cultures around the world contain situations and activities that we would think of as religious but which differ markedly from what we usually identify as religious. Among Australian aborigines, for example, religious beliefs and attitudes pervade every aspect of existence; even objects in nature are vested with religious significance. But the specific organizations and activity associated with religion in Western society are not present. If religion is so variable, yet also a universal feature of human life, then just what is its essence?

One of the earliest efforts by a sociologist to extend the understanding of religion beyond the limited range of Western culture was made by Émile Durkheim. A French Jew living in the nineteenth and early twentieth centuries, Durkheim was familiar with the religious cultures of Europe. He became aware of the growing body of anthropological data on other cultures and sought a way to understand religion, so that the "primitive" religion of the Arunta of Australia and the Roman Catholic Church of France could both be explained. To do this, Durkheim defined religion in a general way that encompassed many different forms and varieties of religious activity and belief. This definition can be found in his classic book, *The Elementary Forms of the Religious Life*.

> A religion is a unified system of beliefs and practices relative to sacred things, that is to say, things set apart and forbidden—beliefs and practices which unite into one single moral community called a Church, all those who adhere to them. (1912: 62)

An important part of Durkheim's definition of religion is the distinction between the *sacred* and the *profane*. Each culture, in Durkheim's view, divides the world into two domains. All ideas, objects, and activities fall under the heading either of sacred or profane. Sacred things can be anything—gods and spirits, pebbles and animals, rituals and practices. For Durkheim, sacred and profane are not simply opposites, but terms representing two totally separate realms. The sacred is set apart, viewed with respect, and protected from the profane. The respect paid to things that are viewed as sacred is illustrated by the reverence that Roman Catholics display for the crucifix or Jews hold for the Torah.

Samuel Heilman's (1976) study of Orthodox Jews illustrates how objects that are normally profane can for specific periods become sacred because they are connected with sacred objects. The Torah—a hand-lettered scroll containing the first five books of the Bible—is a powerful sacred object for Jews, one that generates feelings of love as well as awe. One might say it both repels and attracts. People will touch the Torah with an object such as a prayer shawl or prayer book and then kiss the object, an act that transfers the sacred quality of the Torah through the other object to them. But under no circumstances would an observant Jew ever touch the Torah scroll itself with bare hands. When reading from the Torah, he would use a pointer, rather than his hand, to mark his place. When the Torah scroll is irrevocably harmed, it is accorded a funeral and buried, just as a person would be.

In the synagogue Heilman studied, there are many objects that are generally considered profane, but that become sacred when used in conjunction with the Torah. Among the objects that have this quality is a certain table. On most days, even when religious services are taking place, the table is not sacred. Various profane objects like books and mail are often put on it. However, on the Sabbath and holy days, the Torah is placed on the table while it is being read. When it serves this purpose, the table is sacred, and members of the congregation approach it only in enacting certain specific roles (for example, men saying certain prayers before and after the reading of the Torah). The ability of the Torah to change the table from profane to sacred extends to any object the Torah touches. The cabinet in which it is kept is not any cabinet but is the Holy Ark. The ornaments that adorn it become holy.

Almost anything can be defined as sacred, not only objects such as the Torah or a crucifix, but ideas, animals, and supernatural beings. Among many tribal peoples, specific animals take on special significance and are regarded with respect or treated as especially important. These *totems* may be regarded as the ancestors of the group or of specific clans within the society; they may be worshiped; and they are often felt to possess special powers to aid or harm people. Christians and Jews have a number of sacred objects, but a deity is also a major part of the sacred category for these religions. Whether the one God of Jews or the more complex Trinity of Christians, these religions have a conception of the world in which supernatural power figures very prominently. In contrast, religions such as Buddhism are less concerned with supernatural entities and more focused on the attainment of philosophical or moral ideals. For them, ideas are a major part of what is sacred.

Awa Tsireh, *Green Corn Ceremony* (1935)
Gouache, 19¼ × 27¾ inches. Collection, The Museum of Modern Art, New York. Abby Aldrich Rockefeller Fund.

Among the pueblo Indians, the religious calendar includes public dances that are linked to annual cycles of planting and harvesting. These communal events provide an opportunity not only to reaffirm the moral community of the pueblo, but also to confirm the identities of individual members.

Whatever the specific contents of the sacred category, sociologists since Durkheim have generally agreed that the distinction between sacred and profane is the essence of religion. And they have viewed these categories as having social origins. Sacred objects, ideas, and beings are sacred because they are socially defined as such. The power that lies beneath these objects—and which these objects symbolize—is nothing less than society itself. Moreover, these ideas have consequences for society. For example, Durkheim indicates that religion has a primary role in creating and sustaining social solidarity. That is what he means when he writes about "a single moral community" (1912: 62). For Durkheim, common beliefs about the sacred unite those who share them, bringing them together with common purposes as well as with a sense of belonging. While he uses the term "church" to refer to this moral community, he does not mean it as a building or organization; for Durkheim, the word refers to a moral community, and as such it can encompass a whole society.

The Consequences of Religious Ideas

Durkheim's idea that the sacred represents society and that religion makes important contributions to social solidarity raises the broader questions of the effects of religious ideas upon society. If religious ideas function to organize the moral sentiments of the members of society, and if it is, at bottom, society that we worship when we stand in awe of the sacred, then religion would seem to be a conservative social force. That is, religion would seem to reinforce the status quo, to serve as a force to preserve social arrangements as they are.

Indeed, this is very much the perspective advanced by Karl Marx, in whose view religious ideas serve to justify the existing distribution of power in society, keeping the working classes in their subordinate position and providing a rationale for the dominance of the ruling classes. This, of course, is not quite the same thing as Durkheim had in mind. For Durkheim, religion helped sustain solidarity in a community of persons sharing common beliefs, values, and sentiments. For Marx, religion is a part of the ideological superstructure of society and is controlled by those who rule to justify their power and to keep the masses in their place. From this perspective, religious beliefs that place little emphasis on this world, regarding it as a prelude to life in heaven, can be seen as means used to dampen discontent among those who are without power. For those who share such religious beliefs, life in this world is rather unimportant; what one should do is concentrate on gaining a place in the next. When people lack the necessities of life, religion provides solace—and it also keeps them from rebelling.

Although this idea has considerable validity, the relationship between religion and society is not quite that simple. Marx was probably right in pointing to the frequent subservience of religious ideas (and religious functionaries) to the interests of the ruling class. But religious ideas can have an impact that is independent of social class, and those who hold them can act self-consciously to promote social change. Many American religious leaders were activists in the Civil Rights Movement, for example, and justified their actions in explicitly religious terms, calling for social justice for blacks on the basis of the moral teachings of Christianity and Judaism. In many instances, these leaders took positions that were opposed by their congregations, and sometimes their stands called for such drastic changes in the existing social order that they threatened the social and economic positions of their congregants. A white minister in the South who espoused the cause of blacks, for example, risked being socially ostracized, fired, or even injured. Despite this, many did, and their actions are evidence that religious ideas can be independent of other social forces.

There is another sense in which religious ideas can be a force promoting social change. One of the classic works of Western sociology is Max Weber's book *The Protestant Ethic and the Spirit of Capitalism* (1930). In this work, Weber argued that the emergence of Protestanism paved the way for new beliefs and outlooks that led to the success of capitalism. The early Protestants placed considerable emphasis on the relationship between the individual and God, and the Calvinists in particular emphasized the idea of predestination. They believed that individuals were born predestined either for salvation or damnation, and that nothing people did in their lives would change this fact. But they also believed that the people's earthly successes could be interpreted as signs of their ultimate fate. People who worked hard and were successful could interpret this as a sign that they were among the elect.

At the same time that such beliefs favored hard work, other beliefs encouraged Calvinists to plow the profits of their labors back into the enterprise. A luxurious life style was viewed as sinful, and so the fruits of one's labors were to be reinvested. This combination of beliefs—in hard work, frugality, and individualism—provided a powerful system of motivation that Weber believed to underlie the success of capitalism. Calvinists did not intend to create a capitalist economic system, but their beliefs had this result.

Social Organization of Religion

The relationship between religion, established social institutions, and social change underscores an important point about the study of religion. Religious beliefs, activities, and organization cannot be explained except by examining their relationship to the society in which they occur. Furthermore, it is impossible to create such explanations without looking at the development of religious institutions and meanings over time. Religion, like other institutions, takes many forms in the contemporary world, and these forms have come about through historical processes stretching back over many centuries. We can illustrate these ideas by looking briefly at the emergence of the four major forms of religious organization within Christianity: the church, the sect, the denomination, and the cult.

By the thirteenth century, the Roman Catholic Church dominated Europe. It was "the Church" in the sense that Durkheim used the term. It had a unified system of beliefs adhered to by nearly all, and it was a prime integrating force in society. The Church held secular as well as religious authority; it affected all aspects of life, political and economic as well as spiritual. The Church was universal; except for a relatively few Jews, all Europeans were Catholic, subject to the authority of the Pope in Rome in matters both spiritual and temporal. This meant, for example, that there were no civil marriages or divorces. One could be married only under Church law and the marriage dissolved only by the Church. The Church was also deeply involved in the politics of the day.

As the social and economic structure of Europe was affected by the growth of trade and cities and later by increasing nationalism, the power of the Roman Catholic Church eroded. When Martin Luther posted his Ninety-five Theses on the door of a church in Wittenberg, Germany, in 1517, the Reformation was underway. Throughout Europe, the authority of the Church was questioned and challenged, and new forms of Christianity, today called Protestant, developed. The Lutherans in Germany, Sweden, and Denmark, the Presbyterians in Scotland, the Anglicans in England, and the Huguenots in France all demonstrated that the Christian Church was no longer unified. In Europe, the nationalist and religious differences tended to reinforce one another and often led to conflict and even war.

The various Protestant groups that emerged during the Reformation are called *sects*, a term sociologists use to label religious groups that break off from a dominant church. Unlike the church, sects generally stand in opposition to the society as a whole; that is, instead of supporting and reinforcing secular powers, which are allied with the established church, sects oppose both the church and the state for which it stands.

Sects were first described by scholars studying religious groups that emerged during the Reformation. Ernst Troeltsch, a theologian who was a pioneer in the study of religious organization, noted that the church and the sect were different in several significant ways (1931: II). Where the church was organized as a hierarchy, was ideologically conservative, and appealed to the ruling class, the sect was egalitarian and radical and appealed to the disadvantaged. The church served as an agency of social control, while the sect was an agency of rebellion.

The dichotomy described by Troeltsch is an ideal type, a distillation of important characteristics that are not necessarily fully represented by any one group. People became members of a church at birth or when they were baptized, and they achieved salvation through membership in it. Only in rare cases were members of the church expelled (excommunicated). Before the Reformation and the rise of Protestantism, Europeans (except for Jews) were automatically members of the Roman Catholic Church. It was simply taken for granted.

In contrast, membership in a sect was voluntary, the members of a sect had to *do* something to acquire that status, and their attainment of salvation was dependent upon personal holiness. A sect makes exclusive claims on people, demanding that its members affiliate only with it and with no other religious group, and there is an overriding belief that the members of the sect represent the "true elect." In most cases, sects required every person to submit some proof or test of merit before he or she could be admitted to its membership. In addition, there was expulsion for those who went astray.

As time passed, the conflict between the established Roman Catholic Church and the new Protestant sects was resolved in different ways. In some instances, as in England and the Scandinavian countries, a Protestant sect came to dominate the religious life of the country and itself became the established church. In other areas, such as Germany, local princes utimately acquired the right to choose between Catholicism and Lutheranism, and their subjects had the obligation to adopt the religion of their prince. Here, too, what had been a sect became transformed into a church as it gained dominance within a region.

Because the United States and Canada were settled by people who were already members of many different groups, there was diversity from the start, and the church-sect classification does not really fit. There is no dominant church in the United States. Instead, there is a multiplicity of churches, called *denominations*. In the North American context, a sect is more loosely defined as a "high tension, schismatic religious movement within a conventional religious tradition" (Stark and Bainbridge, 1981: 131).

In societies like the United States and Canada where there are many conventional religious traditions, a more relevant distinction is that between the sect and the cult. The sect breaks off from a religious body but remains within the society's definition of normal religious expression. In contrast, the *cult* develops within a deviant religious tradition. For example, Protestant churches in which the handling of poisonous snakes is part of religious ritual are considered sects because they remain within the broader Protestant Christian tradition. In contrast, Scientology is considered a cult. It is not an offshoot of an established religious group, but an innovative movement viewed by many as a deviant group—that is, one which stands outside the mainstream.

Stark and Bainbridge identified 417 American-born sects. Of these, only 3 percent have more than 500,000 members, and 4 percent have between 100,000 and 500,000 members. The vast majority of sects are very small. Yet sects tend to be larger than cults because the former are generally older and more successful in attracting members. To some extent, the greater success of sects is probably a consequence of the fact that they are a part of the society's general religious traditions, even though they are in tension with the society. The snake-handling sect has continuity with Protestant tradition, even though it engages in rituals not recognized by other Protestants. In contrast, a cult such as Scientology tends to be defined as deviant by others in the society and has no ties with the society's main religious traditions.

As these examples suggest, churches, denominations, sects, and cults are differentiated by their relationship to the society as a whole (and to one another) and not on the basis of any intrinsic characteristics. Just as the Protestant sects of Europe often became established churches themselves, so groups that are today sects may be tomorrow's denominations or churches. Mormons were a sect when they first were formed in the nineteenth century. But the dominance they acquired in Utah transformed them into a church, and one, it should be noted, that since then has had to contend with splinter sects it has itself spawned.

RELIGION AND IDENTITY

Like age, sex, ethnicity, and social class, religion shapes the individual's identity. It establishes who the individual is and how he or she is to be treated, both in the eyes of others and in the person's own eyes. Even in a world as secular as ours, religion continues to play a role in people's lives. It affects the way they celebrate major life-cycle events such as marriage, birth, and death; their attitudes and values; how they vote; their social contacts and opportunities; and it may also be the reason for prejudice and discrimination.

Normally, religious identity is ascribed. The child takes the religious identity of the parents. Although there is obviously nothing in the genes that binds us to a religion at birth, we normally acquire the religious values and affiliation of our parents. We take it for granted that parents will teach their children their religious beliefs and that children are obliged to take them as their own. Indeed, the idea that children should adopt their parents' religion is so strong that few, in fact, change. And when this does occur, it is often a cause of dismay in parents and guilt in their children.

Regardless of where individuals acquire their religious identity—whether they are continuing their family's traditional religion or adopting new beliefs as their own—this identity provides them with a special perspective on the world.

Identity is a powerful influence on how a person perceives the environment, for what seems important and real to us depends upon who we are. Every aspect of our identity affects our interpretation of reality at one time or another, but in any given situation, one aspect of our identity is usually more important than the others. For example, when a twelve-year-old boy walks into a classroom, his identity as a student is likely to be paramount. The fact that he also has the identity of a male, a Lutheran, and the oldest child in his family is less important in this particular situation. In a color war at summer camp, whether one is a "Red" or "Blue" becomes the most important fact of life. Friendships and alliances are formed among those sharing a common color. Regardless of a camper's usual interests, what is important is which color's team is the best. Even family ties become temporarily less important than to which color team the person belongs.

Religion is one of the many aspects of our identity, but there are occasions when religious identity is *the* perspective through which we view and interpret the world. In a society clearly shaped by religious ideas and structures, religious identity must shape our perception of the world. For example, if you live in Northern Ireland and you are a Protestant, you will interpret the fact that you have a job, the presence of the British Army, and the activities of the IRA quite differently than if you are a Catholic. Even where religious differences are not acted out in street battles, religious identity shapes interpretations of life events. For example, if you believe that everything that will happen in life has been predetermined, you will interpret events very differently than if your religion teaches freedom of will.

In contemporary society, religious identity tends to be most important in those situations that are related to home and family. Most life-cycle events are influenced by religious identity. Whether a child is baptized or circumcised, where a marriage ceremony takes place, the age at which the child is considered an adult, and the whole collection of mourning customs will vary according to the individual's religion. Even among people who rarely participate in religious ceremonies and who do not define themselves as religious, these life-cycle events continue to have their roots in religious identity.

Religion in America is generally looked upon as a private matter, and people become uncomfortable when the topic is discussed too seriously in conversations or introduced where it is felt not to belong. Even the invocation of religion by political leaders is carefully circumscribed, not just by constitutional provisions about the separation of church and state but by a sense that that religious expression by politicians should be vague—not too specific and not too personal. Political leaders are expected to discuss the reasons for their actions in secular terms, not religious ones, for in affairs of government a religious "vocabulary of motives," in the words of C. Wright Mills (1940), is viewed as inappropriate.

During the presidency of Jimmy Carter, for example, many people were made uncomfortable when the president spoke of his religious faith. Because religion is thought to be essentially a private matter, the public invocation of religious ideas becomes discomfiting when public officials become too insistent in their pronouncements or appear to be trying to translate specific beliefs into public policy. Similarly, religion briefly became an issue in the 1984 presidential campaign between Ronald Reagan and Walter Mondale, largely because the President and some of his supporters appeared to ally themselves too closely with religious leaders and injected specific religious precepts, such as opposition to abortion, into the campaign. Invoking an ambiguous Judeo-Christian deity in very general terms is an accepted part of American political culture, but claiming that God supports the Republican ticket is not!

In both the Reagan and Carter presidencies, of course, many conservative and fundamentalist Christian groups welcomed the melding of religion and politics. For members of such groups in American society, religious identity is not so limited, for religious interpretations color every aspect of life. If they are successful in their business, fundamentalists believe that that reflects the will of God. If disaster befalls them, they are being tested in their faith. Their very happiness or sadness is due to divine will. The Bible contains all the answers they need. It provides standards of right and wrong, explanations of life's vicissitudes, and a whole vocabulary for perceiving reality.

For all the secularization that exists in American society, it is well to remember that there are large segments of the population for whom religion remains highly significant. There is widespread general acceptance among Protestants and Catholics of the theological tenets of their respective religions. According to sociologist (and Roman Catholic priest) Andrew Greeley, two-fifths to one-half of Americans describe themselves as frequent or weekly church attenders. Moreover, there are periodic revivals of religious activity in this society, some of them accompanied (as was the Moral Majority of the 1980s) by controversial efforts to link the religious and political realms. In the United States, the impact of religion should not be lightly dismissed.

Conversion

Earlier we said that religious identity is similar to sex, age, race, and ethnic identities because all are ascribed; they are acquired at birth and tend to stick. But of all ascribed identities, religious identity is perhaps the easiest to change. Sociologists use the same word as everyone else to describe changes in religious identity: *conversion.* Usually, conversion is said to occur when a person makes a change of religion significant enough that there are important changes in self-concept. If a Baptist were to become a Roman Catholic, for example, or an Orthodox Jew to become an Episcopalian, the change in religious values and beliefs would occasion changes in self-concept. But changes in affiliation from one Protestant denomination to another are, as a rule, not that significant. An individual who changes membership from a Methodist church to a Congregational church down the street has not, ordinarily, undergone a conversion. Similarly, if one switches from a Conservative Jewish synagogue to a Reform Jewish temple, no conversion has occurred. In other words, without a substantive change in the person's identity, conversion has not taken place.

Conversion has an additional, related meaning: an emotional experience in which the individual feels he or she has encountered something otherworldly which then has a pronounced effect upon the person's religious self-concept. When such an event occurs, the individual can be said to have had a conversion experience. This form of conversion does not necessarily involve a change of religious affiliation. Indeed, many people who have such conversion experiences are already active participants in a congregation and, by having the experience, they become more legitimate members of the religious group.

Born-again Christians are an example of this kind of conversion experience. They are people who have been and are Christians but for the first time, they say, they feel the presence of the "Holy Spirit" and come to accept Jesus as their "personal savior." By having this experience, they have become, in their view, not just Christians in name only, but real Christians. This self-designation signals a substantive change in identity, a feeling that their place in the world and the meaning of themselves and their lives have changed.

Whatever the nature of a person's religious identity, it is strengthened when the individual is part of a community. A person who is part of a group in which all the members share a common identity has his or her identity as a member confirmed and reinforced by the others' support. And when this identity is newly acquired, such a community serves a most critical function, since it supports and sustains the new self-concept. As this suggests, religious identity involves more than just beliefs. It also entails membership in a religious community, which can be as large as the Roman Catholic Church or as small as a local Holiness congregation. Converts to any religious group can be made to feel part of the group, and consequently their sense of commitment and affiliation can be strengthened.

This was the case for the converts to many of the new religious groups that flourished in the 1970s. One of the largest and best known of these is the Unification Church, whose adherents are commonly called Moonies. In the 1960s sociologists John Lofland and Rodney Stark studied what was then a small religious group looking for converts. They described the rather unsuccessful attempts of adherents to convince others to join their group. After that study was published, the group refined its techniques and, in the 1970s, attracted thousands to its ranks. The effective recruitment techniques adopted by the Moonies involve making prospective members feel at home and comfortable by providing friendship, kindness, and love. In addition, prospects are generally isolated from the outside world while contacts with others within the community are intensified. In this way, the newly developed religious self-concepts are nurtured and strengthened.

Identity is central in the process of conversion. Lofland and Stark (1965) found that there were conditions that seemed to precede the conversion of people to the "obscure millenarian perspective" of the Unification Church. Converts were seekers of religious solutions to the keenly felt personal problems they were experiencing. Encountering representatives of the Unification Church at a critical point in their lives, they were highly receptive to their appeals. Usually close social ties and affective bonds were formed with one or more members of the new group, while at the same time previous social attachments were reduced. Consequently, there was a redefinition of self, and their identities came to rest upon a sense of membership in the Unification Church.

The removal of the person from prior affective attachments has been called *bridge burning* by some sociologists. Often a single, dramatic act or new form of behavior symbolizes this removal and conversion. Examples of bridge burning include glossolalia (speaking in tongues) among Christian Pentecostals and the adoption by Hare Krishnas of saffron robes, shaved heads, changed dietary habits, and new living styles. Such an act has "cut the performer of it off from the larger society in some significant way, identified him with the group in which the act is valued, and committed him to changed attitudinal and behavioral patterns consistent with group ideals" (Hine, 1970: 63).

The capacity of a religious group to isolate its adherents from their previous attachments is typically greater if the group as a whole can isolate itself from the rest of society. When the Mormons were driven from the East to Utah, their new isolation helped them build a viable and distinct religious group. In their new home, they were able to support one another without outside interference. Although this separation was forced upon the group, other religious groups have recognized the usefulness of isolation. Consequently, many new religious groups move to isolated farm communities where their members are removed from both family (and prior religious attachments) and the temptations of the secular world.

The Dimensions of Religious Commitment

Whether acquired through conversion or ascribed at birth, religious identity is apt to be complex in its meaning to individuals and in its implications for their everyday behavior. As you may well have guessed, religion does not have a single meaning. One person may believe in the theology of a religion; another may know little about its beliefs but take satisfaction from participation in its rituals; others feel a sense of community with fellow religionists, even though they may not define themselves as believers. Many sociologists have looked at this phenomenon and have attempted to differentiate the forms of religious commitment.

In a classic study of the religious factor in Detroit, Lenski (1963) distinguished two aspects of religion: belief and group membership, or in the felicitous terms of Andrew Greeley, "meaning and belonging." Religion involves beliefs and interpretations that give meaning to life; and it involves association with others and a sense of belonging to the group. Group membership can be *asso-*

ciational (emphasizing participation in a religious group itself) or *communal* (having one's friends and spouse come from the same religious group). Lenski also saw that belief might involve a conscious knowledge and acceptance of the doctrines of a particular religion. But people may be oriented less to doctrinal orthodoxy and more to behavior, to acts of private prayer and communion with the deity, an orientation Lenski termed *devotional.* While there are no doubt many more orientations to religion than Lenski studied, his work contributed to the understanding that religion meant more than belonging to a particular church and regularly attending its services.

Not everyone in a secular society is fully socialized in a religious sense. For some, doctrinal exposure is not accompanied by a supporting community that provides continuing support for a religious self-concept. For others, formal membership in a religious group is a requisite to other things—social acceptance or business success in a community—but has little or no value in itself. For some, the theology of a particular religion meets specific personal needs and may be particularly well suited to explaining their life circumstances in a useful way. For others, it is the simple sense of belonging, rather than any specific set of meanings, that forms the impetus for religious attachment and participation.

People thus do not join religious groups simply because of their beliefs and practices. People who convert to Roman Catholicism, Orthodox Judaism, evangelical Protestantism, or the Unification Church do not necessarily do so because they have abandoned the beliefs and values taught by the religion they were raised in. As we have seen, beliefs and values are but part of the reasons a person chooses to accept one religion rather than another.

The success of a new religious group such as the Hare Krishnas in recruiting members gives insight into the various reasons underlying a person's joining a group. While its origin lies in fifth-century India, the current manifestation of Hare Krishna did not develop until 1966, when A. C. Bhaktivedanta started the Krishna Consciousness Movement. Its greatest success seemed to be in places where there were large college-age populations. Within a short time after the movement's formation, there were more than fifty temples throughout the world.

The ability of the Hare Krishnas to recruit members is exemplified by activities of the movement's temple in the Haight-Ashbury section of San Francisco in the 1960s (Johnson, 1976). There, surrounded by the hippie drug culture, the Hare Krishnas offered people an opportunity to "drop out and turn on" to a religious experience devoid of drugs. In contrast to the liberal attitudes of the neighborhood toward sex, drug use, and personal behavior, the Krishna movement had rigid guidelines. No longer could a person drink, smoke cigarettes, use drugs, or gamble. In addition, converts were required to give up their personal property and wealth. Clothing from one's past life was given away, and the convert was only to wear the saffron Hindu robe. Strict dietary rules were imposed—no meat, fish, or eggs could be eaten. Sexual activities were limited to a person's spouse.

The new life style demanded by the group differed greatly from that of the middle-class families in which most converts were raised and the drug-oriented countercultural life style that they had first adopted. (Many converts, however, felt that their earlier experiences with hallucinogens were a necessary precursor to their ability to achieve transcendence through the chanting of their mantra.) It is a fascinating question as to why, in the midst of the cultural freedom and experimentation of Haight-Ashbury, a demanding religious group should have been so successful. One interpretation is that its beliefs and practices provided a structured sense of belonging and a security of meaning not found in any of the recruits' previous experiences. In general, the most successful recent religious groups have been those which have imposed the most demands upon their recruits. This applies as much to fairly conventional groups such as the Mormons as to groups like the Hare Krishna. This suggests that conventional religious groups—indeed, secular society as a whole—may provide neither the meaning nor the belonging that many people crave.

But the emergence of religious groups cannot be explained simply by referring to the social and personal needs they presumably meet. Throughout history many religions have emerged; some have flourished (for example, the Mormons, Pentecostal Protestant churches, and Christian Science); others have disappeared (for example, the Shakers and the Oneida community). Whether the Krishna movement or the Moonies or any other nonmainstream religious group succeeds in recruiting members is not dependent upon any one factor. Indeed, the survival of established religious groups is not simply dependent upon the needs of their members. One factor that bears examination in this context is of importance in any social organization: leadership.

Religious Leadership

Our discussion of the differences between church and sect alluded to differences in religious leadership. These differences include such features as the source of the leader's authority, how leadership is organized, and styles of leadership.

The authority of religious leaders, like other forms of authority, can be traditional, legal, or charismatic. In some highly organized religious groups (for example, the Roman Catholic Church), a clear hierarchy exists. Individuals attend school and are trained to be priests. Following this formal training period, they are ordained by the church, and only then can they assume the duties of the priesthood. This kind of authority is based on a position attained in a formally prescribed way. A man not trained and ordained as a priest does not have the authority of a priest.

A charismatic religious leader's authority is derived from personality and not from the position he or she fills. Unlike priests, charismatic leaders often are the heads of independent religious groups. A priest leads a parish because he has been placed in that position by a superior. Charismatic leaders simply assume the role, and their personal appeal becomes the basis on which a congregation develops. In many cases, new religious groups are led by men and women who have charismatic authority, although such groups typically develop organizations and legal forms of leadership as they become established.

For example, Joseph Smith was a charismatic religious leader during the nineteenth century. Originally only a few people followed his religious teachings, but slowly and constantly the group grew. In time, that group, the Church of Jesus Christ of the Latter-Day Saints (also called Mormons), became a major religious group. Thomas O'Dea's sociological study of the origins of the Mormon Church documents the change from a charismatic to a traditional-rational leadership (O'Dea, 1957). Joseph Smith took over leadership of the Mormons by force of personality, claiming that he had received a revelation that gave him the position of "prophet, seer, and revelator." But he also dominated the church leadership and made himself president of the church. In this way he began the practice of combining charismatic leadership (the prophet) with traditional-rational leadership (the president).

Upon Smith's death, others attempted to replace him as the leader. Some who claimed to be Smith's successor led splinter groups. Others, like Brigham Young and Sidney Rigdon, did not claim to be replacing Smith. Rigdon claimed the right to rule the church as guardian, while Young won the right to rule it as president of the Twelve. It was only after several years and Young's successful leadership of the Mormons in their trek to Utah and in the establishment of their new social organization that he assumed the office of president, along with the title of "prophet, seer, and revelator." Young, like Smith, was able to rule because of the strength of his personality. But he also had the machinery of the church organization to aid him in the legitimization of his position of leadership. Charisma had become *routinized*—that is, identified with whatever person occupied the principal office of church leadership—rather than dependent on the leader's personality.

Most mainstream religious groups have leaders whose authority is legal; they have authority because they have acquired the positions of ministers, rabbis, priests, or nuns in formally prescribed ways. Sects and cults are more likely to have charismatic leadership, since it is often the activity of the individual that creates the group itself.

RELIGION IN CONTEMPORARY AMERICA

Although the United States is frequently described as a secularized society in which religious values and activities have diminished in importance, religion still commands a considerable amount of our attention. We talk about it, debate whether it is about to die out or to make a comeback, form new religious groups and abandon old ones, and in a variety of ways behave as if religion were still of some consequence to us. During the 1950s, for example, it was widely thought that a great religious revival was taking place. In the 1960s, a public controversy erupted when a theologian proclaimed the "death of God," and later in that decade many new religious groups and religions with Eastern origins flourished as a part of the counterculture of that time. In the 1970s, evangelical and pentecostal Christianity enjoyed a resurgence. At any given time, it seems, religion is a topic of considerable social interest. While some are decrying the loss of religious faith, others are proclaiming new religions and the dawning of a new religious age. While some are abandoning religious commitments, new converts are being found to a variety of religious groups, both mainstream and innovative.

The ebb and flow of religious activity and belief is nothing new in American life. Religious revivals have swept the nation several times during our history. From the "Great Awakening" of the eighteenth century, through several periods of intense revivalism in the nineteenth century, to the present, religious movements have had a prominent place in American society. Thus, the resurgent Protestant evangelicals of the 1970s and 1980s are part of a pattern in American history that stretches back to the nation's founding.

Since pre-Revolutionary times, there have been many different religious groups in the United States, some arriving to found colonies of their own, others importing their religious beliefs into the relative tolerance of the New World. At the beginning, there were Puritans in New England; Dutch Reformed in New York; Quakers, Amish, and Brethren in Pennsylvania; Roman Catholics in Maryland; and Anglicans in the South. Later other groups would settle in particular areas of the country: Jews in New York City and other cities of the Northeast; Scandinavian Lutherans in Minnesota, the Dakotas, and elsewhere in the Midwest; Germans in the Midwest; Irish Catholics in the Northeast; and Scotch-Irish Protestants in the Southern Highlands. On the frontier, circuit-riding ministers converted settlers to several different religious groups, especially during periods of religious revivalism.

As populations grew and moved, a variety of religious groups and beliefs became available. In even the smallest of towns, one could find several different denominations. Plurality was and is the prevailing mode of religious organization in this country. The Constitution supported this by establishing a division between church and state. This means no one particular religion has been able to prevail over the others, even in those areas of the country where adherents of one religion numerically predominate. We have become, in Andrew Greeley's words, a "denominational society," one in which it is relatively easy for people to change affiliation from one group to another (1972).

Changing one's religious affiliation from one church to another has occurred throughout American history. In recent years scholars have investigated why some groups are growing more rapidly than others. Dean Kelly (1972) pointed out that during the 1960s it appeared to be those churches which made the greatest demands that were most successful in gaining new adherents. Recent statistics continue to show considerable losses in the membership of mainline Protestant denominations but considerable gains in membership for evangelical

John Steuart Curry, *Baptism in Kansas* (1928)
Oil. 40 × 50 inches. Collection of Whitney Museum of American Art. Acq#31.293.

Like the Tewa Green Corn Ceremony portrayed in Awa Tsireh's drawing, this Kansas baptism is a communal and an individual matter. For the person being baptized, it is a mark of a new identity as a Christian; for the community, it is an occasion for the reaffirmation of a sense of moral community.

and fundamentalist churches. Such mainstream Protestant groups as Methodists, Presbyterians, Episcopalians, and the United Church of Christ showed slight gains from 1940 to 1960, but by 1979 all had lost members. During the same period, more conservative and evangelical groups such as the Church of God, the Lutheran Church-Missouri Synod, Southern Baptist, the Church of Jesus Christ of the Latter-Day Saints (Mormon), and Assemblies of God increased their membership. Southern Baptists, for example, grew from approximately five million members in 1940 to over thirteen million in 1979, and Mormons from three-quarters of a million to two and three-quarter million members.

The growth of demanding, conservative denominations may be due to the same factors that have made some demanding cults so successful. In a society that is today (and has probably always been) characterized by great fluidity and change, the demanding religious organization provides a sense of security and identity for its members. Religion is a response to uncertainty, and the more change (real or apparent) there is in a society, the more likely some will find an uncompromising religious stance to their liking. Yet the past ebb and flow of religious activity should make us wary of predicting the continuation of present trends into the future. On the American religious scene there is usually something new waiting to enter the picture.

Although denomination switching is relatively easy in this society, there is still more constancy than change. In a recent study, Kluegel (1980: 30) found that most people continue to identify with the denomination in which they were raised. He found this to be particularly true among Jews (86.7 percent), Catholics (85.4 percent), Lutherans (77.7 percent), and Baptists (73.8 percent). Other Protestant denominations are somewhat less successful in keeping their adherents, but even among these groups the majority retained their original affiliation. Comparable figures for other groups are as follows: Presbyterians (62 percent), Episcopalians (64 percent), members of the United Church of Christ (64 percent), Methodists (64 percent), and Disciples of Christ (64 percent).

The movement of people from one religious affiliation to another may or may not be associated with the kind of conversion experience we discussed earlier. Some people may experience a change of self-concept when they change religions; for others it may simply be a change of association based on convenience.

Religious change may also entail the abandonment of religious affiliation and belief. A study of college students during the 1960s focused on *apostasy*, "the abandonment of a set of principles or faith, not the replacement of one set of principles with another" (Caplovitz and Sherrow 1977). Caplovitz and Sherrow argue that apostates—individuals who give their religion as "none"—have not only abandoned their religious beliefs and are indicating a loss of religious faith, but they are also rejecting a "particular ascriptive community as a basis for self-identification." For such people, achieved rather than ascriptive status is the preferred basis for self-concept. This explanation is supported by the theory that people more committed to personal achievement are more likely to be apostates. Another theory attributes apostasy to *secularization*, a general decline in the importance of religion as a basis for identity. Still another explanation argues that individuals are expressing alienation and rebellion in their rejection of the values and beliefs of the religion in which they were raised. Certainly many popular articles imply that people who have dropped out of their parents' religion do so because they want to rebel.

Caplovitz and Sherrow's study did not find that one theory was a better explanation than any other. They concluded that all three theories could be supported by their analysis. Whatever their conclusion, answering "none" to a question about religious affiliation may not really mean that the individual has abandoned religious beliefs. Some people seem to maintain religious values, ethics, and conceptions of the world even after they cease to be members of particular churches or synagogues, to attend religious services, or to perform religious rituals.

Born-again Christians

One of the most notable developments of recent years has been the resurgence of Christian evangelicalism. The idea of carrying the gospel to the uninitiated has had a long tradition in American culture, but recently this idea has achieved a new respectability. Television ministers and seminary professors, congressmen and presidential candidates, business leaders and factory workers are among the many people who have been calling themselves born-again Christians. This phrase—"born again"—means that the person has experienced "personal salvation through Christ." In addition to having the born-again experience, evangelical Christians often feel they must share it with others.

Four terms are used to describe born-again Christians: evangelical, pentecostal, charismatic, and fundamentalist. The *fundamentalist* is primarily concerned with the literal interpretation of the Bible. The *pentecostal* and the *charismatic* express validation of salvation and baptism in the Holy Spirit through speaking in tongues and performing other special acts. The *evangelical* is committed to having the conversion experience and then telling others about it. People who call themselves born again can be found in any of these traditions.

Both recruitment and identity maintenance of born-again Christians is achieved through traditional means: membership in fundamentalist churches, revival meetings, attendance at prayer meetings in homes, and personal contacts. Since the late 1970s, these methods have been augmented by the introduction of many Christian television programs and networks. Some of these programs continue the tradition of a minister preaching to a television congregation just as he would in church. Other types of programming include soap operas with a Christian orientation, children's shows, and the born-again talk show.

The Christian talk show is similar to nonreligious talk shows in format. The host is a minister who serves as the central personality on the program. He introduces performers and interviews guests, each a born-again Christian with a story to tell. By hearing each person tell how he or she found salvation, the television viewer learns that the born-again experience is common for many people. Moreover, in addition to hearing how the person "found the Lord," viewers also hear how becoming a born-again Christian affects the individual positively. Participants stress how much their religious rebirth has made them feel happy and at peace with their lives.

This use of personal *witness* is a standard feature of recruitment and member retention in evangelical Christianity. The televised talk-show format enables evangelicals to reach more people than conventional techniques, since Christian television programs, stations, and even cable and satellite networks have proliferated in recent years. Although many nonbelievers wonder about the funding of these enterprises (the appeal for funds is a constant feature of such programs), it is clear that for the actual or potential believer, the electronic church serves a very positive function.

Christian television programs provide an opportunity for individual viewers to achieve salvation through a conversion experience, and they also help sustain a private religious experience. By watching such television programs, each person becomes involved in the expression of the born-again religious experience. The Christian program is an important agent of socialization: roles and patterns of behavior are learned, vocabularies and language worlds become familiar. As the person watches the program and becomes more involved, he or she may have the born-again experience and thus share the experiential identity. Moreover, the single individual is able to establish an individualized definition of the religious experience. Since watching television is basically a one-way communication, each person is able to individually define his or her religious identity. Proof of the adoption of the identity, indeed the born-again experience itself, becomes an internal, individual act that requires no outside validation.

The televised church may thus represent a change in religious activity that requires a revision of some of our ideas about identity and group membership. The person whose conversion experience and contact with others sharing the experience is mainly through television seems to defy the usual expectations. Ordinarily, people are expected to develop and sustain an identity only if they have real contact with others who share it. While many who watch Christian television are affiliated with church groups, there are also many who are not. These more autonomous individuals may nevertheless be able to sustain their born-again identities through an essentially one-way interaction with television personalities.

While many have turned to a religious identity that has its roots in traditional Christianity, others have turned to non-Western religions. We have already discussed the Hare Krishna movement and the Unification Church (Moonies). There are also many countercultural religious movements that began in the 1960s and 1970s and that still exist in the 1980s. TM (Transcendental Meditation), Zen, Yoga, Guru Maharah Ji, and the Divine Light Mission all have followers today, as do "secular" groups like Scientology, Synanon, and EST that have a religious character.

CONCLUSION

The sphere of the sacred in modern life has clearly shrunk, and religious groups and ideas are confronted on all sides with conflicting bases of identity. Nevertheless, religion remains an important factor in modern American society. For some people, it provides an important social anchor, a way of relating socially to others and finding a place in a large, complex, and often impersonal society. For others, religion continues to be a source of meaning, providing ideas and concepts that organize and make sense of life. But whether it provides a sense of belonging or meaning, or both, religion is sought by members of our society and of all societies. From the outback of Australia to the canyons of Manhattan, people consider some things sacred and others profane. They have gods and spirits which are revered and ways of life which are deemed appropriate and right.

SUGGESTED READINGS

BERGER, PETER L. *The Sacred Canopy: Elements of a Sociological Theory of Religion* (New York: Doubleday, 1969).

GLOCK, CHARLES Y. and ROBERT BELLAH, eds. *The New Religious Consciousness* (Berkeley: University of California Press, 1976).

GREELEY, ANDREW M. *The Denominational Society: A Sociological Approach to Religion in America* (Glencoe, Ill.: Scott Foresman, 1972).

HEILMAN, SAMUEL C. *Synagogue Life: A Study in Symbolic Interaction* (Chicago: University of Chicago Press, 1976).

LUCKMANN, THOMAS. *The Invisible Religion* (New York: Macmillan, 1967).

MARTY, MARTIN E. *A Nation of Behavers* (Chicago: University of Chicago Press, 1976).

WEBER, MAX. *The Protestant Ethic and the Spirit of Capitalism* (New York: Scribner, 1930; first published in 1904–5).

14

The World of Politics

WHAT IS POLITICS?
- A Definition of Politics

THE ORGANIZATION OF POLITICAL ACTIVITY
- Interests, Goals, and Conflict
- Political Organizations and Actors
- Negotiations
- Issues
- Political Issues and Social Change
- Political Drama

WHO IS IN CHARGE?
- Power and the Definition of Reality
- Who Controls America?

Politics is a word with paradoxical meaning. On one hand, Americans associate it with law and government—institutions that have an almost sacred character that they often think the rest of the world should emulate. On the other hand, *politics* also denotes the unabashed use of deceit, force, or chicanery in the pursuit of self-interest. Thus, people encourage one another to "get involved in politics"—to vote, write to their elected officials, run for office themselves, and in other ways participate in their democratic institutions. But almost in the same breath, Americans may dismiss politics as a game for the corrupt, deride a governmental decision to build a new bridge or a new weapons system as political, or express contempt for politicians as an unspeakably low form of life.

WHAT IS POLITICS?

These conflicting images of the political process tap two important aspects of its reality. First, the realm of politics is about government and its institutions—legislatures, executives, courts, constitutions, laws, the state, and political parties and philosophies. Government and politics are concerned with social coordination on a large scale, with the resolution of issues that affect society as a whole and the relationships between it and its constituent groups. At the same time, however, politics is also very clearly about the pursuit of self-interest by various groups and collectivities that together make up the society. The large-scale social coordination that is the focus of government and politics involves real or potential conflict—between society and its individual members, between society and its groups, or between one group and other. In a fundamental sense, politics is also about self-interest and conflict.

The aim of this chapter is to examine the realities of political processes and the images people form of politics. These two levels are complex and tightly interwoven. People act in the political realm, as in all others, on the basis of their definitions of situations. Their images of politics and politicians influence their own participation, whether they think they can have an effect on politics, whether they bother to vote, whether they accept the legitimacy of governmental institutions or seek to subvert them. These images are shaped by political reality, but not completely determined by it, for what actually occurs in politics is not always accurately perceived by people. A seething pit of corruption can be concealed or ignored, and conscientious public servants can be deemed wrongheaded and untrustworthy by the voters. And, as is always the case in social life, social reality is shaped by the way people perceive it.

A Definition of Politics

Politics and government are fundamentally concerned with social coordination on a relatively large scale. A modern society is composed of many groups and organizations. Politics is a main arena in which their goals, interests, and activities are coordinated.

Even in the simplest society, where sex and age are the main bases of social differentiation, there will be distinct family groups, perhaps several clans, each with its own lineage, religious symbols, and sense of group cohesiveness. Contemporary societies have a more complex division of labor and greater social differentiation. Inequalities of wealth and power lead to the formation of different groups of people with different life styles, goals, and interests. The many organizations within which people work and play have to be coordinated with one another and with the goals and interests of the society as a whole. Indeed, the very question of societal goals has to be answered: What do the members of a society want? How should its limited resources be used? How are the valued things it produces to be distributed? These questions are answered by society's political institutions.

In simple societies, coordination between different family groups or clans is achieved with relative ease. People live in close contact with one another, they share strong convictions about how people should act, and they evolve ways of handling disputes. As societies become more complex, however, a number of things happen to make social coordination more problematic. Inequalities of wealth and power increase, and with them the growing capacity of some people to achieve social coordination by force. Economic activity comes to depend upon coordinated and more or less stable interchanges among numerous organizations, including factories, corporations, industries, and unions. Societies become larger in territory and population and more heterogeneous in the values and interests of their members.

As societal scale and complexity have increased throughout history, so too have the size and complexity of governmental and political organizations. The state and its many executive, legislative, and judicial organizations and subunits has emerged as the principle agency of social coordination at the societal level. In contemporary American society, local, state, and especially the federal governments have a significant hand in important decisions about societal goals and the distribution of goods and resources. At the same time, related organizations—political lobbies, special interest organizations, and political parties—have also grown in importance. Various groups and organizations contend with one another for influence or control over governmental decisions.

Politics is a process in which a tremendous variety of social activities are coordinated, a process that often involves the resolution of issues: Should the federal government provide financial assistance to the states to support public education? Should industries be left to conduct their affairs without governmental intervention, or should they be regulated in various ways in order to ensure the safety of their products or to prevent them from doing harm to the environment? Should a new highway be built, or should funds be spent instead on public transportation facilities? Should basic levels of welfare support be increased?

Out of such issues emerge the laws, procedures, administrative organizations, and political practices with which people are familiar in their everyday lives. Laws create programs of financial aid for college students or subsidies to farmers. New organizations such as the Environmental Protection Agency emerge as concrete resolutions of questions about how and how much to regulate industry to ensure public health and environmental quality. A road gets built or a new rapid transit system is begun; federal food-stamp programs are expanded or cut back as political decisions about welfare are made and then revised.

As issues arise and are dealt with in the political process, both governmental and nongovernmental organizations are involved. A town or city, for example, may be confronted with a demand by its teachers for higher wages. Formal contract talks will occur between representatives of the teachers and representatives of the local government—between a teacher union that represents the interests of the teachers and a local board of education that represents the community as a whole. But numerous other groups may also be involved in this process. Parents who are dissatisfied with the way their children are being taught may organize to oppose teacher raises, as may taxpayers who do not want to spend more money on education. Neither of these latter groups sits at the bargaining table, yet each can be indirectly involved in the matter by organizing telephone and letter-writing campaigns to pressure school board members or by mounting efforts to defeat school budget proposals.

In an example such as this, *social coordination* is taking place; that is, various groups of people focus their attention and actions upon a single issue, and eventually there is a political outcome of some kind. Teachers do or do not get a raise; a school budget is passed or defeated. Political outcomes are usually visible as decisions made by governmental units with the right and responsibility to make them. But the decisions are typically the outcome of coordinated activities in which both governmental and nongovernmental groups are involved.

Much governmental and political activity is thus focused on the maintenance of *internal order* in the society. Issues arise, decisions are made, and more or less orderly relations among individuals, groups, and organizations are thus ensured for a time. But *external order*—relationships between one society and another—is also a political matter. Just as there are competing and conflicting interests and goals within societies, so too there are conflicts between societies. Social coordination is something that occurs at an international level as well as within societies. For simplicity, however, this discussion of politics will not attempt to deal with international affairs and will consider external relations only when they have a bearing upon the internal political process.

In addition to large-scale social coordination, politics and government have a number of other important features that will be examined in this chapter. First, politics is an activity in which group, organizational, and societal interests and goals are defined and pursued. Politics and government thus invariably involve *social conflict* to one degree or another. People try to foster conflict, reduce it, organize it, use it to secure their ends, or resolve it. Conflict arises out of many factors: the complexity of modern society; the propensity of individuals, groups, and organizations to define their interests differently and to seek to impose their goals on society; and inequalities of wealth and power.

Second, politics and government are associated with the actual or threatened *use of power and authority*, with efforts to get, extend, keep, and exercise power and to have this power defined as legitimate. Because the resources of power are distributed unequally, people seek to impose their will upon one another and upon the society. But whenever people seek to exert power, they also seek to have it defined as just and right; that is, they seek to persuade those over whom power is exercised to accept the legitimacy of their doing so and to give their consent to its exercise. They seek to transform power into authority.

Third, *negotiation* is a key aspect of politics. As people coordinate their activities, pursue interests, come into conflict, and use power and authority, they negotiate a variety of agreements with one another. High-school civics classes may encourage us to view the government as a social mechanism that does its work in a simple and straightforward manner in accordance with established law. And often it appears that some groups get what they want through sheer power. But underlying both the operation of government and the efforts of various groups and organizations to influence it are many contexts and processes of negotiation. Like any other organization, government does not work automatically. It depends upon agreements worked out between real people on a day-to-day basis. And power is likewise never automatic; it rests upon threat, exaggeration, and political maneuvering that result in negotiated agreements.

Last, politics occurs before an *audience*, most of whom are involved as spectators and voters rather than as active participants. Much political activity in modern society has the appearance of performances staged in order to persuade or influence various audiences. Politics is often dramatic, and politicians are like actors on a stage, presenting and developing a character that will convince a skeptical audience. And most people are involved only through their membership in the audience. They vote, but do not join parties, give money to support policies or candidates, or in other ways play a more active role in the political process.

THE ORGANIZATION OF POLITICAL ACTIVITY

Politics and government are thus organized activities involving political organizations and actors, conflict, issues, drama, power and authority, and negotiations. In the following section we will begin to examine the social organization of political life in contemporary society, focusing especially on the United States as an example of a democratic society.

Interests, Goals, and Conflict

If society were a harmonious and stable affair, there would be little need for politics and government. People would share norms and values and would therefore have the same goals for themselves and for society. Their shared commitments to the same ends would lead them voluntarily to regulate their own affairs so as to achieve them. People would obey norms and cooperate with their fellows. Perceiving no differences in goals or interests, they would have no reason to be in conflict with one another. And in the absence of social conflict, there would be no need for organizations such as government to regulate and settle conflicts among groups.

Such perfect harmony and stability have yet to be achieved in a human society. Although some small-scale societies come closer than modern societies to achieving a harmonious, cooperative social life, even they do not attain it. Among the Pueblo Indians of the Southwest, it is important that community life is placid and harmonious; people are not supposed to assert themselves at the expense of the group nor exhibit too much individuality. Among the traditional Zuni of New Mexico, for example, the individual is not supposed to seek opportunities to be a leader, and conflict with others is to be avoided (Benedict, 1934: 95).

But even societies such as the Zuni do not always live up to their ideals. Occasions arise when people must be sanctioned for showing too much pride; individuals do not always avoid conflict when their rights have been infringed by others; and jealousy between families can surface. As a result, social control must now and then be invoked. People have to be criticized or ostracized for their conduct in an effort to reassert group norms and bring the person back within the sphere of group influence. Decisions have to be made to resolve conflicts between individuals and groups, and the scarce resources of the community have to be allocated.

In more complex societies, conflict is more prevalent for two major and closely related reasons: social inequality and social differentiation. Wherever it is possible for people to accumulate wealth, conflicts between the interests of the individual and those of the group or society become possible. Although, as was argued in Chapter 5, there is no need to view human beings as inherently selfish, the accumulation of individual advantage does make it possible for people to choose between self-interest and the needs of others. And as was suggested in Chapter 10, such accumulation generally becomes a matter of group interest. A family may jealously guard its extra production and deny requests for aid from less successful families. Inequality makes possible the idea of self-interest versus group interest, and it creates power resources that some may use to control the actions of others.

Moreover, inequality is generally accompanied by social differentiation. In a traditional society like that of the Zuni, people were basically alike. There was little opportunity for one family to accumulate very much more than another, and strong norms of sharing tended to counteract such inequalities as did occur. Zuni life was so focused on a traditional round of religious ritual that economic activity was of secondary importance; wealth was not perceived as the route to personal or social well-being. There were, of course, lines that divided the experiences, activities, and outlooks of the sexes and of various age groups, but even these were minimized.

Such a society contrasts sharply with our own, where social differentiation is much more pronounced. Social classes develop different life styles and, based upon inequalities of life chances, different perceptions of group interest. The society is heterogeneous in other respects as well. Racial, religious, and ethnic groups exist with sharply contrasting values and definitions of group interest. Such groups are apt to joust with one another as they seek to define and pursue their own goals. Moreover, in a heterogeneous society the interests and goals of the society as a whole are likely themselves to be matters of contention. The basic values of the society, as well as the specific steps that it should take to pursue these values, are not matters of easy agreement because groups have very different perspectives and beliefs. And in a society such as ours, even sex and age divisions may engender differing perspectives, conflicting interests, and organized conflict.

Thus, in the contemporary United States there are many different lines of division and bases of social conflict. Various minority groups contend with dominant groups in the society—and often with one another—for their just share of economic goods and opportunities. They may seek affirmative action hiring, equal employment opportunity legislation, or special funding for minority-run businesses. One state or region of the nation contends with another for government legislation that will affect the local environment. Northeastern governors who want federal legislation to control power plant emissions and reduce acid rain contend with midwestern governors in whose states the offending coal-burning plants are located and who do not wish to impose extra tax burdens on their citizens or costs on local industries. The elderly, who are growing in numbers, seek to retain their share of social services and often meet the resistance of the young, who would rather retain income for themselves than pay higher taxes. Women seek greater equality of opportunity and compensation in the job market. And in all of these particular arenas of conflict, basic societal values are at stake, along with the goals of particular groups.

Political Organizations and Actors

Government and politics can be viewed as organized solutions to the problems associated with conflict among social groups, classes, categories, and organizations. In societies like the United States and Canada, the broad outlines of these solutions are familiar to all of us. In both countries there is a *nation-state*, an encompassing organization that embraces a large territory and passes laws, executes them, and adjudicates disputes in a more or less orderly fashion. In both countries as well, there are lesser governmental organizations—states and provinces—that control territorial divisions of the nation and that have defined and delimited spheres of authority. Each country has smaller political subdivisions—counties, towns, cities, and assorted regional authorities—with specific functions and spheres of authority. And each country has a constitution that sets the basic limits within which laws can be enacted, defines the basic structure of administration, and sets forth the role of the judiciary.

The *state*—the government and its agencies and organizations—ordinarily has a significant advantage in political conflict. First, the state has a near monopoly of force. It controls the police and armed forces, which stand ready to enforce its decisions. In democratic societies, the police power of the state is not highly visible. We have no armed soldiers patrolling the streets and, while the police are armed, there are restrictions on the circumstances in which they may use force as well as on the amount of force they may apply. (Such restrictions are not always obeyed, but they are obeyed more often than not.) Yet the power of the state is nevertheless present as potential, even if it is seldom exercised as naked force.

Second, the state has authority as well as power. That is, the government and its constituent units can implement their decisions not simply because they have the power to do so, but because they are generally accorded the right to do so. As was indicated earlier in this book, authority is legitimate power. That is, an individual, group, or organization can be said to have authority when those over whom it is exercised generally concede that those who exercise it have the right to do so. In constitutional systems such as the United States, authority stems in large part from a constitution and set of laws that, at least in theory, are to be interpreted and executed impartially. But the legitimacy of political actions also stems from other things. Each president of the United States has the same constitutional authority as any other, but some manage to exercise that authority more successfully because the authority of the office is supplemented by their personal, charismatic appeal. Some public officials seem better able than others to have their decisions and policies accepted as legitimate, for reasons we will explore later in this chapter.

Authority is thus neither static nor solely dependent upon the rule of law, even in a society such as ours. And authority that appears well established may decay gradually or disappear swiftly. In the early 1960s, for example, public officials in the South had the authority to enforce segregation laws that denied black people equal access to public facilities such as restaurants and hotels. They could claim legitimacy for their actions not only on the basis of law, but also because of established customs and traditions. When many black and white people began to resist these laws in a nonviolent way, the police frequently responded with brutality, beating civil-rights workers and protesters. They also condoned and sometimes cooperated with acts of murder and arson directed against blacks. These reactions were newsworthy events, and their nightly portrayal on national television did much to undermine the legitimacy of both the segregation laws and the public officials who enforced them.

There is much more to government and politics, however, than the legislative, administrative, and judicial structure of the state. Every social class, category, group, or organization that seeks to pursue its own interests or influence the conduct of the government is a political entity. One of the important features of political life in Canada and the United States, as in all democratic societies, is the emergence of *political parties*. Parties can be defined as organizations that express a general political philosophy, represent or seek to represent the interests of several social categories and collectivities, and participate in an organized way in elections and government. Political life in the United States has long been organized around the activities of two dominant parties. For more than one hundred years, these parties have been the Republican Party and the Democratic Party. Many smaller third parties have emerged over the years, but generally they take a back seat to the major parties and disappear. In Canada, three major parties have dominated political life in recent years: the Liberal Party, the Progressive-Conservative Party, and the New Democratic Party.

Political parties are significant entities in democratic political systems, but their role must be carefully delineated. To begin, few people actually "belong" to political parties in the sense that they pay dues. Neither do most citizens make contributions, regularly attend meetings, or have much of a say in the development of the platform or actions of the party. The majority of people in democratic societies confine their political participation to voting and do not get involved in party politics. Indeed, most people confront political parties only when they participate in voting. And even in voting, the significance of party has declined. The old "party line" vote, whereby one could pull a single lever (or make a single x) and vote for all candidates of a particular party, no longer exists, and voters are more likely to split their vote between members of different parties.

Yet political parties are important. Although not specified in the United States Constitution, American political life has come to depend upon the political party in several ways, particularly in determining candidates for political office. The party provides an organizational framework for political campaigns, as well as for the discussion of political ideology. It nominates candidates for office and supports their campaigns; in many, if not most, states, only citizens who are registered in a particular party can vote in that party's primary. Because of this, people are encouraged to identify themselves with a party. Such party identification is often a general expression of political philosophy and represents only a mild attachment to the organization.

In the past, political parties provided identity in addition to other functions. Recent studies of political party identification have found that fewer people call themselves Democrat or Republican than once did. Party allegiance seems to be on the decline in the United States. Old political machines and coalitions are breaking up, and growing numbers of voters identify themselves as Independents rather than as Democrats or Republicans. People no longer identify themselves with a party as they once did, and no political party can any longer count on people who will automatically vote for party candidates. Where people once valued their identities as Democrats or Republicans loyal to their party's traditions, they now seem to value the independent identity more. To be an Independent, in the contemporary political vocabulary, is to make voting decisions on the basis of issues and candidates rather than blind party loyalty.

In addition, there are typifications associated with a particular political party. Because many people want to disassociate themselves from these typifications, identification with a political party is further eroded. In the past, such typifications as the following were an important part of American identity: "Republicans are rich, conservative businessmen." "Democrats are immigrants, live in cities, and work in factories." "The Democratic Party is the party of white segregationists." "Republicans are an alternative to corrupt urban machines." Such images often drastically oversimplify the relationship between parties and the interests they represent, but they nevertheless do provide people with some basis for political identity and action.

The party label not only reflects upon the individuals who are identified with that party, but it also supplies people with cognitive maps of the political world, providing simplifying themes that explain and order the complexities of political and governmental affairs. For example, most Americans believe the two-party system is best. They do not see contradictions in having a president of one party and the majority of Congress from the other. The political map of citizens of countries with parliamentary governments would find this inconceivable.

Political parties also provide the organizational structure within which various contending interest groups and factions negotiate with one another. The diverse assortment of groups and interests that makes up the Democratic Party, for example, does not easily reach agreement about party goals and philosophy. Rather, the agreements that are reached—for example, on whether the party will seek to expand welfare services or work for a change in foreign policy—are hammered out in party meetings, committees, caucuses, and conventions.

One of the major historic roles played by party organizations in American politics is exemplified by the urban political machine of Mayor Richard Daley, who ruled Chicago from 1955 until his death in 1976. Organizations like Daley's were built on a foundation of loyalty and patronage. Whoever controls a large city controls a great many jobs as well as essential city services—collecting garbage, plowing snow off the streets, fire and police protection, and the like. Loyalty to a political machine in the form of votes, organizational activities, and proper decisions is rewarded by jobs and the delivery of city services. Disloyalty is likewise punished by withholding these desired things. In Daley's day, loyal precinct captains and other workers could round up voters at election time, confident that they could promise potential voters a favor or special treatment here or there, and that loyalty would earn them rewards as well. Urban political machines like Daley's worked especially well in cities with large numbers of second-generation immigrants who felt otherwise alienated from power. The machine provided the people with many needed services; it often functioned more effectively than established social welfare organizations in helping people find jobs or housing or providing temporary assistance.

Voting itself seems to be on the decline in the United States. In European democracies, it is not uncommon for 80 or 90 percent of the electorate to turn out for elections. Figures in the United States are far lower, with turnouts of less than half the electorate common, even for congressional and presidential elections. It is not clear why voting turnout is declining. Some argue that registration procedures are too complex, and that if they were simplified voting would increase. Others believe that low voting rates are an indication of alienation from the political system, that people do not vote because they believe their votes do not make a difference. And it can also be argued that some citizens have found other, more direct avenues of political participation by their involvement in social movements, community organizations, and similar forms of direct action.

Declining voter participation is viewed by many as significant because voting itself is defined as the most important form of political participation. Voting is widely regarded in this society as both a civic duty and a source of political influence. "If you want to make a difference," people are encouraged to believe, "then get out and vote." Organizations like the League of Women Voters promote the view that voting is a good in itself, and that the ideal citizen is one who votes for candidates based on knowledge of them and the issues. Declining voting rates are thus perceived as undesirable because they threaten the legitimacy of the political system as Americans define it. For if democracy requires the consent of the governed, not voting is a way of withholding that consent.

Negotiations

Negotiation is the process in which interests and goals are defined and pursued, social conflict is regulated, power is exercised, and authority is established or undermined. Politics is filled with countless situations where contending parties, groups, and organizations resolve their differences and agree on a course of action through negotiations. Some of these negotiations are public and open, while others occur behind the scene in the proverbial "smoke-filled rooms" of political caucuses and conventions. Some result in long-standing agreements, and others yield short-term alliances. Some exemplify private horse-trading among legislators—"I'll vote for your bill if you'll vote for mine"—while others occur in the more formal settings of constitutional conventions, legislative meetings, and committee hearings.

A few examples will convey the kinds of political negotiations that occur and their contribution to the political process. Vote trading among politicians is a most common form of negotiation. One senator, for example, may favor a bill that will primarily benefit his own state by establishing a military base or building a dam or public building that will benefit the local economy. It is likely that this senator will find that there is a price to be paid for gaining the support of other senators, and the price is likely to be his or her support for bills they favor. Deals of this kind are routinely struck at all levels of politics. Although they seem to violate our expectations about how decisions should ideally be made (bills should be voted for on their merits, people are apt to feel), it seems unlikely that many decisions could be made without such deals. Such negotiations, which emphasize the accomplishment of specific practical objectives, tend to soften

William Gropper, *The Senate* (1935) Oil on canvas, 25⅛ × 33⅛ inches. Collection, the Museum of Modern Art, New York. Gift of A. Conger Goodyear.

Political oratory is part of political life, but as this painting suggests, it may be regarded with boredom. Much of what transpires in legislative bodies occurs behind the scenes, where participants negotiate arrangements they will later publicly confirm by speeches and votes.

ideological conflicts over societal goals. They are an accommodation to the fact that ideal principles, lofty aims, and broad societal goals have to be translated into specific decisions, and that people often disagree about the best means of attaining desired ends.

Negotiations also occur within the arena of intraparty politics. Every four years the people of the United States elect a president—a political event that involves a constant round of activities as individual politicians seek their party's nomination for the office. Much of this activity centers on the candidates' efforts to garner support from other politicians, who will subsequently be counted on to associate themselves and their popularity with the candidate, make speeches, persuade others to lend their support, provide organizational help, and in other ways further the candidacy. Needless to say, many of these negotiations focus on a political *quid pro quo*; in politics as elsewhere there is no such thing as a free lunch. A senator popular in his or her state, for example, may be ideologically inclined toward a given candidate. But there are matters at stake in addition to principle. Will the candidacy of a particular individual hurt or help the reelection chances of the senator? Can the candidate's need for the senator's help be used to extract commitments—whether to adopt a particular policy or find a job for a friend in the new administration?

It is also worth noting that agreements can be struck that involve major social groups, organizations, and social classes. It is frequently pointed out, for example, that during the New Deal years, when Franklin D. Roosevelt was president (1932–1945), the Democratic Party was able to forge an alliance that encompassed several constituencies. Labor, the poor, blacks, Jews, Catholics, and city dwellers were the heart of this alliance, which gave the Democrats a majority in almost every Congress from the 1930s through the 1970s. Although the participants in this alliance were not in agreement on every issue (disagreements over civil rights policies were a major source of friction), there was a working alliance between the party and key members of each of the several constituencies to maintain the Democrats as the majority party in Congress. After Roosevelt, the Democrats had strikingly less success in holding the presidency, with Republicans elected in 1952 and 1956 (Eisenhower), 1968 and 1972 (Nixon), and 1980 and 1984 (Reagan). Negotiated bargains and coalitions at the state level were effective in electing Democrats, but less successful in presidential politics, where additional processes are involved.

Governmental and political party organizations, combined with party affiliation and voting, are the most important elements of political activity, but they are not the only ones. Whenever various groups of people identify their goals and try to attain them, they become involved in the political process. A group of local property owners who want to keep taxes low may organize to present their case to local officials and attempt to persuade or pressure the latter to keep their spending in check. Such activities will probably bring taxpayers into conflict with public employees who want adequate wages or with parents who want to spend more money on schools for their children. Similarly, the desire of highway officials to build a new road through a residential neighborhood puts them in conflict with the residents' desire to keep their homes and preserve their community. Political activities and conflict can involve many different groups, organizations, and governmental bodies.

Moreover, political activity and conflict can focus not only on the incompatible interests of particular groups, but also on the goals and values of the society or community as a whole or upon definitions of social reality. Should a new road be built? Should a decaying section of a city be torn down to make way for new homes and businesses? Should the sale and use of alcohol or other drugs be legal? Should women be allowed to secure abortions without intervention by the state? Should a new nuclear missile system be built by the federal government? Is it realistic to even consider the possibility of "winning" a nuclear war?

Politics is, in some fundamental respect, ultimately about the definition of reality. It is not only an activity in which people decide what is to be done, but also one in which they decide what is good and what is not, how members of society should behave and how they should not, and what is truth and what is falsehood. The struggle of blacks to attain full civil and social rights, for example, has been only partly about the pursuit of group interest by citizens previously deprived of those rights. It has also been a struggle to realize the values of freedom and equality for all that are written into the Constitution of the United States. In this sense, conflict between a deprived group and the dominant society is a stage on which larger issues are at stake, including the very nature of the society itself.

Issues

Regardless of the groups and organizations involved, visible political activity in the United States and other democratic societies tends to focus on the definition and resolution of issues such as those above. Newspapers and the nightly television news report on such issues, as do politicians in their quest for the votes of the public or the support of other politicians. At any given moment, politics seems to consist of intense activity centered on one or a few issues. People take sides, advance arguments, look for support from others, dramatize the importance of the issue, and make claims about the dire consequences that will ensue if their position on the issue is not upheld.

An *issue* can be defined as something about which people acknowledge a right to disagree (Turner and Killian, 1972: 180). Abortion, the Equal Rights Amendment, national defense policy, nuclear power, and the social welfare rights of the poor are issues in this sense. They are matters of public controversy on which there are two (and usually more) positions, and discussion occurs on the basis of widespread agreement that the issue is important and that there are differing points of view.

Defining issues this way emphasizes the fact that issues do not come spontaneously into existence, nor are they a fixed part of the political landscape. For many years, American law simply outlawed abortion. Although many women suffered from this prohibition, it took many years for abortion laws to be overturned by United States Supreme Court decisions. Indeed, abortion did not really become a major political issue until *after* it was legalized, an event that set in motion a vigorous anti-abortion movement. Issues like abortion come and go, with one issue occupying center stage for a time, only to be replaced by another. As a result, political activity often must be directed toward establishing the legitimacy of an issue, toward establishing the idea that the issue is something about which people can legitimately disagree, and that it is worthy of attention and political resolution.

How are issues related to the interests and goals of specific groups and categories in the society? An example like abortion suggests that groups with specific interests try to make issues out of their goals and then work to sustain their position on the issue. Thus, it might be argued, the right to abortion becomes defined as a women's interest, and so various women's organizations seek to have the issue established as legitimate and to advance their side of the matter. Things can work this way, but the politics of issues is considerably more complex.

One reason for this complexity is that issues usually have several layers of meaning to participants. Abortion provides an excellent illustration of this point. Women who favor the removal of restrictions on abortion are apt to define their objective as a matter of civil rights. It is the right of a woman, they feel, to have control over her body, and laws that restrict abortion infringe upon this right. Yet the issue of abortion cuts deeper than this, for it is important for what it stands for, as well as for the straightforward interests that are at stake. Abortion is a symbolic issue. Opposition to abortion symbolizes resistance to a variety of social changes involving the status of women, including equality within marriage as well as equal treatment and opportunity in the workplace. By the same token, right-to-life groups oppose abortion because they think it morally wrong, but also because the idea of abortion, to them, symbolizes declining morals and individual responsibility, as well as the breakdown of the family institution.

Another complicating factor is that issues lend themselves readily to manipulation. Groups have a variety of interests, not all of which are uppermost in the minds of their members at any given time. The vast majority of elder Americans, for example, have a stake in the stability of the Social Security system. This mandatory pension program has been the key reason why the economic status of the aged has improved dramatically since the depression of the 1930s. Yet it is generally only when the system is threatened that it becomes a political issue that mobilizes the participation of the elderly and sharply focuses their consciousness of group interest. Social Security became an issue during the presidential election of 1980 and again in 1984 because candidate Ronald Reagan made some remarks that could be interpreted as hostile to the program, and also because his opponents emphasized the issue, portraying Reagan as someone in whose hands Social Security pensions would not be safe.

Issues are thus an important aspect of political activity in democratic societies, and a great deal of politics is focused upon them. But the relationships between the issues that are current at a given time and the interests and goals of the groups and organizations that take opposing sides on them are far from simple. For issues do not simply follow the dividing lines that exist in a society but have a life of their own, shaping political reality as well as reflecting it.

An understanding of how political issues function in democratic societies depends on the recognition that there is no simple way to measure the real or objective interests of social groups, categories, and organizations. Political actors, like all others, act on the basis of their definitions of situations, including definitions of what is in their interest and what is not. Abortion is an important issue because contending groups have come to define it as such and to believe that the outcome of the issue is important to them and to society as a whole.

Moreover, groups have a variety of interests, so that the lines of social division are rarely simple. American Jews, for example, take a strong interest in the welfare of the state of Israel. When American support for Israel becomes an issue, Jews are often joined by conservative Christian groups in their advocacy of continued political and economic support for that nation. On other issues, such as those involving civil liberties, Jews, who tend on the whole to take liberal stands in matters of civil rights, may find themselves on the opposite side from fundamentalist Christians.

Political Issues and Social Change

In general, the tendency for each issue that arises to attract a somewhat different coalition of supporting and opposing groups exerts a stabilizing force in democratic politics. Groups that are opponents today may be allies tomorrow, a fact that leads them to moderate their conflict tactics and to look for opportunities for compromise. Each group implicitly recognizes that there are limits to how far it should press its claims and how decisive a victory it should seek. Its members' desire to pursue any given interest is moderated by the recognition that victories gained in one sphere may lead to defeats in another.

The political process works differently when a single issue becomes so important that all other issues become subordinate to it. For many partisans in the abortion controversy, for example, this issue is *the* single issue of importance in American society, and a victory is to be sought without regard to other consequences. Something like this happened during the decades preceding the American Civil War, when slavery became the overriding political issue, and each side became prepared to go to any length to secure a victory.

When an issue gains such overwhelming importance, it becomes crucial to the identities of participants. For many prolifers, their anti-abortion activity is probably the single most crucial fact about themselves, organizing the way they see the world and their political role in it. For them, anti-abortion activity is a matter of sustaining and enhancing an important identity. The same is true of members of many social movements, who find their membership in the movement to be the major identifying fact about them and the most important organizer and energizer of their activity.

It is when an individual's position on an issue becomes tied to identity that he or she becomes prepared to take major risks and do anything on behalf of the cause. At the extreme, civil war is one outcome of such total mobilization of personal commitment around a single issue. More typically in American society, the flow of successive issues and the shifting coalitions that arise around them make for moderation. No issue dominates national attention for very long.

But this state of affairs can also impede social change. In American political life, issues tend to be perceived as separate and distinct from one another. Sociologist Peter Hall (1972: 65) argues that the belief that issues are separate is one of the important myths of American political life. Political attention is focused on the parade of issues, and as each one passes from view, it tends to be forgotten by most participants, who turn their attention and energy to the next issue in the parade. Crime, the future of Social Security, the American hostages in Iran, the energy shortage, American policy in Central America, disarmament, the nuclear freeze, and a host of other issues have preoccupied Americans in recent years. Most issues tend to disappear before they have been effectively resolved. Thus, for example, the energy crisis of the 1970s has disappeared in the relative energy abundance of the 1980s. Yet many of the underlying conditions of energy shortage still remain and may well help to precipitate real crises in the future.

American politics tends to focus on separate issues in part because the ideological differences among the major political parties are not very sharply defined. The two parties do tend to represent different coalitions of voters, of course; Democrats are less affluent and powerful, on the whole, and more likely to be minority group members, than are Republicans. Yet both parties subscribe to political philosophies—including support of democratic institutions and capitalism—that are in many ways more similar than different. Unlike Great Britain, where a distinctly socialist, working-class party (the Labour Party) emerged, the United States has produced no politically successful socialist movement. Political philosophies that are similar and tend to stay in the center of the political spectrum rather than moving too far left or right mean that radical proposals for social change do not generally get much of a hearing in American society. From the perspective of radicals, this means that attention is focused on superficial issues, rather than on the underlying social conditions that give rise to them and should be changed. From the dominant centrist perspective, the lack of strong ideological differences means that change can occur gradually and without social upheaval.

Childe Hassam, *Allies Day, May 1917* (1917)
Canvas, 36¾ × 30¼ inches. The National Gallery of Art, Washington. Gift of Ethelyn McKinney in memory of her brother, Glenn Ford McKinney.

Flags are quintessential political symbols, and flag waving is a potent form of symbolic action. Standing as they do for the nation, flags evoke sentiments of resolve and consensus. The politician who manages to "wrap" a program or policy in the flag has found an effective way to dampen opposition.

Political Drama

In order to understand how the American political system works, we must also examine it as a form of dramatic activity. The political world is an arena of illusion and appearances, as much as one of conflict, power, and decision-making. We can begin to grasp the nature of political drama by examining the difference between *symbolic* and *instrumental* actions.

Political leaders at all levels do many things that have real instrumental significance to their cities, states, and nations. A mayor, for example, either signs or vetoes a law that would allocate funds for a new school, library, or bridge. Congress either passes or does not pass tax reform legislation that restricts tax loopholes for the wealthy. Such decisions have real consequences; things do or do not get built, and the rich have their taxes lowered or raised.

But many of the things political leaders do are intended mainly for their symbolic impact. The president of the United States confers with the president of Mexico not just to conduct foreign policy negotiations, but also to show "respect" for the cultural traditions of Mexican Americans and thereby gain their support at the polls. An urban mayor establishes neighborhood offices—little "city halls"—to improve communication with ordinary people. The governor of a state rushes to a disaster scene to signify his concern for the victims and to take steps to assist them. These are symbolic actions, for while they may accomplish little concretely, they do symbolize attention to duty, good intentions, and being on the "right" side of an issue.

The promotion and manipulation of issues is an important way political figures seek support. This can be seen most clearly in presidential politics, but it is evident to some degree at all levels. Candidates for the presidency are faced with the same tasks as any political candidates. They must attract attention to themselves, gain the support of influential politicians as well as potential voters, and become perceived as viable candidates for this high office. How they deal with issues is important in accomplishing these tasks.

In order to focus attention on themselves, candidates for the presidency will often seek to create and gain a monopoly on a particular issue—whether it is law and order, the environment, women's rights, nuclear disarmament, or any other issue. Sometimes candidates seek to popularize issues out of genuine conviction, but sheer expediency also plays an important role. The candidate's task, if he or she is to get elected, is to be perceived as someone who has important things to say on the burning issues of the day. If there are no burning issues, or none on which the candidate's views are likely to earn votes, then new issues have to be created or incipient issues exploited. By seizing the initiative on an issue, the candidate has the chance to influence the definition of the issue and the terms of the debate. During the very early stages of the 1984 presidential campaign, the incumbent President Reagan was able to gain ownership of the "education" issue in this way, making proposals for reform before the Democrats had even chosen their party nominee.

Presidential candidates will also seek to ally themselves with what they perceive to be the winning side of a current issue, if they believe doing so will net them more votes than it loses. If nuclear disarmament is a burning political issue, for example, candidates will have to contend with it, and one way is simply to support the side that appears to have the upper hand. During the contest for the 1984 Democratic Party nomination, most of the candidates recognized that the votes of women would be crucial to their ultimate chances. As a result, they vied with one another for the support of women's groups, occasionally seeming to outdo one another in their willingness to make promises.

Thus, candidates will seek to do things that symbolize their commitment to the "right" side of an issue. They will make dutiful speeches and pledges before the conventions of various interest groups, have their photographs taken with influential leaders, make ritual journeys to foreign lands to learn the realities of international affairs first hand, and in other ways appear to have the "correct" opinions and the "right" commitments. Yet their desire to build broad bases of support will incline them to take as few risks as possible, especially when it comes to offending potential voters. Meanwhile, opposing candidates are seeking to have other issues defined as the significant ones and are engaging in their own symbolic acts designed to attract support.

The importance of political symbols is not confined to the efforts of candidates to capture issues and attract voters through their symbolic acts. In a more basic sense, politics in the United States *is* symbolic activity—a realm of appearances in which political actors seek to define situations, manipulate symbols, manage impressions, and create and sustain the illusion of orderly, rational, and democratic decision-making.

A considerable part of governmental activity seems oriented toward providing the public with reassurance that competent men and women are at the helm, that the city, state, or nation is being held on course by leaders who know what to do and have the courage to do it. In an international crisis, for example, the president will make televised speeches, invite congressional leaders to the White House, and take highly visible and concrete steps, such as placing the armed forces on alert or announcing a willingness to negotiate instead of fight. Part of the impetus for such actions is to reassure the public that a legitimate government is taking decisive and effective action. One of the reasons that the crisis of the American hostages in Iran was so problematic was that there was little the Carter Administration did or could do to provide such assurance.

Symbolic reassurance is important for a number of reasons. Life in modern society is complex, and the average member is beset with a great many anxieties: the likelihood of nuclear war, the safety of consumer products, the perceived threat to law and order by criminals or social dissidents, the possibility of unemployment, and a host of real or perceived changes in economic, familial, and other institutions. A great part of visible political activity seems designed to assuage these anxieties and to encourage people to trust the political system and to grant legitimacy to the activities of leaders.

Many political issues are so complex that the facts are highly ambiguous, and conclusions are difficult to reach with certainty. Will a freeze on the development of nuclear weapons lessen the chances of a nuclear war or encourage the Soviet Union to be more aggressive? Do aggressive affirmative action policies hasten the equalization of employment opportunities between blacks and whites? Issues such as these defy easy solutions, for evidence and arguments can be mounted on both sides.

Many political issues are complex and provoke intense anxieties, but the concrete process by which decisions are made and actions taken are largely invisible. In the eyes of freeze proponents, the continued development of nuclear weapons increases the already alarmingly high risk of nuclear catastrophe; opponents are apt to feel anxiety about the effects on Soviet ambitions. Affirmative action policies may seem reassuring to blacks who see no other way to gain a foothold in the world of work; working-class whites may feel very threatened by the same policies, which they may perceive as designed to achieve gains for blacks at their expense. Both sides in such disputes are far removed from the actual political contexts in which decisions are made and actions taken. International arms negotiations occur in secret and may take years to complete; and the passage of legislation involves complex political negotiations that are largely hidden from the public. Political scientists Murray Edelman and Kenneth Dolbeare summarize the results quite succinctly:

> When hopes and fears are strong and political events cannot be observed directly, governmental acts become especially powerful symbols. (Dolbeare and Edelman, 1979: 464)

Under such conditions, many governmental acts take on an essentially symbolic character. People seek visible cues that will assuage their anxieties or provide evidence that confirms their view of the world. They look for simplifying images and evidence of decisive action. Not surprisingly, political leaders recognize that the symbolic import of their actions is as great as their instrumental value in solving problems. They know that they must do *something* to resolve issues and cope with problems; they also know that they must *appear* to be doing something, even when they are not.

Another notable feature of American politics is its emphasis on the personality and character of political leaders. Observers often comment that Americans dwell more on such matters than on the issues, that they are more interested in the integrity or personal qualities of the leader than in the issues and the leader's position with regard to them. Television campaign commercials and the public relations efforts of elected officials both seem to recognize this fact. Candidates and officials are presented as mature, decisive, reliable, and experienced, with the emphasis decidedly on images of these individuals rather than the positions to which they are committed.

There may be diverse reasons for the emphasis on personality. Although America is a "government of laws, not of men," it is also a highly individualistic society in which individual men and women are held accountable for their actions. The intense focus on individual political leaders may thus be an offshoot of the more general idea that individuals make a difference. Moreover, where issues are complex and the facts are confusing, the character of the individual leader or aspirant may be one of the few things on which the electorate can focus. An additional reason for the emphasis upon personality and character is that issues themselves tend to be personified in American politics. For an issue to attain legitimacy in American politics, it has to be associated with a recognized political spokesman (Hall, 1972: 66).

Since character and personality are important, leaders and candidates must be concerned with the political presentation of self, with the management of their appearances so that the public will attribute a desirable character to them. They must seem to have integrity, strength, imagination, compassion, and other virtues in the right degrees and mixtures. In this realm of appearances, speaking ability, physical looks, an appropriate spouse and family, firmness of demeanor, and other matters unrelated to issues assume an exaggerated significance. As Hall points out, however, elections are more often lost than won on the basis of character. That is, a candidate is vulnerable to accidents and mistakes that may detract from a carefully cultivated appearance. A classic example was Senator Edmund Muskie's campaign for the Democratic presidential nomination in 1972. Muskie had gained a considerable following in his quest for the nomination, but one misstep during the New Hampshire primary undermined his public character. A New Hampshire newspaper with a reputation for political mudslinging had published an article critical of Muskie's wife. The candidate went to the steps of the newspaper's building to denounce it and its publisher, but was apparently overcome with emotion and, reportedly, cried. The event was widely reported and, by undermining a reputation for firmness and resolve, destroyed Muskie's chances for the nomination.

WHO IS IN CHARGE?

Up to this point we have skirted the issue of power, focusing instead on the visible public activity associated with politics and government. But the world of politics is more than drama. It is also a world of struggles in which people seek to enforce their will over others in order to achieve their aims. In the concluding section of this chapter we will examine the question of power and authority and ask "Who is in charge?"

Power and the Definition of Reality

The processes of symbolic action and political impression management do not occur in a vacuum. Some people have more capacity than others to shape political and governmental decisions because they can control the flow of information, manipulate events, and in other ways exert influence over the definition of political situations. The essence of political drama is the control of public perceptions so that people define reality in ways that will lead them to act as leaders wish them to act.

The capacity to influence behavior by controlling definitions of situations is vividly demonstrated in the area of foreign policy. In the fall of 1983 the United States led an invasion of the Caribbean island nation of Grenada. The ostensible reason for the action was to protect several hundred American students who were enrolled in medical school on the island and who were allegedly in danger from the local regime. It was generally acknowledged, however, that the more fundamental reason was to overturn a Marxist government that, after a recent coup, had become even more militant and was on its way to full membership in the Soviet-Cuban camp.

Although there was some evidence of danger to the American students, this factor was made crucial to the Reagan administration's strategy for convincing the American people of the necessity of the invasion, and so it received considerable attention in administration statements about the event. Students were portrayed as helpless in the face of government thugs and madmen who could not be counted on to respect the lives of innocent civilians. Early reports of the invasion emphasized the real, immediate dangers and the compelling urgency of the effort to rescue the students. At first, information about the invasion came exclusively from the military, since independent news reporters were kept off the island for some time. The portrayal of the students' plight contributed significantly to the widespread acceptance of the administration's definition of the situation, which held that the United States is justified in foreign intervention when the lives of its citizens are threatened.

Only later did the more fundamental reason for the invasion—seizing an opportunity to topple an unfriendly Marxist regime—become more readily acknowledged. Once again, the administration was able to use its power to capture the dramatic moment by showing extensive pictures of arms caches and by playing up the eagerness with which the local populace welcomed their liberation by American soldiers. And by the time the more clearly political reasons for the invasion were acknowledged, a climate of acceptance had already been created by the emphasis on rescuing students.

The president of the United States has an enormous capacity to control the definition of political situations in ways suggested by the Grenada invasion. Presidents can call news conferences and be guaranteed coverage by major print and electronic media, as well as a national audience on the evening network television news programs. A single telephone call can arrange time on the three major networks for a special address. The executive branch can control the release of information about its activities and stage its information in ways best calculated to serve its interests.

The capacity to control the flow of information is augmented by the powerful aura of the presidency itself. Regardless of the individual who occupies the White House, Americans are taught to honor the office of the presidency itself. The president of the United States is the only single individual who symbolizes the nation as a whole and whose actions are supposed to reflect the interest of the whole society, rather than one or another special interest. Because of this symbolic leadership role of the president, there is a strong disposition to believe that the president would not knowingly do anything contrary to the national interest. Even when people disagree about the appropriate means of pursuing that interest, they seldom question the motives of the president. This disposition to believe means that information coming from the White House has an edge over conflicting information. In the Grenada invasion, skeptics and critics were few in number, compared with the vast number of people who accepted the administration's definition of the situation.

The power of the presidency, exercised through such symbolic means, thus goes well beyond the specific authority conferred on the president by the Constitution. That authority rests upon law, whereas a considerable amount of presidential power rest upon such symbolic means of controlling definitions of situations. Thus we cannot think of the executive branch of government (or other branches, for that matter) as simply carrying out the wishes of the people by enforcing and passing legislation that meets their needs. To a considerable extent, government is an autonomous social force that attempts to create and manipulate public perceptions, wishes, and motives.

It would be a mistake, however, to argue that government has an unlimited capacity to control the flow of information or an unchecked capacity to define situations. The media operate with considerable autonomy from the government, uncovering facts and developing analyses that often undermine the official point of view. Indeed, "freedom of the press" means, to a considerable extent, the right to challenge official definitions of situations, to present contrary information and alternative interpretations. And while the media always operate at a disadvantage relative to those who hold power, they occasionally play a major role in undermining official definitions or in establishing their own definitions of situations.

The growing disillusionment with the war in Vietnam in the late 1960s and early 1970s, for example, was partly due to media activities. Officials of the Johnson and later the Nixon administrations spoke optimistically about progress in "winning" the war, but Americans saw nightly television news reports replete with horrible pictures of death and devastation. It should be added that both administrations were also unable to use symbolic means very effectively to mobilize public support for the war; they never succeeded in establishing their definition of Vietnam as crucial to America's security. In the same way, the transformation of the Watergate burglary into a major political scandal that led to the resignation of President Richard Nixon was largely the result of persistent media activity. And in more recent years, the intensity of emotions that developed when Americans were held hostage in the United States' embassy in Iran was due in part to the treatment of the event by the media. Passions were inflamed by television pictures of frenzied Iranian mobs burning American flags and by the sheer amount of time devoted to the situation on newscasts.

Who Controls America?

There is more to the question of who runs the United States than mobilization of public support for governmental actions by the control of information and the definition of situations. A more basic question is whether all or most of the decisions reached in the political process reflect the diverse interests of a majority of Americans or, instead, the more narrow interests of a few. Is America a pluralistic society in which any group can organize politically and press its interest in competition with those of others? Is power dispersed widely, even if not equally, among various social groups and categories? Or is there a ruling class, a relatively small number of individuals whose collective will has an effect disproportionate to their small numbers?

Questions such as these have been the topic of a major controversy in American social science, one that involves both conflicting empirical evidence about the society and, to some degree, conflicting political perspectives. On one side are scholars such as C. Wright Mills (1956) and G. William Domhoff (1967, 1978), who argue that the United States is ruled by a national elite or ruling class whose members are both wealthy and powerful. On the other side are those, such as Robert Dahl (1961), who argue that political power is dispersed among a great variety of groups, and that there is no single class or elite that can control decisions.

C. Wright Mills argued that there was a "power elite" consisting of the leaders of three major social spheres: military, government, and business. These individuals think alike in political and social terms, they have similar social class backgrounds, and they tend to move back and forth from one sphere to another. Next year's secretary of defense, in this view, is likely to have been last year's president of Ford Motors or some other industrial firm; the high-ranking Air Force general is apt to find lucrative employment in the defense industry when he retires; and the members and staff of federal regulatory agencies are drawn from the ranks of the very industries they regulate and will return to those industries when they leave government service.

Because of their similarities of orgins and outlook and their movement among elite positions in various spheres, the members of the power elite exert significant control over government. They tend to agree with one another in the decisions they make, and these decisions usually serve the interests of the business, governmental, and military centers of power. The Air Force general with strong ties to the defense industry, for example, recommends defense policies that contribute to the aggrandizement of both his own branch of the service and the economy of that industry. The presidential adviser or cabinet secretary whose closest personal ties are to powerful business leaders perceives the world through the lens of business interests and supports governmental actions that serve these interests. In the eyes of the elite theorists, business dominance over government is growing, and the power elite is setting policies for the society as a whole.

Pluralist theorists disagree. Arguing that there are a great many competing interest groups in American society, they take the view that no single group dominates everything. Elites tend to develop within every major sphere of social activity, they would say, but their interests do not necessarily coincide, nor do their members perceive them as coinciding. There are governmental, military, and business elites—but there are also elites within organized labor, the universities, the mass media, private foundations, and other centers of power. As a result, there is considerable competition among various groups, and as issues shift, the dominant groups tend to shift. At a given point, they might argue, military leaders might gain the upper hand in shaping national policy, while at some other point business or labor might gain in power.

Where does the truth lie? As we pointed out in Chapter 10, it is clear that wealth is disproportionately concentrated in the hands of a few, and wealth is a crucial power resource. Control over major corporations, banks, insurance companies, and other economic enterprises can be readily translated into significant influence over the activities of other centers of power. The "national upper class" detected by William Domhoff (1967) clearly is in a position to influence the decisions of foundations and major private universities because the trustees of such organizations are drawn disproportionately from this class. And an industry that offers the chance of future employment can easily have an impact upon the decisions of a government bureaucrat employed by the Federal Aviation Administration or the Federal Trade Commission. It would be silly to argue that wealth does not confer power.

But even the vast wealth of the corporate elite does not confer unlimited power. Although elections often seem to do little more than legitimize the existing political and social order, their existence does give rise to some forms of competition. At the very least, democratic elections make for competition for mass support among various elites or factions within the elite. This competition for mass support is a reminder that electoral support is required for legitimacy in a democratic system, and that a condition for gaining this support is responsiveness to at least some popular demands. Although, as we have argued, governmental officials play a major role in shaping popular perceptions and controlling the demands of the people, neither they nor any single elite completely control these demands.

The "truth" about power also depends in part on the standard against which we evaluate it. Judged against the ideal of a pluralistic democracy in which each person votes individually to influence equally the decisions of his or her representatives, it is clear that there are significant inequalities. Some people are "more equal" than others in their access to persons in power, in the likelihood of their being chosen for elite positions, and in their capacity to put their own interests ahead of the society as a whole when they make decisions on its behalf. Judged against the standard of a tightly organized national upper class that is able to exert control over every significant decision, there are clear elements of pluralism in the American system. Liberals and leftists can get elected to high office and oppose the goals of the corporate elite; ideas that contradict and expose the power elite can gain circulation; and the balance of power can shift among various groups from time to time. The truth depends in part on how one views it.

CONCLUSION

Americans are encouraged by tradition to maintain a kind of "high school civics" image of politics and government, while at the same time holding politics in contempt and politicians at arm's length. Many of the positive views are based on simplifying images of politics that serve simultaneously to shape our understanding of political process ("This is how we do things") and as a basis for both legitimation and aspiration ("This is how things should be done"). Phrases such as "checks and balances," "the Bill of Rights," "due process," "the rule of law," "the two-party system," and "the system works" are examples of such simplifying images.

At the same time, negative views of politics indicate widespread recognition that the high ideals of the American system are often not met. Social reality often does not correspond with high school civics. We have also characterized politics as an activity that more people watch than participate in. It is, as Edelman (1964: 5) has written, "a passing parade of abstract symbols" in which we look for reassurance, for evidence that competent and reasonable people are making honest and sound decisions in the most rational way possible.

These are fitting, if not highly idealistic, themes with which to approach the end of this book. Symbolic interactionism encourages us to look within the minds and perspectives of people, as well as at their external behavior. It emphasizes that people create the worlds, including the political worlds, in which they live and which constrain them and their acts. And it encourages us to look at the myths people create about reality as well as at reality itself. Politics is a realm of myth as well as objective fact, of hankering after psychic security as well as making decisions and exercising power. And in politics, as in other human spheres, understanding the complexities of human belief and conduct is a prerequisite to, although not a guarantee of, improvements in the human condition.

SUGGESTED READINGS

DAHL, ROBERT A. *Who Governs? Democracy and Power in an American City* (New Haven: Yale University Press, 1961).

DOLBEARE, KENNETH M. and MURRAY EDELMAN. *American Politics: Policies, Power, and Change*, 3rd ed. (Lexington, Mass.: Heath, 1979).

EDELMAN, MURRAY. *The Symbolic Uses of Politics* (Urbana, Ill.: University of Illinois Press, 1964).

HALL, PETER M. "A Symbolic Interactionist Analysis of Politics," *Sociological Inquiry* 42 (1972): 35–75.

MILLS, C. WRIGHT. *The Power Elite* (New York: Oxford University Press, 1956).

ROSE, ARNOLD, M. *The Power Structure: Political Process in American Society* (New York: Oxford University Press, 1967).

15

Symbolic Interactionism and Sociology

The time has come for a summing up, for a last look at sociology and the way symbolic interactionists approach it. The aim here is not to summarize "facts" and "findings" about various topics, but to explore some of the major themes and ideas that guide sociologists, particularly those working from the perspective of symbolic interactionism. One of these themes, the impact of society on the self, merits special attention, for there seem to have been significant historical changes in the relationship between individuals and society. And we will conclude by examining the potential social value of the discipline.

HOW SYMBOLIC INTERACTIONISTS VIEW SOCIETY

As we saw in the first chapter, there are a variety of ways to approach society, the central concept with which sociologists work. Structural functionalists view it as an assembly of functioning parts whose operation can be examined without much regard for the flesh-and-blood human members who are powerfully constrained by its patterns. Other theorists see social conflict as the fundamental process, the motor that drives human beings and shapes the society in which they live. For others, social interaction oriented to the exchange of valued things is the essential process on which society is based.

Symbolic interactionists do not deny that people are constrained by society, that conflict is an important part of social life, or that exchange is a key aspect of social interaction. This book presented many example of these processes. But none of them, by itself, captures the essence of human society as symbolic interactionists see it.

Society and the Individual: A Paradox

The symbolic-interactionist analysis of human society begins with a paradox. Human beings are self-conscious creatures whose social behavior depends upon the exercise of a self-conscious intelligence. And yet society is itself the source of the very qualities of mind people need in order to be social creatures. On the one hand, society *precedes* the individual, in the sense that each person is born into an ongoing stream of social life and must find a place there, adapting to its demands and meeting needs within the limitations it imposes. But the very continuation of that stream depends upon the participation of its members. Human beings are not like molecules of water swept along in a river, contributing to its flow but with no power to change its course. The course and continuation of human society depends upon the actions of its member "molecules."

Symbolic interactionists resolve this paradox by turning to George Herbert Mead's account of the emergence of mind and self. Human beings are creatures with the capacity to make and use symbols, to represent the complex world in which they live with a rich set of linguistic symbols that mediate between them and this world. Symbols, of course, are themselves inherently social; words have meaning because a group of people use and respond to them in the same way. And symbols make it possible to represent the group itself—not just the material world, but the communities in which people live, their individual members, their hopes and fears.

Symbols give rise to self-consciousness. Because human beings can represent the world, including the social world, with symbols, they gain the capacity to "get outside" of themselves. Each individual is not just a subject responding to events in the world, but a person with the capacity to be conscious of himself or herself as a part of that world. Humans gain that capacity because the groups to which they belong give them names and a place within the life of the group. Human beings map their world using symbols, and each person thus gains an identity—a place on that map.

To have consciousness of self is to have a very great capacity for self-control. Human beings can use symbols to anticipate the consequences of their acts—their potential success or failure in securing goals, the approval or condemnation with which others in the group will view them. And even more important, people are able to imagine themselves engaging in various alternative acts, compare the probable results of doing one thing as against another, and choose one act over another on the basis of its anticipated results. Humans are not limited to trial-and-error learning, but can use their symbolic capacity in imaginative ways.

This view of symbols and self-control resolves the paradox of individual and society. On one hand, Mead's approach allows us to explain the very great influence of society on the individual. Individuals do not invent the symbols they use, for the language spoken by the group precedes the individual and is something the individual learns. In this sense, the group confers a world upon us by teaching us its language. Moreover, the group is the source of individual self-consciousness. The person has a self and has the capacity to imagine alternative acts and then select a desired act only because the group has assigned the person a name and a place. Individuals can only imagine themselves and the consequences of their acts by taking the perspectives of others, whether the group as a whole or some specific other within it.

The influence of society upon the individual is thus solid and powerful, but it is by no means total or irresistible. Society shapes the human beings who are its members and whose actions keep it going, but this process of shaping, called socialization, is by no means perfect. It creates people with the capacity to choose otherwise—to rebel, to resist, to innovate. Each mind does not become a duplicate of every other mind, nor are the interests and goals of individuals defined completely by society. As we have pointed out, human needs are individual, but they are met through cooperative activity. The human capacity to choose among alternative courses of action means that sometimes people will choose acts that secure their own goals at the expense of other people. And, finally, symbols are themselves expansive and creative. Language gives human beings the capacity to say things that have never been said before and to invent

Pieter Brueghel the Elder, *The Harvesters*
The Metropolitan Museum of Art, New York

This sixteenth-century painting portrays a society in which the individual was bound closely with others in a commmunity of effort and responsibility. The individual readily found a sense of place and identity, but the community held the upper hand in its relationship to the individual.

new realities by inventing new symbols. Moreover, human beings do not respond automatically or habitually to symbols, but must interpret them before conduct can occur.

As a result, human beings have some degrees of freedom. Their relationships with one another are not mechanically governed by society, but depend upon choice and voluntary conduct. Human society continues to exist because human beings decide to act as they do. This is not to deny that group life has a powerful constraining influence on individuals. Language itself restricts the choices people can make, for they cannot do what they cannot conceive. And the unequal distribution of resources means that some people have the capacity to exact from others the behavior they desire. Society constrains in this sense because people constrain one another. Even so, at bottom the perpetuation of human society and its influence over people rests upon the consciously constructed acts of its members.

The Social Construction of Reality

Although people produce society through their own activities, it is often the power of society over people that seems most visible. Each individual, particularly in modern society, has the everyday experience of choosing between one act and another, but the broader outlines of society and culture often appear to be fixed and natural. Even in the modern world, where people are frequently aware of the diversity of human societies and culture, familiar ways of doing things are taken for granted as inevitable. For example, the nuclear family seems to many people to represent the natural order of things. Similarly, many consider the quest for individual profit to be an inherent human motivation. The rules and procedures of organizations often appear to their members as the only way things can be done.

To put this another way, the members of a society often *reify* it; that is, they see the society, its culture, groups, and organizations as things that are as they are and cannot be altered. The bureaucrat in the university, military, government, or corporation who has learned the rules and who cannot imagine ever bending them or making exceptions engages in reification. Such a bureaucrat perceives the rules as fixed ways of dealing with people and cannot imagine a different set of rules, or even the possibility that human beings, who originally made the rules, can also change them. Indeed, such individuals may so identify with the organization that they cannot take the role of the client and try to perceive how a problem might be solved. "Those are the rules and I have no choice but to enforce them," is a statement that signals that reification is taking place.

Reification is a part of a broader proces of *reality construction*, in which people create the reality of society in part simply through their definitions of it. As we have frequently pointed out, people act on the basis of their definitions of situations. If they believe that women are inferior to men or that homosexuals threaten the social order, they will act on the basis of such conceptions of reality. In doing so, people often create the very conditions they believe factually exist. The bureaucrat who believes the rules are etched in stone helps to create a rigid and immovable organization. Men who believe women are inferior will convey inferior self-images to them and help to create the very disabilities in women that they believe are natural. And if homosexuals or other classes of deviants are feared, such social reactions will help to engender forms of deviant behavior that serve to confirm the original beliefs.

The reification of social life is to some degree an inevitable process. Human beings appear to have a powerful need to live in an orderly and predictable world. They seem, on the whole, to prefer clarity of meaning over ambiguity, certainty about norms over anomie, commitment over ambivalence. They want the world to be an orderly place, feel threatened and upset whenever it is not, and do their best to restore certainty and order when it is threatened.

We have seen this quest for certainty in a number of ways in this book.

In situations of collective behavior, people strongly desire to establish a definition of a situation so they can know their roles and what is required of them. In politics, Americans especially seem to crave symbolic reassurance, to have their leaders engage in symbolic acts that they can interpret as evidence that the frightening and disorderly events that threaten are being brought under control. In dealing with normal everyday behavior as well as deviance, people seem to demand the certainty of familiar typifications.

Why do humans seek order and predictability? One explanation lies in the nature of symbols themselves. The capacity to choose, to react not to a world given in nature but one interpreted through language, gives human beings a great deal of freedom, but it also puts them in a precarious and difficult situation. The members of a species that acts on the basis of symbols and meanings look for meaning in everything. In their everyday relations with their fellows, humans perceive significance in every word and deed. They look for implications of approval or disapproval; they wonder whether they are being told the truth or lied to.

Moreover, as Ernest Becker (1971) has argued, symbols give human beings the capacity to rise above a sheer biological level of existence. We are, in our own eyes, "just a little lower than the angels." At the same time, we are always being reminded of the purely biological basis of our existence. We must eat and breathe, we are driven by powerful sexual urges, and—of great significance in Becker's eyes—we are conscious of our mortality. Human beings, in this view, live in terror of the fact that they will ultimately die—that all of their creations and aspirations will in the end come to nothing.

Human beings thus seek to construct an orderly social reality, and often do so by reifying it, because in a perverse way their sanity depends upon it. Although the effort to construct an image of an orderly and predictable world—or to restore that world when it seems threatened—often leads people to injure one another or to avoid reality, it seems in some degree inevitable that they do so.

The Relevance of History

There is one other major theme that we have emphasized in this book that is implicit in symbolic interactionism: the importance of viewing society in a historical way. Human society is a product of human activity, albeit also a potent influence on that activity. But society is not simply the product of activity by those alive at any given moment, nor can its reality be grasped fully by taking a "snapshot" of it at a particular time. Society exists because people in the past and present have acted and constructed reality as they have, and frequently we must examine the historical development of society if we are to understand its contemporary operation.

Human society is never static, for even the most seemingly stable traditional societies change slowly over time. But for the past three centuries or so, Western society has been in constant flux, and a great deal of the change it has experienced has occurred in the last century and a half. Two hundred years ago, the United States was a small, new nation, mostly agrarian. People lived relatively traditional lives in small communities and cities. Since that time, thunderous changes have occurred. America is now an industrial society whose population is heavily concentrated in urban areas where tradition counts for very little.

As we have attempted to show in a number of chapters, understanding contemporary American society depends upon understanding these changes. It owes its ethnically and racially diverse—and often troubled—population to more than four centuries of forced and voluntary migration and to a succession of efforts to assimilate diverse groups to an image of America as an English-speaking society founded on English culture. Its contemporary class structure was forged during the nineteenth century, as the society industrialized and new social strata emerged. Just as important, America's contemporary culture is a product of historical developments, many of which have by now receded from our collective memories. The fervent belief that men belonged in the harsh world of work and women should be responsible for maintaining home and family as a welcoming haven, for example, was created during the industrialization of the United States during the last century.

The importance of history derives from the fact that human beings are creatures of time. Unlike nonsymbolic creatures who live in the timeless world of the here and now, human beings are very much temporally oriented. We remember our past just as we anticipate the future. Although (for reasons we will explore in the next section of this chapter) Americans have had a tendency to concentrate on the future to the exclusion of the past, we nevertheless resemble all human beings in our orientation to time. Each individual has memories of an individual past that are linked to present and future to form a continuous sense of self. We remember what we used to be, just as we look forward to what we will be in the future. We remember our ancestors, even as we make plans for the future and for our descendents.

Contemporary people are closer to the past than they may sometimes imagine. A person in his or her early twenties now is likely to have had grandparents born near the beginning of the twentieth century. Allowing for about twenty-five years per generation, the grandparents of such a person are about five generations removed from ancestors who were alive at the time of the American Revolution. That seems a very long time ago, for we are talking about the great-great-great-great-great grandparents of a contemporary twenty-five-year-old. Yet, looked at in another way, it is not so long ago. The grandparents of one of this book's authors were born in the 1880s, and he remembers his grandmother telling stories of her childhood, when she was told of the "war of the Blue and the Gray"—the Civil War—that had been concluded scarcely twenty years before her birth. Her parents were born before the Civil War, and her grandparents would have remembered stories from their youth about the American Revolution.

The point to be stressed is that contemporaty societies bear the powerful imprint of past events and of the lives and perspectives of ordinary as well as powerful people from the past. During the nineteenth century, the forebears of people now alive grappled with an economy changing from agriculture to industry; they struggled across oceans and prairies; they sought to Americanize themselves or to defend the "purity" of the United States against "foreigners." The actions of their everyday lives forged the world we now live in. When symbolic interactionists say that people are born into a society, it is a historically created and ongoing society they have in mind, not an abstraction.

THE SELF IN MODERN SOCIETY

Symbolic interactionists place a great deal of emphasis upon the concepts of self and identity. As we have seen, it is the capacity for self-consciousness that gives human beings a great deal of control over their behavior. And it is the person's identity in each situation that provides direction to conduct, for people know what to do only by knowing who they are. The importance of this concept becomes especially visible when we examine the kinds of social changes that have been underway for the past several centuries, for it appears that the relationship between self and society has been changing, with new kinds of people emerging as a result.

From Community to Society

At the risk of oversimplification, we can say that as recently as two centuries ago, around the time of the American Revolution or shortly before, most individuals lived in a very different relationship to the society than at present. Most Americans were farmers or small-town dwellers, as their fathers and mothers had been, and they played out the drama of their lives within or very near the communities in which they were born. The country was homogeneous—people were more like one another than different in cultural and religious terms—and the range of social inequality, although noticeable, was smaller than at present. People lived and died in the company of people familiar to them since birth. They found vocations and a secure place in the communities in which they lived. They knew who they were, and they had strong ideas about right and wrong. Although the severe religious views of the New England Puritans had declined into a softer Congregationalism, Protestantism continued to have a powerful influence upon values and beliefs.

A word that readily conveys the character of life for many people in those times—not only in the United States but in most other societies—is *community*. People lived as a part of communities; they interacted on a daily basis with people they knew well and toward whom they felt a sense of responsibility. Their lives were guided by traditions that were shared by members of the community. People had a more or less secure sense of place as members of a community. Indeed, one could scarcely live in society except as a member of a community, for to be born and to be alive was to associate with others whom one knew, seek their company always, and feel secure only in their midst. There were those, to be sure, who sought the freedom of the frontier in preference to the security of village and town. But for the most part, Americans of that era lived a traditional life within a community, a life not all that unlike the lives their ancestors had led.

For the member of a stable and traditional community, life is often filled with many constraints, for other people are always present to check one's impulses and set forth standards of behavior acceptable to the community. Communities can be oppressive, for they have a strong sense of order and tradition, and often have very little tolerance for those who depart from it. In such societies, the heavy weight of tradition often discourages innovation, and nonconformity carries a high price.

But life within such communities also had many advantages. People who live in stable communities have a secure sense of place. Although they may (and early Americans did) face many material hardships, their identity was seldom in question. Each person knew his or her place, knew what was expected, what could and could not be done, what were the boundaries of appropriate conduct. Such men and women traded a measure of autonomy and freedom for a sense of security. They defined themselves in terms of society and its expectations.

There is a sense, however, in which this picture, while generally true, is somewhat misleading. Although America was then in many respects a traditional society, there were foreshadowings of the future as well. Much happened during the nineteenth century to change very drastically the relationship between individual and society. But most of the developments had at least begun by the time of the Revolution or shortly thereafter.

First, from the very beginning, the United States seems to have been a society whose members were shifting their loyalties from the past to the future. People of two centuries ago were in many ways bound to the past; they conceived of themselves as living a life that would resemble that of their ancestors. But gradually at first and then with increasing rapidity, Americans began to identify with the future. They began to see America as a land of boundless opportunity, a place where they could achieve success they could not have aspired to in England. A secure place in an established community was surely appealing. But for many people, the chance to make a fortune in land speculation or to find opportunities for success in the West were even more enticing. So, throughout the nineteenth century, the community lost its hold on people, who began to define their place less in terms of membership in a community and more in terms of their quest for success.

Second, the United States was, from the first, founded on ideas of equality and liberty. It was not that there was no inequality, or that all people were perfectly free to do what they pleased. The era of the 1830s and 1840s, when the belief in an egalitarian democracy was especially strong, was also the time when inequalities began to increase because a great deal of wealth was being created. And there were many times when ideals of liberty were circumscribed by law or custom, most obviously in the institution of slavery and the treatment of even free blacks. Still, freedom and equality were potent ideals, and as a result, people were less inclined to accept the place assigned them by their communities.

Third, freedom, equality, and the quest for wealth and success became interpreted in very individualistic terms. Americans have tended to think of themselves as a society of individuals in which the individual is responsible for his or her success or failure. The individualization of America was well underway during the nineteenth century. One result of a growing emphasis on the individual was that the person's place in a community became a less sure basis for identity. In a traditional society, people take the places that have been assigned to them, and they see themselves according to their station in life. But in a society where each individual person is free to succeed or not, the qualities of the individual become more important. What one is becomes a result of one's own efforts, rather than a result of where one was born.

Fourth, America steadily became a more industrialized society during the nineteenth century, slowly at first and then with great rapidity after the Civil War. People moved from farms to factories, from towns to cities, from a seamless round of work in the company of spouses, parents, and children to the more isolated and individualized existence of the factory. As the society became an industrial nation, fewer people were tied to the land, and more were dependent upon the great corporations and the factories they owned. More and more people began to work for others rather than for themselves. And at the same time, the division of labor became more complex. Industrialization created new jobs and more specialization. Where once people could know their places within a community built on a human scale, now society became larger and more complicated, and it was harder to have an overall grasp of it and one's place within it.

Industrialization also led in many instances to a growing separation between the worker and his product. The farmer or mechanic of the 1830s saw the end product of his labors—a crop, a wagon, a barrel. Part of himself was expressed in that product; he identified with it, felt pride in it, saw himself in it. As the factory system of production developed, and especially as control over production shifted from the individual worker to an owner or manager, this sense of contact with the fruits of one's labors began to be lost. Workers in factories did not own what they produced or the tools used to produce it, and often they did not see the finished product. They contributed only a small part of the total labor needed to make it. In Marxian terms, people became alienated from their work; they came to find less satisfaction in it.

In short, throughout the nineteenth century, processes were underway that altered the nature of identity and self-image. People began to define themselves in terms of what they might become instead of the communities of which they were a part. They increasingly saw themselves as alike, in potential if not always in fact, rather than as a part of a naturally ordered world in which men and women of different talents and stations were assigned different roles. They began to see themselves increasingly as individuals rather than as members of communities, and they began to seek identities as unique individuals rather than by identifying with others. And, finally, they became accustomed to a complex, often unfriendly, frequently harsh urban industrial world of strangers in which no one had an assured place.

The Quest for Identity

We can summarize these ideas by suggesting that an important characteristic of American society is the uncertainty of its members about their identity. Although the search for identity is often spoken of as something characteristic of the present, anxiety about status and identity has deep roots in American history.

What does it mean in concrete terms to say that people are uncertain about identity? After all, it might be argued, most contemporary Americans manage to cope with life in their society in one way or another. They know they are men or women, Protestants or Jews, assembly-line workers or college professors. They know there are expectations associated with their roles, and they manage to discharge their responsibilities. All of this is true. Yet in several ways, the experience of self in modern society is affected by uncertainties.

Edward Hopper, *Nighthawks* (1942)
Oil on canvas. 33⅛ × 60 inches. Friends of American Art Collection, © The Art Institute of Chicago. All Rights Reserved. Courtesy of The Art Institute of Chicago.

The individual in modern society is in many ways more autonomous and less constrained than were members of a tradional community. The price of individuality, however, is often self-preoccupation, uncertainty about identity, and sheer loneliness.

First, in modern society, and especially contemporary American society, people have a tendency to emphasize the wishes and impulses of the individual rather than the expectations of society. In a traditional society, people tend to identify with the community and its expectations. Although they may sometimes wish to escape its restrictions, they are able to hold in check the impulse to rebel because they believe such impulses are not only wrong but contrary to their own true nature. In modern life, people are more apt to define the real self *as* impulse, and to feel that social norms restrict their capacity to express this self (Turner, 1976). Whereas people in a traditional society identify with the roles assigned them, modern people are more likely to view their roles as artificial impositions on a true self that lies underneath.

Second, modern life seems to generate a constant search for meaning and community, for new beliefs and philosophies that can make life more satisfying, and for new places and groups that can provide people with a sense of place and belonging. Much of the appeal of new religious movements (as well as of some of the more demanding established groups) in recent decades can be traced directly to their capacity to provide a more secure sense of identity for their members. Such groups seem to tap a deep longing for order and certainty, not only about the meaning of life, but about the place of the individual in the social world.

In like manner, during the 1960s and 1970s various kinds of psychotherapy, encounter groups, and human-potential philosophies became very popular. The "person-centered" approach to therapy of Carl Rogers (1951), for example, stressed the need for people to be open and honest in their relationships with one another and emphasized the vast potential for growth and happiness that could be liberated within each individual. Ideas like those of Rogers had considerable appeal because they provided a framework for interpreting the person's experience, they promised a better self in the future, and they offered supporting groups of people who shared those beliefs and could provide fellow believers with a sense of belonging. Ideas like those of Rogers, which emphasize the importance and potential powers of the person, also fit very well with an American emphasis on individualism and the future. Just as earlier generations of Americans were taught that any boy could achieve wealth or grow up to be president, contemporary people often believe that anyone can achieve psychic comfort and social community.

A quest for community and identity is not confined to the twentieth century, of course. American society throughout its transformation during the nineteenth century, and perhaps even before that, spawned numerous social and religious movements. During the first half of the nineteenth century, for example, western New York was so ablaze with religious fervor and revival that it came to be known as the "burned-over district" (Cross, 1950). Many utopian movements also sprang up around this time—the Oneida Community of Vermont and New York State, for example, whose members practiced a kind of "Bible communism" and a system of complex marriage taught by their leader,

John Humphrey Noyes. And throughout the nineteenth century, various fraternal organizations—the Masonic orders, the Moose, Elks, Knights of Pythias, and others—provided a similar sense of social meaning and belonging to their members. Although America was then a society in the process of rejecting tradition, its members also craved some of the security and social connectedness that tradition provided.

Finally, *status anxiety*—a concern about social standing and prestige—is a frequent companion to uncertainty about identity. In a society where every person has a place and knows it, people are not anxious about where they stand. They might not be content with their place in society or feel that it is just, but they are not moved by a need to establish it. In modern societies like the United States, where identity is generally less secure, there is more anxiety about social standing. People are more apt to worry about "keeping up with the Joneses," and they are perhaps more likely to feel threatened by social changes that may affect their sense of status. (We suggested in earlier chapters that such status anxiety may well have been related to the Temperance Movement of the nineteenth century and the abortion controversy of the twentieth.)

In sum, contemporary American society (and, although perhaps to a lesser extent, other modern industrial societies as well) does not easily provide the sense of meaning and place, orderliness and security that people wish. It creates people who often define themselves *against* rather than *in terms of* society. And, if the observations of psychiatrists are correct, it also creates people who often feel a vague anxiety about life in general and their own lives in particular. Some (Lasch, 1979) argue that Americans are self-preoccupied to the point of pathological narcissism. Others (Wheelis, 1958) feel that identity is a major preoccupation, that people feel dissatisfied for reasons they cannot pinpoint, but that reflect the lack of a secure identity.

WHAT GOOD IS SOCIOLOGY?

The topic of identity seems to be a fitting note on which to end this book. Ultimately every academic discipline has to justify itself in some way—to make a case that it has some value, some "redeeming social purpose." In our eyes, sociology justifies itself to a very great extent by contributing to an understanding of the social world—our place in it, the impact of that world upon us, and our possible impact upon it.

There are, of course, many ways to justify the worth of a field of study. In some vague way, most sociologists hope that their discipline will help make the world a better place in which to live. Some sociologists argue more explicitly that sociology should be a discipline that establishes the empirical and theoretical basis on which better social policy can be made. And some of our colleagues believe that the discipline itself should be part of a revolutionary effort, providing a radical analysis of society on the basis of which existing social institutions can be replaced with new ones.

Without disputing the good intentions of such colleagues—although we have serious doubts about either social engineering or social revolution as approaches to social change—we envision a more humble and modest role for sociology. Each of us as members of society must learn to act within it—to make decisions as corporate workers or officers, as practitioners of law or medicine, as teachers or engineers, as parents, as citizens. There are no magical shortcuts to a better society, we believe, only the efforts of conscientious and informed people in a democratic society doing their best to make things better within their various spheres of endeavor.

We conceive of sociology, therefore, as making a contribution to the knowledge and understanding of the people who will create and recreate the society and culture of the next generation. Sociology will not produce the magic tools by which to transform the world instantly into a better place, nor will it train the revolutionary cadres who will overthrow all the evils of present society and replace them with goodness. It may, however, educate people like yourselves, helping to demystify social life, to provide a broader perspective on society and culture, to develop new and enlightening ways of seeing self and others. It will not provide all the tools of understanding, of course, only some of them—and we have sought in this book to provide those we think most crucial. We hope you have and will find them useful.

References

Adorno, Theodor W., et al. *The Authoritarian Personality* (New York: Harper & Row, Pub. 1950).

Allport, Gordon W. *The Nature of Prejudice* (Reading, Mass.: Addison-Wesley, 1954).

Ariès, Phillipe. *Centuries of Childhood: A Social History of Family Life* (New York: Vintage, 1965).

Bandura, Albert. "Social Learning Theory of Identificatory Processes." In D. A. Goslin, ed., *Handbook of Socialization Theory and Research* (Chicago: Rand McNally, 1969).

Becker, Ernest. *The Birth and Death of Meaning*, 2nd ed. (New York: Free Press, 1971).

Becker, Howard S. *Outsiders*, rev. ed. (New York: Free Press, 1973).

Becker, Howard S., et al. *Boys in White: Student Culture in Medical School* (Chicago: University of Chicago Press, 1961).

Bendix, Reinhard, and Seymour M. Lipset. "Karl Marx's Theory of Social Classes." In Reinhard Bendix and Seymour M. Lipset, eds., *Class, Status, and Power*, 2nd ed. (New York: Free Press, 1966).

Benedict, Ruth. *Patterns of Culture* (Boston: Houghton Mifflin, 1934).

Berger, Peter L. *A Rumor of Angels: Modern Society and the Rediscovery of the Supernatural* (New York: Doubleday, 1969).

Berger, Peter L. *The Sacred Canopy: Elements of a Sociological Theory of Religion* (New York: Doubleday, 1967).

Berger, Peter L. *Invitation to Sociology* (Garden City, N.Y.: Anchor Books, 1963).

Berger, Peter L., and Thomas Luckmann. *The Social Construction of Reality* (New York: Doubleday/Anchor, 1967).

Blau, Peter M. *Exchange and Power in Social Life* (New York: John Wiley, 1964).

Blumer, Herbert. *Symbolic Interactionism: Perspective and Method* (Englewood Cliffs, N.J.: Prentice-Hall, 1969).

Bogdan, Robert, and Steven J. Taylor. *An Introduction to Qualitative Research Methods* (New York: John Wiley, 1975).

Bottomore, Thomas B., and Maximilien Rubel, eds. *Karl Marx: Selected Writings in Sociology and Social Philosophy* (New York: McGraw-Hill, 1964).

Bowles, Samuel, and Herbert Gintis. *Schooling in Capitalist America* (New York: Basic Books, 1976).

Bronfenbrenner, Urie. *Two Worlds of Childhood: U.S. and U.S.S.R.* (New York: Russell Sage Foundation, 1970).

Caplovitz, David, and Fred Sherrow. *The Religious Drop-Outs: Apostasy among College Graduates* (Beverly Hills, Calif.: Sage, 1977).

Clausen, John A. "The Life Course of Individuals." In Matilda W. Riley et al., eds., *Aging and Society: A Sociology of Age Stratification* (New York: Russell Sage, 1972).

Cloward, Richard, and Lloyd Ohlin. *Delinquency and Opportunity* (New York: Free Press, 1960).

Cohen, Albert K. *Delinquent Boys* (New York: Free Press, 1955).

Collins, Randall. *Conflict Sociology* (New York: Academic Press, 1975).

Collins, Randall, and Michael Makowsky. *The Discovery of Society*, 2nd ed. (New York: Random House, 1978).

Conklin, John E. *Illegal But Not Criminal: Business Crime in America* (Englewood Cliffs, N.J.: Prentice-Hall, 1977).

CROSS, WHITNEY R. *The Burned-over District* (Ithaca, N.Y.: Cornell University Press, 1950).

CUBER, JOHN, and PEGGY B. HARROFF. *The Significant Americans* (New York: Hawthorn, 1965).

DAHL, ROBERT A. *Who Governs? Democracy and Power in an American City* (New Haven: Yale University Press, 1961).

DEMOS, JOHN. "Myths and Realities in the History of American Family Life." In Arlene S. Skolnick and Jerome H. Skolnick, eds., *Family in Transition*, 2nd ed. (Boston: Little, Brown, 1977).

DEMOS, JOHN. "Images of the American Family, Then and Now." In Virginia Tufte and Barbara Myerhoff, eds. *Changing Images of the Family* (New Haven: Yale University Press, 1979).

DENZIN, NORMAN K. "Play, Games, and Interaction: The Contexts of Childhood Socialization," *Sociological Quarterly*, 16 (Autumn 1975), 458–478).

DENZIN, NORMAN K. *The Research Act* (New York: McGraw-Hill, 1978).

DOLBEARE, KENNETH M., and MURRAY EDELMAN. *American Politics: Policies, Power, and Change*, 3rd ed. (Lexington, Mass.: Heath, 1979).

DOMHOFF, G. WILLIAM. *Who Rules America?* (Englewood Cliffs, N.J.: Prentice-Hall, 1967).

DOMHOFF, G. WILLIAM. *Who Really Rules?* (New Brunswick, N.J.: Transaction Books, 1978).

DOZIER, EDWARD P. *Hano: A Tewa Indian Community in Arizona* (New York: Holt, 1966).

DURKHEIM, ÉMILE. *Suicide* (New York: Free Press, 1966). First published in 1897.

DURKHEIM, ÉMILE. *The Division of Labor in Society* (New York: Free Press, 1965). First published in 1893.

DURKHEIM, ÉMILE. *The Rules of Sociological Method* (New York: Free Press, 1964). First published in 1895.

DURKHEIM, ÉMILE. *The Elementary Forms of the Religious Life* (New York: Collier, 1961). First published in 1912.

EAKINS, BARBARA W., and R. GENE EAKINS. *Sex Differences in Human Communications* (Boston: Houghton Mifflin, 1978).

EDELMAN, MURRAY. *The Symbolic Uses of Politics* (Urbana, Ill.: University of Illinois Press, 1964).

ELKINS, STANLEY. *Slavery: A Problem in American Institutional and Intellectual Life* (Chicago: University of Chicago Press, 1959).

ERIKSON, ERIK H. *Childhood and Society*, rev. ed. (New York: W. W. Norton & Co., Inc., 1964).

ERIKSON, KAI T. *Everything in Its Path* (New York: Simon & Schuster, 1977).

ERIKSON, KAI T. "Notes on the Sociology of Deviance." In Howard Becker, ed., *The Other Side* (New York: Free Press, 1964).

ERIKSON, KAI T. *Wayward Puritans: A Study in the Sociology of Deviance* (New York: John Wiley, 1966).

FARB, PETER. *Word Play* (New York: Knopf, 1973).

FARBERMAN, HARVEY. "A Criminogenic Market Structure: The Automobile Industry," *Sociological Quarterly*, 16 (Autumn 1975), 438–457.

FAULKNER, ROBERT H. "Coming of Age in Organizations: A Comparative Study of Career Contingencies and Adult Socialization," *Sociology of Work and Occupations*, 1 (May 1974), 131–173.

FESTINGER, LEON, HENRY W. RIECKEN, and STANLEY SCHACHTER. *When Prophecy Fails* (New York: Harper & Row, Pub., 1956).

FINE, GARY ALAN. "Impression Management and Preadolescent Behavior: Friends as Socializers." In S. Asher and J. Gottman, eds., *The Development of Friendship* (Cambridge, England: Cambridge University Press, 1980).

FOOTE, NELSON N. "Identification as the Basis for a Theory of Motivation," *American Sociological Review*, 16 (February 1951), 14–21.

GANS, HERBERT. *More Equality* (New York: Pantheon, 1973).

GECAS, VIKTOR. "Contexts of Socialization." In Morris Rosenberg and Ralph Turner, eds., *Social Psychology: Sociological Perspectives* (New York: Basic Books, 1981).

GEER, BLANCHE. *Learning to Work* (Beverly Hills, Calif.: Sage, 1972).

GEERTZ, CLIFFORD. *The Interpretation of Cultures* (New York: Basic Books, 1973).

GELLES, RICHARD J. "Demythologizing Child Abuse," *The Family Coordinator*, 25 (1976), 135–141.

GELLES, RICHARD J. *Family Violence* (Beverly Hills, Calif.: Sage, 1979).

GENOVESE, EUGENE D. *Roll, Jordan, Roll: The World the Slaves Made* (New York: Vintage, 1976).

GERTH, HANS, and C. WRIGHT MILLS. *From Max Weber: Essays in Sociology* (New York: Free Press, 1958).

GILBERT, DENNIS, and JOSEPH A. KAHL. *The American Class Structure: A New Synthesis*, 2nd ed. (Homewood, Ill.: Dorsey, 1982).

GLASER, BARNEY, and ANSELM L. STRAUSS. *The Discovery of Grounded Theory* (Chicago: Aldine, 1967).

GLAZER, NATHAN, and DANIEL PATRICK MOYNIHAN, eds. *Ethnicity: Theory and Experience* (Cambridge, Mass.: Harvard University Press, 1975).

GLOCK, CHARLES Y., ed. *Religion in Sociological Perspective* (Belmont, Calif.: Wadsworth, 1973).

GLOCK, CHARLES Y., and ROBERT N. BELLAH, eds. *The New Religious Consciousness* (Berkeley: University of California Press, 1976).

GOFFMAN, ERVING. *The Presentation of Self in Everyday Life* (New York: Doubleday, 1959).

GOFFMAN, ERVING. *Stigma: Notes on the Management of Spoiled Identity* (Englewood Cliffs, N.J.: Prentice-Hall, 1963).

GOODE, ERICH. *Deviant Behavior: An Interactionist Approach*, rev. ed. (Englewood Cliffs, N.J.: Prentice-Hall, 1984).

GOODE, WILLIAM J. *The Family*, 2nd ed. (Englewood Cliffs, N.J.: Prentice-Hall, 1982).

GORDON, MICHAEL, ed. *The American Family in Social-Historical Perspective*, 2nd ed. (New York: St. Martin's Press, 1978).

GORDON, MILTON. *Assimilation in American Life* (New York: Oxford University Press, 1964).

GOSLIN, D. A., ed. *Handbook of Socialization Theory and Research* (Chicago: Rand McNally, 1969).

GOSSETT, THOMAS F. *Race: The History of an Idea in America* (New York: Schocken, 1965).

GOUGH, KATHLEEN. "The Nayars and the Definition of Marriage," *Journal of the Royal Anthropological Institute*, 85 (1955), 45–80.

GOUGH, KATHLEEN. "The Origin of the Family." In Arlene S. Skolnick and Jerome H. Skolnick, eds., *Family in Transition*, 2nd ed. (Boston: Little, Brown, 1977).

GOULDNER, ALVIN. "The Norm of Reciprocity: A Preliminary Statement," *American Sociological Review*, 25 (February 1960), 161–178.

GREELEY, ANDREW M. *The Denominational Society* (New York: Scott, Foresman, 1972).

GREELEY, ANDREW M., and WILLIAM C. MCCREADY. *Ethnicity in the United States: A Preliminary Reconnaissance* (New York: John Wiley, 1974).

GURR, TED ROBERT. *Why Men Rebel* (Princeton: Princeton University Press, 1971).

GUSFIELD, JOSEPH. *Symbolic Crusade* (Urbana, Ill.: University of Illinois Press, 1963).

GUTMAN, HERBERT D. *The Black Family in Slavery and Freedom: 1750–1925* (New York: Vintage, 1977).

HALL, EDWARD T. *The Hidden Dimension* (New York: Doubleday, 1966).

HALL, EDWARD T. *The Silent Language* (Greenwich, Conn.: Fawcett Books Group–CBS Publications, 1959).

HALL, PETER M. "A Symbolic Interactionist Analysis of Politics," *Sociological Inquiry*, 42 (1972), 35–75.

HALL, PETER M., and DEE ANN SPENCER-HALL. "The Social Conditions of the Negotiated Order," *Urban Life*, 11 (October 1982), 328–349.

HALL, RICHARD M. *Organizations: Structure and Process*, 3rd ed. (Englewood Cliffs, N.J.: Prentice-Hall, 1982).

HAREVEN, TAMARA, ed. *Family and Kin in Urban Communities: 1700–1930* (New York: New Viewpoints, 1978).

HARRINGTON, MICHAEL. *The Other America* (New York: Macmillan, 1962).

HARRIS, MARVIN. *Cannibals and Kings: The Origins of Culture* (New York: Random House, 1977).

HEILMAN, SAMUEL C. *Synagogue Life: A Study in Symbolic Interaction* (Chicago: University of Chicago Press, 1976).

HERBERG, WILL. *Protestant, Catholic, Jew* (Garden City, N.Y.: Doubleday, 1960).

HEWITT, JOHN P. *Self and Society: A Symbolic Interactionist Social Psychology*, 3rd ed. (Boston: Allyn & Bacon, 1984).

HEWITT, JOHN P., and PETER M. HALL. "Social Problems, Problematic Situations, and Quasi-theories," *American Sociological Review*, 38 (June 1973), 367–374.

HEWITT, MYRNA LIVINGSTON. ". . . But They're Still Jews: Jewish Identity, Assimilation, and the Ethnogenesis Model." Unpublished doctoral dissertation, Department of Sociology. Amherst, Mass.: University of Massachusetts, 1980.

HINE, VIRGINIA H. "Bridge Burners: Commitment and Participation in a Religious Movement," *Sociological Analysis*, 31 (Summer 1970), 61–66.

HIRSCHI, TRAVIS. *Causes of Delinquency* (Berkeley: University of California Press, 1969).

HOCKETT, CHARLES F., and ROBERT ASCHER. "The Human Revolution," *Current Anthropology*, 5 (1964), 135–168.

HODGE, ROBERT, et al. "Occupational Prestige in the United States, 1925–1963," *American Journal of Sociology*, 70 (November 1964), 286–302.

HOLMBERG, ALAN R. *People of the Long Bow* (New York: Natural History Press, 1969).

HOMANS, GEORGE C. *Social Behavior: Its Elementary Forms*, rev. ed. (New York: Harcourt Brace Jovanovich, Inc., 1974).

HUMPHRIES, LAUD. *Tearoom Trade: Impersonal Sex in Public Places* (Chicago: Aldine, 1970).

HUNDLEY, JAMES R., JR. "The Dynamics of Recent Ghetto Riots," *Detroit Journal of Urban Law*, 45 (1968), 627–639.

HURN, CHRISTOPHER. *The Limits and Possibilities of Schooling* (Boston: Allyn & Bacon, 1978).

INKELES, ALEX. *What Is Sociology?* (Englewood Cliffs, N.J.: Prentice-Hall, 1964).

JACQUET, C. H., ed. *Yearbook of American and Canadian Churches* (New York: National Council of Churches of Christ in the U.S.A., 1981).

JENCKS, CHRISTOPHER. *Who Gets Ahead?* (New York: Basic Books, 1979).

JOHNSON, GREGORY. "The Hare Krishna in San Francisco." In Charles Y. Glock and Robert N. Bellah, eds., *The New Religious Consciousness* (Berkeley: University of California Press, 1976).

KANTER, ROSABETH MOSS, and BARRY A. STEIN, eds. *Life in Organizations* (New York: Basic Books, 1979).

KARDINER, ABRAHAM, and LIONEL OVESEY. *The Mark of Oppression* (New York: W.W. Norton & Co., Inc., 1951).

KATZ, JACK. "Deviance, Charisma, and Rule-Defined Behavior," *Social Problems*, 20 (Fall 1972), 186–202.

KELLEY, DEAN M. *Why Conservative Churches Are Growing* (New York: Harper & Row, Pub., 1972).

KERCKHOFF, ALAN C., et al. "Sociometric Patterns in Hysterical Contagion," *Sociometry*, 28 (1965), 2–15.

KERCKHOFF, ALAN C., and KURT W. BACK. *The June*

Bug: A Study of Hysterical Contagion (New York: Appleton-Century-Crofts, 1968).

KILLIAN, LEWIS M. *The Impossible Revolution: Phase II* (New York: Random House, 1975).

KITANO, HARRY H. L. *Race Relations*, 3rd ed. (Englewood Cliffs, N.J.: Prentice-Hall, 1985).

KLUCKHOHN, CLYDE, and W. H. KELLEY. "The Concept of Culture." In Ralph Linton, ed., *The Science of Man in the World Crisis* (New York: Columbia University Press, 1945).

KLUEGEL, JAMES R. "Denominational Mobility: Correct Patterns and Recent Trends," *Journal for the Scientific Study of Religion*, 19 (1980), 26–39.

KOHLBERG, LAWRENCE. "Stage and Sequence: The Cognitive Developmental Approach to Socialization." In D. A. Goslin, ed., *Handbook of Socialization Theory and Research* (Chicago: Rand McNally, 1969).

KOHLBERG, LAWRENCE. "A Cognitive-Developmental Analysis of Children's Sex Role Concepts and Attitudes." In Eleanor Maccoby, ed., *The Development of Sex Differences* (Stanford, Calif.: Stanford University Press, 1966).

KOHN, MELVIN. *Class and Values: A Study in Conformity* (Homewood, Ill.: Dorsey, 1969).

KOLLER, MARVIN R., and OSCAR W. RITCHIE. *Sociology of Childhood* (Englewood Cliffs, N.J.: Prentice-Hall, 1978).

LAKOFF, ROBIN. *Language and Women's Place* (New York: Harper & Row, Pub., 1975).

LAKOFF, ROBIN. "Language and Woman's Place," *Language in Society*, 2 (1973), 65.

LARKIN, ROBERT. *Suburban Youth in Cultural Crisis* (New York: Oxford University Press, 1978).

LASCH, CHRISTOPHER. *The Culture of Narcissism* (New York: W. W. Norton & Co., Inc., 1979).

LASCH, CHRISTOPHER. *Haven in a Heartless World* (New York: Basic Books, 1977).

LAWS, JUDITH LONG, and PEPPER SCHWARTZ. *Sexual Scripts: The Social Construction of Female Sexuality* (Hinsdale, Ill.: Dryden Press, 1977).

LEMERT, EDWIN. *Social Pathology* (New York: McGraw-Hill, 1951).

LENSKI, GERHARD. *Power and Privilege: A Theory of Social Stratification* (New York: McGraw-Hill, 1966).

LENSKI, GERHARD. *The Religious Factor*, rev. ed. (Garden City, N.Y.: Doubleday, 1963).

LEVINSON, DANIEL J. *The Seasons of a Man's Life* (New York: Knopf, 1978).

LEWIS, MICHAEL. *The Culture of Inequality* (Amherst, Mass.: University of Massachusetts Press, 1978).

LINDESMITH, ALFRED, ANSELM L. STRAUSS, and NORMAN K. DENZIN. *Social Psychology*, 5th ed. (New York: Holt, Rinehart, & Winston, 1977).

LINTON, RALPH, ed. *The Science of Man in the World Crisis* (New York: Columbia University Press, 1945).

LOFLAND, JOHN. "'Becoming a World-Saver' Revisited," *American Behavioral Scientist*, 20 (1977), 805–818.

LOFLAND, JOHN, and RODNEY STARK. "Becoming a World-Saver: A Theory of Conversion to a Deviant Perspective." In Charles Y. Glock, ed., *Religion in Sociological Perspective* (Belmont, Calif.: Wadsworth, 1973). Originally published in *American Sociological Review*, 30 (1965), 862–874.

LOFLAND, JOHN. *Analyzing Social Settings* (Beverly Hills, Calif.: Wadsworth, 1971).

LOFLAND, JOHN. *Doomsday Cult* (Englewood Cliffs, N.J.: Prentice-Hall, 1966).

LUCKMANN, THOMAS. *The Invisible Religion* (New York: Macmillan, 1967).

MADGE, JOHN. *The Origins of Scientific Sociology* (New York: Free Press, 1962).

MARTY, MARTIN E. *A Nation of Behavers* (Chicago: University of Chicago Press, 1976).

MARX, KARL, and FRIEDRICH ENGELS. *The Communist Manifesto* (London: Allen and Unwin, 1848). In print edition (Baltimore: Penguin, 1969).

MCHUGH, PETER. *Defining the Situation* (Indianapolis: Bobbs-Merrill, 1968).

MEAD, GEORGE HERBERT. *The Philosophy of the Act* (Chicago: University of Chicago Press, 1938).

MEAD, GEORGE HERBERT. *Mind, Self, and Society* (Chicago: University of Chicago Press, 1934).

MERTON, ROBERT K. *Social Theory and Social Structure*, rev. ed. (New York: Free Press, 1957).

MILGRAM, STANLEY. *Obedience to Authority* (New York: Harper & Row Pubs., 1974).

MILLS, C. WRIGHT. *The Sociological Imagination* (New York: Oxford University Press, 1959).

MILLS, C. WRIGHT *The Power Elite* (New York: Oxford University Press, 1956).

MILLS, C. WRIGHT. *White Collar* (New York: Oxford University Press, 1951).

MILLS, C. WRIGHT. "Situated Actions and Vocabularies of Motive," *American Sociological Review*, 5 (October 1940), 904–913.

MOORE, JOAN W. *Mexican Americans*, 2nd ed. (Englewood Cliffs, N.J.: Prentice-Hall, 1976).

MOORE, JOAN W. "Colonialism: The Case for Mexican Americans," *Social Problems*, 17 (Spring 1970), 463–472.

NATIONAL OPINION RESEARCH CENTER. *General Social Survey, 1975–82 Cumulative Codebook* (Chicago: N.O.R.C., 1982).

NIEBUHR, H. RICHARD. *The Social Sources of Denominationalism* (New York: World, 1929).

NIXON, HOWARD L. *The Small Group* (Englewood Cliffs, N.J.: Prentice-Hall, 1979).

NOCK, STEVEN L., and PETER H. ROSSI. "Household Types and Social Standing," *Social Forces*, 57 (June 1979), 1325–1345.

OAKLEY, ANN. *The Sociology of Housework* (New York: Pantheon, 1975).

O'DEA, THOMAS F. *The Mormons* (Chicago: University of Chicago Press, 1957).

PARK, ROBERT E. "Our Racial Frontier on the Pacific," *Survey Graphic*, 55, (May 1926), 192–196. Reprinted in Robert E. Park, *Race and Culture* (New York: Free Press, 1950).

PINCKNEY, ALPHONSE. *Black Americans*, 2nd ed. (Englewood Cliffs, N.J.: Prentice-Hall, 1975).

PIVEN, FRANCES FOX, and RICHARD A. CLOWARD. *Poor People's Movements: Why They Succeed, How They Fail* (New York: Vintage, 1979).

QUARANTELLI, ELI, and RUSSELL R. DYNES. "When Disaster Strikes: It Isn't Much Like What You've Heard and Read About," *Psychology Today*, 5 (February 1972), 67–70.

ROBBOY, HOWARD, and CANDACE CLARK, eds. *Social Interaction: Readings in Sociology* (New York: St. Martin's Press, 1983).

ROGERS, CARL R. *Client Centered Therapy* (Boston: Houghton-Mifflin, 1951).

ROHNER, RONALD P., and EVELYN C. ROHNER. *The Kwakiutl: Indians of British Columbia* (New York: Holt, Rinehart, & Winston, 1970).

ROSE, ARNOLD M. *The Power Structure: Political Process in American Society* (New York: Oxford University Press, 1967).

ROSE, PETER I., ed. *Socialization and the Life Cycle* (New York: St. Martin's Press, 1979).

ROSENBERG, MORRIS. "The Self-Concept: Social Product and Social Force." In Morris Rosenberg and Ralph Turner, eds., *Social Psychology: Sociological Perspectives* (New York: Basic Books, 1981).

ROSENBERG, MORRIS, and LEONARD PEARLIN. "Social Class and Self-Esteem among Children and Adults," *American Journal of Sociology*, 84 (1978), 53–77.

ROSENBERG, MORRIS, and RALPH TURNER, eds. *Social Psychology: Sociological Perspectives* (New York: Basic Books, 1981).

ROSNOW, RALPH, and GARY A. FINE. *Rumor and Gossip: The Social Psychology of Hearsay* (New York: Elsevier North-Holland, 1976).

ROSSI, ALICE. "A Biosocial Perspective on Parenting," *Daedalus* 106 (1977), 1–31.

ROSSI, ALICE. "Transition to Parenthood," *Journal of Marriage and the Family*, 30 (1968), 334–343.

ROSSI, PETER H., RICHARD BERK, and KENNETH J. LENIHAN. *Money, Work and Crime* (New York: Academic Press, 1980).

ROTHMAN, DAVID. *The Discovery of the Asylum* (Boston: Little, Brown, 1971).

RUBIN, JEFFREY Z., FRANK J. PROVENZANO, and ZELLA LURIA. "The Eye of the Beholder: Parents' Views on Sex of Newborns" *American Journal of Orthopsychiatry*, 44 (1974), 512–519.

RUBIN, LILLIAN. *Worlds of Pain* (New York: Basic Books, 1976).

SACHS, JACQUELINE. "Cues to the Identification of Sex in Children's Speech." In Barrie Thorne and Nancy Hanley, eds., *Language and Sex: Difference and Dominance* (Rowley, Mass.: Newbury House, 1975).

SCHATZMAN, LEONARD, and ANSELM L. STRAUSS. *Field Research: Strategies for a Natural Sociology* (Englewood Cliffs, N.J.: Prentice-Hall, 1973).

SCHEFF, THOMAS. *Being Mentally Ill: A Sociological Theory* (Chicago: Aldine, 1966).

SCHEIN, EDGAR H. "Organizational Socialization and the Profession of Management," *Industrial Management Review*, 9 (1968), 1–15.

SCHULZ, MURIEL R. "The Semantic Derogation of Women." In Barrie Thorne and Nancy Hanley, eds., *Language and Sex: Difference and Dominance* (Rowley, Mass.: Newbury House, 1975).

SCHUR, EDWIN. *Crimes without Victims* (Englewood Cliffs, N.J.: Prentice-Hall, 1965).

SCOTT, MARVIN, and STANFORD LYMAN. "Accounts," *American Sociological Review*, 33 (December 1968), 46–62.

SENNETT, RICHARD, and JONATHAN COBB. *The Hidden Injuries of Class* (New York: Vintage, 1972).

SHIBUTANI, TAMOTSU. *Improvised News* (Indianapolis: Bobbs-Merrill, 1966).

SHIBUTANI, TAMOTSU. *Society and Personality* (Englewood Cliffs, N.J.: Prentice-Hall, 1961).

SHORTER, EDWARD. *The Making of the Modern Family* (New York: Basic Books, 1975).

SIMMEL, GEORG. *Conflict and the Web of Group Affiliations* (New York: Free Press, 1955). First published in 1908.

SKLARE, MARSHALL. *American Jews* (New York: Random House, 1971).

SKOLNICK, ARLENE S., and JEROME H. SKOLNICK, eds. *Family in Transition*, 2nd ed. (Boston: Little, Brown, 1977).

SMELSER, NEIL J. *A Theory of Collective Behavior* (New York: Free Press, 1963).

SPENCER, BALDWIN, and F. J. GILLEN. *The Arunta: A Study of a Stone Age People* (London, Macmillan, 1927).

SPIRO, MEDFORD E. *Children of the Kibbutz* (Cambridge, Mass.: Harvard University Press, 1965).

STARK, RODNEY, and WILLIAM S. BAINBRIDGE. "Secularization and Cult Formation in the Jazz Age," *Journal for the Scientific Study of Religion*, 20 (December 1981), 360–373.

STARK, RODNEY, and CHARLES Y. GLOCK. *American Piety: The Nature of Religious Commitment* (Berkeley: University of California Press, 1968).

STEIN, PETER J., ed. *Single Life: Unmarried Adults in Social Context* (New York: St. Martin's Press, 1981).

STOKES, RANDALL G., and JOHN P. HEWITT. "Aligning Actions," *American Sociological Review*, 46 (October 1976), 838–849.

STONE, GREGORY P., and HARVEY A. FARBERMAN, eds. *Social Psychology through Symbolic Interaction*, 2nd ed. (New York: John Wiley, 1981).

STRAUSS, ANSELM L. *Negotiations* (San Francisco: Jossey-Bass, 1978).

SUTHERLAND, EDWIN H. *White Collar Crime*, 3rd ed.

(New York: Holt, Rinehart, & Winston, 1967). Originally published in 1949.

TAUSKY, CURT, and ROBERT DUBIN. "Career Anchorage: Managerial Mobility Aspirations," *American Sociological Review*, 30 (1965), 725–735.

THOMAS, DARWIN L., et al. "Role-taking and Power in Social Psychology," *American Sociological Review*, 37 (October 1972), 605–614.

THORNE, BARRIE, and NANCY HANLEY, eds. *Language and Sex: Difference and Dominance* (Rowley, Mass.: Newbury House, 1975).

TRAVISANO, RICHARD V. "Alternation and Conversion as Qualitatively Different Transformations." In Gregory P. Stone and Harvey A. Farberman, *Social Psychology through Symbolic Interaction*, 2nd ed. (New York: John Wiley, 1981).

TREIMAN, DONALD J. *Occupational Prestige in Perspective* (New York: Academic Press, 1977).

TROELTSCH, ERNST. *The Social Teachings of the Christian Churches*, 2 vols. Translated by Olive Wyon. (New York: Macmillan, 1931).

TUCHMAN, GAYE, ARLENE KAPLAN DANIELS, and JAMES BENET, eds., *Hearth and Home: Images of Women in the Mass Media* (New York: Oxford University Press, 1978).

TUFTE, VIRGINIA, and BARBARA MEYERHOFF. *Changing Images of the Family* (New Haven: Yale University Press, 1979).

TURNBULL, COLIN. *The Forest People* (New York: Simon & Schuster, 1961).

TURNER, RALPH H. "The Real Self: From Institution to Impulse," *American Journal of Sociology*, 81 (March 1976), 989–1016.

TURNER, RALPH H. "Role-taking: Process versus Conformity." In Arnold M. Rose, ed., *Human Nature and Social Processes* (Boston: Houghton Mifflin, 1962).

TURNER, RALPH H., and LEWIS M. KILLIAN. *Collective Behavior*, 2nd ed. (Englewood Cliffs, N.J.: Prentice-Hall, 1972).

UNITED STATES BUREAU OF THE CENSUS. *Money Income of Families and Persons in the United States: 1980 Current Population Reports*, P-60, No. 132, 1982.

UNITED STATES OFFICE OF MANAGEMENT AND BUDGET. *Social Indicators, 1973* (Washington, D.C.: U.S. Government Printing Office, 1973).

WEBER, MAX. *The Protestant Ethic and the Spirit of Capitalism* (New York: Scribner's, 1930). Translated by Talcott Parsons. First published 1904–05.

WENGER, DENNIS E., et al. "It's a Matter of Myths: An Empirical Examination of Individual Insight into Disaster Response," *Mass Emergencies*, 1 (1976), 33–46.

WEYER, E. M. *The Eskimos* (New Haven: Yale University Press, 1924).

WHEELIS, ALLEN. *The Quest for Identity* (New York: W. W. Norton & Co., Inc., 1958).

WILSON, BRYAN. *Religious Sects* (New York: World University Library, 1970).

WILSON, JOHN. *Religion in American Society: The Effective Presence* (Englewood Cliffs, N.J.: Prentice-Hall, 1978).

WILSON, WILLIAM J. *The Declining Significance of Race*, 2nd ed. (Chicago: University of Chicago Press, 1980).

WIRTH, LOUIS. "The Problem of Minority Groups." In Ralph Linton, ed., *The Science of Man in the World Crisis* (New York: Columbia University Press, 1945).

WRIGHT, ERIK O. *Class Structure and Income Determination* (New York: Academic Press, 1979).

ZUCKERMAN, HARRIET. *Scientific Elite: Nobel Laureates in the United States* (New York: Free Press, 1977).

Index